A Brief History of
WESTERN
PHILOSOPHY

FOR NORMAN KRETZMANN

A Brief History of

WESTERN PHILOSOPHY

ANTHONY KENNY
University of Oxford

First published 1998

Reprinted 1998, 1999, 2000, 2001

Blackwell Publishers Ltd
108 Cowley Road
Oxford OX4 1JF, UK

Blackwell Publishers Inc
350 Main Street
Malden, Massachusetts 02148, USA

British Library Cataloguing in Publication Data
A CIP catalogue record for this book is available from the British Library

Library of Congress Cataloging in Publication Data
Kenny, Anthony John Patrick.
A brief history of western philosophy / Anthony Kenny.
p.   cm.
Includes bibliographical references and index.
ISBN 0–631–18791-X (alk. paper) — ISBN 0–631–20132–7 (pbk. :
alk. paper)
1. Philosophy—History. Title.
B72.K44 1998
190—dc21
98–20921 CIP

Typeset in 10 on 13 pt Galliard
by Graphicraft Typesetters Limited, Hong Kong
Printed and bound in Great Britain by MPG Books, Bodmin, Cornwall

This book is printed on acid-free paper

CONTENTS

PREFACE

Fifty-two years ago Bertrand Russell wrote a one-volume *History of Western Philosophy*, which is still in demand. When it was suggested to me that I might write a modern equivalent, I was at first daunted by the challenge. Russell was one of the greatest philosophers of the century, and he won a Nobel Prize for Literature: how could anyone venture to compete? However, the book is not generally regarded as one of Russell's best, and he is notoriously unfair to some of the greatest philosophers of the past, such as Aristotle and Kant. Moreover, he operated with assumptions about the nature of philosophy and philosophical method which would be questioned by most philosophers at the present time. There does indeed seem to be room for a book which would offer a comprehensive overview of the history of the subject from a contemporary philosophical viewpoint.

Russell's book, however inaccurate in detail, is entertaining and stimulating and it has given many people their first taste of the excitement of philosophy. I aim in this book to reach the same audience as Russell: I write for the general educated reader, who has no special philosophical training, and who wishes to learn the contribution that philosophy has made to the culture we live in. I have tried to avoid using any philosophical terms without explaining them when they first appear. The dialogues of Plato offer a model here: Plato was able to make philosophical points without using any technical vocabulary, because none existed when he wrote. For this reason, among others, I have treated several of his dialogues at some length in the second and third chapters of the book.

The quality of Russell's writing which I have been at most pains to imitate is the clarity and vigour of his style. (He once wrote that his own models as prose writers were Baedeker and John Milton.) A reader new to philosophy is bound to find some parts of this book difficult to follow. There is no shallow end in philosophy, and every novice philosopher has to struggle to keep head above water. But I have done my best to ensure that the reader does not have to face any difficulties in comprehension which are not intrinsic to the subject matter.

It is not possible to explain in advance what philosophy is about. The best way to learn philosophy is to read the works of great philosophers. This book is meant to show the reader what topics have interested philosophers and what methods they have used to address them. By themselves, summaries of philosophical doctrines are of little use: a reader is cheated if merely told a philosopher's conclusions without an indication of the methods by which they were reached. For this reason I do my best to present, and criticize, the reasoning used by philosophers in support of their theses. I mean no disrespect by engaging thus in argument with the great minds of the past. That is the way to take a philosopher seriously: not to parrot his text, but to battle with it, and learn from its strengths and weaknesses.

Philosophy is simultaneously the most exciting and the most frustrating of subjects. Philosophy is exciting because it is the broadest of all disciplines, exploring the basic concepts which run through all our talking and thinking on any topic whatever. Moreover, it can be undertaken without any special preliminary training or instruction; anyone can do philosophy who is willing to think hard and follow a line of reasoning. But philosophy is also frustrating, because, unlike scientific or historical disciplines, it gives no new information about nature or society. Philosophy aims to provide not knowledge, but understanding; and its history shows how difficult it has been, even for the very greatest minds, to develop a complete and coherent vision. It can be said without exaggeration that no human being has yet succeeded in reaching a complete and coherent understanding even of the language we use to think our simplest thoughts. It is no accident that the man whom many regard as the founder of philosophy as a self-conscious discipline, Socrates, claimed that the only wisdom he possessed was his knowledge of his own ignorance.

Philosophy is neither science nor religion, though historically it has been entwined with both. I have tried to bring out how in many areas philosophical thought grew out of religious reflection and grew into empirical science. Many issues which were treated by great past philosophers would nowadays no longer count as philosophical. Accordingly, I have concentrated on those areas of their endeavour which would still be regarded as philosophical today, such as ethics, metaphysics, and the philosophy of mind.

Like Russell I have made a personal choice of the philosophers to include in the history, and the length of time to be devoted to each. I have not, however, departed as much as Russell did from the proportions commonly accepted in the philosophical canon. Like him, I have included discussions of non-philosophers who have influenced philosophical thinking; that is why Darwin and Freud appear on my list of subjects. I have devoted considerable space to ancient and medieval philosophy, though not as much as Russell, who at the mid-point of his book had not got further than Alcuin and Charlemagne. I have ended the story at the time of the Second World War, and I have not attempted to cover twentieth-century continental philosophy.

Again like Russell, I have sketched in the social, historical, and religious background to the lives of the philosophers, at greater length when treating of remote periods and very briefly as we approach modern times.

I have not written for professional philosophers, though of course I hope that they will find my presentation accurate, and will feel able to recommend my book as background reading for their students. To those who are already familiar with the subject my writing will bear the marks of my own philosophical training, which was first in the scholastic philosophy which takes its inspiration from the Middle Ages, and then in the school of linguistic analysis which has been dominant for much of the present century in the English-speaking world.

My hope in publishing this book is that it may convey to those curious about philosophy something of the excitement of the subject, and point them towards the actual writings of the great thinkers of the past.

I am indebted to the editorial staff at Blackwells, and to Anthony Grahame, for assistance in the preparation of the book; and to three anonymous referees who made helpful suggestions for its improvement. I am particularly grateful to my wife, Nancy Kenny, who read the entire book in manuscript and struck out many passages as unintelligible to the non-philosopher. I am sure that my readers will share my gratitude to her for sparing them unprofitable toil.

January 1998

ACKNOWLEDGEMENTS

The author and publishers gratefully acknowledge the following for permission to reproduce copyright material:

T. S. Eliot: for an excerpt from Part IV of 'The Dry Salvages' from *Four Quartets*, copyright © 1941 by T. S. Eliot and renewed 1969 by Esme Valerie Eliot, and for an excerpt from Part II of 'Little Gidding' from *Four Quartets*, copyright © 1943 by T. S. Eliot and renewed 1971 by Esme Valerie Eliot, to Harcourt Brace & Company and Faber & Faber Ltd. (Reprinted by Faber in *Collected Poems 1909–1962* by T. S. Eliot).

W. B. Yeats: for lines from 'Among School Children' from *The Collected Works of W. B. Yeats, Volume 1: The Poems*, revised and edited by Richard J. Finneran, copyright © 1928 by Macmillan Publishing Company, renewed © 1956 by Georgie Yeats, to A. P. Watt Ltd., on behalf of Michael Yeats, and Scribner, a division of Simon & Schuster.

The publishers apologize for any errors or omissions in the above list and would be grateful to be notified of any corrections that should be incorporated in the next edition or reprint of this book.

I
PHILOSOPHY
IN ITS INFANCY

The earliest Western philosophers were Greeks: men who spoke dialects of the Greek language, who were familiar with the Greek poems of Homer and Hesiod, and who had been brought up to worship Greek Gods like Zeus, Apollo, and Aphrodite. They lived not on the mainland of Greece, but in outlying centres of Greek culture, on the southern coasts of Italy or on the western coast of what is now Turkey. They flourished in the sixth-century BC, the century which began with the deportation of the Jews to Babylon by King Nebuchadnezzar and ended with the foundation of the Roman Republic after the expulsion of the young city's kings.

These early philosophers were also early scientists, and several of them were also religious leaders. In the beginning the distinction between science, religion, and philosophy was not as clear as it became in later centuries. In the sixth century, in Asia Minor and Greek Italy, there was an intellectual cauldron in which elements of all these future disciplines fermented together. Later, religious devotees, philosophical disciples, and scientific inheritors could all look back to these thinkers as their forefathers.

Pythagoras, who was honoured in antiquity as the first to bring philosophy to the Greek world, illustrates in his own person the characteristics of this early period. Born in Samos, off the Turkish coast, he migrated to Croton on the toe of Italy. He has a claim to be the founder of geometry as a systematic study. His name became familiar to many generations of European schoolchildren because he was credited with the first proof that the square on the long side of a right-angled triangle is equal in area to the sum of the squares on the other two sides. But he also founded a religious community with a set of ascetic and ceremonial rules, the best-known of which was a prohibition on the eating of beans. He taught the doctrine of the transmigration of souls: human beings had souls which were separable from their bodies, and at death a person's soul might migrate into another kind of animal. For this reason, he taught his disciples to abstain from meat; once, it is said, he stopped a man whipping a puppy, claiming to have

---

1

recognized in its whimper the voice of a dear dead friend. He believed that the soul, having migrated into different kinds of animal in succession, was eventually reincarnated as a human being. He himself claimed to remember having been, some centuries earlier, a hero at the siege of Troy.

The doctrine of the transmigration of souls was called in Greek 'metempsychosis'. Faustus, in Christopher Marlowe's play, having sold his soul to the devil, and about to be carried off to the Christian Hell, expresses the desperate wish that Pythagoras had got things right.

> Ah, Pythagoras' metempsychosis, were that true
> This soul should fly from me, and I be chang'd
> Unto some brutish beast.

Pythagoras' disciples wrote biographies of him full of wonders, crediting him with second sight and the gift of bilocation, and making him a son of Apollo.

THE MILESIANS

Pythagoras' life is lost in legend. Rather more is known about a group of philosophers, roughly contemporary with him, who lived in the city of Miletus in Ionia, or Greek Asia. The first of these was **Thales**, who was old enough to have foretold an eclipse in 585. Like Pythagoras, he was a geometer, though he is credited with rather simpler theorems, such as the one that a circle is bisected by its diameter. Like Pythagoras, he mingled geometry with religion: when he discovered how to inscribe a right-angled triangle inside a circle, he sacrificed an ox to the gods. But his geometry had a practical side: he was able to measure the height of the pyramids by measuring their shadows. He was also interested in astronomy: he identified the constellation of the little bear, and pointed out its use in navigation. He was, we are told, the first Greek to fix the length of the year as 365 days, and he made estimates of the sizes of the sun and moon.

Thales was perhaps the first philosopher to ask questions about the structure and nature of the cosmos as a whole. He maintained that the earth rests on water, like a log floating in a stream. (Aristotle asked, later: what does the water rest on?) But earth and its inhabitants did not just rest on water: in some sense, so Thales believed, they were all made out of water. Even in antiquity, people could only conjecture the grounds for this belief: was it because all animals and plants need water, or because the seeds of everything are moist?

Because of his theory about the cosmos Thales was called by later writers a physicist or philosopher of nature ('*physis*' is the Greek word for 'nature'). Though he was a physicist, Thales was not a materialist: he did not, that is to say, believe that nothing existed except physical matter. One of the two sayings which have come down from him verbatim is 'everything is full of gods'. What he meant is perhaps indicated by his claim that the magnet, because it moves iron, has a soul. He did not believe in Pythagoras' doctrine of transmigration, but he did maintain the immortality of the soul.

Thales was no mere theorist. He was a political and military adviser to King Croesus of Lydia, and helped him to ford a river by diverting a stream. Foreseeing an unusually good olive crop, he took a lease on all the oil-mills, and made a fortune. None the less, he acquired a reputation for unworldly absent-mindedness, as appears in a letter which an ancient fiction-writer feigned to have been written to Pythagoras from Miletus:

> Thales has met an unkind fate in his old age. He went out from the court of his house at night, as was his custom, with his maidservant to view the stars, and forgetting where he was, as he gazed, he got to the edge of a steep slope and fell over. In such wise have the Milesians lost their astronomer. Let us who were his pupils cherish his memory, and let it be cherished by our children and pupils.

The pretended writer of this letter was a younger contemporary and pupil of Thales called **Anaximander**, a savant who made the first map of the world and of the stars, and invented both a sundial and an all-weather clock. He taught that the earth was cylindrical in shape, like a section of a pillar. Around the world were gigantic tyres, full of fire; each tyre had a hole through which the fire could be seen, and the holes were the sun and moon and stars. The largest tyre was twenty-eight times as great as the earth, and the fire seen through its orifice was the sun. Blockages in the holes explained eclipses and the phases of the moon. The fire within these tyres was once a great ball of flame surrounding the infant earth, which had gradually burst into fragments which enrolled themselves in bark-like casings. Eventually the heavenly bodies would return to the original fire.

> The things from which existing things come into being are also the things into which they are destroyed, in accordance with what must be. For they give justice and reparation to one another for their injustice in accordance with the arrangement of time.

Here physical cosmogony is mingled not so much with theology as with a grand cosmic ethic: the several elements, no less than men and gods, must keep within bounds everlastingly fixed by nature.

Though fire played an important part in Anaximander's cosmogony, it would be wrong to think that he regarded it as the ultimate constituent of the world, like Thales' water. The basic element of everything, he maintained, could be neither water nor fire, nor anything similar, or else it would gradually take over the universe. It had to be something with no definite nature, which he called the 'infinite' or 'unlimited'. 'The infinite is the first principle of things that exist: it is eternal and ageless, and it contains all the worlds.'

Anaximander was an early proponent of evolution. The human beings we know cannot always have existed, he argued. Other animals are able to look after themselves, soon after birth, while humans require a long period of nursing; if humans had originally been as they are now they could not have survived. He maintained that in an earlier age there were fish-like animals within which human embryos grew to puberty before bursting forth into the world. Because of this thesis, though he was not otherwise a vegetarian, he preached against the eating of fish.

The infinite of Anaximander was a concept too rarefied for some of his successors. His younger contemporary at Miletus, **Anaximenes**, while agreeing that the ultimate element could not be fire or water, claimed that it was air, from which everything else had come into being. In its stable state, air is invisible, but when it is moved and condensed it becomes first wind and then cloud and then water, and finally water condensed becomes mud and stone. Rarefied air, presumably, became fire, completing the gamut of the elements. In support of his theory, Anaximenes appealed to experience: 'Men release both hot and cold from their mouths; for the breath is cooled when it is compressed and condensed by the lips, but when the mouth is relaxed and it is exhaled it becomes hot by reason of its rareness'. Thus rarefaction and condensation can generate everything out of the underlying air. This is naive, but it is naive science: it is not mythology, like the classical and biblical stories of the flood and of the rainbow.

Anaximenes was the first flat-earther: he thought that the heavenly bodies did not travel under the earth, as his predecessors had claimed, but rotated round our heads like a felt cap. He was also a flat-mooner and a flat-sunner: 'the sun and the moon and the other heavenly bodies, which are all fiery, ride the air because of their flatness'.

XENOPHANES

Thales, Anaximander, and Anaximenes were a trio of hardy and ingenious speculators. Their interests mark them out as the forebears of modern scientists rather more than of modern philosophers. The matter is different when we come to **Xenophanes** of Colophon (near present-day Izmir), who lived into the fifth century. His themes and methods are recognizably the same as those of philosophers through succeeding ages. In particular he was the first philosopher of religion, and some of the arguments he propounded are still taken seriously by his successors.

Xenophanes detested the religion found in the poems of Homer and Hesiod, whose stories blasphemously attributed to the gods theft, trickery, adultery, and all kinds of behaviour that, among humans, would be shameful and blameworthy.

A poet himself, he savaged Homeric theology in satirical verses, now lost. It was not that he claimed himself to possess a clear insight into the nature of the divine; on the contrary, he wrote, 'the clear truth about the gods no man has ever seen nor any man will ever know'. But he did claim to know where these legends of the gods came from: human beings have a tendency to picture everybody and everything as like themselves. Ethiopians, he said, make their gods dark and snub-nosed, while Thracians make them red-haired and blue-eyed. The belief that gods have any kind of human form at all is childish anthropomorphism. 'If cows and horses or lions had hands and could draw, then horses would draw the forms of gods like horses, cows like cows, making their bodies similar in shape to their own.'

Though no one would ever have a clear vision of God, Xenophanes thought that as science progressed, mortals could learn more than had been originally revealed. 'There is one god,' he wrote, 'greatest among gods and men, similar to mortals neither in shape nor in thought.' God was neither limited nor infinite, but altogether non-spatial: that which is divine is a living thing which sees as a whole, thinks as a whole and hears as a whole.

In a society which worshipped many gods, he was a resolute monotheist. There was only one God, he argued, because God is the most powerful of all things, and if there were more than one, then they would all have to share equal power. God cannot have an origin; because what comes into existence does so either from what is like or what is unlike, and both alternatives lead to absurdity in the case of God. God is neither infinite nor finite, neither changeable nor changeless. But though God is in a manner unthinkable, he is not unthinking. On the contrary, 'Remote and effortless, with his mind alone he governs all there is'.

Xenophanes' monotheism is remarkable not so much because of its originality as because of its philosophical nature. The Hebrew prophet Jeremiah and the authors of the book of Isaiah had already proclaimed that there was only one true God. But while they took their stance on the basis of a divine oracle, Xenophanes offered to prove his point by rational argument. In terms of a distinction not drawn until centuries later, Isaiah proclaimed a revealed religion, while Xenophanes was a natural theologian.

Xenophanes' philosophy of nature is less exciting than his philosophy of religion. His views are variations on themes proposed by his Milesian predecessors. He took as his ultimate element not water, or air, but earth. The earth, he thought, reached down beneath us to infinity. The sun, he maintained, came into existence each day from a congregation of tiny sparks. But it was not the only sun; indeed there were infinitely many. Xenophanes' most original contribution to science was to draw attention to the existence of fossils: he pointed out that in Malta there were to be found impressed in rocks the shapes of all sea-creatures. From this he drew the conclusion that the world passed through a cycle of alternating terrestrial and marine phases.

HERACLITUS

The last, and the most famous, of these early Ionian philosophers was **Heraclitus**, who lived early in the fifth century in the great metropolis of Ephesus, where later St Paul was to preach, dwell, and be persecuted. The city, in Heraclitus' day as in St Paul's, was dominated by the great temple of the fertility goddess Artemis. Heraclitus denounced the worship of the temple: praying to statues was like whispering gossip to an empty house, and offering sacrifices to purify oneself from sin was like trying to wash off mud with mud. He visited the temple from time to time, but only to play dice with the children there – much better company than statesmen, he said, refusing to take any part in the city's politics. In Artemis' temple, too, he deposited his three-book treatise on philosophy and politics, a work, now lost, of notorious difficulty, so puzzling that some thought it a text of physics, others a political tract. ('What I understand of it is excellent,' Socrates said later, 'what I don't understand may well be excellent also; but only a deep-sea diver could get to the bottom of it.')

In this book Heraclitus spoke of a great Word or Logos which holds forever and in accordance with which all things come about. He wrote in paradoxes, claiming that the universe is both divisible and indivisible, generated and ungenerated, mortal and immortal, Word and Eternity, Father and Son, God and Justice. No wonder that everybody, as he complained, found his Logos quite incomprehensible.

If Xenophanes, in his style of argument, resembled modern professional philosophers, Heraclitus was much more like the popular modern idea of the philosopher as guru. He had nothing but contempt for his philosophical predecessors. Much learning, he said, does not teach a man sense; otherwise it would have taught Hesiod and Pythagoras and Xenophanes. Heraclitus did not argue, he pronounced: he was a master of pregnant dicta, profound in sound and obscure in sense. His delphic style was perhaps an imitation of the oracle of Apollo, which, in his own words, 'neither speaks, nor conceals, but gestures'. Among Heraclitus' best-known sayings are these:

> The way up and the way down is one and the same.
> Hidden harmony is better than manifest harmony.
> War is the father of all and the king of all; it proves some people gods, and
>   some people men; it makes some people slaves and some people free.
> A dry soul is wisest and best.
> For souls it is death to become water.
> A drunk is a man led by a boy.
> Gods are mortal, humans immortal, living their death, dying their life.
> The soul is a spider and the body is its web.

That last remark was explained by Heraclitus thus: just as a spider, in the middle of a web, notices as soon as a fly breaks one of its threads and rushes thither as if in grief, so a person's soul, if some part of the body is hurt, hurries quickly there as if unable to bear the hurt. But if the soul is a busy spider, it is also, according to Heraclitus, a spark of the substance of the fiery stars.

In Heraclitus' cosmology fire has the role which water had in Thales and air had in Anaximenes. The world is an ever-burning fire: all things come from fire and go into fire; 'all things are exchangeable for fire, as goods are for gold and gold for goods'. There is a downward path, whereby fire turns to water and water to earth, and an upward path, whereby earth turns to water, water to air, and air to fire. The death of earth is to become water, and the death of water is to become air, and the death of air is to become fire. There is a single world, the same for all, made neither by god nor man; it has always existed and always will exist, passing, in accordance with cycles laid down by fate, through a phase of kindling, which is war, and a phase of burning, which is peace.

Heraclitus' vision of the transmutation of the elements in an ever-burning fire has caught the imagination of poets down to the present age. T. S. Eliot, in *Four Quartets*, puts this gloss on Heraclitus' statement that water was the death of earth.

> There are flood and drouth
> Over the eyes and in the mouth,
> Dead water and dead sand
> Contending for the upper hand.
> The parched eviscerate soil
> Gapes at the vanity of toil,
> Laughs without mirth
> This is the death of earth.

Gerard Manley Hopkins wrote a poem entitled 'That Nature is a Heraclitean Fire', full of imagery drawn from Heraclitus.

> Million fueled, nature's bonfire burns on.
> But quench her bonniest, dearest to her, her clearest-selved spark,
> Man, how fast his firedint, his mark on mind, is gone!
> Both are in an unfathomable, all is in an enormous dark
> Drowned. O pity and indignation! Manshape, that shone
> Sheer off, disseveral, a star, death blots black out . . .

Hopkins seeks comfort from this in the promise of the final resurrection – a Christian doctrine, of course, but one which itself finds its anticipation in a passage of Heraclitus which speaks of humans rising up and becoming wakeful guardians of the living and the dead. 'Fire', he said, 'will come and judge and convict all things.'

In the ancient world the aspect of Heraclitus' teaching which most impressed philosophers was not so much the vision of the world as a bonfire, as the corollary that everything in the world was in a state of constant change and flux. Everything moves on, he said, and nothing remains; the world is like a flowing stream. If we stand by the river bank, the water we see beneath us is not the same two moments together, and we cannot put our feet twice into the same water. So far, so good; but Heraclitus went on to say that we cannot even step twice into the same river. This seems false, whether taken literally or allegorically; but, as we shall see, the sentiment was highly influential in later Greek philosophy.

THE SCHOOL OF PARMENIDES

The philosophical scene is very different when we turn to **Parmenides**, who was born in the closing years of the sixth century. Though probably a pupil of Xenophanes, Parmenides spent most of his life not in Ionia but in Italy, in a town called Elea, seventy miles or so south of Naples. He is said to have drawn up an excellent set of laws for his city; but we know nothing of his politics or political philosophy. He is the first philosopher whose writing has come down to us in any quantity: he wrote a philosophical poem in clumsy verse, of which we possess about a hundred and twenty lines. In his writing he devoted himself not to cosmology, like the early Milesians, nor to theology, like Xenophanes, but to a new and universal study which embraced and transcended both: the discipline which later philosophers called 'ontology'. Ontology gets its name from a Greek word which in the singular is '*on*' and in the plural '*onta*': it is this word – the present participle of the Greek verb 'to be' – which defines Parmenides' subject matter. His remarkable poem can claim to be the founding charter of ontology.

To explain what ontology is, and what Parmenides' poem is about, it is necessary to go into detail about points of grammar and translation. The reader's patience with this pedantry will be rewarded, for between Parmenides and the present-day, ontology was to have a vast and luxuriant growth, and only a sure grasp of what Parmenides meant, and what he failed to mean, enables one to see one's way clear over the centuries through the ontological jungle.

Parmenides' subject is '*to on*', which translated literally means 'the being'. Before explaining the verb, we need to say something about the article. In English we sometimes use an adjective, preceded by the definite article, to refer to a class of people or things; as when we say 'the rich' to mean people who are rich, and 'the poor' to mean those who are poor. The corresponding idiom was much more frequent in Greek than in English: Greeks could use the expression 'the hot' to mean things that are hot, and 'the cold' to mean things that are cold. Thus, for instance, Anaximenes said that air was made visible by the hot and the cold and the moist and the moving. Instead of an adjective after 'the' we may use a participle: as when we speak, for instance, of a hospice for the dying, or a playgroup for the rising fours. Once again, the corresponding construction was possible, and frequent, in Greek; and it is this idiom which occurs in 'the being'. 'The being' is that which is be-ing, in the same way as 'the dying' are those who are dying.

A verbal form like 'dying' has, in English, two uses: it may be a participle, as in 'the dying should not be neglected', or it may be a verbal noun, as in 'dying can be a long-drawn-out business'. 'Seeing is believing' is equivalent to 'To see is to believe'. When philosophers write treatises about being, they are commonly using the word as a verbal noun: they are offering to explain what it is for something *to be*. That is not, or not mainly, what Parmenides is about: he is concerned with *the being*, that is to say, with whatever is, as it were, doing the be-ing. To distinguish this sense of 'being' from its use as a verbal noun, and to avoid the strangeness of the literal 'the being' in English, it has been traditional to dignify Parmenides' topic with a capital 'B'. We will follow this convention, whereby 'Being' means whatever is engaged in being, and 'being' is the verbal noun equivalent to the infinitive 'to be'.

Very well; but if that is what Being is, in order to make out what Parmenides is talking about we must also know what being is, that is to say, what it is for something to be. We can understand what it is for something to be blue, or to be a puppy: but what is it for something to just be, period? One possibility which suggests itself is this: being is existing, or, in other words, to be is to exist. If so, then Being is all that exists.

In English 'to be' can certainly mean 'to exist'. When Hamlet asks the question 'to be or not to be?' he is debating whether or not to put an end to his existence. In the Bible we read that Rachel wept for her children 'and would not be comforted because they are not'. This usage in English is poetic and archaic, and it is not natural to say such things as 'The Tower of London is, and the Crystal Palace is not', when we mean that the former building is still in existence while the latter is no longer there. But the corresponding statement would be quite natural in ancient Greek; and this sense of 'be' is certainly involved in Parmenides' talk of Being.

If this were all that was involved, then we could say simply that Being is all that exists, or if you like, all that there is, or again, everything that is in being. That is a broad enough topic, in all conscience. One could not reproach Parmenides, as Hamlet reproached Horatio, by saying:

> There are more things in heaven and earth
> Than are dreamt of in your philosophy.

For whatever there is in heaven and earth will fall under the heading of Being.

Unfortunately for us, however, matters are more complicated than this. Existence is not all that Parmenides has in mind when he talks of Being. He is interested in the verb 'to be' not only as it occurs in sentences such as 'Troy is no more' but as it occurs in any kind of sentence whatever – whether 'Penelope is a woman' or 'Achilles is a hero' or 'Menelaus is gold-haired' or 'Telemachus is six-feet high'. So understood, Being is not just that which exists, but that of which any sentence containing 'is' is true. Equally, being is not just existing (being, period) but being anything whatever: being red or being blue, being hot or being cold, and so on *ad nauseam*. Taken in this sense, Being is a much more difficult realm to comprehend.

After this long preamble, we are in a position to look at some of the lines of Parmenides' mysterious poem.

> What you can call and think must Being be
> For Being can, and nothing cannot, be.

The first line stresses the vast extension of Being: if you can call Argos a dog, or if you can think of the moon, then Argos and the moon must be, must count as part of Being. But why does the second line tell us that nothing cannot be? Well, anything that can be at all, must be something or other; it cannot be just nothing.

Parmenides introduces, to correspond with Being, the notion of Unbeing.

> Never shall this prevail, that Unbeing is;
> Rein in your mind from any thought like this.

If Being is that of which something or other, no matter what, is true, then Unbeing is that of which nothing at all is true. That, surely, is nonsense. Not only can it not exist, it cannot even be thought of.

> Unbeing you won't grasp – it can't be done –
> Nor utter; being thought and being are one.

Given his definition of 'being' and 'Unbeing' Parmenides is surely right here. If I tell you that I am thinking of something, and you ask me what kind of thing I'm thinking of, you will be puzzled if I say that it isn't any kind of thing. If you then ask me what it is like, and I say that it isn't like anything at all, you will be quite baffled. 'Can you then tell me anything at all about it?' you may ask. If I say no, then you may justly conclude that I am not really thinking of anything or indeed thinking at all. In that sense, it is true that to be thought of and to be are one and the same.

We can agree with Parmenides thus far; but we may note that there is an important difference between saying

Unbeing cannot be thought of

and saying

What does not exist cannot be thought of.

The first sentence is, in the sense explained, true; the second is false. If it were true, we could prove that things exist simply by thinking of them; but whereas lions and unicorns can both be thought of, lions exist and unicorns don't. Given the convolutions of his language, it is hard to be sure whether Parmenides thought that the two statements were equivalent. Some of his followers have accused him of that confusion; others have seemed to share it themselves.

We have agreed with Parmenides in rejecting Unbeing. But it is harder to follow Parmenides in some of the conclusions he draws from the inconceivability of Unbeing and the universality of Being. This is how he proceeds.

> One road there is, signposted in this wise:
> Being was never born and never dies;
> Foursquare, unmoved, no end it will allow
> It never was, nor will be; all is now,
> One and continuous. How could it be born
> Or whence could it be grown? Unbeing? No –
> That mayn't be said or thought; we cannot go
> So far ev'n to deny it is. What need,
> Early or late, could Being from Unbeing seed?
> Thus it must altogether be or not.
> Nor to Unbeing will belief allot
> An offspring other than itself . . .

'Nothing can come from nothing' is a principle which has been accepted by many thinkers far less intrepid than Parmenides. But not many have drawn the conclusion that Being has no beginning and no end, and is not subject to temporal change. To see why Parmenides drew this conclusion, we have to assume that he thought that 'being water' or 'being air' was related to 'being' in the same way as 'running fast' and 'running slowly' is related to 'running'. Someone who first runs fast and then runs slowly, all the time goes on running; similarly, for Parmenides, stuff which is first water and then is air goes on being. When a kettle of water boils away, this may be, in Heraclitus' words, the death of water and the birth of air; but, for Parmenides, it is not the death or birth of Being. Whatever changes may take place, they are not changes from being to non-being; they are all changes within Being, not changes of Being.

Being must be everlasting; because it could not have come from Unbeing, and it could never turn into Unbeing because there is no such thing. If Being could – *per impossibile* – come from nothing, what could make it do so at one time rather than another? Indeed, what is it that differentiates past from present and future? If it is no kind of being, then time is unreal; if it is some kind of being, then it is all part of Being, and past, present and future are all one Being.

By similar arguments Parmenides seeks to show that Being is undivided and unlimited. What would divide Being from Being? Unbeing? In that case the division is unreal. Being? In that case there is no division, but continuous Being. What could set limits to Being? Unbeing cannot do anything to anything; and if we imagine that Being is limited by Being, then Being has not yet reached its limits.

> To think a thing's to think it is, no less.
> Apart from Being, whate'er we may express,
> Thought does not reach. Naught is or will be
> Beyond Being's bounds, since Destiny's decree
> Fetters it whole and still. All things are names
> Which the credulity of mortals frames –
> Birth and destruction, being all or none,
> Changes of place, and colours come and gone.

Parmenides' poem is in two parts: the Way of Truth and the Way of Seeming. The Way of Truth contains the doctrine of Being, which we have been examining; the Way of Seeming deals with the world of the senses, the world of change and colour, the world of empty names. We need not spend time on the Way of Seeming, since what Parmenides tells us about this is not very different from the cosmological speculations of the Ionian thinkers. It was his Way of Truth which set an agenda for many ages of subsequent philosophy.

The problem facing future philosophers was this. Common sense suggests that the world contains things which endure, such as rocky mountains, and things which constantly change, such as rushing streams. On the one hand, Heraclitus had pronounced that at a fundamental level, even the most solid things were in perpetual flux; on the other hand, Parmenides had argued that even what is most apparently fleeting is, at a fundamental level, static and unchanging. Can the doctrines of either Heraclitus or Parmenides be refuted? Is there any way in which they can be reconciled? For Plato, and his successors, this was a major task for philosophy to address.

Parmenides' pupil **Melissus** (*fl.* 441) put into plain prose the ideas which Parmenides had expounded in opaque verse. From these ideas he drew out two particular shocking consequences. One was that pain was unreal, because it implied a deficiency of being. The other was that there was no such thing as an empty space or vacuum: it would have to be a piece of Unbeing. Hence, motion was impossible, because the bodies which occupy space have no room to move into.

Zeno, a friend of Parmenides some twenty-five years his junior, developed an ingenious series of paradoxes designed to show beyond doubt that movement was inconceivable. The best known of these purports to prove that a fast mover can never overtake a slow mover. Let us suppose that Achilles, a fast runner, runs a hundred-yard race with a tortoise which can only run a quarter as fast, giving the tortoise a forty-yard start. By the time Achilles has reached the forty-yard mark, the tortoise is still ahead, by ten yards. By the time Achilles has run those ten yards, the tortoise is ahead by two-and-a-half yards. Each time Achilles makes up the gap, the tortoise opens up a new, shorter, gap ahead of him; so it seems that he can never overtake him. Another, simpler, argument sought to prove that no one could ever run from one end of a stadium to another, because to reach the far end you must first reach the half-way point, to reach the half-way point you must first reach the point half way to that, and so *ad infinitum*.

These and other arguments of Zeno assume that distances are infinitely divisible. This assumption was challenged by some later thinkers, and accepted by others. Aristotle, who preserved the puzzles for us, was able to disentangle some of the ambiguities. However, it was not for many centuries that the paradoxes were given solutions that satisfied both philosophers and mathematicians.

Plato tells us that Parmenides, when he was a grey-haired sixty-five-year-old, travelled with Zeno from Elea to a festival in Athens, and there met the young Socrates. This would have been about 450 BC. Some scholars think the story a dramatic invention; but the meeting, if it took place, was a splendid inauguration of the golden age of Greek philosophy in Athens. We shall turn to Athenian philosophy shortly; but in the meantime there remain to be considered another Italian thinker, Empedocles of Acragas, and two more Ionian physicists, Leucippus and Democritus.

EMPEDOCLES

Empedocles flourished in the middle of the fifth century and was a citizen of the town on the south coast of Sicily which is now Agrigento. He is reputed to have been an active politician, an ardent democrat who was offered, but refused, the kingship of his city. In later life he was banished and practised philosophy in exile. He was renowned as a physician, but according to the ancient biographers he cured by magic as well as by drugs, and he even raised to life a woman thirty days dead. In his last years, they tell us, he came to believe that he was a god, and met his death by leaping into the volcano Etna to establish his divinity.

Whether or not Empedocles was a wonder-worker, he deserved his reputation as an original and imaginative philosopher. He wrote two poems, longer than Parmenides' and more fluent if also more repetitive. One was about science and one about religion. Of the former, *On Nature*, we possess some four hundred lines from an original two thousand; of the latter, *Purifications*, only smaller fragments have survived.

Empedocles' philosophy of nature can be regarded as a synthesis of the thought of the Ionian philosophers. As we have seen, each of them had singled out some one substance as the basic stuff of the universe: for Thales it was water, for

Anaximenes air, for Xenophanes earth, for Heraclitus fire. For Empedocles, all four of these substances stood on equal terms as the basic elements ('roots', in his word) of the universe. These elements have always existed, he believed, but they mingle with each other in various proportions to produce the furniture of the world.

> From these four sprang what was and is and ever shall
> Trees, beasts, and human beings, males and females all
> Birds of the air, and fishes bred by water bright,
> The age-old gods as well, long worshipped in the height.
> These four are all there is, each other interweaving
> And, intermixed, the world's variety achieving.

The interweaving and intermingling of the elements, in Empedocles' system, is caused by two forces: Love and Strife. Love combines the elements together, making one thing out of many things, and Strife forces them apart, making many things out of one. History is a cycle in which sometimes Love is dominant, and sometimes Strife. Under the influence of Love, the elements unite into a homogeneous and glorious sphere; then, under the influence of Strife, they separate out into beings of different kinds. All compound beings, such as animals and birds and fish, are temporary creatures which come and go; only the elements are everlasting, and only the cosmic cycle goes on for ever.

Empedocles' accounts of his cosmology are sometimes prosaic and sometimes poetic. The cosmic force of Love is often personified as the joyous goddess Aphrodite, and the early stage of cosmic development is identified with a golden age over which she reigned. The element of fire is sometimes called Hephaestus, the sun-god. But despite its symbolic and mythical clothing, Empedocles' system deserves to be taken seriously as an exercise in science.

We are accustomed to think of solid, liquid, and gas as three fundamental states of matter. It was not unreasonable to think of fire, and in particular the fire of the sun, as being a fourth state of matter of equal importance. Indeed, in our own century, the emergence of the discipline of plasma physics, which studies the properties of matter at the temperature of the sun, may be said to have restored the fourth element to parity with the other three. Love and Strife can be recognized as the ancient analogues of the forces of attraction and repulsion which have played a significant part in the development of physical theory through the ages.

Empedocles knew that the moon shone with reflected light; however, he believed the same to be true of the sun. He was aware that eclipses of the sun were caused by the interposition of the moon. He knew that plants propagated sexually, and he had an elaborate theory relating respiration to the movement of the blood within the body. He presented a crude theory of evolution. In a primitive stage of the world, he maintained, chance formed matter into isolated limbs and organs: arms without shoulders, unsocketed eyes, heads without necks. These

Lego-like animal parts, again by chance, linked up into organisms, many of which were monstrosities such as human-headed oxen and ox-headed humans. Most of these fortuitous organisms were fragile or sterile; only the fittest structures survived to be the human and animal species we know.

Even the gods, as we have seen, were products of the Empedoclean elements. *A fortiori*, the human soul was a material compound, composed of earth, air, fire, and water. Each element – and indeed the forces of love and strife – had its role in the operation of our senses, according to the principle that like is perceived by like.

> We see the earth by earth, by water water see
> The air of the sky by air, by fire the fire in flame
> Love we perceive by love, strife by sad strife, the same.

Thought, in some strange way, is to be identified with the movement of the blood around the heart: blood is a refined mixture of all the elements, and this accounts for thought's wide-ranging nature.

Empedocles' religious poem *Purifications* makes clear that he accepted the Pythagorean doctrine of metempsychosis, the transmigration of souls. Strife punishes sinners by casting their souls into different kinds of creatures on land or sea. Empedocles told his followers to abstain from eating living things, for the bodies of the animals we eat are the dwelling-places of punished souls. It is not clear whether, in order to avoid the risks here, vegetarianism would be sufficient, since on his view a human soul might migrate into a plant. The best fate for a human, he said, was to become a lion if death changed him into an animal, and a laurel if he became a plant. Best of all was to be changed into a god: those most likely to qualify for such ennoblement were seers, hymn-writers, and doctors.

Empedocles, who fell into all three of these categories, claimed to have experienced metempsychosis in his own person.

> I was once in the past a boy, once a girl, once a tree
> Once too a bird, and once a silent fish in the sea.

Our present existence may be wretched, and after death our immediate prospects may be bleak; but after the punishment of our sins through reincarnation, we can look forward to eternal rest at the table of the immortals, free from weariness and suffering. No doubt this was what Empedocles looked forward to as he plunged into Etna.

THE ATOMISTS

Democritus was the first significant philosopher to be born in mainland Greece: he came from Abdera, in the north-eastern corner of the country. He was a pupil of one Leucippus, about whom little is known. The two philosophers are commonly mentioned together in antiquity, and the atomism which made both of them famous was probably Leucippus' invention. Aristotle tells us that Leucippus was trying to reconcile the data of the senses with Eleatic monism, that is, the theory that there was only one everlasting, unchanging Being.

> Leucippus thought he had a theory which was consistent with sense-perception and would not do away with coming to be and passing away or with motion and the multiplicity of things. He conceded thus much to appearances, but he agreed with the Monists that there could be no motion without void, and that the void was Unbeing and no part of Being, since Being was an absolute plenum. But there was not just one Being, but many, infinite in number and invisible because of the minuteness of their mass.

However, no more than one line of Leucippus survives verbatim, and for the detailed content of the atomic theory we have to rely on what we can learn from his pupil. Democritus was a polymath and a prolific writer, author of nearly eighty treatises on topics ranging from poetry and harmony to military tactics and Babylonian theology. But it is for his natural philosophy that he is most remembered. He is reported to have said that he would rather discover a single scientific explanation than become King of the Persians. But he was also modest in his scientific aspirations: 'do not try to know everthing,' he warned, 'or you may end up knowing nothing.'

The fundamental tenet of Democritus' atomism is that matter is not infinitely divisible. According to atomism, if we take any chunk of any kind of stuff and divide it up as far as we can, we will have to come to a halt at some point at which we will reach tiny bodies which are indivisible. The argument for this conclusion seems to have been philosophical rather than experimental. If matter is divisible to infinity, then let us suppose that this division has been carried out – for if matter is genuinely so divisible, there will be nothing incoherent in this supposition. How large are the fragments resulting from this division? If they have any magnitude at all, then, on the hypothesis of infinite divisibility, it would be possible to divide them further; so they must be fragments with no extension, like a geometrical point. But whatever can be divided can be put together again: if we saw a log into many pieces, we can put the pieces together into a log of the same size. But if our fragments have no magnitude then how can they ever have added up to make the extended chunk of matter with which we began? Matter cannot consist of mere geometrical points, not even of an infinite number of them; so we have to conclude that divisibility comes to an end, and the smallest possible fragments must be bodies with sizes and shapes.

It is these bodies which Democritus called 'atoms' ('atom' is just the Greek word for 'indivisible'). He believed that they are too small to be detected by the senses, and that they are infinite in number and come in infinitely many different kinds. They are scattered, like motes in a sunbeam, in infinite empty space, which he called 'the void'. They have existed for ever, and they are always in motion. They collide with each other and link up with each other; some of them are concave and some convex; some are like hooks and some are like eyes. The middle-sized objects with which we are familiar are complexes of atoms thus randomly united; and the differences between different kinds of substances are due to the differences in their atoms. Atoms, he said, differed in shape (as the letter A differs from the letter N), in order (as AN differs from NA), and in posture (as N differs from Z).

Critics of Democritus in antiquity complained that while he explained everything else in terms of the motion of atoms, he had no explanation of this motion itself. Others, in his defence, claimed that the motion was caused by a force of attraction whereby each atom sought out similar atoms. But an unexplained attraction is perhaps no better than an unexplained motion. Moreover, if an attractive force had been operative for an infinite time without any counteracting force (such as Empedocles' Strife), the world would now consist of congregations of uniform atoms; which is very different from the random aggregates with which Democritus identified the animate and inanimate beings with which we are familiar.

For Democritus, atoms and void are the only two realities: all else was appearance. When atoms approach or collide or entangle with each other, the aggregates appear as water or fire or plants or humans, but all that really exists are the underlying atoms in the void. In particular, the qualities perceived by the senses are mere appearances. Democritus' most often quoted dictum was:

> By convention sweet and by convention bitter; by convention hot, by convention cold, by convention colour: in reality atoms and void.

When he said that sensory qualities were 'by convention', ancient commentators tell us, he meant that the qualities were relative to us and did not belong to the natures of the things themselves. By nature nothing is white or black or yellow or red or bitter or sweet.

Democritus explained in detail how different flavours result from different kinds of atom. Sharp flavours arise from atoms which are small, fine, angular and jagged. Sweet tastes, on the other hand, originate from larger, rounder atoms. If something tastes salty, that is because its atoms are large, rough, jagged and angular.

Not only tastes and smells, but colours, sounds, and felt qualities are similarly to be explained by the properties and relationships of the underlying atoms. The knowledge which is given us by all these senses – taste, smell, sight, hearing, and touch – is a knowledge which is darkness. Genuine knowledge is altogether different, the prerogative of those who have mastered the theory of atoms and void.

Democritus wrote on ethics as well as physics: the sayings which have been handed down to us suggest that as a moralist he was edifying rather than inspiring. The following remark, sensible but unexciting, is typical of many:

> Be satisfied with what you have, and do not spend your time dreaming of acquisitions which excite envy and admiration; look at the lives of those who are poor and in distress, so that what you have and own may appear great and enviable.

A man who is lucky in his son-in-law, he said, gains a son, while one who is unlucky loses a daughter – a remark that has been quoted unwittingly, and often in garbled form, by many a speaker at a wedding breakfast. Many a political reformer, too, has echoed his sentiment that it is better to be poor in a democracy than prosperous in a dictatorship.

The sayings which have been preserved do not add up to a systematic morality, and they do not seem to have any connection with the atomic theory which underlies his philosophy. However, some of his dicta, brief and banal as they may appear, are sufficient, if true, to overturn whole systems of moral philosophy. For instance,

> The good person not only refrains from wrongdoing but does not even desire it.

conflicts with the often held view that virtue is at its highest when it triumphs over conflicting passion. Again,

> It is better to suffer wrong than to inflict it.

cannot be reconciled with the utilitarian view, widespread in the modern world, that morality should take account only of the consequences of an action, not the identity of the agent.

In late antiquity, and in the Renaissance, Democritus was known as the laughing philosopher, while Heraclitus was known as the weeping philosopher. Neither description seems very solidly based. However, there are remarks attributed to Democritus which support his claim to cheerfulness, notably

> A life without feasting is like a highway without inns.

II

THE ATHENS OF SOCRATES

THE ATHENIAN EMPIRE

The most glorious days of Ancient Greece fell in the fifth-century BC, during fifty years of peace between two periods of warfare. The century began with wars between Greece and Persia, and ended with a war between the city states of Greece itself. In the middle period flowered the great civilization of the city of Athens.

Ionia, where the earliest philosophers had flourished, had been under Persian rule since the mid-sixth century. In 499 the Ionian Greeks rose in revolt against the Persian king, Darius. After crushing the rising, Darius invaded Greece to punish those who had assisted the rebels from the mainland. A mainly Athenian force defeated the invading army at Marathon in 490. Darius' son Xerxes launched a more massive expedition in 484, defeated a gallant band of Spartans at Thermopylae, and forced the Athenians to evacuate their city. But his fleet was defeated by a united Greek navy near the offshore island of Salamis, and a Greek land victory at Platea in 479 put an end to the invasion.

After the invasions, Athens assumed the leadership of the Greek allies. It was the Athenians who liberated the Ionian Greeks, and it was Athens, supported by contributions from other cities, which controlled the navy that kept the freedom of the Aegean and Ionian seas. What began as a federation grew into an Athenian Empire.

Internally, Athens was a democracy, the first authenticated example of such a polity. 'Democracy' is the Greek word for the rule of the people, and Athenian democracy was a very thoroughgoing form of that rule. Athens was not like a modern democracy, in which the citizens elect representatives to form a government. Rather, each citizen had the right personally to take part in government by attending a general assembly, where he could listen to speeches by political leaders and then cast his vote. To see what this would mean in modern terms, imagine that members of the cabinet and shadow cabinet speak on television for two hours, after which a motion is put and a decision taken on the basis of votes recorded by each viewer pressing either a 'yes' or 'no' button on the television set. To make the parallel precise, one would have to add that only male citizens over 20 are allowed to press the button; and no women or children, or slaves or foreigners.

The judiciary and the legislature in Athens were drawn by lot from members of the assembly over thirty; laws were passed by a panel of 1,000 chosen for one day only, and major trials were conducted before a jury of 501. Even the magistrates – the executives charged with carrying out the decisions of government, whether judicial, financial, or military – were largely chosen by lot; only about one hundred were elected officers.

Never before or since have the ordinary people of a state taken so full a part in its government. It is important to remember this when reading what Greek philosophers have to say about the merits and demerits of democratic institutions. Athenians dated their constitution to the reforms of Cleisthenes in 508 BC, and that year is often taken to be the birthdate of democracy.

Athenian democracy was not incompatible with aristocratic leadership, and during its period of empire Athens, by popular choice, was governed by Pericles, the great-nephew of Cleisthenes. He instituted an ambitious programme to re-build the city's temples which had been destroyed by Xerxes. To this day, visitors travel across the world to see the ruins of the buildings he erected on the Acropolis, the city's citadel. The sculptures with which these temples were decorated are among the most treasured possessions of the museums in which they are now scattered. The Parthenon, the temple of the virgin goddess Athena, was a thank-offering for the victories of the Persian wars. The Elgin marbles in the British Museum, brought from the temple ruins by Lord Elgin in 1803, represent a great Athenian festival, the Panathenaea, just such a one as Parmenides and Zeno saw in the years when the building works were beginning. When Pericles' programme was complete, Athens was unrivalled anywhere in the world for architecture and sculpture.

Athens held the primacy too in drama and literature. Aeschylus, who had fought in the Persian wars, was the first great writer of tragedy: he brought onto the stage the heroes and heroines of Homeric epic, and his re-enactment of the homecoming and murder of Agamemnon can still fascinate and horrify. Aeschylus also represented the more recent catastrophes which had afflicted King Xerxes. Younger dramatists, the pious conservative Sophocles and the more radical and sceptical Euripides, set the classical pattern of tragic drama. Sophocles' plays about King Oedipus, killer of his father and husband of his mother, and Euripides' portrayal of the child-murderer Medea, not only figure in the twentieth-century repertoire but strike disturbing chords in the twentieth-century psyche. The serious writing of history, also, began in this century, with Herodotus' Chronicles of the Persian Wars written in the early years of the century, and Thucydides' narrative of the war between the Greeks as it came to an end.

ANAXAGORAS

Philosophy, too, came to Athens in the age of Pericles. **Anaxagoras** of Clazomenae (near Izmir) was born about 500 BC and was thus about forty years older than Democritus. He came to Athens after the end of the Persian wars, and became a friend and associate of Pericles. He wrote a book on natural philosophy in the style of his Ionian predecessors, acknowledging a particular debt to Anaximenes; it was the first such treatise, we are told, to contain diagrams.

Anaxagoras' account of the origin of the world is strikingly similar to a model which is popular today. At the beginning, he said, 'all things were together', in a unit infinitely complex and infinitely small which lacked all perceptible qualities. This primeval pebble began to rotate, expanding as it did so, and throwing off air and ether, and eventually the stars and the sun and the moon. In the course of the rotation, what is dense separated off from what is rarefied, and so did the hot from the cold, the bright from the dark, and the dry from the wet. Thus the articulated substances of our world were formed, with the dense and the wet and the cold and the dark congregating where our earth now is, and the rare and the hot and the dry and the bright moving to the outermost parts of the ether.

In a manner, however, Anaxagoras maintained, 'as things were in the beginning, so now they are all together': that is, in every single thing there is a portion of everything else; there is a little whiteness in what is black, and something lightweight in whatever is heavy. This was clearest in the case of semen, which must contain hair and nails and muscles and bones and ever so much else. The expansion of the universe, according to Anaxagoras, has continued until the present, and will continue in the future, and perhaps it is even now generating inhabited worlds other than our own.

The motion which generates the development of the universe is set in train by Mind. Mind is something entirely different from the matter over whose history it presides. It is infinite and separate, and has no part in the general commingling of elements; if it did, it would get drawn into the evolutionary process and could not control it.

In the 430s, when the popularity of Pericles began to wane, his protégé Anaxagoras was targeted for attack. He had said that the sun was a fiery lump, somewhat larger than the Peloponnesus. This was taken as inconsistent with worship of the sun as a god, and was made the basis of a charge of impiety. He fled to Lampsacus on the Hellespont and lived there in honourable exile until his death in 428.

THE SOPHISTS

Anaxagoras, during the rule of Pericles, was without rival as a resident philosopher in Athens. But during the same period the city received visits from a number of itinerant purveyors of learning who left behind reputations not inferior to his. These peripatetic teachers, or advisers, were called sophists: they were willing, for a fee, to impart many different skills and to act as consultants on a variety of topics.

As there was no public system of higher education in Athens, it fell to the sophists to instruct those young men who could afford their services in the arts and information which they would need in their adult life. Given the importance of public pleading in the assembly and before the courts, rhetorical skill was at a premium, and sophists were much in demand to teach, and assist with, the presentation of a case in the most favourable possible light. Critics alleged that because they were more concerned with persuasiveness than with the pursuit of truth, the sophists were no true philosophers. None the less, the best of them were quite capable of holding their own in philosophical argument.

The most famous of the sophists was **Protagoras** of Abdera, who visited Athens several times during the mid-fifth century, and was employed by Pericles to draw up a constitution for an Athenian colony. Most of what we know of Protagoras comes from the writings of Plato, who disapproved of sophists and regarded them as a bad influence on the young, encouragers of scepticism, relativism, and cynicism. None the less, Plato took Protagoras seriously and endeavoured to provide answers to his arguments.

Protagoras was agnostic in religion. 'About the gods,' he said, 'I cannot be sure whether they exist or not, or what they are like to see; for many things stand in the way of knowledge of them, both the opacity of the subject and the shortness of human life.' He was more a humanist than a theist: 'Man is the measure of all things,' ran his most famous saying, 'both of things that are that they are, and of things that are not that they are not.'

On the most likely interpretation, this means that whatever, whether through perception or through thought, appears to a particular person to be true, *is* true for that person. This does away with objective truth: nothing can be true absolutely, but only true relative to an individual. When people differ in belief, there is no way in which one of them is right and the other wrong. Democritus, and later Plato, objected that Protagoras' doctrine destroyed itself. For if all beliefs are true, then among true beliefs is the belief that not every belief is true.

Another sophist, **Gorgias** of Leontini, had been a pupil of Empedocles. He was first and foremost a teacher of rhetoric, whose essays on the polishing of style influenced the history of Greek oratory. But he was also a philosopher, of a tendency even more sceptical than that of Protagoras. He is said to have maintained that there is nothing, that if there is anything it cannot be known, and if anything can be known it cannot be communicated by one person to another.

By the time Gorgias visited Athens, in 427, a war had commenced between Athens and Sparta, known as the Peloponnesian war. Shortly after the outbreak of war, Pericles died, and campaign after campaign went badly for Athens. Defeat and plague brutalized the Athenians, and they became cruel and unscrupulous in warfare. They forfeited all claim to moral grandeur in 416 when they occupied the island of Melos, slaughtered all the adult males and enslaved the women and children. The later tragedies of Euripides, and some of the comedies of his contemporary Aristophanes, expressed an eloquent protest against the Athenian conduct of the war. It concluded with a crushing naval defeat at Aegospotami in 405 BC. The Athenian empire came to an end, and the leadership of Greece passed to Sparta. But the great days of Athenian philosophy were still to come.

SOCRATES

Among those who served in the Athenian heavy infantry was **Socrates** the son of Sophroniscus, who was thirty-eight when the war began. He was present at three of the important battles in the earlier years of the war and won a reputation for bravery. Back in Athens in 406, he held office in the Assembly at a time when a group of generals was put on trial for abandoning the bodies of the dead at the sea-battle of Arginusae. It was illegal to try the generals collectively rather than individually, but Socrates was the only person to vote against doing so, and they were executed.

When the war ended in 404, the Spartans replaced the Athenian democracy with an oligarchy known as the Thirty Tyrants, who instituted a reign of terror. Socrates was ordered to arrest an innocent man, but disregarded the order. He would soon pay the price of the uprightness which had made him unpopular now with both democrats and aristocrats.

Socrates' importance in the development of philosophy is such that all the philosophers we have considered hitherto are lumped together by historians under the title 'Pre-Socratics'. Yet he left no written work, and the details of his life, apart from its main dramatic events, remain obscure, a subject of controversy among scholars. He did not lack biographers, and indeed many of his contemporaries and successors wrote dialogues in which he took the leading part. The difficulty is to sort out sober fact from admiring fiction. His biographers all tell us that he was shabby and ugly, pot-bellied and snub-nosed; but agreement goes little further than that. The two authors whose works survive intact, the military historian Xenophon and the idealist philosopher Plato, paint pictures of Socrates which differ from each other as much as the picture of Jesus given by St Mark differs from that given by St John.

In his lifetime, Socrates was mocked by the comic dramatist Aristophanes, who portrayed him as a bumbling and corrupt eccentric, pursuing scientific curiosities with his head literally in the clouds. But rather than a natural philosopher, Socrates seems to have been a sophist of an unusual kind. Like the sophists, he spent much of his time in discussion and debate with rich young men (some of whom came to positions of power when oligarchy replaced democracy). But unlike others he charged no fees, and his method of education was not to instruct but to question; he said that he drew out, like a midwife, the thoughts with which his young pupils were pregnant. Unlike the sophists he made no claim to the possession of any special knowledge or expertise.

In classical Greece great attention was paid to the oracles uttered in the name of the god Apollo by the entranced priestesses in the shrine of Delphi. When asked if there was anyone wiser than Socrates, a priestess replied that there was no one. Socrates professed to be puzzled by this oracle, and questioned, one after another, politicians, poets, and experts claiming to possess wisdom of various kinds. None of them were able to defend their reputation against his cross-questioning, and Socrates concluded that the oracle was correct in that he alone realized that his own wisdom was worth nothing.

It was in matters of morality that it was most important to pursue genuine knowledge and to expose false pretensions. For according to Socrates moral know-ledge and virtue were one and the same thing. Someone who really knew what it was right to do could not do wrong; if anyone did what was wrong, it must be because he did not know what was right. No one goes wrong on purpose, since everyone wants to lead a good life and thus be happy. Those who do wrong unintentionally are in need of instruction, not punishment. This remarkable set of doctrines is sometimes called by historians 'The Socratic Paradox'.

Socrates did not claim to possess himself the degree of wisdom which would keep him from wrongdoing. Instead, he said that he relied on an inner divine voice, which would intervene if ever he was on the point of taking a wrong step.

Authorities who disagree about the content of Socrates' teaching agree about the manner of his death. The enemies whom he had made by his political probity, and his gadfly-like puncturing of reputations, ganged together to bring against him, at the age of seventy, a series of capital charges, accusing him of impiety, the introduction of strange gods, and the corruption of Athenian youth. Plato, who was present at his trial, wrote, after his death, a dramatized version of his speech in his defence, or *Apology*.

His accuser, Meletus, claims that he corrupts the young. Who then are the people who improve the young? In answer Meletus suggests, first, the judges, then the members of the legislative council, then the members of the assembly, and finally every single Athenian except Socrates. What a surprising piece of good fortune for the city's young people! Socrates goes on to ask whether it is better to live among good men than among bad men? Anyone would obviously prefer to live among good men, since bad men are likely to do him harm; if so he himself can have no motive for corrupting the young on purpose, and if he is doing so unwittingly, he should be educated rather than prosecuted.

Socrates turns to the charge of impiety. Is he being accused of atheism, or of introducing strange gods? The two charges are not consistent with each other;

and in fact, Meletus seems to be confusing him with Anaxagoras who said the sun was made of stone and the moon of earth. As for the charge of atheism, Socrates can reply that his mission as a philosopher was given him by God himself, and his campaign to expose false wisdom was waged in obedience to the Delphic oracle. What would really be a betrayal of God would be to desert his post through fear of death. If he were told that he could go free on condition of abandoning philosophical inquiry, he would reply, 'Men of Athens, I honour and love you; but I shall obey God rather than you, and while I have life and strength I shall never cease from the practice and teaching of philosophy'.

Socrates concludes his defence by pointing to the presence in court of many of his pupils and their families, none of whom has been called on to testify for the prosecution. He refuses to do as others and produce in court his weeping children as objects of compassion: at the hands of the judges he seeks justice and not mercy.

When the verdict was delivered, he was condemned by a slender majority of the 501 judges. The prosecution called for the death penalty; it was for the accused to propose an alternative sentence. Socrates considered asking for an honourable pension, but was willing to settle for a moderate fine – one too large for him to pay himself, but which Plato and his friends were willing to pay on his behalf. The judges regarded the fine as unrealistically small, and passed sentence of death.

In his speech after sentence, Socrates told the judges that it would not have been difficult for him to frame a defence which would have secured acquittal; but the kind of tactics required would have been beneath him. 'The difficulty, my friends, is not to avoid death, but to avoid unrighteousness; for that runs faster than death'. Socrates, old and slow, has been overtaken by the slower runner; his sprightly accusers have been overtaken by the faster. During the trial his divine voice has never once spoken to him to hold him back, and so he is content to go to his death.

Is death a dreamless sleep? Such a sleep is more blessed than most nights and days in the life of even the most fortunate mortal. Is death a journey to another world? How splendid, to be able to meet the glorious dead and to converse with Hesiod and Homer! 'Nay. if this be true, let me die again and again.' He has so many questions to put to the great men and women of the past: and in the next world no one will be put to death for asking questions. 'The hour of departure has arrived, and we go our ways – I to die, and you to live. Which is better God only knows.'

THE *EUTHYPHRO*

After the trial portrayed in the *Apology*, there was a delay before sentence of death was carried out. A sacred ship had set out on its annual ceremonial voyage to the island of Delos, and until it returned to Athens the taking of human life was taboo. Plato has represented these days between condemnation and execution in a pair of unforgettable dialogues, the *Crito* and the *Phaedo*. No one knows how much in these dialogues is history, and how much invention; but the picture which they paint has fired the imagination of many who lived centuries and millennia after Socrates' death.

Before considering these works, we should turn to a short dialogue, the *Euthyphro*, which Plato situates immediately before the trial. However fictional in detail, this probably gives a fair picture of Socrates' actual methods of discussion and cross-examination.

Socrates, awaiting trial outside the courthouse, meets young Euthyphro from Naxos, who has come to bring a private prosecution. Euthyphro's father had apprehended a farm-labourer who had killed a servant in a brawl; while sending to Athens for an authoritative ruling about his punishment, he had had him tied up and thrown into a ditch, where he died of hunger and exposure. The son had now come to Athens to prosecute a charge of murder against his father.

The case is obviously intended by Plato to be a difficult one: did the father really kill the labourer? If he did, is killing a murderer really murder? If it is, is a son a proper prosecutor of a father? But Euthyphro has no doubts, and regards his action as the performance of a religious duty. The case provides the setting for a discussion between Socrates and Euthyphro on the relation between religion and morality. The nature of piety, or holiness, is of keen interest to Socrates who is himself about to stand trial on a charge of impiety. So he asks Euthyphro to tell him the nature of piety and impiety.

Piety, replies Euthyphro, is doing as I am doing, prosecuting crime; and if you think I should not take my father to court, remember that the supreme god Zeus punished his own father, Cronos. Socrates expresses some distaste for such stories of conflicts between the gods, and takes a while to ascertain that Euthyphro really believes them. But his real difficulty with Euthyphro's account of piety or holiness is that it merely gives a single example, and does not tell us what is the standard by which actions are to be judged pious or impious. Euthyphro obliges with a definition: holiness is what the gods love, and unholiness is what they hate.

Socrates points out that, given the stories about quarrels between the gods, it may not be easy to secure a consensus about what the gods love; if something is loved by some gods and hated by others, it will turn out to be both holy and unholy. Such may be the case with Euthyphro's own action of prosecuting his father. But let us waive this, and amend the definition so that it runs: what all the gods love is holy, and what all the gods hate is unholy. A further question arises: do the gods love what is holy because it is holy, or is it holy because the gods love it?

In order to get Euthyphro to grasp the sense of this question, Socrates offers a number of examples which turn on points of Greek grammar. His point could be made in English by saying that in a criminal case, 'the accused' is so called because someone accuses him; it is not that people accuse him because he is the accused. Now is the holy, similarly, so called because the gods love it? Once he understands the question, Euthyphro rejects it: on the contrary, the gods love what is holy because it is holy.

Socrates now slyly offers 'godly' as an abbreviation for 'what is loved by the gods'. Since Euthyphro maintains that holiness and godliness are the same, we can substitute 'godly' for 'holy' in Euthyphro's thesis that what is holy is loved by the gods because it is holy. We get this result:

(A) The godly is loved by the gods because it is godly

On the other hand it seems clear that

(B) The godly is godly because it is loved by the gods

since 'godly' was introduced precisely as a synonym for 'loved by the gods'. Socrates claims to have reduced Euthyphro to inconsistency, and urges him to withdraw his claim that godliness and holiness are identical.

Euthyphro in the dialogue concedes that his definitions have not turned out as he wished. We may well think, however, that he should have stood his ground, and pointed out that Socrates was equivocating with the word 'because', using it in two different senses. If we say that the godly is the godly because it is loved by the gods, we are talking about the word 'godly'; the 'because' invokes our stipulation about its meaning. If we say that the gods love the holy because it is holy, the 'because' introduces the motive of the gods' love, and we are not talking about the meanings of words. In fact, once we realize the ambiguity of 'because' there is no conflict between (A) and (B). The point can be made in English by pointing out that it is true both that

(C) A judge is a judge because he judges

(that is why he is called a judge); and also that

(D) A judge judges because he is a judge

(he does it because it is his job).

So Euthyphro should not have been checkmated so easily. However, even if Socrates was persuaded to agree that there was nothing inconsistent in saying that what is holy is loved by the gods because it is holy, he could still go on to say, as he does in the dialogue, that even if that is so, being loved by the gods is only something that happens to what is holy: it does not tell us the essential nature of holiness in itself.

Instead of godliness, should holiness be identified with justice? Socrates and Euthyphro agree that holiness seems to be only one part of justice, and Euthyphro suggests that it is justice in the service of the gods, rather than justice in the service of humans. Socrates latches onto the word 'service'. When we take care of horses, or dogs, or oxen, we do them various services which improve their condition. Can we in a similar way do services to the gods? Can we make them any better than they are? Euthyphro points out that servants do not necessarily aim to improve their masters by serving them, but simply to assist them in their work. What then, Socrates asks, is the gods' work, in which we can offer service? Euthyphro is unable to reply, and falls back on a definition of holiness as divine service in the form of prayer and sacrifice.

So then, Socrates says, holiness is giving things to the gods in the hope of getting something back from them; a kind of trade. But a trader can only hope to strike a bargain by offering his customer something which he needs or wants; so we must ask what good the gods gain from our gifts? Euthyphro cannot answer except by falling back on his earlier claim that holiness is something which the gods love. He refuses to take the discussion further, and hastens on to his self-appointed task.

The *Euthyphro* probably gives a realistic picture of the strengths and weaknesses of Socrates' methods of cross-examination. It also, whether this was Plato's intention or not, enables us to understand why religious folk in Athens might in good faith regard Socrates as a danger to the young and a purveyor of impiety.

THE *CRITO*

The *Crito* is a much easier dialogue to read. Socrates is now in prison, waiting for the execution of his sentence. A number of his friends, led by Crito, have devised a plan for him to escape and flee to Thessaly. The plan had a good chance of success, but Socrates would have no part in it. Life was only worth striving for if it was a good life; and life purchased by disobedience to the laws was not a life worth living. Even if he has been wronged, he should not render evil for evil. But in fact he has been condemned by due process, and he should remain obedient to the law.

Socrates imagines the laws of Athens addressing him. 'Did we not bring you into existence? By our aid your father married your mother and begat you.' We also commanded your father to educate you in body and mind. 'Has a philosopher like you failed to discover that our country is more precious and higher and holier far than mother or father or any ancestor? . . . Having brought you into the world, and nurtured and educated you, and given you and every other citizen a share in every good which we had to give, we further proclaim to any Athenian by the liberty which we allow him, that if he does not like us, the laws, when he has become of age and seen the ways of the city, and made our acquaintance, he may go where he pleases and take his goods with him.'

By remaining in Athens continuously through his long life Socrates has entered into an implied contract that he will do as the laws command. By refusing at his trial to accept exile rather than death, he has renewed that commitment. Will he now, at the age of seventy, turn his back on the covenants he has made and run away? 'Think not of life and children first, and of justice afterwards, but of justice first; for if you leave the city, returning evil for evil and breaking the contracts you have made with us, our brethren, the laws in the world below, will give you no friendly welcome.' Crito has no answer and Socrates concludes, 'Let us fulfil the will of God and follow whither he leads'.

THE *PHAEDO*

The dialogue with which Plato concludes his account of Socrates' last days is called the *Phaedo*, after the name of the narrator, a citizen of Parmenides' city of Elea, who claims, with his friends Simmias and Cebes, to have been present with Socrates at his death. The drama begins as news arrives that the sacred ship has returned from Delos, which brings to an end the stay of execution. Socrates' chains are removed, and he is allowed a final visit from his weeping wife Xanthippe with their youngest child in her arms. After she leaves, the group turns to a discussion of death and immortality.

A true philosopher, Socrates maintains, will have no fear of death; but he will not take his own life, either, even when dying seems preferable to going on living. We are God's cattle, and we should not take ourselves off without a summons from God. Why, then, ask Simmias and Cebes, is Socrates so ready to go to his death?

In response Socrates takes as his starting point the conception of a human being as a soul imprisoned in a body. True philosophers care little for bodily pleasures such as food and drink and sex, and they find the body a hindrance rather than a help in the pursuit of scientific knowledge. 'Thought is best when the mind is gathered into itself, and none of these things trouble it – neither sounds nor sights nor pain, nor again any pleasure – when it takes leave of the body and has as little as possible to do with it.' So philosophers in their pursuit of truth continually try to keep their souls detached from their bodies. But death is the full separation of soul from body: hence, a true philosopher has, all life long, been in effect seeking and craving after death.

Hunger and disease and lust and fear obstruct the study of philosophy. The body is to blame for faction and war, because the body's demands need money for their satisfaction, and all wars are caused by the love of money. Even in peacetime the body is a source of endless turmoil and confusion. 'If we would have pure knowledge of anything we must be quit of the body – the soul by itself must behold things by themselves: and then we shall attain that which we desire, and of which we say that we are lovers – wisdom; not while we live but, as the argument shows, only after death.' A true lover of wisdom, therefore, will depart this life with joy.

So far, it is fair to say, Socrates has been preaching rather than arguing. Cebes brings him up short by saying that most people will reject the premiss that the soul can survive the body. They believe rather that on the day of death the soul comes to an end, vanishing into nothingness like a puff of smoke. 'Surely it requires a great deal of proof to show that when a man is dead his soul yet exists, and has any strength or intelligence.' So Socrates proceeds to offer a set of proofs of immortality.

First, there is the argument from opposites. If two things are opposites, each of them comes into being from the other. If someone goes to sleep, she must have been awake. If someone wakes up, he must have been asleep. Again, if A becomes greater than B, then A must have been less that B. If A becomes better than B, then A must have been worse than B. Thus, these opposites, *greater* and *less,* plus *better* and *worse,* just like *sleeping* and *waking,* come into being from each other. But death and life are opposites, and the same must hold true here also. Those who die, obviously enough, are those who have been living; should we not conclude that dying in its turn is followed by living? Since life after death is not visible, we must conclude that souls live in another world below, perhaps to return to earth in some latter day.

The second argument sets out to prove the existence of a non-embodied soul not after, but before, its life in the body. The proof proceeds in two steps: first, Socrates seeks to show that knowledge is recollection; second, he urges that recollection involves pre-existence.

The first step in the argument goes like this. We constantly see things which are more or less equal in size. But we never see two stones or blocks of wood or other material things which are absolutely equal to each other. Hence, our idea of absolute equality cannot be derived from experience. The approximately equal things we see merely remind us of absolute equality, in the way that a portrait may remind us of an absent lover.

The second step is this. If we are reminded of something, we must have been acquainted with it beforehand. So if we are reminded of absolute equality, we must have previously encountered it. But we did not do so in our present life with our ordinary senses of sight and touch. So we must have done so, by pure intellect, in a previous life before we were born – unless, improbably, we imagine that the knowledge of equality was infused into us at the moment of our birth. If the argument works for the idea of absolute equality, it works equally for other similar ideas, such as absolute goodness and absolute beauty.

Socrates admits that this second argument, even if successful in proving that the soul exists before birth, will not show its survival after death unless it is reinforced by the first argument. So he offers a third argument, based on the concepts of dissolubility and indissolubility.

If something is able to dissolve and disintegrate, as the body does at death, then it must be something composite and changeable. But the objects with which the soul is concerned, such as absolute equality and beauty, are unchangeable, unlike the beauties we see with the eyes of the body, which fade and decay. The visible world is constantly changing; only what is invisible remains unaltered. The invisible soul suffers change only when dragged, through the senses of the body, into the world of flux.

Within that world, the soul staggers like a drunkard; but when it returns into itself, it passes into the world of purity, eternity, and immortality. This is the world in which it is at home. 'The soul is in the very likeness of the divine, and immortal, and rational, and uniform, and indissoluble and unchangeable, and the body is in the very likeness of the human, and mortal, and irrational, and multi-form, and dissoluble, and changeable.' Hence, Socrates concludes, the body is liable to dissolution, while the soul is almost totally indissoluble. If even bodies, when mummified in Egypt, can survive for many years, it must be totally improbable that the soul dissolves and disappears at the moment of death.

The soul of the true philosopher will depart to an invisible world of bliss. But impure souls, who in life were nailed to the body by rivets of pleasure and pain, and are still wedded to bodily concerns at the moment of death, will not become totally immaterial, but will haunt the tomb as shadowy ghosts, until they enter the prison of a new body, perhaps of a lascivious ass, or a vicious wolf, or at best, a sociable and industrious bee.

Simmias now undermines the basis of Socrates' argument by offering a differ-ent, and subtle, conception of the soul. Consider, he says, a lyre made out of wood and strings. The lyre may be in tune or out of tune, depending on the tension of the strings. A living human body may be compared to a lyre that is in tune, and a dead body to a lyre out of tune. Suppose someone were to claim that, while the strings and the wood were gross material composites, being in tune was something which was invisible and incorporeal. Would it not be foolish to argue that this attunement could survive the smashing of the lyre and the rending of its strings? Of course; and we must conclude that when the strings of the body lose their tone through injury or disease, the soul must perish like the tunefulness of a broken lyre.

Cebes too still needs convincing that the soul is immortal, but his criticism of Socrates is less radical than that of Simmias. He is prepared to agree that the soul is more powerful than the body, and need not wear out when the body wears out. In the normal course of life, the body suffers frequent wear and tear and needs constant restoration by the soul. But may not the soul itself eventually come to die in the body, just as a weaver, who has made and worn out many coats in his lifetime, may die and be survived by the last of them? Even on the hypothesis of transmigration, a soul might pass from body to body, and yet not be imperishable but eventually meet its death. So, concludes Simmias, 'he who is confident about death can have but a foolish confidence, unless he is able to prove that the soul is altogether immortal and imperishable'.

In response to Simmias, Socrates first falls back on the argument from recollection which required the soul's pre-existence. This is quite unintelligible if having a soul is simply having one's body in tune; a lyre has to exist before it can be tuned. More importantly, being in tune admits of degrees: a lyre can be more or less in tune. But souls do not admit of degrees; no soul can be more or less a soul than another soul. One might say that a virtuous soul was a soul in harmony with itself: but if so, it would have to be an attunement of an attunement. Again, it is the tension of the strings which causes the lyre to be in tune, but in the human case the relationship is the other way round: it is the soul which keeps the body in order. Under this battery of arguments, Simmias admits defeat.

Before answering Cebes, Socrates offers a long narrative of his own intellectual history, leading up to his acceptance of the existence of absolute ideas, such as absolute beauty and absolute goodness. Only by sharing in beauty itself can something be beautiful. The same goes for the tall and short: a tall man is tall through tallness, and a short man is short through shortness. An individual may grow or shrink, and indeed if he becomes taller he must have been shorter, as was agreed earlier; but though he is first short and then tall, his shortness can never become tallness, nor his tallness shortness. This is so even in the case of a person like Simmias, who, as it happens, is taller than Socrates and shorter than Phaedo.

The relevance of these remarks to immortality takes some time to become clear. Socrates goes on to make a distinction between what later philosophers would call the contingent and necessary properties of things. Human beings may or may not be tall, but the number three cannot but be odd, and snow cannot but be cold: these properties are necessary to them, and not just contingent. Now just as coldness cannot turn into heat, so too snow, which is necessarily cold, must either retire or perish at the approach of heat; it cannot remain and become hot snow. Socrates generalizes: not only will opposites not receive opposites, but nothing which necessarily brings with it an opposite will admit the opposite of what it brings.

Now Socrates draws his moral. The soul brings life, just as snow brings cold. But death is the opposite of life, so that the soul can no more admit death than snow can admit heat. But what cannot admit death is immortal, and so the soul is immortal. But there is a difference between the soul and snow: when heat arrives, the snow simply perishes. But since what is immortal is also imperishable, the soul, at the approach of death, does not perish, but retires to another world.

It is not at all clear how this is an answer to Cebes' contention that the soul might be able to survive one or more deaths without being everlasting and imperishable. But in the dialogue Socrates' conclusion that the soul is immortal and imperishable and will exist in another world is greeted with acclamation, and the audience settles down to listen to Socrates as he narrates a series of myths about the soul's journeys in the underworld.

The narration over, Crito asks Socrates whether he has any last wishes, and how he should be buried. He is told to bear in mind the message of the dialogue: they will be burying only Socrates' body, not Socrates himself who is to go to the joys of the blessed. Socrates takes his last bath, and says farewell to the women and children of his family. The gaoler arrives with the cup of the poison, hemlock, which was given to condemned prisoners in Athens as the mode of their execution. After a joke to the gaoler, Socrates drains the cup and composes himself serenely for death as sensation gradually deserts his limbs. His last words are puzzling: 'Crito, I owe a cock to Aesculapius; will you remember to pay the debt'. Aesculapius was the god of healing. Perhaps the words mean that the life of the body is a disease, and death is its cure.

The *Phaedo* is a masterpiece: it is one of the finest surviving pieces of Greek prose, and even in translation it moves and haunts the reader. Two questions arise: what does it tell us about Socrates? What does it tell us about the immortality of the soul?

The narrative framework provided by Socrates' imprisonment and death is commonly accepted by scholars as authentic; and certainly it is Plato's account of these last hours which has held the imagination of writers and artists through the centuries. But several of the speeches propounding the soul's immortality are couched in language more appropriate to Plato's own philosophical system than to the cross-examination techniques of the historic Socrates. The confidence in survival expressed in the *Phaedo* is in sharp contrast with the agnosticism attributed to Socrates in Plato's own *Apology*.

The arguments for immortality, cut out of the pattern of ancient myth into which they are interwoven, are unlikely to convince a modern reader. But even in antiquity, counterarguments would come quickly to mind. Is it true that opposites always come from opposites? Did not Parmenides show that Being could not come from Unbeing? And even where opposites come from opposites, must the cycle continue for ever? Even if sleeping has to follow waking, may not one last waking be followed by everlasting sleep? And however true it may be that the soul cannot abide death, why must it retire elsewhere when the body dies, rather than perish like the melted snow?

The most interesting topics of the dialogue are the argument from recollection, and the criticism of the idea that the soul is an attunement of the body. Both of these themes have a long history ahead of them. But the first will be best pursued when we have examined its place in Plato's own developed system, and the second is best evaluated when we consider the account of the soul given by Plato's successor Aristotle.

In the works of philosophers through the ages, the name 'Socrates' occurs on many a page. More often than not, however, it is not a reference to the Athenian who drank the hemlock. It came into common use as a dummy name to be used in the formalization of arguments; as in the syllogism:

> All men are mortal
> Socrates is a man
> Therefore Socrates is mortal.

Particularly in the Middle Ages the name was used daily by writers who knew very little of the story told in the *Apology*, *Crito*, and *Phaedo*. In this, as in more solemn ways, the mortality and death of Socrates has echoed through the philosophical literature of the West.

III

THE PHILOSOPHY OF
PLATO

LIFE AND WORKS

Plato was born into a wealthy family in the last days of the Athenian Empire.
When the Peloponnesian war ended in 405 he was in his early twenties, just old
enough to have fought in it, as his brothers certainly did. His uncles, Critias and
Charmides, were two of the Thirty Tyrants. Socrates' execution in 399 under a
restored democracy gave Plato a lifelong distrust of demagogues, and a distaste
for a political career in Athens.

When he was forty Plato went to Sicily and formed a close association with
Dion, the brother-in-law of the reigning monarch Dionysius I. On his return to
Athens he founded a school, the Academy, in a private grove beside his own
house. It was modelled on the Pythagorean communities in Italy, a group of like-
minded thinkers interested in mathematics, metaphysics, morality and mysticism.
At the age of sixty Plato was invited back to Sicily as an adviser to Dion's nephew,
who had now succeeded to the throne as Dionysius II. His career as a royal
adviser was not successful, either politically or philosophically, and in 360 he
returned home. He died peacefully at a wedding-feast in Athens, himself unmarried, in his eighty-first year (347).

Apart from these few facts, which were embroidered by fiction writers in later
antiquity, we know little about Plato's life. However, unlike Socrates, Plato left
behind many writings on philosophy, all of which survive today. But these works
are in dialogue form, and Plato himself never appears in them as a speaker.
Hence, it is difficult to be sure which of the varied and often conflicting philosophical positions propounded by the characters in the dialogues are ones to
which Plato was himself committed. When we seek to discover his own philosophical standpoint, we can achieve little certainty; but commentators have reached
a tentative consensus about the general lines along which his thought developed.

Plato's dialogues fall into three classes. The first group, commonly thought to
have been written earliest, are called 'Socratic' dialogues because in each of them
Socrates appears in his historic role as the questioner and deflater of spurious

claims to knowledge. The *Euthyphro* illustrates the pattern common to most of these dialogues: some person, usually the one named in the title, professes to be knowledgeable about a particular art or virtue or excellence, and Socrates' cross-questioning shows up the pretended knowledge as mere prejudice. In this manner the topic of courage is treated in the *Laches*, temperance in the *Charmides*, friendship in the *Lysis*, beauty in the *Hippias Major* and poetic recitation in the *Ion*, just as piety was in the *Euthyphro*. The *Hippias Minor*, another dialogue of this period, addresses the Socratic theme of intentional and unintentional wrongdoing.

In the central group of dialogues, dating from Plato's maturity, Socrates is again the principal figure; but he is no longer simply an attorney prosecuting prejudices that masquerade as knowledge. He now appears as a teacher in his own right, expounding elaborate philosophical ideas. The dialogues are longer, and their content is more difficult to master. We have already met one dialogue of this group, the *Phaedo*. Others are the *Gorgias*, the *Protagoras*, the *Meno*, the *Symposium*, the *Phaedrus*, and, best known of all, the *Republic*. Common to most of these is a preoccupation with the famous Theory of Ideas, which we must shortly explain.

In the final group of dialogues, the role of Socrates diminishes; sometimes he is only a minor figure, and sometimes he does not appear at all. A bridge between the middle and the later dialogues is given by the *Theaetetus*, which seeks a definition of knowledge: Socrates is still to be seen in his familiar role as the midwife of thought. In the *Parmenides* Socrates appears as a young man in awe of the aged Parmenides while dense and complicated arguments are presented against the Theory of Ideas. In the *Philebus*, whose topic is pleasure, Socrates once again has the chief part; in the *Sophist*, on Being and Unbeing, and in the *Statesman*, about the best form of government, he is present, but takes no effective part in the discussion. In the latest and longest of this group, *The Laws*, which sets out a detailed constitution for an imaginary state, Socrates does not appear at all.

Scholars do not agree how to interpret the cool and critical view which these late dialogues take of the Theory of Ideas. Are the arguments against it meant to be convincing, and did Plato abandon the theory in mid-life? Or did he think the arguments were only sophistries, and simply leave it as an exercise for the reader to work out how they could be refuted? The uncertainty here is compounded by the existence of another dialogue, the *Timaeus*, which sets out Plato's cosmology, and which, until the Renaissance, was the best known of all his dialogues. In the *Timaeus* the Theory of Ideas appears unchallenged in all its original glory; what is in question is whether the dialogue belongs to the middle or the later period of Plato's life. Plato's philosophical development is easier to understand if we place the *Timaeus* with dialogues like the *Republic*; but if we compare the dialogues on the basis of style, it seems to resemble more the group containing the *Sophist*. The question of its dating is unresolved, and will no doubt continue to be debated among scholars.

But let us look more closely at the Theory of Ideas which underpins the middle dialogues and provides the bone of contention concerning the later dialogues. We have already met it briefly, when Socrates spoke of absolute beauty and absolute goodness in the *Phaedo*. But I tried to expound the arguments of that dialogue so far as possible without elaborating on the nature of Ideas. It is now time to fill that gap.

The Theory of Ideas

Plato's theory arises as follows. Socrates, Simmias, and Cebes are all called 'men'; they have it in common that they are all men. Now when we say 'Simmias is a man' does the word 'man' stand for something in the way that the word 'Simmias' stands for the individual man Simmias? If so, what? Is it the same thing as the word 'man' stands for in the sentence 'Cebes is a man'? Plato's answer is yes: in each case in which such an expression occurs it stands for the same thing, namely, that which makes Simmias, Cebes, and Socrates all men. This is given by Plato various designations, Greek phrases corresponding for instance to 'the man himself', or 'that very thing which is man'. Because, in calling Socrates a man, Plato meant not that he was male, but that he was human, the common thing meant by 'man' can be called – by analogy with Plato's use in other cases – 'humanity'. But its best known designation is 'The Idea (or Form) of Man'.

Generalizing, in any case where A,B,C, are all F, Plato is likely to say that they are related to a single Idea of F. Sometimes he states the principle universally, sometimes, in particular cases, he hesitates about applying it. In various places he lists Ideas of many different types, such as the Idea of Good, the Idea of Bad, the Idea of Circle, the Idea of Being, the Idea of Sameness. And as long as he held the theory at all Plato seems to have continued to believe in the Ideas of Good and Beauty and Being. But he seems to have been unsure whether there was an Idea of Mud.

If we search through the Platonic texts, we discover a number of theses about Ideas and their relations to ordinary things in the world.

(1) Wherever several things are F, this is because they participate or imitate a single Idea of F.

(2) No Idea is a participant or imitator of itself.

(3) (a) The Idea of F is F.
    (b) The Idea of F is nothing but F.

(4) Nothing but the Idea of F is really and truly altogether F.

(5) Ideas are not in space or time, they have no parts and do not change, they are not perceptible to the senses.

Theses (1), (2) and (3) make up an inconsistent triad. The difficulty to which they lead was first expounded by Plato himself in the *Parmenides*. Let us suppose we have a number of individuals each of which is F. Then, by (1), there is an Idea of F. This, by (3), is itself F. But now the Idea of F and the original F things make up a new collection of F things. By (1) again, this must be because they participate in an Idea of F. But, by (2), this cannot be the Idea first postulated. So there must be another Idea of F; but this in its turn, by (3), will be F; and so on ad infinitum. So, against (1), there will be not a single Idea but infinitely many.

The problem can be illustrated by substituting 'Man' for 'F' in the above pattern of argument. If there are a number of men, then, by (1) there is an Idea of Man. But this, by (3) is itself man. The Idea of Man, plus the original men, therefore form a new collection of men. By (1), therefore, there must be an Idea of Man to correspond to this collection. But, by (2) this cannot be the Idea we have already met; so it must be a new Idea. But this, in its turn, will be another man; and so on ad infinitum; we cannot stop just with one or two Ideas of Man. Aristotle was to call this refutation of the Theory of Ideas 'The Third Man argument'. The problem was never resolved by Plato; and, as already said, it is a matter of dispute between scholars whether he shrugged the objection off or abandoned all or part of his theory as a consequence.

The problem to which Plato's theory is an inadequate solution is sometimes called 'the problem of universals'. In modern discussions of this problem, four notions can be discerned which bear some resemblance to Plato's Ideas.

(A) *Concrete Universals.* In a sentence such as 'water is fluid' the word 'water' is treated by some philosophers as the name of a single scattered object, the aqueous part of the world, made up of puddles, rivers, lakes and so on. Such a concrete universal would have a certain similarity with Plato's Ideas. It would explain Plato's preference (not always shared by his commentators) for referring to his Ideas by a concrete mode of speech (e.g. 'the beautiful') rather than an abstract one ('beauty'). It would give a clear sense to his theory that particulars participate in Ideas: this particular bottle of water is quite literally a part of all-the-water-in-the-world. Theses (2), (3a) and (4) are easily shown to be true. However, a concrete universal is very unlike a Platonic Idea in respect of (3b) and (5) – the water in the universe can be located and can change in quantity and distribution, it can be seen and touched, and has many other properties besides that of being water.

(B) *Paradigms.* It has more than once been suggested that Platonic forms might be looked on as paradigms or standards: the relation between individuals and Ideas may be thought to be similar to that between particular metre-long objects and the Standard Metre in Paris by which the metre length was formerly defined. This brings out well the imitation and resemblance aspect of Plato's theory: to be a metre long is, precisely, to resemble in length the Standard Metre; and if two things are each a metre long it is in virtue of this common resemblance to the paradigm. Like a concrete universal, a paradigm object fits those aspects of Plato's ideas which make them seem substantial entities; like a concrete universal, it fails to have the properties by which Platonic Ideas transcend the sensible world. The Standard Metre is not in heaven, but in Paris, and is discerned not by intellectual vision but by the eyes in one's head.

(C) *Attributes and Properties.* Logicians sometimes talk of attributes, such as humanity, or the property of being divisible by seven. These abstract entities share the more transcendental aspects of Plato's ideas; humanity does not grow or die as human beings do, and nowhere in the world could one view or handle divisibility by seven. All men, we might say, are human by virtue of sharing a common humanity; this humanity, we might say, is the attribute for which the predicate '. . . is a man' stands in the sentences 'Peter is a man' and 'John is a man'. But if we think of Platonic ideas in this way as attributes, it is very hard to see how Plato could ever have thought that humanity itself, and only humanity itself, was really a human being. Is it not clear that humanity is an abstraction, and that only a concrete individual can be a human being?

(D) *Classes.* Attributes serve as principles according to which objects can be collected into classes: objects which possess the attribute of humanity, for instance, can be grouped into the class of human beings. In some ways classes seem closer than attributes to Platonic Ideas: participation in an Idea can be understood without too much difficulty as membership of a class. Classes, like attributes, and unlike paradigms and concrete universals, resemble Ideas in their abstract properties. However, there is an important difference between attributes and classes. Two classes with the same members (the same *extension*, as philosophers sometimes say) are identical with each other, whereas attribute A need not be identical with attribute B even though all and only those who possess A possess also B. Being a human, for instance, is not the same attribute as being a featherless biped, though the class of featherless bipeds may well be the same class as the class of human beings. Philosophers express this difference by saying that classes are *extensional*, while attributes are not. It is not clear whether Plato's Ideas are extensional like classes, or non-extensional like attributes. The difficulty in identifying Ideas with classes arises over theses (2) and (3). The class of men is not a man and we cannot say in general that the class of Fs is F; some classes are members of themselves and some are not. There are problems in this area which only became fully obvious more than two millennia later.

Concepts such as those of *attribute* and *class* are more or less sophisticated descendants of Plato's notion; none of them, however, does justice to the many facets of his Ideas. If one wants to see how the theses (1) to (5) seemed plausible to Plato, it is better to take, not any modern logician's technical concept, but some more unreflective notion. Consider one of the points of the compass, North, South, West, and East. Take the notion of the East, for instance, not as one might try to explain it in virtue of an abstract notion, e.g. eastwardness, but as one might conceive it by naive reflection on the various locutions we in Britain use about the East. There are many places which are east of us, e.g. Belgrade, Warsaw, and Hong Kong. Anything which is thus east is in the East, is indeed a part of The East (participation); or, if you prefer, it is in more or less the same direction as The East (imitation). It is by virtue of being in The East, or by virtue of being in the same direction as that point of the compass, that whatever is east of us is east (Thesis 1). Now The East cannot be identified with any of the places which are east of us: it is provincial to think that 'The East' means a place such as India, since from some other point of view, e.g. that of Beijing, India is part of The West (Thesis 2). The East itself, of course, is east of us – to walk towards The East you must walk eastwards – and The East is nothing but east; we may say 'The East is red' but we really mean that the eastern sky is red (Thesis 3). Nothing but The East is unqualifiedly east: the sun is sometimes east and sometimes west, India is east of Iran but west of Vietnam, but in every time and every place The East is east (Thesis 4). Moreover, The East cannot be identified with any point in space, nor has it any history in time, nor can it be seen, handled, or parcelled out (Thesis 5).

I am not, of course, suggesting that points of the compass will supply an interpretation of Plato's Ideas which will make all theses (1) to (5) come out true. No interpretation could do this since the theses are not all compatible with each other. I am merely saying that this interpretation will make the theses look *prima facie* plausible in a way in which the interpretations previously considered will not. Concrete universals, paradigms, attributes, and classes all raise problems of their own, as philosophers long after Plato discovered, and though we cannot go back to Plato's solutions, we have yet to answer many of his problems in this area.

PLATO'S *REPUBLIC*

Plato relied on the Theory of Ideas not only in the area of logic and metaphysics, but also in the theory of knowledge and in the foundations of morality. To see the many different uses to which he put it in the years of his maturity, we cannot do better than to consider in detail his longest and most famous dialogue, *The Republic*.

The official purpose of the dialogue is to seek a definition of justice, and the thesis which it propounds is that justice is the health of the soul. But that answer takes a long while to reach, and when it is reached it is interpreted in many different ways.

The dialogue's first book offers a number of candidate definitions which are, one after the other, exploded by Socrates in the manner of the early dialogues. The book indeed, may at one time have existed separately as a self-contained dialogue.

But it also illustrates the essential structure of the entire *Republic*, which is dictated by a method to which Plato attached great importance and to which he gave the name 'dialectic'.

A dialectician operates as follows. He takes a hypothesis, a questionable assumption, and tries to show that it leads to a contradiction: he presents, in the Greek technical term, an *elenchus*. If the elenchus is successful, and a contradiction is reached, then the hypothesis is refuted; and the dialectician next puts to the test the other premisses used to derive the contradiction, subjecting them in turn to elenchus until he reaches a premiss which is unquestionable.

All this can be illustrated from the first book of the *Republic*. The first elenchus is very brief. Socrates' old friend Cephalus puts forward the hypothesis that justice is telling the truth and returning whatever one has borrowed. Socrates asks: is it just to return a weapon to a mad friend? Cephalus agrees that it is not; and so Socrates concludes 'justice cannot be defined as telling the truth and returning what one has borrowed'. Cephalus then withdraws from the debate and goes off to sacrifice.

In pursuit of the definition of justice, we must next examine the further premisses used in refuting Cephalus. The reason why it is unjust to return a weapon to a madman is that it cannot be just to harm a friend. So next, Polemarchus, Cephalus' son and the heir to his argument, defends the hypothesis that justice is doing good to one's friends and harm to one's enemies. The refutation of this suggestion takes longer; but finally Polemarchus agrees that it is not just to harm any man at all. The crucial premiss needed for this elenchus is that justice is human excellence or virtue. It is preposterous, Socrates urges, to think that a just man could exercise his excellence by making others less excellent.

Polemarchus is knocked out of the debate because he accepts without a murmur the premiss that justice is human excellence; but waiting in the wings is the sophist Thrasymachus, agog to challenge that hypothesis. Justice is not a virtue or excellence, he says, but weakness and foolishness, because it is not in anyone's interest to possess it. On the contrary, justice is simply what is to the advantage of those who have power in the state; law and morality are only systems designed for the protection of their interests. It takes Socrates twenty pages and some complicated forking procedures to checkmate Thrasymachus; but eventually, at the end of Book One, it is agreed that the just man will have a better life than the unjust man, so that justice is in its possessor's interests. Thrasymachus is driven to agree by a number of concessions he makes to Socrates. For instance, he agrees that the gods are just, that human virtue or excellence makes one happy. These and other premisses need arguing for; all of them can be questioned and most of them are questioned elsewhere in the *Republic*, from Book Two onwards.

Two people who have so far listened silently to the debate are Plato's brothers Glaucon and Adeimantus. Glaucon intervenes to suggest that while justice may not be a positive evil, as Thrasymachus had suggested, it is not something worthwhile for its own sake, but something chosen as a way of avoiding evil. To avoid being oppressed by others, weak human beings make compacts with each other neither to suffer nor to commit injustice. People would much prefer to act unjustly, if they could do so with impunity – the kind of impunity a man would have, for instance, if he could make himself invisible so that his misdeeds passed undetected. Adeimantus supports his brother, saying that among humans the rewards of justice are the rewards of seeming to be just rather than the rewards of actually being just, and with regard to the gods the penalties of injustice can be bought off by prayer and sacrifice. If Socrates is really to defeat Thrasymachus, he must show that quite apart from reputation, and quite apart from sanctions, justice is in itself as much preferable to injustice as sight is to blindness and health is to sickness.

In response, Socrates shifts from the consideration of justice in the individual to the consideration of justice in the city-state. There, he says, the nature of justice will be written in larger letters and easier to read. The purpose of living in cities is to enable people with different skills to supply each others' needs. Ideally, if people were content with the satisfaction of their basic needs, a very simple community would suffice. But citizens demand more than mere subsistence, and this necessitates a more complicated structure, providing, among other things, for a well-trained professional army.

Socrates describes a city in which there are three classes. Those among the soldiers most fitted to rule are selected by competition to form the upper class, called guardians; the remaining soldiers are described as auxiliaries; and the rest of the citizens belong to the class of farmers and artisans. The consent of the governed to the authority of the rulers is to be secured by propagating 'a noble falsehood', a myth according to which the members of each class have different metals in their souls: gold, silver, and bronze respectively. Membership of classes is in general conferred by birth, but there is scope for a small amount of promotion and demotion from class to class.

The rulers and auxiliaries are to receive an elaborate education in literature (based on a censored version of the Homeric poems), music (only edifying and martial rhythms are allowed) and gymnastic activity (undertaken by both sexes in common). Women as well as men are to be rulers and soldiers, but the members of these classes are not allowed to marry. Women are to be held in common, and all intercourse is to be public. Procreation is to be strictly regulated in order that the population remains stable and healthy. Children are to be brought up in public creches without contact with their parents. Guardians and auxiliaries are to be debarred from possessing private property, or touching precious metals; they will live in common like soldiers in camp, and receive, free of charge, adequate but modest provisions.

The life of these rulers may not sound attractive, Socrates concedes, but the happiness of the city is more important than the happiness of a class. If the city itself is to be happy it must be a virtuous city, and the virtues of the city depend on the virtues of the classes which make it up.

Four virtues stand out as paramount: wisdom, courage, temperance, and justice. The wisdom of the city is the wisdom of its rulers; the courage of the city is the courage of its soldiers; and the temperance of the city consists in the submissiveness of the artisans to the rulers. Where then is justice? It is rooted in the principle of the division of labour from which the city-state originated: every citizen, and each class, doing that for which they are most suited. Justice is doing one's own thing, or minding one's own business: it is harmony between the classes.

The state which Socrates imagines is one of ruthless totalitarianism, devoid of privacy, full of deceit, in flagrant conflict with the most basic human rights. If Plato meant the description to be taken as a blueprint for a real-life polity, then he deserves all the obloquy which has been heaped on him by conservatives and liberals alike. But it must be remembered that the explicit purpose of this constitution-mongering was to cast light on the nature of justice in the soul; and that is what Socrates goes on to do.

He proposes that there are three elements in the soul corresponding to the three classes in the imagined state. 'Do we,' he asks, 'gain knowledge with one part, feel anger with another, and with yet a third desire the pleasures of food, sex and so on? Or is the whole soul at work in every impulse and in all these forms of behaviour?' To settle the question he appeals to phenomena of mental conflict. A man may be thirsty and yet unwilling to drink; what impels to an action must be distinct from what restrains from it; so there must be one part of the soul which reflects and another which is the vehicle of hunger, thirst, and sexual desire. These two elements can be called reason and appetite. Now anger cannot be attributed to either of these elements; for anger conflicts with appetite (one can be disgusted with one's own perverted desires) and can be divorced from reason (children have tantrums before they reach the years of discretion). So we must postulate a third element in the soul, temper, to go with reason and appetite.

This division is based on two premises: the principle of non-contrariety, and the identification of the parts of the soul by their desires. If X and Y are contrary relations, nothing can unqualifiedly stand in X and Y to the same thing; and desire and aversion are contrary relations. The desires of appetite are clear enough, and the desires of temper are to fight and punish; but we are not at this point told anything about the desires of reason. No doubt the man in whom reason fights with thirst is one who is under doctor's orders not to drink; in which case the opponent of appetite will be the rational desire for health.

Socrates' thesis is that justice in an individual is harmony, and injustice is discord, between these three parts of the soul. Justice in the state meant that each of the three orders was doing its own proper work. 'Each one of us likewise will be a just person, fulfilling his proper function, only if the several parts of our nature fulfil theirs.' Reason is to rule, educated temper to be its ally, both are to govern the insatiable appetites and prevent them going beyond bounds. Like justice, the other three cardinal virtues relate to the psychic elements: courage will be located in temper, temperance will reside in the unanimity of the three elements, and wisdom will be in 'that small part which rules . . . possessing as it does the knowledge of what is good for each of the three elements and for all of them in common'.

Justice in the soul is a prerequisite even for the pursuits of the avaricious and ambitious man, the making of money and the affairs of state. Injustice is a sort of civil strife among the elements when they usurp each other's functions. 'Justice is produced in the soul, like health in the body, by establishing the elements concerned in their natural relations of control and subordination, whereas injustice is like disease and means that this natural order is subverted.' Since virtue is the health of the soul, it is absurd to ask whether it is more profitable to live justly or to do wrong. All the wealth and power in the world cannot make life worth living when the bodily constitution is going to rack and ruin; and can life be worth living when the very principle whereby we live is deranged and corrupted?

We have now reached the end of the fourth of the ten books of the *Republic*, and the dialectical process has moved on several stages. One of the hypotheses assumed against Thrasyumachus was that it is the soul's function to deliberate, rule, and take care of the person. Now that the soul has been divided into reason, appetite, and temper, this is abandoned: these functions belong not to the whole soul but only to reason. Another hypothesis is employed in the establishment of the trichotomy: the principle of non-contrariety. This, it turns out, is not a principle which can be relied on in the everyday world. In that world, whatever is moving is also in some respect stationary; whatever is beautiful is also in some way ugly. Only the Idea of Beauty neither waxes nor wanes, is not beautiful in one part and ugly in another, nor beautiful at one time and ugly at another, nor beautiful in relation to one thing and ugly in relation to another. All terrestrial entities, including the tripartite soul, are infected by the ubiquity of contrariety. The theory of the tripartite soul is only an approximation to the truth, because it makes no mention of the Ideas.

In the *Republic* these make their first appearance in Book Five, where they are used as the basis of a distinction between two mental powers or states of mind, knowledge and opinion. The rulers in an ideal state must be educated in such a way that they achieve true knowledge; and knowledge concerns the Ideas, which alone really *are* (i.e., for any F, only the idea of F is altogether and without qualification F). Opinion, on the other hand, concerns the pedestrian objects which both are and are not (i.e., for any F, anything in the world which is F is also in some respect or other not F).

These powers are in turn subdivided, with the aid of a line diagram (see below), in Book Six: opinion includes two items, (a) imagination, whose objects

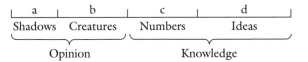

are 'shadows and reflections', and (b) belief, whose objects are 'the living creatures about us and the works of nature or of human hands'. Knowledge, too, comes in two forms. Knowledge *par excellence* is (d) philosophical understanding, whose method is dialectic and whose object is the realm of Ideas. But knowledge also includes (c), mathematical investigation, whose method is hypothetical and whose objects are abstract items like numbers and geometrical figures. The objects of mathematics, no less than the Ideas, possess eternal unchangeability: like all objects of knowledge they belong to the world of being, not of becoming. But they have in common with terrestrial objects that they are not single, but many, for the geometers' circles, unlike The Ideal Circle, can intersect with each other, and the arithmeticians' twos, unlike the one and only Idea of Two, can be added to each other to make four.

Philosophical dialectic is superior to mathematical reasoning, according to Plato, because it has a firm grasp of the relation between hypothesis and truth. Mathematicians treat hypotheses as axioms, from which they draw conclusions and which they do not feel called upon to justify. The dialectician, in contrast, though starting likewise from hypotheses, does not treat them as self-evident axioms; he does not immediately move downwards to the drawing of conclusions, but first ascends from hypotheses to an unhypothetical principle. Hypotheses, as the Greek word suggests, are things 'laid down' like a flight of steps, up which the dialectician mounts to something which is not hypothetical. The upward path of dialectic is described as a course of 'doing away with assumptions – unhypothesizing the hypotheses – and travelling up to the first principle of all, so as to make sure of confirmation there'. We have seen in the earlier parts of the *Republic* how hypotheses are unhypothesized, either by being abandoned or by being laid on a more solid foundation. In the central books of the *Republic* we learn that the hypotheses are founded on the Theory of Ideas, and that the unhypothetical principle to which the dialectical ascends is the Idea of the Good.

Light is thrown on all this by the allegory of the cave, which Plato uses as an illustration to supplement the abstract presentation of his line-diagram. We are to imagine a group of prisoners chained in a cave with their backs to its entrance, facing shadows of puppets thrown by a fire against the cave's inner wall. Education in the liberal arts of arithmetic, geometry, astronomy, and harmony is to release the prisoners from their chains, and to lead them, past the puppets and the fire in the shadow-world of becoming, into the open sunlight of the world of being. The whole course of this education, the conversion from the shadows, is designed for the best part of the soul – i.e. for reason; and the chains from which the pupil must be released so as to begin the ascent are the desires and pleasures of appetite. The prisoners have already had training in gymnastics and music according to the syllabus of Books Two and Three. Even to start the journey out of the cave you must already be sound of mind and limb.

The four segments of the line-diagram are the four stages of the education of the philosopher. Plato illustrates the stages most fully in connection with the course in mathematics. If a child reads a story about a mathematician, that is an exercise of the imagination. If someone use arithmetic to count the soldiers in an army, or any other set of concrete objects, that will be what Plato calls mathematical belief. Mature study of arithmetic will lead the pupil out of the world of becoming altogether, and teach him to study the abstract numbers, which can be multiplied but cannot change. Finally, dialectic, by questioning the hypotheses of arithmetic – researching, as we should say, into the foundations of mathematics – will give him a true understanding of number, by introducing him to the Ideas, the men and trees and stars of the allegory of the cave.

The *Republic* is concerned more with moral education than with mathematical education; but it turns out that this follows a parallel path. Imagination in morals consists of the dicta of poets and tragedians. If the pupil has been educated in the bowdlerized literature recommended by Plato, he will have seen justice triumphing on the stage, and will have learned that the gods are unchanging, good, and truthful. This he will later see as a symbolic representation of the eternal idea of Good, source of truth and knowledge. The first stage of moral education will make him competent in the human justice which operates in courts of law. This will give him true belief about right and wrong; but it will be the task of dialectic to teach him the real nature of justice and to display its participation in the Idea of the Good at the end of dialectic's upward path. Every Idea, for Plato, depends hierarchically on the Idea of the Good: for the Idea of X is the perfect X, and so each Idea participates in the Idea of Perfection or Goodness. In the allegory of the cave, it is the Idea of the Good which corresponds to the all-enlightening sun.

A philosopher who had contemplated that Idea would no doubt be able to replace the hypothetical definition of justice as psychic health with a better definition which would show beyond question the mode of its participation in goodness. But Socrates proves unable to achieve this task: his eyes are blinded by the dialectical sun, and he can talk only in metaphor, and cannot give even a provisional account of goodness itself. When next we see clearly in the *Republic*, dialectic has begun its downward path. We return to the topics of the earlier books – the natural history of the state, the divisions of the soul, the happiness of the just, the deficiencies of poetry – but we study them now in the light of the Theory of Ideas. The just man is happier than the unjust, not only because his soul is in concord, but because it is more delightful to fill the soul with understanding than to feed fat the desires of appetite. Reason is no longer the faculty which takes care of the person, it is a faculty akin to the unchanging and immortal world of truth. And the poets fall short, not just because – as Socrates insisted when censoring their works for the education of the guardians – they spread unedifying stories and pander to decadent tastes, but because they operate at the third remove from the reality of the Ideas. For the items in the world that poets and painters copy are themselves only copies of Ideas: a picture of a bed is a copy of a copy of the Ideal Bed.

The description of the education of the philosopher in the central books of the *Republic* was meant to establish the characteristics of the ideal ruler, the philosopher king. The best constitution, Socrates claims, is one ruled by the wisdom thus acquired – it may be either monarchy or aristocracy, for it does not matter whether wisdom is incarnate in one or more rulers. But there are four inferior types of constitution: timocracy, oligarchy, democracy, and despotism. And to each of these degraded types of constitution in the state, there corresponds a degraded type of character in the soul.

If there are three parts of the soul, why are there four cardinal virtues, and five different characters as constitutions? The second part of this question is easier to answer than the first. There are five constitutions and four virtues because each constitution turns into the next by the downgrading of one of the virtues; and it takes four steps to pass from the first constitution to the fifth. It is when the rulers cease to be men of wisdom that aristocracy gives place to timocracy. The oligarchic rulers differ from the timocrats because they lack courage and military virtues. Democracy arises when even the miserly temperance of the oligarchs is abandoned. For Plato, any step from aristocracy is a step away from justice; but it is the step from democracy to despotism that marks the enthronement of injustice incarnate. So the aristocratic state is marked by the presence of all the virtues, the timocratic state by the absence of wisdom, the oligarchic state by the decay of courage, the democratic state by contempt for temperance, and the despotic state by the overturning of justice.

But how are these vices and these constitutions related to the parts of the soul? The pattern is ingeniously woven. In the ideal constitution the rulers of the state are ruled by reason, in the timocratic state the rulers are ruled by temper, and in the oligarchic state appetite is enthroned in the rulers' souls. But now within the third part of the tripartite soul a new tripartition appears. The bodily desires which make up appetite are divided into necessary, unnecessary, and lawless desires. A desire for plain bread and meat is a necessary desire; a desire for luxuries is an unnecessary desire. Lawless desires are those unnecessary desires which are so impious, perverse, and shameless that they find expression normally only in dreams. The difference between the oligarchic, democratic, and despotic constitutions arises from the different types of desire which dominate the rulers of each state. The few rulers of the oligarchic state are themselves ruled by a few necessary desires; each of the multitude dominant in the democracy is dominated by a multitude of unnecessary desires; the sole master of the despotic state is himself mastered by a single dominating lawless passion.

Socrates makes further use of the tripartite theory of the soul to prove the superiority of the just man's happiness. Men may be classified as avaricious, ambitious, or academic according to whether the dominant element in their soul is appetite, temper, or reason. Men of each type will claim that their own life is best: the avaricious man will praise the life of business, the ambitious man will praise a political career, and the academic man will praise knowledge and understanding and the life of learning. It is the academic, the philosopher, whose judgement is to be preferred: he has the advantage over the others in experience, insight, and reasoning. Moreover, the objects to which the philosopher devotes his life are so much more real than the objects pursued by the others that their pleasures seem illusory by comparison. To obey reason is not only the most virtuous course for the other elements in the soul, it is also the pleasantest.

In Book Ten Plato redescribes, once again, the anatomy of the soul. He makes a contrast between two elements within the reasoning faculty of the tripartite soul. There is one element in the soul which is confused by straight sticks looking bent in water, and another element which measures, counts, and weighs. Plato uses this distinction to launch an attack on drama and literature. In the actions represented by drama, there is an internal conflict in a man analogous to the conflict between the contrary opinions induced by visual impressions. In tragedy, this conflict is between a lamentation-loving part of the soul and the better part of us which is willing to abide by the law that says we must bear misfortune quietly. In comedy this noble element has to fight with another element which has an instinctive impulse to play the buffoon.

Plato's notion of justice as psychic health makes its final appearance in a new proof of immortality which concludes the *Republic*. Each thing is destroyed by its characteristic disease: eyes by ophthalmia, and iron by rust. Now vice is the characteristic disease of the soul; but vice does not destroy the soul in the way disease destroys the body. But if the soul is not killed by its own disease, it will hardly be killed by diseases of anything else – certainly not by bodily disease – and so it must be immortal.

The principle that justice is the soul's health is now finally severed from the tripartite theory of the soul on which it rested. An uneasily composite entity like the threefold soul, Socrates says, could hardly be everlasting. The soul in its real nature is a far lovelier thing in which justice is much more easily to be distinguished. The soul in its tripartite form is more like a monster than its natural self, like a statue of a sea-god covered by barnacles. If we could fix our eye on the soul's love of wisdom and passion for the divine and everlasting, we would realize how different it would be, once freed from the pursuit of earthly happiness.

By defining justice as the health of the soul Plato achieved three things. First, he provided himself with an easy answer to the quesion 'why be just?' Everyone wants to be healthy, so if justice is health, everyone must really want to be just. If some do not want to behave justly, this can only be because they do not understand the nature of justice and injustice, and lack insight into their own condition. Thus, the doctrine that justice is mental health rides well with the Socratic theses that no one does wrong voluntarily, and that vice is fundamentally ignorance. Secondly, if injustice is a disease, it should be possible to eradicate it by the application of medical science. So Plato can offer the strict training programme and educational system of the *Republic* as the best preventative against an epidemic of vice. Thirdly, if every vicious man is really a sick man, then the virtuous philosopher can claim over him the type of control which a doctor has over his patients. To treat injustice as mental sickness is to assimilate vice to madness; and the point is made very early on in the *Republic* that madmen have no rights; they may not claim their property, they are not entitled to be told the truth. But of course by Plato's lights, all who fall short of the standards of the philosopher king are more or less mad: and thus the guardians in the totalitarian state are allowed to use the 'drug of falsehood' on their subjects. The thesis that madmen need restraint is lethal when combined with the view that all the world is mad but me and possibly thee.

That justice is the health of the soul is the unifying theme of the *Republic*; but, as we have seen, Plato ranges in the dialogue over philosophy of mind, moral philosophy, political philosophy, philosophy of education, aesthetics, theory of knowledge, and metaphysics. In all these areas the Theory of Ideas is brought to bear. It remains for us to consider some of Plato's later writings in which his philosophy is no longer anchored to that theory.

THE *THEAETETUS* AND THE *SOPHIST*

The *Theaetetus* begins in the manner of an early dialogue. The question set is 'What is knowledge?', and Socrates offers to act as midwife to enable the bright young mathematician Theaetetus to bring the answer to birth. The first suggestion is that knowledge consists of things like geometry and carpentry; but this will not do as a definition, for the word 'knowledge' itself would turn up if we tried to give definitions of geometry and carpentry. What Socrates is looking for is what is common to all these different kinds of knowledge.

Theaetetus' second proposal is that knowledge is perception: to know something is to encounter it with the senses. Socrates observes that different people's senses are differently affected: the same wind may be felt by one person as warm and by another as chilly. 'It feels cold' means 'it seems cold', so that perceiving is the same thing as seeming. Only what is true can be known, so if knowledge is perceiving, we will have to accept the doctrine of Protagoras that whatever seems is true, or at least that what seems to a particular person is true for him.

Behind Protagoras lies Heraclitus. If it is true that everything in the world is constantly undergoing change, then the colours we see and the qualities we feel cannot be objective, stable realities. Rather, each is the offspring of a momentary meeting between one of our senses and some corresponding transitory item in the universal flux. When an eye, for instance, comes into contact with an appropriate visible counterpart, the eye begins to see whiteness and the object begins to look white. The whiteness itself is generated by the intercourse between these two parents, the eye and the object. The eye and its object, no less than the whiteness they beget, are themselves involved in the universal flux; they are not motionless, but their motion is slow by comparison with the speed with which the sense-impressions come and go. The eye's seeing of the white object, and the whiteness of the object itself, are two twins which are born and die together. A similar story can be told of the other senses: and thus we can see, at least in the realm of the sensation, why Protagoras should say that whatever seems, is; for the existence of a quality, and its appearance to the appropriate sense, are inseparable from each other.

But life is not all sensation. We have dreams, in which we have wings and fly; madmen suffer delusions in which they feel themselves gods. Surely these are seemings which do not accord with reality? Half our life is spent asleep, and perhaps we can never be sure whether we are awake or dreaming; so how can any of us say that whatever seems to him at any given moment is true?

For answer, Protagoras can again appeal to Heraclitus. Suppose Socrates falls ill and sweet wine begins to taste sour to him. On the account given above, the sourness is the offspring of two parents, the wine and the taster. But Socrates sick is a different taster from Socrates healthy, and with a different parent the offspring is naturally different. As every perceiver is constantly changing, each perception is a unique, unrepeatable experience. It may not be true that the wine is sour, but it is true that it is sour for Socrates. No one else is in a position to correct the sick Socrates on this point, and so here too Protagoras is vindicated: whatever seems *to me*, is true *for me*. Theaetetus can continue to maintain that perception is knowledge.

But is all knowledge perception? Knowing a language, for instance, is more than just hearing the sounds uttered, which we can do in a language we do not know. It is true, of course, that I often learn something – say that the Parthenon is on the Acropolis – by seeing it with my own eyes. But even after I shut my eyes, or go away, I continue to know that the Parthenon is on the Acropolis. So memory provides an example of knowledge without perception. But perhaps Theaetetus is not yet beaten: Protagoras might come to his aid by replying that it is possible to know and not know something at the same time, just as, if you clap your hand over one of your eyes, you can both see and not see the same thing at the same time.

Socrates seems to be reduced to an *ad hominem* riposte. How can Protagoras claim to be a teacher, and charge fees, if no one is in a better position than anyone else with regard to knowledge, since what appears to each man is true for him? Protagoras would reply that while there is no such thing as teaching someone to give up false thoughts for true thoughts, a teacher can make him give up bad thoughts for good thoughts. For though all seemings are equally true, not all seemings are equally good. A sophist like Protagoras can bring a pupil into a better state, just as a doctor might cure Socrates of the illness that affected his palate, so that the wine would come to taste sweet again.

In response to this, Socrates draws on the argument of Democritus to show that Protagoras' doctrine is self-refuting. It seems true to all men that some men know better than others about various matters of skill and expertise; if so, that must be true for all men. It seems to the majority of people that Protagoras' thesis is false; if so then his thesis must be more false than true, since the unbelievers outnumber the believers. Protagoras' theory may seem on a firm footing as applied to sense-perception, but it is quite implausible if applied to medical diagnosis or political prediction. Each man may be the measure of what *is*, but even in the case of sensations he is not the measure of what *will be*: a physician knows better than a patient whether he will feel hot, and a vintner will know better than a drinker whether a wine will turn out sweet or dry.

But even at its strongest, in the realm of sensation, Protagoras' claim is vulnerable, Socrates argues, for it depends on the thesis of the universal flux, which is itself incoherent. According to the Heracliteans, everything is always changing, in respect both of local motion (movement from place to place) and qualitative alteration (such as the change from white to black). Now if something stayed put, we could describe how it changed in quality, and if we had a patch of constant colour, we could describe how it moved from place to place. But if both kinds of change are taking place simultaneously, we are reduced to speechlessness; we cannot say *what* is moving, or *what* is altering. Sense-perception itself will be in flux: an episode of seeing will turn instantly into an episode of non-seeing; hearing and not hearing will follow each other incessantly. This is so unlike what we take knowledge to be, that if knowledge is identical with perception, knowledge will not be knowledge any more than non-knowledge.

Socrates finally moves in for the kill by turning to examine the bodily organs of the senses: the eyes and ears, the channels through which we see colours and hear sounds. The objects of one sense cannot be perceived with another: we cannot hear colours or see sounds. But in that case, the thought that a sound and a colour are not the same as each other, but two different things, cannot be the product of either sight or hearing. Theaetetus has to concede that there are no organs for perceiving sameness and difference or unity and multiplicity; the mind itself contemplates the common terms which apply to everything. But the truth about the most tangible bodily properties can only be reached by the use of these common terms, which belong not to the senses but to the mind. Knowledge resides not in the sense-impressions but in the mind's reflection upon them.

At last Theaetetus gives up the thesis that knowledge is perception: he proposes instead that it consists in the judgements of the reflecting mind. Socrates approves of this change of course. When the mind is thinking, he says, it is as if it were talking to itself, asking questions and answering them, saying yes or no. When it concludes its internal discussion with itself, and comes out silently with its answer, that is a judgement.

Knowledge cannot be identified outright with judgement, because there is such a thing as false judgement as well as true judgement. It is not easy to give an account of false judgement: how can I make the judgement that A = B unless I know what A is and what B is, and if I know that, how can I get the judgement wrong? The possibility of false judgement seems to threaten us with having to admit that someone can know and not know the same thing at the same time.

Let us suppose, Socrates now suggests, that the mind is a wax tablet. When we want to commit something to memory we stamp an impression or an idea on this tablet, and so long as the stamp remains we remember. False judgement may occur in the following way. Socrates knows Theaetetus and his tutor Theodorus and he has images of each of them stamped on the tablet of his memory; but seeing Theaetetus at a distance, he mistakenly matches him not to his own image, but to the image of Theodorus. The more indistinct the images on the wax become, the more possible it is that such mistakes are made. False judgement, then, comes about through a mismatch between perception and thought.

But are there not cases where we make false judgements when no perception is in question: when we make a mistake in working out a sum in arithmetic, for instance? In order to take account of these cases, Socrates says that it is possible to possess knowledge without holding it in your mind on a particular occasion, just as you can possess a coat without wearing it. Think of the mind now not as a waxen tablet, but as an aviary. We are born with a mind which is an empty cage; as we learn new things we capture new birds, and knowing something is having the corresponding bird in our collection. But if you want to make use of a piece of knowledge, you have to catch the appropriate bird and hold him in your hand before letting him go again. Thus we explain mistakes in arithmetic: someone who knows no arithmetic has no number birds in his aviary; a person who judges that 7 + 5 = 11 has all the right birds fluttering around, but catches the eleventh bird instead of the twelfth bird.

Whether or not these similes are sufficient to make clear the nature of false judgement, there is a difficulty, Socrates points out, with the thesis that knowledge is true judgement. If a jury is persuaded by a clever attorney to bring in a certain verdict, then even though the verdict accords with the facts, the jurors do not have the knowledge that an eye-witness would have. Theaetetus then modifies his definition so that knowledge is a judgement or belief which is not only true but articulate.

Socrates then explores three different ways in which a belief about something might be said to be articulate. Most obviously, someone has an articulate belief if he can express it in words; but anyone with a true belief who is not deaf and dumb can do this, so it can hardly make the difference between true belief and knowledge.

The second way is the one which Socrates takes most seriously: to have an articulate belief about an object is to be able to offer an analysis of it. Knowledge of a thing is acquired by reducing it to its elements. But in that case there can be no knowledge of any of the ultimate, unanalysable elements. The elements which make up the substances of the world are like the letters which make up the words in a language, and analysing a substance may be compared with spelling a word. But while one can spell 'Socrates' one cannot spell the letter 'S'. Just as a letter cannot be spelt, the elements of the world cannot be analysed and therefore cannot be known. But if the elements cannot be known, how can complexes made out of them be known? Moreover, while knowledge of elements may be necessary if we are to have knowledge of complexes, it is not sufficient; a child might know all his letters, and yet not be able to spell consistently.

On the third interpretation someone has an articulate belief about an object if he can spell out a description which is uniquely true of it. Thus, the sun may be described as the brightest of the heavenly bodies. But on this view, how can one have any idea at all of something without having an articulate belief about it? I cannot really be thinking of Theaetetus himself if the only things I can say in description of him are things he has in common with others, like having a nose and eyes and a mouth.

Socrates concludes, a little precipitately, that Theaetetus' third definition of knowledge is no better than his two previous ones. The dialogue ends in bafflement, like the Socratic dialogues of Plato's early period. But in fact, it has achieved a great deal. The account which it gives of the nature of sense-perception, modified by Aristotle, became standard until late in the Middle Ages. The definition of knowledge as articulate true belief, interpreted as meaning justified true belief, was still accepted by many philosophers in the present century. But what Plato probably saw as the dialogue's greatest achievement was the cure which it provided for the scepticism of Heraclitus, by showing that the doctrine of universal flux was self-refuting.

In the *Theaetetus* Socrates expresses himself too much in awe to take on in argument the philosopher who stands at the opposite extreme from Heraclitus, the venerable Parmenides. This task Plato undertakes in the dialogue *The Sophist*. In this dialogue, though Theaetetus and Socrates reappear, the chief speaker is not Socrates, but a stranger from Parmenides' town of Elea. The ostensible purpose of the dialogue is to provide a definition of the sophist. The definition is pursued by the method popular in our own day in the game of Twenty Questions. In that game the questioner divides the world into two portions, say animate and inanimate; if the object sought is animate, then the animate world is divided into two further portions, say plants and animals; and thus by further dichotomies the object is uniquely identified. By similar methods the Eleatic stranger defines first the art of angling, and then, more than once, the art of the sophist. The account of sophistry which concludes the dialogue is this: 'the art of contradiction-making, descended from an insincere kind of conceited mimicry, of the semblance-making breed, derived from image-making, distinguished as a portion, not divine but human, of production, that presents a shadow-play of words'.

This is, of course, a joke. The serious business of the dialogue is carried out on the way. One line of thought runs as follows. Sophistry is bound up with falsehood; but how is it possible to talk about falsehood without falling foul of the revered Parmenides? To say what is false is to say what is not: does that mean that it is tantamount to uttering Unbeing? That would be nonsense, for the reasons Parmenides gave. Shall we be more careful, then, and maintain that to say what is false is to say that what is, is not, or that what is not, is? Will this avoid Parmenides' strictures?

We have to disarm Parmenides by forcing him to agree that what is not, in some respect is, and what is, in a manner is not. Motion, for instance, is not rest; but that does not mean that motion is not anything at all. There are many things which even Being is not: for instance, Being is not motion and Being is not rest. When we speak of what is not, we are not talking of Unbeing, the contrary of Being; we are speaking simply of something which is different from one of the things there are. The non-beautiful differs from the beautiful, and the unjust differs from the just; but the non-beautiful and the unjust are no less real than the beautiful and the just. If we lump together all the things which are non-something, or unsomething, then we get the category of non-being, and this is just as real as the category of Being. So we have blown open the prison into which Parmenides had confined us.

We are now in a position to give an account of falsehood in thought and speech. The problem was that it was not possible to think or say what was not, because Unbeing was nonsense. But now that we have found that non-being is perfectly real, we can use this to explain false thoughts and false sentences.

A typical sentence consists of a noun and a verb, and it says something about something. 'Theaetetus is sitting' and 'Theaetetus is flying' are both sentences about Theaetetus, but one of them is true and one false. They say different things about Theaetetus, and the true one says a thing about him which is among the things that he is, while the false one says a thing about him which is among the things that he is not. Flying is not Unbeing, it is a thing that is – there is quite a lot of it about – but it is a thing that is different from the things that Theaetetus is, the things that can be truly said of Theaetetus.

This account of the falsehood of a false sentence can be adapted to fit false thought and judgement also; for thinking is the silent inward utterance of the mind, and judgement is the mental equivalent of assertion and denial. When we speak of 'seeming' and 'appearance' we are referring to judgement which is caused by the operation of the senses, and the same treatment is appropriate here too.

The line of thought we have followed is just one strand in a dense web of argument in which the stranger seeks to trap the monists of his native city Elea. The *Theaetetus* and *Sophist*, between them, enable Plato to take a middle road between the opposed and stultifying philosophies of Heraclitus and Parmenides. But what is remarkable about the *Sophist* is that among the philosophers who are criticized as inadequate are some called 'the friends of the Forms'. These are described in such a way as to leave no doubt that they are proponents of Plato's own Theory of Ideas. The Stranger says that the true philosopher

> must refuse to accept from the champions either of the one or of the many Forms their doctrine that all reality is changeless, and he must turn a deaf ear to the other party who represent reality as everywhere changing. Like a child who wants to have his cake and eat it he must say that Being, the sum of all, is both at once – all that is unchangeable, and all that is in change.

In this passage Heraclitus is the party of change, and Parmenides the champion of the one Form. The champion of the many Forms is none other than Plato himself in his younger days. As we have said, we do not know for certain whether in later life Plato retained or abandoned his belief in the Ideas. But it is difficult to find any other philosopher in the history of the subject who has presented with similar clarity and eloquence such powerful arguments against his own most darling theories.

IV
THE SYSTEM OF ARISTOTLE

PLATO'S PUPIL, ALEXANDER'S TEACHER

Aristotle was not an Athenian; he was born, fifteen years after the death of Socrates, at Stagira in the kingdom of Macedonia in northern Greece. The son of a court physician, he migrated to Athens in 367 at the age of seventeen, and joined Plato's Academy, where he remained for twenty years. Many of Plato's later dialogues date from this period, and some of the arguments they contain may reflect Aristotle's contributions to debate. By a flattering anachronism, Plato introduces a character called 'Aristotle' into the *Parmenides* (dramatic date *c.*450), which is the dialogue most critical of the Theory of Ideas. Probably some of Aristotle's own works on logic and disputation, the *Topics* and the *Sophistical Refutations*, belong to this period.

While Aristotle was at the Academy, Macedonia grew from being an unstable border province to become the greatest power in Greece. King Philip II, who came to the throne in 359, waged war against a series of hostile powers including Athens. The Athenians, despite the orator Demosthenes' martial patriotic speeches (the 'Philippics'), defended their interests only half-heartedly, and after a succession of humiliating concessions they allowed Philip to become, by 338, master of the Greek world.

The period was a difficult one for a Macedonian resident in Athens, and in 347 when Plato died and his nephew Speusippus became head of the Academy, Aristotle moved to Assos on the north-western coast of what is now Turkey. The city was under the rule of Hermias, a graduate of the Academy, who had already invited a number of Academicians to form a new philosophical school there. Aristotle became an intimate friend of Hermias, and married his adopted daughter Pythias, by whom he had two children. During this period he carried out extensive scientific research, particularly in marine biology. This was written up in a book misleadingly entitled *The History of Animals*. It contains detailed, and mainly accurate, observations of the anatomy, diet, and reproductive systems of mammals, birds, reptiles, fish, and crustacea; observations which were quite without precedent and which were not superseded until the seventeenth century.

Aristotle remained at Assos until the death of Hermias, executed in 341 by the King of Persia, to whom he had been treacherously betrayed. Aristotle saluted his memory in an *Ode to Virtue* which is his only surviving poem. After Hermias' death he was invited to the Macedonian capital by Philip II as tutor to his son, the future Alexander the Great, who succeeded as king in 336. We have little solid information about Aristotle's relation to his distinguished pupil, who in the course of ten years made himself master of an empire that stretched from the Danube to the Indus and included Libya and Egypt. Ancient sources tell us that during his early campaigns Alexander arranged for a team of research assistants to send his tutor biological specimens from all parts of Greece and Asia Minor; but we can tell from Aristotle's own writings that the relationship between the two cooled markedly as the conquering monarch grew ever more megalomaniac and finally proclaimed himself divine.

While Alexander was conquering Asia, Aristotle was back in Athens, where he established his own school in the Lyceum, just outside the city boundary. Here he built up a substantial library, and gathered around him a group of brilliant research students. The Lyceum was not a private club like the Academy; many of the lectures were open to the general public, without fee.

Aristotle always acknowledged a great debt to Plato, whom on his death he described as the best and happiest of mortals 'whom it is not right for evil men even to praise'. His main philosophical writings show the influence of his master on almost every page. But he was not an uncritical disciple, and in antiquity some called him an ungrateful foal, who had kicked his mother.

Since the Renaissance it has been traditional to regard the Academy and the Lyceum as two opposite poles of philosophy. Plato, according to this tradition, was idealistic, Utopian, other-worldly; Aristotle was realistic, utilitarian, common-sensical. Thus in Raphael's *School of Athens*, Plato, wearing the colours of the volatile elements air and fire, points heavenwards; Aristotle, clothed in watery blue and earthy green, has his feet firmly on the ground. 'Every man is born an Aristotelian or a Platonist,' said S. T. Coleridge. 'They are the two classes of men, besides which it is next to impossible to conceive a third.' In our own age W. B. Yeats pointed the contrast:

> Plato thought nature but a spume that plays
> Upon a ghostly paradigm of things;
> Solider Aristotle played the taws
> Upon the bottom of a king of kings.

In fact, as we shall see, Aristotle took a large part of his philosophical agenda from Plato, and his teaching is more often a modification than a refutation of Plato's doctrines. Modern historians of ideas were less perceptive than the many commentators in late antiquity who saw it as their duty to construct a harmonious concord between the two greatest philosophers of the ancient world.

Alexander the Great died in 323. Democratic Athens rejoiced, and once again it became an uncomfortable home for even an anti-imperialist Macedonian. Saying that he did not wish the city which had executed Socrates 'to sin twice against philosophy', Aristotle escaped to Chalcis, on a nearby Greek island, where he died a year after Alexander.

Aristotle left his papers to Theophrastus, his successor as head of the Lyceum. They were enormous in volume and in scope, including writings on constitutional history and the history of sport and the theatre, and works of botany, zoology, biology, psychology, chemistry, meteorology, astronomy, and cosmology, as well as more strictly philosophical treatises of logic, metaphysics, ethics, aesthetics, political theory, theory of knowledge, philosophy of science, and the history of ideas.

It was some centuries before these works were properly catalogued, and it has been calculated that four-fifths of what he wrote has been lost. What survives amounts to about one million words, twice the extent of the Platonic corpus. Most of this material appears to be in the form of notes for lectures, sometimes in more than one draft. Aristotle's style was admired in the ancient world; but the writings we possess, though packed with ideas and full of energy, lack the kind of polish which makes for easy reading. What has been delivered to us across the centuries are telegrams from Aristotle rather than epistles.

The Foundation of Logic

Many of the sciences to which Aristotle contributed were disciplines which he himself founded. He makes the claim explicit only in one case: that of logic. At the end of one of his logical works he wrote:

> In the case of rhetoric there were many old writings to draw upon, but in the case of logic we had absolutely nothing at all to mention until we had spent much time in laborious research.

Aristotle's principal logical investigations concerned relations between sentences which make statements. Which of them are consistent or inconsistent with each other? When we have one or more true statements, what further truths can be inferred from them by reasoning alone? These questions are answered in his *Posterior Analytics*.

Unlike Plato, Aristotle does not take a simple noun–verb sentence such as 'Theaetetus is sitting' as the basic element of logical structure. He is much more interested in classifying sentences beginning with 'all' 'no' and 'some', and evaluating inferences between them. Consider the following two inferences.

(1) All Greeks are Europeans
   Some Greeks are male
   Therefore, some Europeans are male.

and

(2) All cows are mammals
   Some mammals are quadrupeds
   Therefore, all cows are quadrupeds.

These two inferences have a lot in common with each other. They are both inferences which draw a conclusion from a pair of premisses. In each inference a keyword which appears in the grammatical subject of the conclusion appears in one of the premisses, and a keyword which appears in the grammatical predicate of the conclusion appears in the other premiss. Aristotle devoted much attention to inferences displaying this feature, which are nowadays called 'syllogisms' after the Greek word which he used for them. The branch of logic which studies the validity of inferences of this kind, which was initiated by Aristotle, is called 'syllogistic'.

A valid inference is an inference of a form which will never lead from true premisses to a false conclusion. Of the two inferences set out above, the first is valid and the second is invalid. It is true that in each of the cases given the premisses are true and the conclusion is true. One cannot fault the second inference on the ground that the sentences occurring in it are false. What one can fault is the 'therefore': the conclusion may be true, but it does not follow from the premisses.

We can bring this out by constructing a parallel inference which leads from true premisses to a false conclusion. For instance:

(3) All whales are mammals
   Some mammals are land-animals
   Therefore, all whales are land-animals.

The inference is of the same form as inference (2), as can be brought out by exhibiting the structure of the inference by schematic letters.

(4) All As are Bs
   Some Bs are Cs
   Therefore all As are Cs.

Because inference (3) leads from true premisses to a false conclusion, we can see that the argument-form of (4) cannot be relied upon. Hence, inference (2), though its conclusion is in fact true, is not a valid inference.

Logic could never have proceeded past its first steps without schematic letters, and their use is something now taken absolutely for granted; but it was Aristotle who first began to use them, and his invention was as important to logic as the invention of algebra was to mathematics.

One way to define logic is to say that it is the discipline which sorts out good inferences from bad. Aristotle examines all the possible forms of syllogistic inference and frames a set of principles which would sort out good syllogisms from bad syllogisms. He begins by classifying the individual sentences or propositions in the premisses. Ones beginning 'all' are universal propositions; ones beginning 'some' are particular propositions. Ones containing 'not' are negative propositions; others are affirmative propositions. Aristotle then uses these classifications to draw up rules to evaluate inferences. For instance, if a syllogism is to be valid, at least one premiss must be affirmative, at least one premiss must be universal, and if either premiss is negative the conclusion must be negative. Aristotle's rules, in their totality, are sufficient to validate sound syllogisms and eliminate invalid ones. They are sufficient, for instance, to accept inference (1) and reject inference (2).

Aristotle believed that his syllogistic was sufficient to deal with every possible valid inference. This was an error; in fact, the system, though complete in itself, was only a fragment of logic. It had two weaknesses. First, it did not deal with inferences depending not on words like 'all' and 'some', which attach to nouns, but on words like 'if' and 'then', which link sentences. It was some centuries later before anyone formalized patterns of inference such as 'If it is not day, it is night; but it is not day; therefore it is night'. Secondly, even within its own field, Aristotle's logic could not cope with inferences in which words like 'all' or 'some' (or 'every' and 'any') occurred not in the subject place but somewhere in the grammatical predicate. The rules would not permit one to determine, for instance, the validity of inferences containing premisses such as 'every schoolchild knows some dates' or 'some people hate all policemen'. It was not until twenty-two centuries after Aristotle's death that this gap was filled.

Logic is used in all the various sciences which Aristotle studied; perhaps it is not so much a science itself as an instrument or tool of the sciences. That was the view taken of Aristotle's logical works by his successors, who called them the 'Organon' after the Greek word for tool.

The *Prior Analytics* tells us how logic functions in the sciences. Those who learnt Euclidean geometry at school will recall how many geometrical truths, or theorems, were derived by deductive reasoning from a small initial set of other truths called axioms. Though Euclid himself was not born until late in Aristotle's life, this axiomatic method was already familiar to geometricians, and Aristotle believed it to be very widely applicable. Logic provided the rules for the derivation of theorems from axioms, and each science would have its own special set of axioms. The sciences could be ordered in hierarchies, with sciences lower down a hierarchy treating as axioms propositions which might be theorems of a higher science.

If we take 'science' in a broad sense, Aristotle says, there are three kinds of sciences: productive, practical, and theoretical. Productive sciences include engineering and architecture, and also disciplines such as rhetoric and playwriting whose products are less concrete. Practical sciences are ones which guide behaviour, most notably ethics and politics. Theoretical sciences are those which have no product and no practical goal, but pursue truth for its own sake.

Theoretical science, in its turn, is threefold. Aristotle names the three divisions 'Physics, Mathematics, Theology'; but in this classification only mathematics is what it seems to be. 'Physics' means natural philosophy or the study of nature (*physis*); it includes, in addition to the disciplines which we would nowadays think of as part of physics, chemistry and biology plus animal and human psychology. 'Theology' is, for Aristotle, the study of entities above and superior to human beings, that is to say, the starry skies as well as whatever divinities may inhabit heaven. 'Metaphysics' is not a name which occurs in Aristotle; indeed the word means simply 'after physics' and it was coined to refer to those works of his own which were catalogued after his *Physics*. But much of what Aristotle wrote would nowadays naturally be described as metaphysics; and he did have his own name for the discipline, as we shall see later.

THE THEORY OF DRAMA

In the realm of productive sciences, Aristotle wrote two works: the *Rhetoric* and the *Poetics*, designed to assist barristers and playwrights in their respective tasks. The *Rhetoric* has interested modern philosophers chiefly on account of the detailed and sensitive examination, in the second book, of the human emotions on which the orator has to play. The *Poetics*, throughout history, has interested a much wider audience. Only its first book survives, a treatment of epic and tragic poetry. The second book, on comedy, is lost. Umberto Eco, in *The Name of the Rose*, wove a dramatic fiction around its imagined survival and then destruction in a medieval abbey.

The surviving first book deals principally with the nature of tragic drama. Six things, Aristotle says, are necessary for a tragedy: plot, character, diction, thought, spectacle, and melody. The elements appear to be listed in order of importance. The melodies sung by the choruses in a Greek drama, and the setting of the stage by the director, are, he says, no more than pleasurable accessories: what is really great in tragedy can be appreciated by listening to an unadorned reading of the text no less than by watching the play on the stage. Thought and diction are more important: it is the thoughts expressed by the characters that arouse emotion in the hearer, and if they are to do so successfully they must be presented convincingly by the actors. But it is character and plot which really bring out the genius of a tragic poet.

The main character, or tragic hero, must be neither supremely good nor extremely bad: he should be a person of rank who is basically good, but comes to grief through some great error. Every one of the *dramatis personae* should possess some good features, and all should act consistently. What they do should be in character, and what happens to them should be a necessary or probable outcome of their behaviour.

The most important of the six elements, Aristotle says, is plot: the characters are introduced for the sake of the plot, not the other way round. The plot must be a self-contained story with a clearly marked beginning, middle, and end; it must be sufficiently short and simple for the spectator to hold all its details in mind. Tragedy must have a unity. It is no good stringing together a set of episodes connected only by a common hero; rather, there must be a single significant action on which the whole plot turns. Typically, the story will get ever more complicated up to a turning-point in the story, which Aristotle calls a 'reversal' (*peripeteia*). That is the moment at which the apparently fortunate hero falls to disaster, perhaps through a 'revelation' (*anagnorisis*), the discovery of some crucial but hitherto unknown piece of information. After the reversal comes the dénouement, in which the complications earlier introduced are gradually unravelled.

Aristotle says that the story must arouse pity and fear: that is the whole point of tragedy. It is most likely to do so if it shows people as the victims of hatred and murder where they could most expect to be loved and cherished. That is why so many tragedies concern feuds within a single family.

All these observations are illustrated by constant reference to actual Greek plays; the one most often cited is Sophocles' tragedy of King Oedipus. Oedipus, at the beginning of the play, enjoys reputation and prosperity. But he has the fatal flaw of impetuosity, which has led him to kill a stranger in a scuffle, and marry a bride without sufficient inquiry into her origins. The 'revelation' that the man was his father and the woman his mother leads to the 'reversal' of his fortune, as he is banished from his kingdom and blinds himself in shame and remorse.

Why should we seek to arouse pity and fear, which we are told is the purpose of tragedy? 'In order to purify our emotions' is Aristotle's answer. No one is quite sure what he meant by this: but most probably the point is that watching tragedy helps us to put our own sorrows and worries into due proportion. Aristotle's account of tragedy enables him to answer Plato's complaint that artists, poets, and playwrights were only imitators of everyday life, which was itself only an imitation of the real world of the Ideas. Tragedy, he says, is in fact closer to the ideal than history is. Much of what happens to people in everyday life is a matter of sheer accident: only in fiction can we see the working out of character and action into their natural consequences. 'Hence poetry is more philosophical and more important than history; for poetry tells us of the universal, while history tells us of the individual.'

Moral Philosophy: Virtue and Happiness

Aristotle's contribution to the practical sciences was made by his writings on moral philosophy and political theory. We possess his moral philosophy in three different versions, two of them his own notes for lecturing, and the third probably notes of his lectures made by a pupil. The dating of the two authentic treatises, the *Eudemian* and *Nicomachean Ethics*, is a matter of controversy; most scholars, for no good reason, regard the *Eudemian Ethics* as a youthful and inferior work. There is much better reason for the consensus that the third work, the *Magna Moralia*, is not from Aristotle's own hand. Whatever its intrinsic merits, the *Eudemian Ethics* has never been studied by more than a handful of scholars; it is the *Nicomachean Ethics* which, since the beginning of the Christian era, has been regarded as *the* Ethics of Aristotle, and it is from there that I will take my account of his moral philosophy.

Since ethics is a practical science, the treatise concerns the nature and purpose of human action. When we ask for the why and wherefore of any human action, we can be told that it is to be done for the sake of something else; we can ask in turn for the why and wherefore of that something else; sooner or later we reach a point where there is no further answer to the question. This is the goal or end of an action, and it is the worthwhileness of this end of an action which makes the actions leading to it themselves worthwhile. The best of all human goods would be a good which appeared at the origin of every chain of practical reasoning: that would be an absolute good, an independent good on which the goodness of every other human good depended, as the goodness of health-producing drugs or regimes depends on the goodness of health itself. It is this supreme good that is the subject matter of the science of ethics, which is the supreme practical science.

The *Nicomachean Ethics* covers much the same ground as Plato's *Republic*; with some exaggeration one could say that Aristotle's moral philosophy is Plato's moral philosophy with the Theory of Ideas stripped out. Right at the beginning, Aristotle explains why the supreme good of which ethics treats cannot be identified with the Idea of the Good. Plato was his friend, he says, but truth is a greater friend, and truth obliges him to bring forward no less than eight arguments to show the incoherence of this part of the Theory of Ideas. Most of the arguments are highly technical, and bear the marks of esoteric discussions in the Academy: but perhaps the clinching one is that ethics is a practical science, about what is within human power to achieve, whereas an everlasting and unchanging Idea of the Good could only be of theoretical interest.

Aristotle agrees, however, with the central contention of the *Republic* that there is an intimate connection between living virtuously and living happily, and that morality is to the soul what health is to the body. Indeed it is happiness (*eudaimonia*) which he puts in place of the Idea of the Good as the supreme good with which ethics is concerned. What then is happiness? To elucidate this we have to consider the function or characteristic activity (*ergon*) of man. Man must have a function, because particular types of men (e.g. sculptors) do, and parts and organs of human beings do. What is this function? Not life, not at least the life of growth and nourishment, for this is shared by plants, nor the life of the senses, for this is shared by animals. It must be a life of reason concerned with action: the activity of soul in accordance with reason. So human good will be good human functioning: namely, Aristotle says, 'activity of soul in accordance with virtue, and if there are several virtues, in accordance with the best and most perfect'.

Well, how many virtues are there, and what is the best of them? Aristotle starts to answer the first question at the end of the first book of the *Nicomachean Ethics*; it takes nine further books to answer the second. Like Plato, Aristotle begins by analysing the structure of the soul, and he offers his own division into three elements: a vegetable element, an appetitive element, and a rational element. The vegetable element is responsible for nourishment and growth; it is irrelevant to ethics. The second element in the soul is one which, unlike the vegetable part, is under the control of reason. It is the part of the soul for desire and passion, corresponding to appetite and temper in the Platonic tripartite soul. This part of the soul has its own virtues: the moral virtues, such as courage, temperance, and liberality. The rational part of the soul, later to be itself subdivided, is the seat of the intellectual virtues like wisdom and understanding.

Books II to V of the *Ethics* deal with the moral virtues, first in general and then individually. Moral virtues are not innate, nor are they simply passed on by a teacher to a pupil; they are acquired by practice and lost by disuse. A moral virtue, Aristotle says, is not a faculty (like intelligence or memory) nor a passion (like a rush of anger or a tug of pity). Neither the simple possession of faculties nor the simple occurrence of passions make people good or bad, praiseworthy or blameworthy. What makes a man a good man is the abiding state of his soul; or, as we would more naturally say in English, the state of his character.

A moral virtue is a state of character which makes a person choose well and act well. Choosing well is a matter of choosing a good way of life; acting well consists in avoiding excess and defect in particular kinds of action. If you are to be virtuous you must, for instance, avoid eating and drinking too much; you must also avoid eating and drinking too little. In your intercourse with others, you may go wrong by talking too much, or by talking too little; by being too solemn or too frivolous; by being too trusting, or not trusting enough.

Virtue, Aristotle says, chooses the mean or middle ground between excess and defect: the virtuous man eats and drinks the right amount, talks the right amount and so on. Such is Aristotle's celebrated doctrine of the mean. It is often mocked because it is often misunderstood. Rightly understood, it is a fine piece of conceptual analysis.

Aristotle is not praising a golden mediocrity, nor is he encouraging us to stay in the middle of the herd. What constitutes the right amount of something, he says expressly, may differ from person to person, in the way that the right amount of food for an Olympic champion differs from the right amount of food for a novice athlete. The doctrine of the mean is not meant as a recipe for correct living: we have to find out for ourselves what is the right amount in each case. But we do so by learning to avoid excess and defect; as, nowadays, we learn to steer a car along the correct part of the road by mastering our initial swerves towards the kerb and towards the oncoming traffic. Once we have learnt, by whatever means, the right amount of some kind of action – whether it is the right length of an after-dinner speech, or the right proportion of one's income to give to charity – then, Aristotle says, we have 'the right prescription' (*orthos logos*) in our mind. Virtue is the state which enables us to act in accordance with the right prescription.

Virtue concerns not only actions, but also passions. We can have too many fears, and we can have too few fears; we can be excessively concerned with sex or insufficiently interested in it. The virtuous person is fearless when appropriate, and fearful when appropriate, and is neither lustful nor frigid. Virtue is concerned with the mean of passion as well as the mean of action.

The virtues, besides being concerned with means of action and passion, are themselves means, in the sense that they occupy a middle ground between two contrary vices. Thus generosity is a mean between prodigality and miserliness; courage is a mean between cowardice and rashness. But virtues do not admit of the mean in the way that actions do: there cannot be too much of a virtue. If we say seriously that someone is over-generous, we mean that he has crossed the boundary between the virtue of generosity and the vice of prodigality. The mayor who said that he did his best to walk the narrow path between partiality and impartiality had misunderstood Aristotle's doctrine.

While all moral virtues are means, and concerned with means, not all actions and passions, Aristotle says, are the kinds of things that can have means. He gives as examples of excluded actions murder and adultery: we could never justly compain that somebody had committed too few murders, and there is no such thing as committing adultery with the right person at the right time in the right way. Among excluded passions he lists envy and spite: *any* amount of these sentiments is too much.

Aristotle's account of virtue as a mean often strikes people as a set of truisms, devoid of moral import. On the contrary, his doctrine sets him in conflict with several highly influential moral systems. Many people nowadays, for instance, accept a utilitarian viewpoint from which there is no class of actions which are ruled out in advance; the morality of each action is to be judged by its consequences. These people would oppose Aristotle's exclusions from the application of the mean; for them there can, in the appropriate circumstances, be the right amount of adultery or murder. On the other hand, some ascetic religious systems have ruled out whole classes of actions to which Aristotle applied the mean: for them any enjoyment of sex, or any eating of meat, is wrong, and there could be no right amount of such actions. We might say that from Aristotle's point of view, the utilitarians are guilty of excess in the application of the doctrine of the mean: they apply it to too many kinds of action. The ascetics, on the contrary, are guilty of defect in its application; they apply it to too few kinds of action.

In being neither innate nor wholly taught, but acquired by a kind of training, and in being concerned with a mean of action, moral virtues resemble skills like the ability to play the harp or the practice of medicine. Socrates and Plato constantly emphasized these similarities. They did so over much in Aristotle's view, and he is at pains to emphasize the differences between skills and virtues. If someone plays the harp beautifully, or effects a successful cure, it makes no difference to the evaluation of their skill what was the motive from which they acted. But if someone is to be accounted virtuous, it is not enough to perform actions which are objectively irreproachable; they must be performed for the right motive (which, for Aristotle, means that they must spring from the choice of an appropriate way of life). For this reason, virtue has a much closer connection than skill has with pleasure in action: a virtuous person, Aristotle believed, must enjoy doing what is right, and a grudging performance of duty is not truly virtuous. Again, a skill can be exercised in wrong actions as well as in right actions. A tennis player may serve a double fault on purpose, perhaps to avoid too humiliating a defeat for her opponent, and the double fault may be no less a use of her skill than an ace would have been. But no one could exercise the virtue of honesty by, once in a while, bringing off a shrewd swindle.

Aristotle treats many individual virtues in detail, defining their area of operation, and showing how they conform to the theory of the mean. In Book III he deals at length with courage and temperance, the virtues of the parts of the soul which Plato called temper and appetite. He deals also with the vices which flank these virtues: cowardice and rashness on the one hand, and self-indulgence and insensitivity to bodily pleasures on the other. Book IV offers a briefer treatment of a long series of virtues: generosity, munificence, greatness of soul, proper ambition, good temper, sociability, candour, readiness of wit.

The types of character which Aristotle has in mind are described shrewdly and vividly; but his descriptions reflect the social customs and institutions of his age, and not all his preferred virtues would appear nowadays on anyone's list of the ten most valuable or attractive traits of character. Both merriment and revulsion have been caused, for instance, by the picture of the great-souled man, who is very conscious of his own worth, who always demands his deserts but is too proud to accept gifts, who is reluctant to admire but swift to despise, and who always speaks with a deep voice and walks with a slow step. Aristotle's contribution to moral philosophy here is not through the individual traits of character he commends, but rather in providing a conceptual structure into which virtues of the most different ages and societies can be fitted with remarkable ease.

Aristotle's shorthand account of moral virtue is that it is a state of character expressed in choice, lying in the appropriate mean, determined by the prescription that a wise person would lay down. To complete his account, he needs to say what wisdom is, and how a wise person lays down prescriptions. This he does in Book VI, where he treats of the intellectual virtues.

Moral Philosophy: Wisdom and Understanding

Wisdom is a practical virtue which is concerned with what is good for human beings. Wisdom is expressed in practical reasoning: reasoning which starts from a general conception or pattern of human well-being, considers the circumstances of particular cases calling for decision, and concludes with a prescription for action. Aristotle envisages the ethical reasoning of the wise person on the model of the professional reasoning of a physician, who starts with his knowledge of the medical art, applies it to the condition of the particular patient, and then issues, literally, a prescription.

Wisdom, then, is an essential prerequisite for the exercise of moral virtue; without it, the most well-intentioned person may do wrong. But moral virtue is also required for the possession of wisdom; for only the virtuous person has the sound conception of human well-being which is the first premiss of practical reasoning: wickedness perverts us and deludes us about the ultimate grounds of action. So wisdom is impossible without moral virtue.

Wisdom and moral virtue are both acquired characteristics which build upon natural qualities. On the one hand, wisdom demands inborn intelligence; but intelligence can be used for evil purposes as well as good ones, and only moral virtue will ensure that the good wins out. On the other hand, children at an early age may have a sense of fairness and be attracted to brave or generous actions; but such good tendencies, without wisdom, can be positively harmful, like the strength of a blind man. Only wisdom will turn these natural virtuous inclinations into genuine moral virtue. So for real virtue and virtuous action, moral virtue and wisdom must be united with each other.

If we have to acquire virtue in order to become wise, and we cannot become wise without virtue, how can we ever acquire either virtue or wisdom? Are we not trapped in a vicious circle? The difficulty is a spurious one. It is as if someone were to allege a difficulty about getting married. How can anyone ever become a husband? To be a husband you need to have a wife; but a woman cannot be a wife unless she has a husband! As one and the same union simultaneously turns a man into a husband and a woman into a wife, so the wedding of wisdom and virtue makes what was intelligence into wisdom and what was natural virtue into full-fledged virtue.

In Aristotle as in Plato, wisdom is a virtue of the reasoning part of the soul; but, again like Plato, Aristotle divides the reasoning part of the soul into two parts. Wisdom (*phronesis*) is the virtue of the lower part, the deliberating part; the virtue of the superior or scientific part of the soul is understanding (*sophia*), which consists in the grasp of the axioms, and the knowledge of the theorems, of the sciences.

Aristotle's teaching that the mastery of a science is an intellectual virtue brings out the fact that his Greek word for virtue, '*arete*', has a broader range than the English word. 'Virtue' is an appropriate enough translation when what is in question is moral virtue; but the Greek word really means just 'goodness', 'excellence', and has a much broader range, so that we can speak of the *arete* of a knife or a horse. I will, however, continue to use the traditional translation and to speak of intellectual virtues. What is common to all intellectual virtues – whether deliberative, like wisdom, or theoretical, like the sciences – is that they are concerned with truth. To have an intellectual virtue is to be in the secure possession of truth about some field of knowledge.

It is not until Book X of the *Nicomachean Ethics* that the relationship between wisdom and understanding is tied up. In the intervening books Aristotle discusses other human characteristics and relationships that are neither virtues nor vices, but are closely related to them. Between the vice of intemperance and the virtue of temperance, for instance, there are two intermediate states and characters: there is the continent man, who exercises self-control in the pursuit of bodily pleasures, but does so only with reluctance; and there is the incontinent man, who pursues pleasures he should not pursue, but through weakness of will, not, like the intemperate man, out of a systematic policy of self-indulgence. Closely allied to virtues and vices, also, are friendships, good and bad. Under this heading Aristotle includes a wide variety of human relationships ranging from business partnerships to marriage. The connection which he sees with virtue is that only virtuous people can have the truest and highest friendship.

In Book X Aristotle finally answers his long-postponed question about the nature of happiness. Happiness, we were told early on in the treatise, is the activity of soul in accordance with virtue, and if there are several virtues, in accordance with the best and most perfect virtue. Now we know that there are both moral and intellectual virtues, and that the latter are superior; and among the intellectual virtues, understanding is superior to wisdom. Supreme happiness, then, is activity in accordance with understanding; it is to be found in science and philosophy. Happiness is not exactly the same as the pursuit of science and philosophy, but it is closely related to it: we are told that understanding is related to philosophy as knowing is to seeking. Happiness, then, in a way which remains to some extent obscure, is to be identified with the enjoyment of the fruits of philosophical inquiry.

To many people this seems an odd, indeed perverse, thesis. It is not quite as odd as it sounds, because the Greek word for happiness, '*eudaimonia*', does not mean quite the same as its English equivalent, just as '*arete*' did not mean quite the same as virtue. Perhaps 'a worthwhile life' is the closest we can get to its meaning in English. Even so, it is hard to accept Aristotle's thesis that the philosopher's life is the only really worthwhile one, and this is so whether one finds the claim endearing or finds it arrogant. Aristotle himself seems to have had second thoughts about it. Elsewhere in the *Nicomachean Ethics* he says that there is another kind of happiness which consists in the exercise of wisdom and the moral virtues. In the *Eudemian Ethics* his ideal life consists of the exercise of all the virtues, intellectual and moral; but even there, philosophical contemplation occupies a dominant position in the life of the happy person, and sets the standard for the exercise of the moral virtues.

> Whatever choice or possession of natural goods – health and strength, wealth, friends and the like – will most conduce to the contemplation of God is best: this is the finest criterion. But any standard of living which either through excess or defect hinders the service and contemplation of God is bad.

Both of Aristotle's *Ethics* end on this exalted note. The contemplation commended by the *Nicomachean Ethics* is described as a superhuman activity of a divine part of us. Aristotle's final word here is that in spite of being mortal, we must make ourselves immortal so far as we can.

POLITICS

When we turn from the *Ethics* to their sequel, the *Politics*, we come down to earth with a bump. 'Man is a political animal' we are told: humans are creatures of flesh and blood, rubbing shoulders with each other in cities and communities. The most primitive communities are families of men and women, masters and slaves; these combine into a more elaborate community, more developed but no less natural, the state (*polis*). A state is a society of humans sharing in a common perception of what is good and evil, just and unjust: its purpose is to provide a good and happy life for its citizens. The ideal state should have no more than a hundred thousand citizens, small enough for them all to know one another and to take their share in judicial and political office. It is all very different from the Empire of Alexander.

In the *Politics* as in the *Ethics* Aristotle thought of himself as correcting the extravagances of the *Republic*. Thus as in Aristotle's ethical system there was no Idea of the Good, so there are no philosopher kings in his political world. He defends private property and attacks the proposals to abolish the family and give women an equal share of government. The root of Plato's error, he thinks, lies in trying to make the state too uniform. The diversity of different kinds of citizen is essential to a state, and life in a city should not be like life in a barracks.

However, when Aristotle presents his own views on political constitutions he makes copious use of Platonic suggestions. Three forms of constitution are tolerable, which he calls monarchy, aristocracy, and polity; and these three have their perverted and intolerable counterparts, namely tyranny, oligarchy, and democracy. If a community contains an individual or family of an excellence far superior to everyone else, then monarchy is the best system. But such a fortunate circumstance is necessarily rare, and Aristotle pointedly refrains from saying that it occurred in the case of the royal family of Macedon. In practice he preferred a kind of constitutional democracy: for what he calls 'polity' is a state in which rich and poor respect each others' rights, and in which the best-qualified citizens rule with the consent of all the citizens. The state which he calls 'democracy' is one of anarchic mob rule.

Two elements of Aristotle's political teaching affected political institutions for centuries to come: his justification of slavery, and his condemnation of usury.

A slave, Aristotle says, is someone who is by nature not his own but another man's property. To those who say that all slavery is a violation of nature, he replies that some men are by nature free and others by nature slaves, and that for the latter slavery is both expedient and right. He agrees, however, that there is such a thing as unnatural slavery: victors in an unjust war, for instance, have no right to make slaves of the defeated. But some men are so inferior and brutish that it is better for them to be under the rule of a kindly master than to be free.

When Aristotle wrote, slavery was well-nigh universal; and his approval of the system is tempered by his observation that slaves are living tools, and that if non-living tools could achieve their purposes, there would be no need for slavery.

> If every instrument could achieve its own work, obeying or anticipating the will of others, like the statues of Daedalus . . . if, likewise the shuttle could weave and the plectrum touch the lyre, overseers would not want servants nor would masters slaves.

If Aristotle were alive today, in the age of automation, there is no reason to believe that he would defend slavery.

Aristotle's remarks on usury were brief, but very influential. Wealth, he says, can be made either by farming, or by trade; the former is more natural and more honourable. But the most unnatural and hateful way of making money is by charging interest on a loan.

> For money was intended to be used in exchange, but not to increase at interest. And this term interest (*tokos*), which means the birth of money from money, is applied to the breeding of money because the offspring resembles the parent. That is why of all modes of getting wealth this is the most unnatural.

Aristotle's words were one reason for the prohibition, throughout medieval Christendom, of the charging of interest even at a modest rate. They lie behind Antonio's reproach to the moneylender Shylock in *The Merchant of Venice*:

When did friendship take
A breed for barren metal of his friend?

SCIENCE AND EXPLANATION

We now turn to Aristotle's work in the theoretical sciences. He contributed to many sciences, but with hindsight we can see that his contribution was uneven. His chemistry and his physics were much less impressive than his inquiries into the life sciences. In particular, partly because he lacked precise clocks and any kind of thermometer, he was unaware of the importance of the measurement of velocity and temperature. While his zoological writings were still found impressive by Darwin, his physics was already superannuated by the sixth century AD.

In works such as *On Generation and Corruption* and *On the Heavens* Aristotle bequeathed to his successors a world-picture which included many features inherited from his pre-Socratic predecessors. He took over the four elements of Empedocles: earth, water, air, and fire, each characterized by the possession of a unique pair of the primary qualities of heat, cold, wetness and dryness. Each element had its natural place in an ordered cosmos, towards which it tended by its own characteristic movement: thus earthy solids fell while fire rose ever higher. Each such motion was natural to its element; other motions were possible, but were 'violent'. (We preserve a relic of Aristotle's distinction when we contrast natural with violent death.) The earth was in the centre of the universe: around it a succession of concentric crystalline spheres carried the moon, the sun and the planets in their journeys across the heavens. Further out, another sphere carried the fixed stars. The heavenly bodies did not contain the four terrestrial elements, but were made of a fifth element or quintessence. They had souls as well as bodies: living divine intellects, guiding their travel across the sky. These intellects were movers which were themselves in motion, and behind them, Aristotle argued, there must be a source of movement not itself in motion. That was the ultimate, unchanging, divinity, moving all other beings 'as an object of love' – the love which, in the final words of Dante's *Paradiso*, moved the sun and the first stars.

Even the best of Aristotle's scientific work now has only a historical interest, and rather than record his theories in detail I will describe the common notion of science which underpins his researches in diverse fields. Aristotle's conception of science can be summed up by saying that it is empirical, explanatory, and teleological.

Science begins with observation. In the course of our lives we notice things through our senses, we remember them, we build up a body of experience. Our concepts are drawn from our experience, and in science observation has the primacy over theory. Though a mature science can be set out and transmitted to others in the axiomatic form described in the *Posterior Analytics*, it is clear from

Aristotle's detailed works that the order of discovery is different from the order of exposition.

If science begins with sense-perception it ends with intellectual knowledge, which Aristotle sees as having a special character of necessity. Necessary truths are such as the unchanging truths of arithmetic: two and two make four, and always have and always will. They are contrasted with contingent truths, such as that the Greeks won a great naval victory at Salamis; something which could have turned out otherwise. It seems strange to say, as Aristotle does, that what is known must be necessary: cannot we have knowledge of contingent facts of experience, such as that Socrates drank hemlock? Some have thought that he was arguing, fallaciously, from the truth:

Necessarily, if p is known, p is true

to

If p is known, p is necessarily true

which is not at all the same thing. (It is a necessary truth that if I know there is a fly in my soup, then there is a fly in my soup. But even if I know that there is a fly in my soup, it is not a necessary truth that there is a fly in my soup: I can fish it out.) But perhaps Aristotle was defining the Greek word for 'knowledge' in such a way that it was restricted to scientific knowledge. This is much more plausible, especially if we notice that for Aristotle necessary truths are not restricted to truths of logic and mathematics, but include all propositions that are true universally, or even 'true for the most part'. But the consequence remains, and would be accepted by Aristotle, that history, because it deals with individual events, cannot be a science.

Science, then, is empirical: it is also explanatory, in the sense that it is a search for causes. In a philosophical lexicon in his *Metaphysics*, Aristotle distinguishes four types of causes, or explanations. First, he says, there is that of which and out of which a thing is made, such as the bronze of a statue and the letters of a syllable. This is called the material cause. Secondly, he says, there is the form and pattern of a thing, which may be expressed in its definition: his example is that the proportion of the length of two strings in a lyre is the cause of one being the octave of the other. The third type of cause is the origin of a change or state of rest in something: he gives as examples a person reaching a decision, and a father who begets a child, and in general anyone who makes a thing or changes a thing. The fourth and last type of cause is the end or goal, that for the sake of which something is done; it is the type of explanation we give if someone asks us why we are taking a walk, and we reply 'in order to keep healthy'.

The fourth type of cause (the 'final cause') plays a very important role in Aristotle's science. He inquires for the final causes not only of human action, but also of animals' behaviour ('why do spiders weave webs?') and of their structural features ('why do ducks have webbed feet?'). There are final causes also for the activities of plants (such as the downward pressure of roots) and those of inanimate elements (such as the upward thrust of flame). Explanations of this kind are called 'teleological', from the Greek word *telos*, which means the end or final cause. When Aristotle looks for teleological explanations, he is not attributing intentions to unconscious or inanimate objects, nor is he thinking in terms of a Grand Designer. Rather, he is laying emphasis on the *function* of various activities and structures. Once again, he was better inspired in the area of the life sciences than in chemistry and physics. Even post-Darwinian biologists are constantly on the look-out for function; but no one after Newton has sought a teleological explanation of the motion of inanimate bodies.

WORDS AND THINGS

Unlike his work in the empirical sciences, there are aspects of Aristotle's theoretical philosophy which still have much to teach us. In particular, he says things of the highest interest about the nature of language, about the nature of reality, and about the relationship between the two.

In his *Categories* Aristotle drew up a list of different types of things which might be said of an individual. It contains ten items: substance, quantity, quality, relation, place, time, posture, clothing, activity, and passivity. It would make sense to say of Socrates, for instance, that he was a human being (substance), was five feet tall (quantity), was gifted (quality), was older than Plato (relation), lived in Athens (place), was a man of the fifth-century BC (time), was sitting (posture), had a cloak on (clothing), was cutting a piece of cloth (activity), was killed by a poison (passivity). This classification was not simply a classification of predicates in language: each irreducibly different type of predicate, so Aristotle believed, stood for an irreducibly different type of entity. In 'Socrates is a man', for instance, the word 'man' stood for a substance, namely Socrates. In 'Socrates was poisoned' the word 'poisoned' stood for an entity called a passivity, namely the poisoning of Socrates. Aristotle perhaps believed that every possible entity, however it might initially be classified, would be found ultimately to belong to one and only one of the ten categories. Thus, Socrates is a man, an animal, a living being, and ultimately a substance; the murder committed by Aigisthos is a murder, a homicide, a killing, and ultimately an activity.

The category of substance was of primary importance. Substances are things like women, lions, and cabbages which can exist independently, and can be identified as individuals of a particular kind; a substance is, in Aristotle's homely phrase, 'a this such-and-such' – this cat, or this carrot. Things falling into the other categories (which Aristotle's successors would call 'accidents') are not separable; a size, for instance, is always the size *of* something. Items in the 'accidental' categories exist only as properties or modifications of substances.

Aristotle's categories do not seem exhaustive, and appear to be of unequal importance. But even if we accept them as one possible classification of predicates, is it correct to regard predicates as *standing for* anything? If 'Socrates runs' is true, must 'runs' stand for an entity of some kind in the way that 'Socrates' stands for Socrates? Even if we say yes, it is clear that this entity cannot be the *meaning* of the word 'runs'. For 'Socrates runs' makes sense even if it is false; and so 'runs' here has meaning even if there is no such thing as the running of Socrates for it to stand for.

If we take a sentence like 'Socrates is white' we may, on Aristotelian lines, think of 'white' as standing for Socrates' whiteness. If so, what does the 'is' stand for? To this question several answers seem possible. (i) We may say that it stands for nothing, but simply marks the connection between subject and predicate. (ii) We may say that it signifies existence, in the sense that if Socrates is white then there exists something – perhaps white Socrates, perhaps the whiteness of Socrates – which does not exist if Socrates is not white. (iii) We may say that it stands for *being*, where 'being' is to be taken as a verbal noun like 'running'. If we say this, it seems that we must add that there are various types of being: the being that is denoted by 'is' in the substantial predicate '. . . is a horse' is substantial being, while the being that is denoted by 'is' in the accidental predicate '. . . is white' is accidental being. In different places Aristotle seems to favour now one, now another, of these interpretations. His favourite is perhaps the third. In the passages where he expresses it, he draws the consequence from it that 'be' is a verb of multiple meaning, a homonymous term with more than one sense (just as 'healthy' has different, but related, senses when we speak of a healthy person, a healthy complexion, or a healthy climate).

I said above that in 'Socrates is a man', 'man' was a predicate in the category of substance which stood for the substance Socrates. But that is not the only analysis which Aristotle gives of such a sentence. Sometimes it appears that 'man' stands rather for the humanity which Socrates has. In such contexts, Aristotle distinguishes two senses of 'substance'. A this such-and-such, e.g. this man Socrates, is a first substance; the humanity he has is a second substance. When he talks like this, Aristotle commonly takes pains to avoid Platonism about universals. The humanity that Socrates has is an individual humanity, Socrates' own humanity; it is not a universal humanity that is participated in by all men.

MOTION AND CHANGE

One of the reasons why Aristotle rejected Plato's Theory of Ideas was that, like Eleatic metaphysics, it denied, at a fundamental level, the reality of change. In his

Physics and his *Metaphysics* Aristotle offered a theory of the nature of change intended to take up and disarm the challenge of Parmenides and Plato. This was his doctrine of potentiality and actuality.

If we consider any substance, such as a piece of wood, we find a number of things which are true of that substance at a given time, and a number of other things which, though not true of it at that time, can become true of it at some other time. Thus, the wood, though it *is* cold, *can* be heated and turned into ash. Aristotle called the things which a substance is, its 'actualities', and the things which it can be, its 'potentialities': thus the wood is actually cold but potentially hot, actually wood, but potentially ash. The change from being cold to being hot is an accidental change which the substance can undergo while remaining the substance that it is; the change from wood to ash is a substantial change, a change from being one kind of substance to another. In English, we can say, very roughly, that predicates which contain the word 'can', or a word with a modal suffix such as 'able' or 'ible', signify potentialities; predicates which do not contain these words signify actualities. Potentiality, in contrast to actuality, is the capacity to undergo a change of some kind, whether through one's own action or through the action of other agents.

The actualities involved in changes are called 'forms', and 'matter' is used as a technical term for what has the capacity for substantial change. In everyday life we are familiar with the idea that one and the same parcel of stuff may be first one kind of thing and then another kind of thing. A bottle containing a pint of cream may be found, after shaking, to contain not cream but butter. The stuff that comes out of the bottle is the same stuff as the stuff that went into the bottle: nothing has been added to it and nothing has been taken from it. But what comes out is different in kind from what goes in. It is from cases such as this that the Aristotelian notion of substantial change is derived.

Substantial change takes place when a substance of one kind turns into a substance of another kind. The stuff which remains the same parcel of stuff throughout the change was called by Aristotle *matter*. The matter takes first one form and then another: first it is cream and then it is butter. A thing may change without ceasing to belong to the same natural kind, by a change falling not under the category of substance, but under one of the other nine categories: thus a human may grow, learn, blush and be vanquished without ceasing to be a human. When a substance undergoes an accidental change there is always a form which it retains throughout the change, namely its substantial form. A man may be first P and then Q, but the predicate '. . . is a man' is true of him throughout. What of substantial change? When a piece of matter is first A and then B, must there be some predicate in the category of substance, '. . . is C', which is true of the matter all the time? In many cases, no doubt, there is such a predicate: when copper and tin change into bronze the changing matter remains metal throughout. It does not seem necessary, however, that there should in all cases be such a predicate; it seems logically conceivable that there should be stuff which is first A and then B without there being any substantial predicate which is true of it all the time. At all events, Aristotle thought so; and he called stuff-which-is-first-one-thing-and-then-another-without-being-anything-all-the-time 'prime matter'.

Form makes things belong to a certain kind; it is matter, according to Aristotle, that makes them individuals of that kind. As philosophers put it, matter is the principle of individuation in material things. This means, for instance, that two peas of the same size and shape, however alike they are, however many properties or forms they may have in common, are two peas and not one pea because they are two different parcels of matter.

It should not be thought that matter and form are parts of bodies, elements out of which they are built or pieces to which they can be taken. Prime matter could not exist without form: it need not take any particular form, but it must take some form or other. The forms of changeable bodies are all forms *of* particular bodies; it is inconceivable that there should be any such form which was not the form of some body. Unless we are to fall into the Platonism which Aristotle frequently explicitly rejected, we must accept that forms are logically incapable of existing without the bodies of which they are the forms. Forms indeed do not themselves exist, nor come to be, in the way in which substances exist and come to be. Forms, unlike bodies, are not made out of anything; and for a form of A-ness to exist is simply for there to be some substance which is A; for *horseness* to exist is simply that there are horses.

The doctrine of matter and form is a philosophical account of certain concepts which we employ in our everyday description and manipulation of material substances. Even if we grant that the account is philosophically correct, it is still a question whether the concepts which it seeks to clarify have any part to play in a scientific explanation of the universe. It is notorious that what in the kitchen appears as a substantial change of macroscopic entities may in the laboratory appear as an accidental change of microscopic entities. It remains a matter of opinion whether a notion such as that of prime matter has any application to physics at a fundamental level, where we talk of transitions between matter and energy.

Form is a particular kind of actuality, and matter a particular kind of potentiality. Aristotle believed that his distinction between actuality and potentiality offered an alternative to the sharp dichotomy of Being vs. Unbeing on which the Parmenidean rejection of change had been based. Since matter underlay and survived all change whether substantial or accidental, there was no question of Being coming from Unbeing, or anything coming from nothing. But it was a consequence of Aristotle's account that matter could not have had a beginning. In later centuries this set a problem for Christian Aristotelians who believed in the creation of the material world out of nothing.

Soul, Sense, and Intellect

One of the most interesting applications of Aristotle's doctrine of matter and form is found in his psychology, which is to be found in his treatise *On the Soul*. For Aristotle it is not only human beings which have a soul, or psyche; all living beings have one, from daisies and molluscs upwards. A soul is simply a principle of life: it is the source of the characteristic activities of living beings. Different living beings have different abilities: plants can grow and reproduce, but cannot move or feel; animals perceive, and feel pleasure and pain; some but not all animals can move around; some very special animals, namely human beings, can also think and understand. Different kinds of soul are diversified by these different activities in which they find expression. The most general definition which Aristotle gives of a soul is that it is the form of an organic body.

As a form, a soul is an actuality of a particular kind. Aristotle at this point introduces a distinction between two kinds of actuality. Someone who knows no Greek is in a state of sheer potentiality with regard to the use of Greek. To learn Greek is to take a step from potentiality in the direction of actuality. But someone who has learnt Greek, but is not at a given time making use of that knowledge, is in a state of both actuality and potentiality: actuality by comparison with the initial position of ignorance, potentiality by comparison with someone actually speaking Greek. Simply knowing Greek Aristotle called 'first actuality'; currently speaking Greek he called 'second actuality'. He uses this distinction in his account of the soul: the soul is the first actuality of an organic body. The actual vital operations of living creatures are second actualities.

An Aristotelian soul is not, as such, a spirit. It is not, indeed, a tangible object; but that is because it is (like all first actualities) a potentiality. Knowledge of Greek is not a tangible object, either; but it is not anything ghostly. If there are any souls which are capable, in whole or in part, of existing without a body – a point on which Aristotle found it difficult to make up his mind – disembodiment is possible, not because they are souls, but because they are souls of a particular kind with specially impressive vital activities.

Aristotle gives straightforwardly biological accounts of the activities of nutrition, growth, and reproduction which are common to all living things. Matters become more complicated, and more interesting, when he turns to explain sense-perception (peculiar to higher animals) and intellectual thought (peculiar to human beings).

In explaining sense-perception, Aristotle adapts the account in Plato's *Theaetetus* according to which sensation is the outcome of an encounter between a sense-faculty (such as vision) and a sense-object (such as a visible object). Only, whereas on Plato's account the eye's seeing a white object, and the whiteness of the object itself, are two twins begotten of the same intercourse, for Aristotle the seeing and the being seen are one and the same thing. He propounds the general thesis: a sense-faculty in actuality is identical with a sense-object in actuality.

This initially obscure thesis is yet another application of Aristotle's theory of actuality and potentiality. Let me illustrate its meaning by taking the example of taste. The sweetness of a piece of sugar, something which can be tasted, is a sense-object, and my sense of taste, my ability to taste things, is a sense-faculty. The operation of my sense of taste upon the sensible object is the same thing as the action of the sense-object upon my sense. That is to say, the sugar's tasting sweet to me is one and the same event as my tasting the sweetness of the sugar. The sugar itself is actually sweet all the time; but until the sugar is put into the mouth its sweetness is not actually, but only potentially, tasting sweet. (Being sweet is a first actuality, tasting sweet a second actuality.)

The sense of taste is nothing other than the power to do such things as taste the sweetness of sweet objects. The sensory property of sweetness is nothing other than the power to taste sweet to a suitable taster. Thus Aristotle is correct to say that the property in action is one and the same thing as the faculty in operation. Of course the power to taste and the power to be tasted are two very different things, the one in the taster and the other in the sugar.

This account of sense-perception is superior to the Platonic one, because it allows us to say that things in the world really do have sensory qualities, even when not being sensed. Things not being looked at are really coloured, things not being sniffed really do smell sour, sounds unheard may really be deafening. Aristotle can say this because his analysis of actuality and potentiality allows him to explain that sensory qualities are really powers of a certain kind.

Aristotle draws on his theory also when dealing with the rational and intellectual abilities of the human soul. He made a distinction between natural powers, such as the power of fire to burn, and rational powers, like the ability to speak Greek. If all the necessary conditions for the exercise of a natural power were present, then, he maintained, the power was necessarily exercised. Put the wood, appropriately dry, on the fire, and the fire will burn it; there are no two ways about it. Rational powers, however, are essentially, he argued, two-way powers, powers which can be exercised at will. A physician who possesses the power to heal may refuse to exercise it, if his patient is insufficiently wealthy; he may even exercise his medical skill to poison rather than to cure. Aristotle's theory of rational powers was to be used by many of his successors in order to give an account of human freedom of the will.

Aristotle's teaching about the intellectual powers of the soul is inconstant. Sometimes the intellect appears to be a part of the soul, and since the soul is the form of the body, the intellect, so conceived, will perish with the body. At other times he argues that since the intellect is capable of grasping necessary and eternal truths, it must itself, by affinity, be something independent and indestructible; and at one point he suggests that the capacity for thought is something divine which comes from outside the body. And in one baffling passage, the subject of endless discussion in succeeding centuries, he appears to divide the intellect into two faculties, one perishable and the other imperishable.

Thought, as we have described it, is what it is by virtue of becoming all things; while there is another which is what it is by virtue of making all things: this is a sort of positive state like light; for in a sense light makes potential colours into actual colours. Thought in this sense is separable and impassive and unmixed, being essentially actuality. And when separate it is just what it is, and it alone is immortal and eternal.

The feature of the human intellect which tempted Aristotle, at times, to think of it as disembodied and divine was its ability to pursue philosophy and especially metaphysics; and so we must finally explain how he saw the nature of this sublime discipline.

METAPHYSICS

'There is a discipline,' Aristotle says in the fourth book of his *Metaphysics*, 'which theorizes about Being qua being, and the things which belong to Being taken in itself.' This discipline is called 'first philosophy', which he elsewhere describes as the knowledge of first principles and supreme causes. Other sciences, he says, deal with a particular kind of being, but the science of the philosopher concerns Being universally and not merely partially. However, in other places Aristotle seems to restrict the object of first philosophy to a particular kind of being, namely divine, independent and immutable substance. There are three theoretical philosophies, he says in one place – mathematics, physics, and theology; and the first, or most honourable philosophy, is theology. Theology is the best of the theoretical sciences because it deals with the most honourable among beings; it is prior to, and more universal than, physics or natural philosophy.

Both sets of definitions so far considered treat of first philosophy as concerned with Being or beings; it is also spoken of as the science of substance or substances. In one place Aristotle tells us that the old question, what is Being?, comes to the same as the question, what is substance? So that first philosophy can be called the theory of first and universal substance.

Are all these definitions of the subject matter of philosophy equivalent to each other – or indeed compatible with each other? Some historians, thinking them incompatible, have attributed the different kinds of definition to different periods of Aristotle's life. But with an effort we can show that the definitions can be reconciled.

Before asking what Being qua being is, we need to settle what Being is. Aristotle is using the Greek phrase *to on* in the same way as Parmenides did: Being is whatever is anything whatever. Whenever Aristotle explains the senses of 'to on' he does so by explaining the sense of 'einai', the verb 'to be'. Being, in its broadest sense, is whatever can appear, in some true sentence, followed by 'is'. On this view, a science of being would be less like a science of the existent than a science of true predication.

All the categories, Aristotle tells us, signify being, because any verb can be replaced by a predicate which will contain the verb 'to be': 'Socrates runs', for instance, can be replaced by 'Socrates is a runner'. And every being in any category other than substance is a property or modification of substance. This means that wherever you have a subject–verb sentence in which the subject is not a term for a substance, you can turn it into another subject–verb sentence in which the subject term does denote a substance – a first substance, like a particular man or cabbage.

With Aristotle, as with Parmenides, it is a mistake simply to equate being with existence. When he discusses the senses of 'being' and 'is' in his philosophical lexicon in the *Metaphysics* Aristotle does not even mention existence as one of the senses of the verb 'to be', a use to be distinguished from the use of the verb with a complement in a predicate, as in 'to be a philosopher'. This is surprising, because he seems himself to have made the distinction in earlier books. In the *Sophistical Refutations*, to counter the sophism that whatever is thought of must exist in order to be thought of, Aristotle distinguishes between 'to be F', where the verb is followed by a predicate (e.g. 'to be thought of') and 'to be' period. He makes a similar move in connection with the being F of that which has ceased to be, period: e.g. from 'Homer is a poet' it does not follow that he is.

It is a mistake, perhaps, to look in Aristotle for a single treatment of existence. When philosophers pose problems about what things really exist and what things do not, they may have three different contrasts in mind: that between the abstract and the concrete (e.g. wisdom vs. Socrates), that between the fictional and the factual (e.g. Pegasus vs. Bucephalus), and that between the extant and the defunct (e.g. the Great Pyramid vs. the Colossus of Rhodes). In different places, Aristotle treats of all three problems. He deals with the problem about abstractions when he discusses accidents: they are all modifications of substance. Any statement about abstractions (such as colours, actions, changes) must be analysable into one about concrete first substances. He deals with the problem about fictions by introducing a sense of 'is' in which it means 'is true': a fiction *is* a genuine thought, but it *is not*, i.e. is not true. The problem about the extant and the defunct, problems about things which come into existence and go out of existence, are solved by the application of the doctrine of matter and form. To exist, in this sense, is to be matter under a certain form, it is to be a thing of a certain kind: Socrates ceases to exist if he ceases to be a human being. Being, for Aristotle, includes anything that exists in any of these ways.

If that is what Being is, what then is Being qua Being? The answer is that there is no such thing. Certainly, you can study Being qua being, and you can look for causes of Being qua being. But this is to engage in a special sort of study, to look for a special sort of cause. It is not to study a special kind of Being, or to look for the causes of a special kind of Being. Aristotle more than once insisted that 'An A qua F is G' must be regarded as consisting of a subject A, and a predicate 'is, qua F, G'. It should not be regarded as consisting of a predicate 'is G' which is attached to a subject An-A-qua-F. One example he gives is that 'A good can be known as good' should not be analysed as 'a good as good can be known', because 'a good as good' is nonsense.

But if 'A qua F' is a pseudo-subject in 'An A qua F is G', equally, 'A qua F' is a pseudo-object in 'We study A qua F'. The object of that sentence is A, and the verb is 'study qua F'. We are talking, not of the study of a special kind of object, but of a special kind of study, a study which looks for special kinds of explanation and causes, causes qua F. For instance, when we do human physiology, we study men qua animals, that is to say, we study the structures and functions which humans have in common with animals. There is no object which is a man qua animal, and it would be foolish to ask whether all men, or only some specially brutish men, are men qua animals. It is equally foolish to ask whether Being qua Being means all beings or only some specially divine beings.

However, you can study any being from the particular point of view of being, that is you can study it in virtue of what it has in common with all other beings. That, one might think, is surely very little: and indeed Aristotle himself says that nothing has being as its essence or nature: there is nothing which is just a being and nothing else. But to study something *as a being* is to study something about which true predications can be made, precisely from the point of view of the possibility of making true predications of it. Aristotle's first philosopher is not making a study of some particular kind of being; he is studying everything, the whole of Being, precisely as such.

Now an Aristotelian science is a science of causes, so that the science of Being qua being will be a science which assigns the causes of there being any truths whatever about anything. Can there be such causes? It is not too difficult to give sense to a particular being's having a cause qua being. If I had never been conceived, there would never have been any truths about me; Aristotle says that if Socrates had never existed neither 'Socrates is well' nor 'Socrates is unwell' would ever have been true. So my parents who brought me into existence are causes of me, qua being. (They are, of course, also causes of me qua human.) So also are their parents, and their parents in turn, and ultimately, Adam and Eve, if we are all descended from a single pair. And if there was anything which produced Adam and Eve, that would be the cause of all human beings, qua beings.

We can see from this clearly enough how the Christian God, the maker of the world, could be regarded as the cause of Being qua being – the cause, in his own existence, of truths about himself, and as creator the efficient cause of the possibility of any truth about anything else. But what is the cause of Being qua being in Aristotle's system, in which there is no maker of the world?

At the supreme point of Aristotle's hierarchy of beings are the moved and unmoved movers which are the final causes of all generation and corruption. They are therefore in one respect the causes of all perceptible and corruptible beings, in so far as they are beings. The science which reaches up to the unmoved mover will be studying the explanation of all true predication whatever, and therefore will be studying every being qua being. In his *Metaphysics* Aristotle explains that there are three kinds of substances: perishable bodies, eternal bodies, and immutable beings. The first two kinds belong to natural science and the third to first philosophy. Whatever explains substances, he says, explains all things; since without substances there would be neither active nor passive change. He then goes on to prove the existence of an unmoved mover; and concludes 'on such a principle the heavens and nature depend' – i.e. eternal bodies and perishable bodies alike depend on immutable being. And this is the divine, the object of theology.

The unmoved mover is prior to other substances and substances are prior to all other beings. 'Prior' is here used not in a temporal sense, but to denote dependency: A is prior to B if you can have A without B and you cannot have B without A. If there was no unmoved mover, there would be no heavens and no nature; if there were no substances there would be no other beings. We can see now why Aristotle says that what is prior has greater explanatory power than what is posterior, and why the science of the divine beings can be said to be the most universal science because it is prior: it deals with beings which are prior, i.e. further back in the chain of dependence. The science of divine beings is more universal than the science of physics because it explains both divine beings and natural beings; the science of physics explains only natural beings and not also divine beings.

We can at last see how the different definitions of first philosophy cohere together. Any science can be defined either by giving the field it is to explain, or by specifying principles by which it explains. First philosophy is universal in its field: it undertakes to offer one kind of explanation of everything whatever, to assign one of the causes of the truth of every true predication. It is the science of Being qua being. But if we turn from the explicandum to the explicans, we can say that first philosophy is the science of the divine; for what it explains, it explains by reference to the divine unmoved mover. It does not deal just with a single kind of Being, for it gives an account not only of the divine itself, but of everything else that exists or is anything. But it is *par excellence* the science of the divine, because it explains everything not, like physics, by reference to nature, but by reference to the divine. Thus theology and the science of Being qua being are one and the same first philosophy.

One is sometimes invited to believe that the final stage in the understanding of Aristotle's metaphysics is an appreciation of the profound and mysterious nature of Being qua Being. Rather, the first step towards such an understanding is the realization that Being qua Being is a chimerical spectre engendered by inattention to Aristotle's logic.

V

GREEK PHILOSOPHY AFTER ARISTOTLE

THE HELLENISTIC ERA

When Alexander the Great died in Bablyon in 323 his vast empire was divided up between his senior officers, who founded a number of independent realms. The most long lasting of these was the kingdom of Ptolemy and his family in Egypt and Libya, which survived until Antony and Cleopatra were defeated by the Roman Emperor Augustus in 31 BC. In the centuries between the death of Alexander and the death of Cleopatra the domains of Alexander's other generals broke up into smaller kingdoms which, one by one, came under the sway of Rome and eventually became provinces of its Empire. These centuries, in which Greek civilization flourished throughout all the lands around the Eastern Mediterranean, are known to historians as the Hellenistic age.

In this period Greek colonists came into contact with widely different systems of thought. In Bactria, at the far eastern end of the former Empire, Greek philosophy encountered the religion of Buddha, energetically propagated by the devout Indian king, Asoka; two surviving dialogues tell the story of the conversion to Buddhism of the Greek king, Menander. In Persia Greeks encountered the already ancient religion of Zarathustra (whose name they Hellenized as Zoroaster); this saw the world as a battlefield between two powerful divine principles, one good and one evil. In Palestine they met the Jews, who since their return in 538 from their Babylonian exile had formed a strictly monotheistic community centred on the Temple worship in Jerusalem. The books of the Maccabees, among the apocrypha in the Bible, tell of their resistance to assimilation by Greek culture under the rule of Antiochus IV of Syria. The first Ptolemies in Egypt built up the new city of Alexandria, whose citizens were drawn from every part of the Greek world. They founded a magnificent and well-catalogued library, which became the envy of the world, rivalled only, at a later date, by the library of King Attalus at Pergamum in Asia Minor. It was in Alexandria that the Hebrew Bible was translated into Greek; the version was known as the Septuagint, a word meaning seventy, after the number of scholars said to have collaborated in the translation.

A series of brilliant mathematicians and scientists in Alexandria competed with, and in time surpassed, the scholars in the Academy and the Lyceum who, in Athens, carried on the work of their founders Plato and Aristotle.

The best-known philosophers in Athens in the generation after Alexander's death were members neither of the Academy nor of the Lyceum, but founders of new rival institutions: Epicurus, who established a school known as 'The Garden', and Zeno, whose followers were called 'Stoics' because he taught in the *Stoa* or painted portico. The multiplication of schools in Athens reflected an increasing interest in philosophy as an essential part of the education of the upper classes.

EPICUREANISM

Epicurus, born into a family of Athenian expatriates in Samos, set up house in Athens about 306 BC, and lived there until his death in 271. His followers in the Garden, who included women and slaves, lived on simple fare and kept away from public life. Epicurus wrote three hundred books, but except for a few letters almost all that he wrote has been lost. Fragments from his treatise *On Nature* were buried in volcanic ash at Herculaneum when Vesuvius erupted in AD 79; in modern times they have been painstakingly unrolled and deciphered. To this day, however, we depend for our knowledge of Epicurus' teachings principally on a long Latin poem written in the first century BC by his follower Lucretius, entitled *On the Nature of Things* (De Rerum Natura).

The aim of Epicurus' philosophy is to make happiness possible by removing the fear of death which is its greatest obstacle. Because men are afraid of death, they struggle for wealth and power in the hope of postponing it, and throw themselves into frenzied activity so that they can forget its inevitability. The fear of death is instilled in us by religion, which holds out the prospect of suffering and punishment after death. But this prospect is illusory. The point is eloquently made by Lucretius (in Dryden's translation): there is no need to fear either death, or survival, or reincarnation.

> What has this bugbear, death, to frighten man,
> If souls can die, as well as bodies can?
> For, as before our birth we felt no pain
> When Punic arms infested land and main,
> So, when our mortal frame shall be disjoined,
> The lifeless lump uncoupled from the mind,
> From sense of grief and pain we shall be free
> We shall not feel, because we shall not be.
> Though earth in seas, and seas in heaven were lost
> We should not move, we only should be tossed.
> Nay, e'en suppose when we have suffered fate,

The soul could feel in her divided state,
What's that to us? for we are only we
While souls and bodies in one frame agree.
Nay, though our atoms should revolve by chance,
And matter leap into the former dance;
Though time our life and motion could restore,
And make our bodies what they were before;
What gain to us would all this bustle bring?
The new-made man would be another thing.

It was to cure the fear of death, and in order to show that the terrors held out by religion were only fairy-tales, that Epicurus set out his account of the nature and structure of the world.

He took over, with some modifications, the atomism of Democritus. Indivisible unchanging units move in void and infinite space; initially they all move downwards at constant and equal speed, but from time to time they swerve and collide with each other. From their collisions everything in heaven and earth has come into being. The soul, too, like everything else, consists of atoms, which differ from other atoms only in being smaller and subtler. At death the atoms of the soul are dispersed, and cease to be capable of sensation because they no longer occupy their appropriate place in a body. The gods themselves are compounded of atoms, just like humans and animals; but because they live in less turbulent regions they are free from the danger of dissolution. Epicurus was no atheist, but he believed that the gods took no interest in the affairs of this world, and lived a life of their own in uninterrupted tranquillity. For this reason, belief in divine providence was superstition, and religious rituals were worthless at best.

Unlike Democritus, Epicurus believed that the senses were reliable sources of information, and he gave an atomistic account of their operation. Bodies in the world throw off thin films of the atoms of which they are made, which retain their original shape and thus serve as images (*eidola*) of their parent bodies. Sensation occurs when these images make contact with the atoms in the soul. The appearances which reach the soul are never false; they always correspond exactly to their source. If we are misled about reality it is because we have used these genuine appearances as a basis for false judgements. If appearances conflict, as when an oar looks bent when in the water and straight when outside it, the two appearances are to be regarded as honest witnesses between which the mind must give judgement. If appearances are insufficient to settle the issue between competing theories (e.g. about the real size of the sun) then the mind should suspend judgement and exercise an equal tolerance to all.

The keystone of Epicurus' moral philosophy is the doctrine that pleasure is the beginning and end of the happy life. He makes a distinction, however, between pleasures which are the satisfaction of desires, and pleasures which come when all desires have been satisfied. The pleasures of satisfying our desires for food and drink and sex are inferior pleasures, because they are bound up with pain: the desire which they satisfy is itself painful, and its satisfaction leads to a renewal of desire. We should aim, therefore, at quiet pleasures such as those of private friendship.

Though he was an atomist, Epicurus was not a determinist; he believed humans enjoyed freedom of the will, and he sought to explain it by appealing to the random swerve of the atoms. Since we are free we are masters of our own fate: the gods neither impose necessity nor interfere with our choices. We cannot escape death, but if we take a truly philosophical view of it, death is no evil.

STOICISM

Epicureanism survived for six hundred years after Epicurus' death; but despite finding incomparable expression in Lucretius' great poem, it was never as popular as the Stoicism founded by his contemporary **Zeno** of Citium. Zeno came from Cyprus, where, having read a book about Socrates, he acquired a passion for philosophy which led him to emigrate to Athens, at about the same time as Epicurus. There he was to study under a number of teachers, but on his first arrival he became a pupil of the Cynic Crates, who, he was told, was the nearest contemporary equivalent of Socrates. Cynicism was not a school of philosophy, but a bohemian way of life, based on contempt for material wealth and conventional propriety. Its founder had been Diogenes of Sinope, who lived like a dog ('cynic' means 'dog-like') in a tub for a kennel. When visited by the great Alexander, who asked what favour he could do him, Diogenes replied 'you could move out of my light'. Zeno's encounter with Cynicism taught him to give a prominent place in his philosophy to the ideal of self-sufficiency.

Unlike Diogenes, who loved teasing Plato, and Crates, who liked writing poetic satire, Zeno took systematic philosophy seriously. His writings have not survived, and for our knowledge of his teaching we rely on writers from the Roman period, such as Nero's court philosopher Seneca and the Emperor Marcus Aurelius. We do know that he founded the Stoic tradition of dividing philosophy into three main disciplines, logic, ethics and physics. His followers said that logic was the bones, ethics the flesh, and physics the soul of philosophy. Zeno himself was concerned principally with ethics, but he was a close associate of two dialecticians from Megara, Diodorus Cronus and Philo, who had taken over from the Lyceum the task of filling the gaps which Aristotle had left in logic.

When Zeno died the leadership of the Stoa passed to **Cleanthes**, a converted boxer who specialized in physics and metaphysics. Cleanthes was a devout man who wrote a remarkable hymn to Zeus, whom he addresses in terms which would be appropriate enough for a Jewish or Christian monotheist addressing the Lord God.

Zeus all powerful,
Author of Nature, named by many names, all hail.
Thy law rules all; and the world's voice may cry to thee.
For from thee we are born, and alone of living things
That move on earth are we created in God's image.

The hymn was known to St Paul, and quoted by him when preaching in Athens.

Zeno was succeeded by **Chrysippus**, who was head of the school from 232 to 206. He took ethics as his own speciality, but he also built up and extended the work of his predecessors, and was the first to present Stoicism as a fully integrated system. Since the works of these three early Stoics have all been lost, it is difficult to determine precisely the contribution each of them made, and their doctrines are best considered together.

The logic of the Stoics differed from that of Aristotle in various ways. Aristotle used letters as variables, while they used numbers; a typical sentence-frame in an Aristotelian inference would run 'every A is B'; a typical sentence-frame in a Stoic inference would be 'If the first, then the second'. The difference between letters and numbers is trivial: what is important is that Aristotle's variables stand in for terms (subjects and predicates), while the Stoic variables stand in for whole sentences. Aristotle's syllogistic formalizes what nowadays would be called predicate logic; Stoic logic formalizes what is nowadays called propositional logic. A typical inference considered by the Stoics is

If Plato is living, then Plato is breathing
Plato is living
Therefore, Plato is breathing.

It is an important feature of Stoic logic that the validity of the argument does not depend on the content of the individual sentences. According to the Stoic view, the following argument is no less sound than the one above.

If Plato is dead, then Athens is in Greece
Plato is dead
Therefore Athens is in Greece.

The first premiss of this argument comes out true if, like the Stoics, we accept a particular definition of 'if . . . then' first suggested by Philo. According to this a sentence of the form 'if the first then the second' is to be taken as true in every case except when the first is true and the second is false. In everyday life, we usually make use of 'if . . . then' when there is some connection between the content of the sentences thus linked together. But we do sometimes make use of Philo's definition – e.g. when we say 'If Athens is in Turkey, then I am a Dutchman' as a way of denying that Athens is in Turkey. It turns out that the Stoics' minimal definition of 'if' is the one most useful for the technical development of propositional logic, and it is the one which logicians use today. The Stoic propositional logic is nowadays taken as the basic element in logic, upon which the predicate logic of Aristotle is built as a superstructure.

Under the heading 'logic' the Stoics investigated also the philosophy of language. They had an elaborate theory of signs, which studied both things signifying and things signified. Things signifying were classified as voice, speech, and discourse. Voice might be inarticulate sound, speech was sound which was articulate but might lack meaning, and discourse was both articulate and meaningful. Things signified might be bodies or statements (*lekta*). By 'statement' is meant, not a sentence, but what is said by a sentence. If I say 'Dion is walking', the word 'Dion' signifies the body which I see; but what I mean by the sentence is not a body, but a statement about a body.

In this respect, there is a clash between Stoic logic and Stoic physics: the statements of Stoic logic are non-bodily entities, while Stoic physics recognizes no existents other than bodies. Once upon a time, Stoics believed, there was nothing but fire; gradually there emerged the other elements and the familiar furniture of the universe. Later, the world will return to fire in a universal conflagration, and then the whole cycle of its history will be repeated over and over again. All this happens in accordance with a system of laws which may be called 'fate', because the laws admit of no exception, or 'providence', because the laws were laid down by God for beneficent purposes.

The Stoics accepted the Aristotelian distinction between matter and form; but as conscientious materialists they insisted that form too was bodily – a fine and subtle body which they called breath (*pneuma*). The human soul and mind are made out of this *pneuma*; so too is God, who is the soul of the cosmos, which, in its entirety, constitutes a rational animal. If God and the soul were not themselves bodily, Stoics argued, they would not be able to act upon the material world.

The divinely designed system is called Nature, and our aim in life should be to live in accordance with Nature. Since all things are determined, nothing can escape Nature's laws. But human beings are free and responsible, despite the determinism of fate. The will must be directed to live in accordance with human nature by obeying reason. It is this voluntary acceptance of Nature's laws which constitutes virtue, and virtue is both necessary and sufficient for happiness. Poverty, imprisonment, and suffering, since they cannot take away virtue, cannot take away happiness; a good person cannot suffer any real harm. Does this mean that we should be indifferent to the misfortunes of others? Well, health and wealth are in truth matters of indifference, but the Stoics, in order to be able to co-operate at all with non-Stoics, were forced to concede that some matters were more indifferent than others.

Because society is natural to human beings, the Stoic, in his aim to be in harmony with Nature, will play his part in society and cultivate the social virtues.

Though slavery and freedom are alike indifferent, it is legitimate to prefer one to the other, even though virtue may be practised in either state. What of life itself? Is that a matter of indifference? The virtuous Stoic will not lose his virtue whether he lives or dies; but it is legitimate for him, when faced with what the non-Stoic would regard as intolerable evils, to make a rational choice to depart from life.

SCEPTICISM

The English language preserves traces of both Epicureanism and Stoicism, but with different degrees of accuracy. An epicure would find little satisfaction in the bread and cheese diet of Epicurus; but a stoic attitude to suffering and death fairly reflects one aspect of Stoic philosophy. A third contemporary school, however, made its mark on the language unambiguously: the basic meaning of Scepticism has not changed since the Sceptics of the third century BC.

The founder of Scepticism was **Pyrrho** of Elis, a soldier in Alexander's army, who was an older contemporary of Epicurus. Pyrrho taught that nothing could be known and, consistently with that view, wrote no books; but his teaching was brought to Athens in the early years of the third century by his pupils Timon and Arcesilaus. Timon denied the possibility of finding any self-evident principles to serve as the foundation of sciences: and in the absence of such axioms, all lines of reasoning must be either circular or endless. Arcesilaus became head of the Platonic Academy about 273 and turned its attention from the later dogmatic works of Plato to the earlier Socratic dialogues. He himself, like Socrates, used to demolish theses put forward by his pupils; the proper attitude for the philosopher was to suspend judgement on all important topics. Arcesilaus' impact on the Academy was great, and it remained the home of Scepticism for two hundred years.

The Sceptics of the Academy took the Stoic system as their major target for attack. The Stoics were empiricists; that is to say, they claimed that all knowledge derived from sensory experience of concrete individuals. The appearances which things present to our senses are the foundation of all science; but appearances may mislead, and we need a test, or 'criterion', to decide which appearances are reliable and justify us in assenting to them. The Sceptics insisted that things appear differently to different species (woodlice taste good to bears but not to people), and differently to different members of the same species (honey seems bitter to some and sweet to others), and differently to the same person at different times (wine tastes sour after figs and sweet after nuts). How can conflicts between them be resolved?

The Stoics say that knowledge must be based not just on any old appearance, but upon appearance of a particular kind, a 'cognitive appearance' (*phantasia kataleptike*) – an appearance of the kind which comes from a real object and compels our assent. The Sceptic counters by asking how we can tell which appearances are cognitive appearances. It is no good defining them as ones which compel assent, since people often feel compelled to assent to appearances which turn out to have been misleading. The Stoics respond that a truly wise person can just tell which appearances are cognitive and which are not. But how can you tell whether you are a truly wise person? The Stoic search for a criterion seems doomed to failure: even if we found a criterion which worked, how would we know we had found it?

The debate between Scepticism and Stoicism continued for several centuries, and most of our knowledge of the arguments used on either side comes from the works of a leading Sceptic of the second century AD, the physician Sextus Empiricus. Sextus presented the Sceptical system in his *Outlines of Pyrrhonism* and set out to refute the non-sceptical, or 'dogmatic', schools in the eleven books of his *Against the Professors*.

ROME AND ITS EMPIRE

The period of Hellenistic philosophy coincided with the extraordinary growth of the power of the Roman Republic. Since its rejection of monarchy in 510, the city state of Rome had been governed by annually elected officers, headed by a pair of consuls, and advised by a Senate of some 300 wealthy aristocrats. At the death of Alexander the Republic was already in control of the greater part of mainland Italy; but it had no overseas dominions, not even in Sicily or Sardinia. Expansion began with two victorious wars against the great Phoenician empire of Carthage, which had hitherto dominated the Western Mediterranean. In the first war (264–238) Rome acquired Sardinia and Corsica; in the second (218–201) it conquered Sicily and took over the eastern seaboard of Spain, from which it expanded its rule into the whole Iberian peninsula and the area of Provence in France. During the second century Rome picked quarrels with successive kings of Macedon and after the defeat of the last of them it occupied the whole of Greece in 146. At the same time, after a brief third war, it destroyed the city of Carthage and took over its North African hinterland. By the end of the second century many parts of Asia Minor also were Roman provinces or client kingdoms.

In the first century further expansion was accompanied by a series of bitter civil wars. Julius Caesar (100–44) extended Roman rule northward from Provence to the English Channel, killing a million Gauls and enslaving a million others. Threatened with prosecution by his enemies at home, he invaded Italy in 49 and made himself master of Rome in defiance of the Senate. Having defeated the Senatorial general Pompey at Pharsalus in 48, and taken over, one by one, the Republic's overseas possessions, he returned to Rome and ruled as perpetual Dictator. He refused the title of King, but was willing to accept divine honours. He was assassinated in the Senate House by a group of conspirators headed by Brutus and Cassius on 15 March 44.

One of the most distinguished members of the party opposed to Caesar was the orator Marcus Tullius **Cicero**. In his late twenties Cicero had been a student of philosophy first in Athens, where he made himself acquainted with the various schools, and then at Rhodes under the Stoic Posidonius. A self-made man, he was consul for the year 63, in which he suppressed a conspiracy in which he believed Caesar to have been implicated. He governed the province of Cilicia in Asia Minor from 51 to 50, and supported the Senatorial party during the Civil War. Pardoned by Caesar, he returned to Italy and spent the period of the Dictatorship writing philosophy.

Cicero was not of the first rank as a philosopher, but he is important in the history of philosophy in several ways. He set himself the task of creating a Latin philosophical vocabulary, so that Romans could study philosophy in their own language. He wrote voluminous accounts of the teaching of Greek and Hellenistic philosophers which have ever since been one of the major sources of instruction in their doctrines. His works *On the Nature of the Gods* and *On Fate* contain interesting discussions of philosophical theology and the issue of determinism. His *De Finibus* was an encyclopedia of the opinions of philosophers on the nature of the supreme good.

In his own opinions, Cicero was eclectic. In epistemology, he adopted a moderate Sceptical position which he had learnt from Philo of Larissa, the last head of the Academy. In ethics, he favoured the Stoic rather than the Epicurean teaching. Writing in a time of unpheaval and stress, he looked to philosophy for consolation and reassurance. He wrote without great profundity, but with warmth and elegance, and his essays on friendship and old age have been popular through the ages. His main work on moral philosophy, *On Duties* (*De Officiis*), was addressed to his son just after Caesar's death; it was, during various periods of history, regarded as an essential item in the education of a gentleman.

Cicero rejoiced at Caesar's death, and returned to politics with a series of bitter attacks on the Caesarian consul Mark Antony. For a while he found a political ally in Caesar's adopted son Octavian. But Antony and Octavian went into partnership to defeat Caesar's murderers Brutus and Cassius at Philippi in 42 BC. By the time of the battle, Cicero was already dead, executed on the orders of Antony.

The alliance between Antony and Octavian did not last. Antony, having married Octavian's sister, deserted her for the last of the Ptolemies, Queen Cleopatra of Egypt. Influential Romans switched their allegiance to Octavian, and having defeated Antony and Cleopatra at Actium in 31 BC he became the first Roman Emperor, changing his name to Augustus.

JESUS OF NAZARETH

Augustus reigned as Emperor for forty-five years, until AD 14. It was in his reign that **Jesus** of Nazareth was born, and under the reign of his successor Tiberius that

Jesus was crucified, probably about AD 30. This Jewish teacher, living in a remote province of the Empire far from the centres of Greek learning, and unconcerned with issues which had preoccupied Plato and Aristotle, was to have an effect on the history of philosophy no less decisive than theirs. But the impact of his teaching was delayed and indirect.

Jesus' own moral doctrine, as reported in the Gospels, was not without precedent. In the Sermon on the Mount, he taught that we should not render evil for evil; but that had been the teaching of Socrates in the *Republic*. He urged his hearers to love their neighbours as themselves; but he was quoting from the Hebrew book of Leviticus, written many centuries earlier. He insisted that we must refrain not just from wrongdoing, but from the thoughts and desires which lead to wrongdoing; in this he was in accord with Aristotle's teaching that virtue concerns passion as well as action, and that the truly virtuous person is not just continent but temperate. He taught his disciples to despise the pleasures and honours of the world; but so, in their different ways, did the Epicureans and the Stoics.

The framework of Jesus' teaching was the world-view of the Hebrew Bible, according to which the Lord God Yahweh had created heaven and earth and all that was in them. The Jews were Yahweh's chosen people, uniquely privileged by the possession of a divine Law, revealed to Moses when Israel had first become a nation. Like Heraclitus, and other Greek and Jewish thinkers, Jesus predicted that there would be a divine judgement on the world, to take place amid catastrophe on a cosmic scale. What made him different was that he saw that judgement as an imminent and localized event, in which he would himself play a crucial role; he was the Messiah, the divinely appointed liberator for whose coming devout Jews had been looking for centuries. When, after his death, heaven and earth continued on their accustomed courses, his followers had to come to terms with a problem which was not faced by others such as the Stoics who placed the end of the cosmic drama in the indefinite and distant future.

Jesus' account of his own identity, as presented and developed by his earliest followers, was pregnant with philosophical problems. St Paul, whose letters are the earliest evidence we possess for the beliefs of the first Christians, saw Jesus' death on the cross as liberating the human race from a curse which had laid upon it since the first human pair whose creation was described at the beginning of the Hebrew Bible. He saw it also as freeing the disciples of Christ, whether Jewish or Gentile, from the obligation to obey the detailed commands of the law of Moses. Paul's understanding of the death on the cross became indissolubly linked with the ceremonial meal instituted by Jesus on the night before his death and repeated in his memory by his followers from that day to this.

According to Paul, a blessed afterlife awaited those whom God had chosen out, as objects of his grace and favour, to be faithful followers of the Saviour. The future life promised by Paul was not the immortal life of a Platonic soul, but a glorified bodily existence such as Jesus himself had enjoyed when he had risen from the tomb three days after his death on the Cross. Paul's letters were to be quoted for centuries to come whenever theologians and philosophers debated the problems of sin and grace, fate and predestination, and the nature of the world to come.

The *Acts of the Apostles* tells us that St Paul, on a preaching journey, visited Athens and held a debate with Epicurean and Stoic philosophers. The sermon St Luke places in his mouth is skilfully crafted, and shows an awareness of matters at issue between the philosophical sects.

> As I passed by and beheld the manner how ye worship your gods, I found an altar wherein was written: unto the unknown god. Whom ye then ignorantly worship, him shew I unto you. God that made the world and all that are in it, seeing that he is Lord of heaven and earth, he dwelleth not in temples made with hands, neither is worshipped with men's hands, as though he needed of any thing, seeing he himself giveth life and breath to all men everywhere and hath made of one blood all nations of men, for to dwell on all the face of the earth, and hath assigned, before now long time, and also the ends of their inhabitation, that they should seek God, if they might feel and find him, though he be not far from every one of us. For in him we live, move, and have our being as certain of your own poets said. For we are also his generation. Forasmuch then as we are the generation of God, we ought not to think that the godhead is like unto gold, silver or stone, graven by craft and imagination of men.

Later legend imagined Paul in philosophical discourse with the Stoic philosopher Seneca. The idea was not wholly fanciful; St Paul once appeared in court before Seneca's brother Gallio, and he had friends in the palace of Nero where Seneca was long influential. Both men died at about the same time, Paul probably in the persecution of Christians which followed the Great Fire of Rome in 64, and Seneca by Socratic suicide in 65.

It was probably around this time that the Christian gospels began to be written. All the gospels represent Jesus as the Son of God. The gospel of St John calls Jesus also the Word of God, the instrument of divine creation. John's language resembles that of the Jewish philosopher Philo, a contemporary of Jesus who had written treatises reconciling Platonism with the Hebrew Bible. But John's fundamental message is very different from Philo's: the Word of God, one with God before the world began, is the very same as the human being Jesus who had lived and died in Galilee and Judea. Greek mythology knew incarnate gods a-plenty, and Alexander persuaded himself that he was the son of Zeus. But there was no precedent for the idea that the God of monotheistic Judaism, a transcendent God as far from anthropomorphism as the God of Xenophanes, Parmenides, and Plato, could take flesh and live among men. This Christian doctrine of the Incarnation, as we shall see, provided fertile ground for the development of subtle new philosophical concepts which affected people's thinking not only about divinity but about human nature itself.

CHRISTIANITY AND GNOSTICISM

In the second and third centuries Christianity, now organized into a disciplined Church, spread across the Roman Empire. It took hold mainly in the cities, in communities presided over by bishops: the Christian word for non-Christians, 'pagan', was originally just the Latin word for a countryman. During this period Christian attitudes to philosophy varied. Some of the early Christian writers, such as Justin Martyr, a convert to the new religion from Platonism, used texts from Plato's dialogues to Christian purposes, claiming that Plato had been influenced by the Hebrew Bible. Others, such as the African writer Tertullian, claimed that Athens and Jerusalem had nothing in common, and condemned all attempts to produce a Stoic, Platonic, or dialectical Christianity.

Orthodox Christian theologians in the second century, however, were engaged in battle less with hostile systems of pagan philosophy than with groups within the Church who devised heady mixtures of Platonic cosmology, Jewish prophecy, Christian theology, and Oriental mystery-mongering. Whereas both Jesus and Paul had preached a message that was available to the poor and unlearned no less than to scholarly rabbis or erudite philosophers, the members of these groups, known collectively as Gnostics, claimed to be in possession of special mysterious knowledge ('*Gnosis*') which had been handed down in secret by the first apostles and which set its possessors in a privileged position apart from the simple faithful.

Gnostics did not believe that the material world was created by the good God; it was the work of lesser, malevolent powers, and its creation was an utter disaster. The cosmos was governed by evil powers living in the planetary spheres, and during life a good Gnostic should shun any involvement in the business of the world. At death the soul, if properly purified by Gnostic ritual, would fly to God's heaven, armed with incantations which would open the barriers placed in its way by the evil powers. Because the world was evil, it was sinful to marry and beget children. Some Gnostics practised an ascetic discipline, others were riotously promiscuous; in both cases the basic premise was that sex was contemptible.

Mainstream Christian writers denounced Gnosticism as heresy (using the word '*hairesis*' – the Greek word for a philosophical sect). They were more at ease with philosophers totally outside the Church, such as members of the Stoic school, which had returned to popularity under the rule of the Roman Emperors. However, the adherents of such classical philosophical traditions commonly despised Christianity, which they did not always clearly distinguish from Gnostic heresy or traditional Judaism. When the Stoic philosopher Marcus Aurelius became Emperor in 161 he proved himself a callous persecutor of the Christians.

The Roman Empire had now reached its greatest extent. By the death of Augustus its northern frontier had been consolidated along the Danube and the Rhine; under his immediate successors the province of Britain had been added to the Empire and imperial rule extended along the whole of the North African coast so that the Mediterranean became a Roman Sea. Under Marcus Aurelius himself its eastern frontier was extended to the Euphrates.

For a hundred years after the defeat of Mark Antony the Empire had been ruled by members of the family of Caesar and Augustus. Successive Emperors had illustrated in their persons, in varying degrees, the adage that absolute power corrupts absolutely. For those within the immediate reach of the Emperors the age was one of captious cruelty, interspersed with periods of clemency, torpidity, and lunacy. But while the court of Rome was a cauldron of vice, hatred, and terror, the imperial peace brought unprecedented blessings to the millions living in the far-flung provinces. Europe, North Africa, and the Near East enjoyed centuries of tranquillity such as they never experienced before or after. This was achieved with a standing army of no more than 120,000, assisted by local auxiliaries. Roman civic and legal institutions maintained order in communities across three continents, and Roman roads provided a network over which travellers brought Latin literature and Greek philosophy to remote corners of the Empire.

The Caesarian dynasty had come to an end with the death of Nero in 69. After a year in which three Emperors siezed power and died after brief inglorious reigns, stability was restored by Vespasian, a general who had spent the last years of Nero's reign suppressing a Jewish revolt in Palestine. Vespasian's son Titus, who was later to succeed him as Emperor, sacked Jerusalem in 70 and dispersed its inhabitants. Henceforth, throughout the Empire, it was the Christians who were the main preservers of Jewish traditions and Jewish values.

Though Titus' brother and successor, Domitian, rivalled Nero in vanity and cruelty, he was followed by a series of comparatively admirable Emperors who presided, between the years 96 and 180, over the greatest period of the Roman Empire. It was at the end of this period that the first substantial attempt was made to harmonize Christianity with Greek philosophy. **Clement of Alexandria**, at the turn of the century, published a set of Miscellanies (*Stromateis*), written in the style of table talk, in which he argues that the study of philosophy is not only permissible, but necessary, for the educated Christian. The Greek thinkers were pedagogues for the world's adolescence, divinely appointed to bring it to Christ in its maturity. Clement enrolled Plato as an ally against the dualism of the Gnostics, he experimented with Aristotelian logic, and he praised the Stoic ideal of freedom from passion. He explained away, as allegorical, aspects of the Bible and especially the Old Testament which educated Greeks found crude and offensive. In this he founded a tradition which was to have a long history in Alexandria.

Clement was an anthologist and a popularizer; his younger Alexandrian contemporary, **Origen** (185–254), was an original thinker. The son of a Christian martyr, Origen felt less at home than Clement in the cultural world of his time. Though massively learned in Greek philosophy, which he had learnt at the feet of the Alexandrian Platonist Ammonius Saccas, he saw himself first and foremost as a student of the Bible, whose authentic text he took great scholarly pains to establish.

None the less, Origen incorporated into his system many philosophical ideas which mainstream Christians regarded as heretical. For instance, he believed, with Plato, that human souls existed before birth or conception. God's first creation had been a world of free spirits; when these became bored with endless worship, he created the present world, in which embodied human souls were in their turn given freedom which they could use to ascend, aided by the grace of Christ, to a heavenly destiny. Origen also maintained, in conflict with Christian orthodoxy, that all rational beings, sinners as well as saints, and devils as well as angels, would finally be saved and find blessedness. He modified St Paul's doctrine of the resurrection of the body, teaching, according to some of his disciples, that the dead would rise in an ethereal form, and according to others, that the resurrection body would take the form of a sphere, which, so Plato had said, was the most perfect of all shapes.

On a visit to Athens Origen proclaimed his vision of final universal salvation. Condemned as a heretic by a synod of Egyptian bishops, he went into exile in Palestine, saying that he would not wish to speak evil of the devil any more than of the bishops who condemned him. In his exile he wrote a vindication of Christianity against his pagan fellow-Platonist, Celsus. *Against Celsus* uses philosophical arguments in support of Christian belief in God, freedom, and the afterlife, and appeals to the fulfilment of prophecy and the working of miracles as testimony to the authenticity of the Christian revelation. Origen died in 254 after repeated torture during the persecution under the Emperor Decius.

NEO-PLATONISM

Contemporary with Origen, and a fellow pupil of Ammonius Saccas, was the last great pagan philosopher, **Plotinus** (205–70). Plotinus was an admirer of Plato, but gave his philosophy such a novel cast that he is known not as a Platonist, but as the founder of Neo-Platonism. After a brief military career he settled in Rome, toying with the idea of founding, with imperial support, a Platonic Republic in Campania. His works were edited after his death, in six groups of nine treatises (*Enneads*), by his disciple and biographer Porphyry. Written in a taut and difficult style, they cover a wide variety of philosophical topics: ethics and aesthetics, physics and cosmology, psychology, metaphysics, logic, and epistemology.

The dominant place in Plotinus' system is occupied by 'the One'. 'One', in ancient philosophy, is not to be thought of as a name for the first of the natural numbers in the series 1,2,3,4; rather, it is an adjective meaning 'united' or 'all in one piece'. Plotinus' use derives, through Plato, from Parmenides, where Oneness is a key property of Being. We cannot, strictly, utter any true sentences about the One, because the use of a subject distinct from a predicate would imply division and plurality. In a way which remains mysterious, The One is identical with the Platonic Idea of the Good. As The One, it is the basis of all reality; as The Good, it is the standard of all value; but it is itself beyond being and beyond goodness.

Below this supreme and ineffable summit, the next level of reality is occupied by Mind or Intellect (*nous*). This is the product of the One's reflection on itself. It is the locus of the Platonic Ideas, which both depend on it for their existence and form an essential part of its own structure. In contemplating the Ideas, Mind knows itself, not by a discursive process, but in a timeless intuition.

The next place below Mind is occupied by Soul. Soul, unlike Mind, operates in time; indeed, it is the creator of time and space. Soul looks in two directions: it looks upward to Mind, and it looks downward to Nature, where it sees its own reflection. Nature in turn creates the physical world, full of wonder and beauty even though its substance is such as dreams are made of. At the lowest level of all is bare matter, the outermost limit of reality.

These levels of reality are not independent of each other. Each level is dependent, causally but not temporally, on the level above it. Everthing has its place in a single downward progress of successive emanations from the One. The system is impressive: but how ever, we may wonder, did Plotinus convince his hearers of the truth of these mysterious, if exalted, docrines?

To see how he attempted to do so, we must retrace our steps and follow the upward path from base matter to the supreme One. Plotinus takes as his starting point Platonic and Aristotelian arguments which we have already met. The ultimate substratum of change, Aristotle had argued, must be something which, of itself, possesses none of the properties of the changeable bodies we see and handle. But a matter which possesses no material properties, Plotinus argued, is inconceivable, like the Unbeing of Parmenides.

We must dispense, therefore, with Aristotelian matter; we are left with Aristotelian forms. The most important of these was the soul, which was the form of the human being; and it is natural for us to think that there are as many souls as there are individual people. But here Plotinus appeals to another Aristotelian thesis: the principle that forms are individuated by matter. If we have given up matter, there is nothing to distinguish Socrates' soul from Xanthippe's soul; and so we conclude that there is only one single soul.

To prove that this soul exists before and after being linked to any particular body, and is independent of body, Plotinus uses very much the same arguments as Plato used in the *Phaedo*. He neatly reverses the argument of those who claim that soul is dependent on body because it is nothing more than an attunement of the body's sinews. When a musician plucks the strings of a lyre, he says, it is the strings, not the melody, that he acts upon; but the strings would not be plucked unless the melody called for it.

But now the problem arises: how can a world soul, transcendent and incorporeal, be in any way present to individual corruptible and composite bodies? To solve the problem, Plotinus says, we have to reverse the question, and ask not how soul can be in body, but how body can be in soul? The answer is that body is in soul by depending upon it for its organization and continued existence.

Soul, then, governs and orders the world of bodies. It does so wisely and well. But the wisdom which it exercises in the governance of the world is not native to it: it must come from outside. It cannot come from the material world, since that is what it shapes; it must come from something which is by nature linked to the Ideas which are the models or patterns for intelligent activity. This can only be the World-Mind, which both constitutes and is constituted by the Ideas, which are the objects of its thought.

In all thinking, Plotinus continues, there must be a distinction between the thinker and what he is thinking of; even when a thinker is thinking of himself there remains this duality of subject and object. Moreover, the Ideas which are the objects of Mind are many in number. In more than one way, then, Mind contains multiplicity and is therefore composite. Like many other ancient philosophers, Plotinus accepted as a principle that whatever was composite must depend on something more simple. And thus we reach, at the end of our journey upward from formless matter, the one and only One.

Though Plotinus' school in Rome did not survive his death, his pupils and their pupils carried his ideas elsewhere. Porphyry's pupil Iamblichus inspired a Neo-Platonic school in Athens. There the industrious and erudite Proclus (410–85), who each day gave five lectures and wrote seven hundred lines, kept Plotinus' memory green with a detailed commentary on the *Enneads*. Proclus was famous in his time as the author of eighteen separate refutations of the Christian doctrine of creation. This Neo-Platonic school of Athens was the last flowering of pagan Greek philosophy, and one of the most encyclopaedic commentators on Aristotle, Simplicius, was working there when the school came to an end in 529, forty-four years after Proclus' death. An edict of the Christian Emperor Justinian, in the words of Gibbon, 'imposed a perpetual silence on the schools of Athens and excited the grief and indignation of the few remaining votaries of Grecian science and superstition'.

VI
EARLY CHRISTIAN PHILOSOPHY

Arianism and Orthodoxy

When Justinian closed the schools at Athens, the Roman world had been officially Christian for some two hundred years. During the third century AD the Empire suffered a number of invasions and began to show signs of disintegration. Effective government was reimposed by Diocletian, who reigned from 284 to 305; as part of his campaign to restore imperial unity he ordered the rooting out of the Christian Church. Only ten years after this last great persecution, Diocletian's successor Constantine issued the Edict of Milan establishing freedom of worship for Christians. Constantine attributed his own success in achieving imperial power to the aid of the God of the Christians, and he founded magnificent churches in Rome before, late in life, becoming a Christian himself.

Diocletian's reforms had divided the Empire into two halves, a Latin-speaking West and a Greek-speaking East. Constantine established the capital of the Eastern part at Byzantium, at the mouth of the Black Sea; he renamed the city Constantinople, and it was known as the New Rome. In the nearby town of Nicaea, in 325, he presided over the first General Council of the bishops of the newly liberated Christian Church.

A General Council was needed in order to determine officially the sense in which, for Christians, Jesus was divine. All Christians agreed that Jesus was the Son of God; the question was whether the Son was equal to, or inferior to, the Father. A priest of Alexandria named Arius taught that the Son was inferior: while the Father had always existed, there had been a time when the Son did not exist; the Son was a creature, subject to change no less than other creatures. Arius' teaching caused debate and division throughout the Church; but when the bishops came to vote at Nicaea they condemned his views by an overwhelming majority, and drew up a creed, or official statement of belief. The expression which the Nicene creed used to affirm the orthodox view was that the Son was '*homoousion*', of the same *ousia* as, the Father.

Ousia was a word much used by Greek philosophers, often translated in English versions of their texts by the word 'essence'. Two human beings, such as Peter and Paul, share the same essence, namely humanity; a man and a dog have two different essences. Essence, thus explained, is the same as Aristotle's second substance; and in the Latin version of the Creed the relation of the Son to the Father was described by saying that he was of the same substance, or consubstantial, with him. The Council of Nicaea was the first, but not the last, occasion on which the universal Church sought to bring precision into Christian doctrine by the introduction of philosophical technicalities.

The Christianization of the Empire affected the course of philosophy in several ways. The most important, paradoxically, was that it gave universal currency to Jewish ideas. The clash between Christianity and paganism was first of all a clash between monotheism and polytheism: and the one God whom Christianity proclaimed was Yahweh, the God who had singled out the Jews and given his law to Moses. That God, unlike the gods of Parmenides or Plato or Aristotle or the Epicureans and the Stoics, had created the world out of nothing; he had, so Christians taught, an overriding claim on the allegiance and worship not only of the Jews but of all human beings.

In this way the spread of Christianity brought about a revolution in metaphysics. But it also changed the character of ethics. Central to Jewish morality is the notion of obedience to a divine Law; and correlated with this notion of Law, as St Paul emphasized, was the notion of sin, which is disobedience to divine Law. There is nothing similar in classical Greek ethical treatises: the Greek word '*hamartia*', which was St Paul's word for sin, is used in Aristotle's works indiscriminately for any form of error, from a murder to a spelling mistake. The Stoics, it is true, spoke of a divine law, but this was largely metaphorical. They would have been at a loss if you had asked them where this law was promulgated. Put the same question to a Jew or Christian, and you would be pointed to the Ten Commandments in the book of Exodus. St Paul had taught that Christians could disregard many specific prescriptions in the Jewish Bible, such as the food laws and the requirement of circumcision. But that there was a divine Law binding on the human race, and that transgression of that Law was the greatest evil, was the common teaching of the Christian Fathers.

Philosophers in most ages have philosophized within a framework set by sacred texts. One way of describing the change from Greek to Christian thought is to say that the Homeric poems were replaced by the Bible as the sacred text which provided the backcloth against which philosophy is discussed. But of course Christian philosophers took their sacred text much more seriously than the Greeks did. Plato feels obliged to state his position on many issues by reference to Homer and Hesiod; but he feels free to censor their texts and eliminate parts of them as false and disgusting. Christian writers who find difficulties with passages in the Bible may give them mystical or allegorical interpretations; but in whatever way they are interpreted, the texts must emerge as truthful and edifying. Moreover, the philosopher's liberty of interpretation is not unlimited, for the Church claims the right not only to uphold the authority of Scripture but also to decide between conflicting interpretations. There was some precedent for this in Judaism, but not in classical Greece. Greek philosophers whose beliefs were unorthodox might suffer, as Anaxagoras and Socrates did; but they were punished under the ordinary laws of the State, and there was no body, independent of the State, specifically charged with the preservation of orthodoxy.

Finally, specific Christian doctrines raised issues which were of philosophical interest far beyond the Christian context within which they arose. The Christian belief that Jesus would return to preside over a bodily resurrection of the dead transformed the nature of philosophical inquiry into death and immortality and the relationship between body and soul. Reflection on the Christian sacraments of baptism and eucharist led to general theories of the nature and efficacy of signs which were much broader in scope than semantic studies of language in the ancient world. The Pauline teaching on grace and predestination led to centuries of inquiry into the compatibility of free-will and determinism. Most immediately, in the centuries following the conversion of Constantine, further debate about the relation between Jesus and the Godhead led to the development of a set of new concepts for the understanding of personal identity.

The Council of Nicaea did not end the disputes about the person and nature of Christ. The supporters of Arius rallied, and after Constantine's death in 337 their party secured the favour of his son Constantius. They rejected the Nicaean teaching that the Son and the Father shared the same essence: they objected to this as implying that the two were not really distinct from each other, but just two aspects of a single reality. Instead, they preferred the formula that the Son's essence was *similar* to the Father's (*homoiousion* rather than *homoousion*). 'The profane of every age,' writes Gibbon, 'have derided the furious contests which the difference of a single diphthong excited between the Homoousians and the Homoiousians.' The derision is misplaced; the presence or absence of the Greek letter iota in the Creed made as much difference as would the presence or absence of 'not' in a United Nations Resolution. Some Arians were unwilling to admit that the Son's essence was even *like* the Father's. In councils in East and West, Constantius imposed a compromise, and at the dedication of the new church of Sancta Sophia in Constantinople a Creed was recited in which the Son was said to be 'like' the Father, with the philosophical term *ousia* altogether dropped. In the time of Constantius and his successors, except for the brief reign of the Emperor Julian who attempted to restore the pagan religion, Arianism was the dominant religion of the Empire. This state of affairs lasted until the accession in 378 of the Emperor Theodosius I who had been brought up in the West in loyalty to the doctrine of Nicaea.

In the meantime, a new dimension had been added to the theological debate. The formula with which Christians were baptized spoke of 'The Father, the Son, and the Holy Spirit'. The Holy Spirit mentioned often in the New Testament was regarded by many Christian thinkers as being divine: so the question arose not only of the relation between Father and Son, but also of the relation between each of them and the Holy Spirit. The formula which came to be preferred in the Greek Church was that they were three separate, but equally divine *hypostases*. The word was the one which Plotinus had used to refer to the One, the Mind, and the Soul. The literal Latin equivalent is the word 'substantia'. It seemed confusing, however, to say that Father, Son, and Holy Spirit were three substances, while the Son was consubstantial with the Father. But the double sense of the word 'substance' is simply a revival of the Aristotelian distinction between first substance (e.g. Socrates) and second substance (e.g. humanity). The relationship between the three members of what came to be called the Trinity was determined by the Council of Constantinople in 381.

That Council reaffirmed the Nicaean understanding of the relation between Son and Father, and reinstated the term 'consubstantial'. It declared that the Holy Spirit was worshipped along with Father and Son; while the Son was begotten of the Father, the Holy Spirit proceeded from the Father. On the relation between the Son and the Holy Spirit it was silent. It did not use the word 'hypostasis'; and Latin explanations of its doctrine began to prefer the word 'persona' – a word originally meaning a mask in a stage-play, but the ancestor of our word 'person'.

THE THEOLOGY OF INCARNATION

The Council of Constantinople put an end to Arianism in the Eastern Empire; Theodosius backed its decrees with persecution. The heresy survived, however, among the barbarian Goths, who had recently mounted a successful invasion across the Danube and were shortly to conquer much of the West. In addition to its doctrinal decisions the Council issued a decree that 'the bishop of Constantinople shall have rank after the bishop of Rome because it is the new Rome'.

During the second and third centuries the Bishop of Rome had come to be accepted as the senior bishop in the Church, even by such churches as Antioch and Alexandria, which had been founded by Apostles. From time to time interventions by Roman bishops in the affairs of other churches had been accepted and sometimes welcomed. This Papal authority had been strengthened when Constantine offered Pope Silvester a position of dignity and a handsome palace in Rome, though not (as later Papal forgery had it) substantial dominions throughout Italy and the West. Silvester had sent representatives to the Council of Nicaea, and his successors remained steadfast to its doctrines. The Roman Church resented the canon which promoted Constantinople to the second place among bishoprics, because it implied that its own traditional authority derived from its location in the Empire's capital rather than because of its claim to be the foundation of the Apostles Peter and Paul.

Rivalry between the leading sees of Christendom played its part in the doctrinal controversies of the fifth century, which concerned not the relationships between the persons of the Trinity, but the intersection of divinity and humanity in Jesus himself. Jesus, as all agreed, was God, and Mary, as all agreed, was the mother of Jesus. Did this mean that Mary was the mother of God? Many popular preachers thought so, but Nestorius, the Bishop of Constantinople from 428 onwards, thought otherwise. According to him, what Mary gave to Jesus was humanity, not divinity, and to call her the Mother of God was to confuse the two. The bishop of Alexandria of the time was Cyril, a fierce and intolerant figure who had already been responsible for the murder of Hypatia, a Neo-Platonist who was the one female philospher of antiquity. He at once denounced Nestorius as a heretic: if he did not believe that the Mother of Jesus was the Mother of God, then he must not really believe that Jesus was God.

As the dispute spread and became increasingly bitter, the Emperor Theodosius II called a Council at Ephesus in 431. By a mixture of theological argument, bribery, intimidation, and populist devotion, Cyril persuaded a doubtfully quorate assembly to condemn Nestorius. The bishops present accepted Cyril's formula that while the divinity and humanity were indeed two distinct natures in Christ, yet in union they constituted a single *hypostasis*. Because of this, human properties (such as being born of Mary and dying on the Cross) could be attributed to the Son of God, and divine properties (such as having created the world and worked miracles) could be attributed to the man Jesus.

In the disputes about the Trinity, the philosophical question had been: if Father, Son, and Holy Ghost are not three Gods, what are they three of? The answer had been: *hypostasis* or person. Here the question was: if Jesus' humanity is distinct from his divinity, what is he only one of? Again, the answer was *hypostasis* or person. The concept of person, now so familiar in everyday life, owes its origin to this pair of theological disputes.

Just as the Council of Nicaea failed to settle the dispute about the relation between the Son and the Father in heaven, so the Council of Ephesus failed to settle the dispute about the Son incarnate on earth. Some of Cyril's Alexandrian supporters thought he had been wrong to concede that there were two natures in Jesus; the Son of God had for eternal ages possessed a divine nature not yet united to a human nature, but once incarnate he possessed only a single nature formed by a union of the two. These extremists, at a second Council at Ephesus, secured the endorsement of the Alexandrian doctrine of the single nature ('monophysitism').

Pope Leo of Rome had not attended this Council, but had submitted written evidence, known as his Tome, which was a firm statement of the doctrine of two natures. When he heard of the result of the Council, Leo denounced it as a den of robbers. Strengthened by the support of Rome, Constantinople struck back at Alexandria; and at a Council at Chalcedon in 451 the monophysite opinion was condemned and the doctrine of the double nature reaffirmed. Christ was perfect God and perfect man, with a human body and a human soul, consubstantial with the Father in his divinity, and consubstantial with us in our humanity, to be acknowledged in two natures without confusion, change, division, or separation.

The definitions of the first Council of Ephesus and the Council of Chalcedon henceforth provided the test of orthodoxy. But they were not accepted immediately or universally, and to this day communities of Nestorian and Monophysite Christians testify to the strength of conviction of the defeated parties. But in the history of philosophy the importance of the early Church Councils is that as a result of their deliberations, the meanings of the terms 'essence', 'substance', 'nature', and 'person' were never quite the same again.

THE LIFE OF AUGUSTINE

While, in the East, a succession of Councils determined the doctrines of the Trinity and the Incarnation, in the West the Church had been ringing with debate about the relation between the purposes of God and the freedom of human beings. The decisive influence in these debates was a man who was to prove the most influential of all Christian philosophers, **St Augustine** of Hippo.

Augustine was born in a small town in present-day Algeria in 354. The son of a Christian mother and a pagan father, he was not baptized as an infant, though he received a Christian education in Latin literature and rhetoric. Having acquired a smattering of Greek he qualified in rhetoric and taught the subject at Carthage. At the age of eighteen, on reading Cicero's lost *Hortensius,* he was fired with a love of philosophy, and especially of Plato. For about ten years he was a follower of Manicheism, a syncretic religion which drew elements from Zoroastrianism, Buddhism, Judaism, and Christianity. The Manichees believed that there were two worlds, a world of spiritual goodness and light created by God, and a world of evil fleshly darkness created by the devil. Their distaste for sex left a permanent mark on Augustine, though for several years in early manhood he lived with a mistress, and had by her a son Adeodatus.

In 383 he crossed the sea to Rome, and quickly moved on to Milan, then the capital of the Western Empire. There he became disillusioned with Manicheism, and began to think of a career in the Imperial administration, dismissing his provincial mistress and engaging himself to an heiress. But he also became friendly with Ambrose, the Bishop of Milan, a great champion of the claims of religion and morality against the secular power represented by the Emperor Theodosius. The influence of Ambrose, and of his mother Monica, along with his studies of Plato and the Neo-Platonists, influenced Augustine in the direction of Christianity. After a period of painful hesitation he was baptized in 387.

In his first years as a Christian, Augustine wrote a number of works of philosophy. A set of dialogues on God and the human soul articulated his reasons for rejecting Manicheism and formulated a Christian Neo-Platonism. *Against the Academics* set out a detailed line of argument against Academic scepticism. In *On Ideas* Augustine presented his own version of Plato's Theory of Ideas: the Ideas have no existence independent of the mind of God, but they exist, eternal and unchangeable, in him, and they are communicated to human souls not through any recollection of pre-existence, but by direct divine illumination. The young Augustine also wrote a treatise on the origin of evil and on free choice, *De Libero Arbitrio* – a book still used as a text in a number of University philosophy departments.

After his mother died at Ostia in 388, Augustine returned to Africa, and formed a philosophical community in his birthplace, Tagaste. The problems they discussed, with Augustine's solutions to them, were published under the title *On 83 Different Questions*. During this period Augustine also wrote six books on music, and an energetic work *On the Teacher* (*de Magistro*), which contains much imaginative reflection on the nature and power of words. He wrote also a treatise *On True Religion*, which, among other things, urges philosophers to make the move from the Trinity of Plotinus to the Christian Trinity. All these works were written before Augustine found his final vocation and was ordained as a priest in 391. Within a very short time he was made an under-bishop, and in 396 he became Bishop of Hippo in Algeria, where he resided until his death in 430.

As bishop he wrote a prodigious amount. Apart from two hundred letters and five hundred sermons, there were about a hundred books, including three expositions of the creation account in Genesis, and fifteen volumes on the Trinity. It has been said that Augustine's output is equal in volume to the entire surviving corpus of previous Latin literature.

The best known of his writings is his autobiography, the *Confessions*, which he wrote shortly after becoming a bishop. Addressed to God in the second person, it produces an effect of candour and psychological intensity never previously achieved, and hardly surpassed since. Interspersed between narrative and prayer, there are many acute philosophical observations.

Consider, for instance, this passage in which Augustine narrates how he learnt to speak.

> It was not that my elders taught me words in a set order as they later taught me the alphabet; I learnt them by myself, with the intelligence which you gave me, my God. I did my best to express the feelings of my heart, by crying and making noises and moving my limbs, trying to get my way, and yet unable to express all I wanted to everyone I wanted. I took the words into my memory: when they called an object by its name, and as they spoke turned toward it, I saw and remembered that the thing was called by the sound they uttered when they wanted to draw attention to it. That this was what they meant was plain from the motion of their body, the natural language, as it were, of all nations, in their facial expressions, the direction of their eyes, the gestures of their limbs, and the tone of their voice, indicating the sentiments of the mind, seeking and possessing, or rejecting and avoiding. And thus

by constantly hearing words, as they occurred in various sentences, I gathered what they signified and once I had trained my mouth to make the sounds I gave expression to my wishes. Thus I began to share with those about me the signs of our wills, and so launched deeper into the stormy intercourse of human life.

Not until the twentieth century did philosophers again take such a sensitive interest in the acquisition of language by infants.

In the eleventh book of the *Confessions* Augustine makes his celebrated inquiry into the nature of time. The peg on which the discussion hangs is the question of an objector: what was God doing before the world began? Rejecting the answer 'Preparing hell for people who ask inquisitive questions', Augustine responds that before heaven and earth were created, there was no time. We cannot ask what God was doing then, because there was no 'then' when there was no time. Equally, we cannot ask why the world was not created sooner, for before the world, there was no sooner. It is misleading to say even of God that he existed at a time earlier than the world's creation, for there is no succession in God. In him today does not replace yesterday, nor give way to tomorrow; there is only an eternal present.

In order to defend his account of eternity, Augustine has to argue that time is unreal. 'What *is* time?' he asks. 'If no one asks me, I know; if I wish to explain to one that asks, I know not.' Time consists of past, present, and future. But only the present exists, for the past is no longer, and the future is not yet. But a present that is only present is not time, but eternity.

We speak of longer and shorter times; but how can we measure time? Suppose we say of a past period that it was long: do we mean that it was long when it was past, or long when it was present? Only the latter makes sense; but how can anything be long in the present, since what is present is instantaneous? No collection of instants can add up to more than an instant. The stages of any period of time never co-exist; how then can they be added up to form a whole? Any measurement we make must be made in the present: how then can we measure what has already gone or is not yet there?

Augustine's solution to these perplexities is to say that time is really only in the mind. The past is not, but I behold it in the present because it is, at this moment, in my memory. The future is not; all that there is, is our present foreseeing. Instead of saying that there are three times, past, present and future, we should say that there is a present of things past (which is memory), a present of things present (which is sight), and a present of things future (which is expectation). A length of time is not really a length of time, but a length of memory, or a length of expectation.

Augustine's account does not truly solve all the perplexities he has raised; nor does he pretend it does. But he was not the last philosopher to put forward a subjective theory of time, and his arguments in its favour are as subtle as anything later propounded.

THE CITY OF GOD AND THE MYSTERY OF GRACE

Thirteen years after the writing of the *Confessions*, the city of Rome was sacked by invading Goths under Alaric. Pagans blamed this disaster on the Christians' abolition of the worship of the city's gods, who had therefore deserted it in its hour of need. In response, Augustine spent thirteen years writing a treatise *The City of God*, which set out a Christian analysis of the history of the Roman Empire and of much else in the ancient world.

Augustine contrasts the City of God, symbolized by Jerusalem, with the city of the world, symbolized by Babylon. The inhabitants of Babylon despise God and are motivated by self-love; the inhabitants of Jerusalem, forgetful of self, are moved by love of God. Both cities aim at justice and peace, but they have different conceptions of these common goals. Babylon is not to be identified with the pagan Empire, nor Jerusalem with the Christian Empire. Not everything was wrong in the Empire in pagan days; and Christian Emperors could be sinners too – as Ambrose had shown when he had excluded the Emperor Theodosius from the Church in punishment for a fearsome massacre at Thessalonica in 391.

The City of God is not the same as the Christian Church on earth, though Augustine's book was often, in later centuries, taken to be a guide to relations between Church and State. Like Plato's Utopian *Republic* – with which Augustine sets himself in explicit conflict – the City of God is not fully realized anywhere this side of heaven.

Augustine's treatise is rambling and sometimes tedious; but it contains many passages of great insight and influence. To take one example among many, it is in this book that Augustine defined for future generations the way in which Christians should interpret the biblical command 'Thou shalt not kill'. First of all, the law does not admit of exception in the case of self-killing: suicide is ruled out for Christians, even if their motive is to avoid sin or shame. On the other hand, the prohibition of killing does not extend to non-human creatures.

> When we read 'Thou shalt not kill' we assume that this does not refer to bushes, which have no feelings, nor to irrational creatures, flying, swimming, walking or crawling, since they have no rational association with us, not having been endowed with reason as we are, and hence it is by a just arrangement of the Creator that their life and death is subordinate to our needs.

What, then, are we to say of the morality of the death penalty, or of warfare, in which human beings deliberately take each other's lives? In contrast to the pacifism of some other early Christian thinkers, Augustine thinks that war is not always wrong. The commandment forbidding killing is not broken by those who wage war, if on divine authority, or those who carry out the death penalty in accordance with the State's laws. But Augustine is not one to glorify war for its own sake: the only purpose of war is to bring a just peace, and even in a just war at least one side is acting sinfully. And only a state in which justice prevails has the right to order its soldiers to kill. 'Remove justice, and what are kingdoms but gangs of criminals on a large scale?'

The *City of God* ends with an exposition of the way in which the two cities reach their culmination, one in heaven and one in hell. Christ will come at the end of time to judge the living and the dead, to rectify the iniquity of the present time, in which the good suffer and the wicked prosper. After the resurrection of the body, good Christians who have died in the love of God will enjoy everlasting happiness in the heavenly City of God; Christians who are unrepentant, heretics, and all those who died unbaptized, whether as adults or as children, will be damned, and their bodies will burn for ever in hell. The choice of those who were to be saved, and implicitly also of those who were damned, was made by God long before they had come into existence or had done any deeds good or bad.

The relation between divine predestination and human virtue and vice pre-occupied Augustine's last years. After the sack of Rome there escaped to Africa a British ascetic named Pelagius, who held a passionate belief in the liberty and autonomy of human beings, even in their relation to God. The sin of Adam, he taught, had not damaged his heirs except by setting them a bad example; human beings, throughout their history, retained full freedom of the will for the practice of virtue or vice. Death was a natural necessity, not a punishment for sin, and pagans who had used their freedom virtuously went at death to a place of beatitude; Christians were given by God the special grace of baptism, which entitled them to the superior happiness of heaven. Such special graces were allotted by God to those he foresaw would deserve them.

All this was anathema to Augustine, who believed that the whole human race had, in some way, taken part in the sin of Adam, so that all human beings descended from him by sexual propagation inherited sinfulness as well as mortality in their genes. We corrupt humans after the Fall have no freedom, unaided, to do good deeds; we need God's grace not only to gain heaven, but to avoid a life of continual sinning. Augustine who, in his youth, had offered to prove philosophically that humans enjoyed freedom of choice, now maintained that the only freedom of the will which we retain is the freedom to choose one sin rather than another. Grace is allotted to some people rather than others not on the basis of any merits, actual or foreseen, but simply by the inscrutable good pleasure of God. As we children of Adam are all members of a cursed mass of perdition, none of us has any grounds to complain if only a few of us, by God's mercy, have the sentence of damnation remitted.

The teaching of Pelagius was condemned at a Council at Carthage in 418, but the debate went on and Augustine's position continually hardened. Monks in monasteries in Africa and France complained that if Augustine's minimal view of human freedom was correct, then exhortation and rebuke were vain, and indeed the whole discipline of monastic life was pointless. In response Augustine insisted that not only the initial call to Christianity, but even the perseverance in virtue of the most devout Christian approaching death was a matter of sheer grace: he pointed to the example of an eighty-four-year-old monk who had just taken a concubine.

If predestination was necessary for salvation, critics asked, was it also sufficient? Could someone, offered grace, reject it? If so, then human freedom would indeed play an important part in the individual's destiny. There would then, at the end of history, be three classes of people: those who were in heaven because they had been offered grace and accepted it; those who were in hell because they had been offered and refused the offer; and those who were in hell because they had never had the offer at all. Augustine in the end denied even this vestige of human choice: grace cannot be declined, cannot be overcome. Humans are free in respect of salvation, on this account, only if freedom is compatible with determinism. In the end there are only two classes of people: those who have been given grace and those who have not; the predestined and the reprobate. Why one person is predestined and another is reprobate is an unanswerable question.

> If we take two babies, equally in the bonds of original sin, and ask why one is taken and the other left; if we take two sinful adults, and ask why one is called and the other not; in each case the judgements of God are inscrutable. If we take two holy men, and ask why the gift of perseverance to the end is given to one and not to the other, the judgements of God are even more inscrutable.

All this teaching about original sin, grace, and predestination is based on texts of St Paul, especially the Epistle to the Romans. Augustine, however, went further than St Paul, and his teaching about predestination led him to explain away, in less and less convincing ways, the statement in the first Epistle to Timothy that God wills all men to be saved and to come to the knowledge of the truth.

Augustine died in 430, leaving it to his successors to continue the battle against Pelagius and his followers, which continued until 529 when the Council of Orange condemned even a much modified version of Pelagianism. The crabbed and embattled theorist of predestination is very different from the endearing autobiographer of the *Confessions*, but it was the aged Augustine who was to have the greater significance for the history of the Church. Throughout the Catholic Middle Ages, Augustine enjoyed greater authority than any of the other Church Fathers, and at the Reformation his influence increased rather than diminished. John Calvin sharpened and hardened Augustine's teaching just as Augustine had sharpened and hardened that of Paul. Even at the present time, when many more people hate him than read him, Augustine's influence on Christian thought is inescapable, and his genius continues to fascinate or repel many outside the Christian tradition.

BOETHIUS AND PHILOPONUS

The sack of Rome by the Goths, which stimulated *The City of God*, was only the first of a series of barbarian attacks on the Western Empire and its metropolis. While Augustine was dying, the Vandals were at the gates of Hippo; before long they were masters of much of Africa and Spain. In mid-century the Huns invaded Gaul and Italy and only the eloquence of Pope Leo prevented them from attacking Rome. The Franks occupied Gaul, the Anglo-Saxons invaded Britain. In 476 the Western Roman Empire came to an end, and its last Emperor, Romulus Augustulus, was packed off into exile. Italy became a Gothic province, under Arian Christian kings.

The most vigorous of the Gothic kings of Italy was Theoderic, who ruled from 493 to 526. One of his ministers was a Roman nobleman and senator, Manlius Severinus **Boethius**. Boethius had in youth written handbooks on music and mathematics, drawn from Greek sources, and he projected a complete translation of Plato and Aristotle. This was never completed, but it was Boethius' translations of Aristotle's logical works that ensured their availability in the West during the early Middle Ages. Boethius also gave canonical status to an introduction to logic by Plotinus' pupil Porphyry, adding it as an appendix to the Aristotelian *Organon*. He made his own modest contribution to the subject, writing commentaries on several Aristotelian treatises, and linking his work with the Stoic development of propositional logic.

Boethius' logical works have been the subject of recent studies by scholars, and his theological treatises on the Trinity contain passages of philosophical interest; but throughout history he has been best known for a single work, *The Consolation of Philosophy*. This was written in 524 while he was under sentence of death, having been imprisoned by Theoderic on suspicion of having taken part in an anti-Arian conspiracy. The work has been widely read, first because of its considerable literary beauty; secondly, because it was the most subtle treatment to date of the problems of human freedom and divine foreknowledge. The book is not at all what one would expect from a devout Catholic facing martyrdom: while it dwells on the comfort offered by philosophy, there is no reference to the consolations of the Christian religion.

The Consolation is in five books; in each, passages of verse and prose alternate, and Boethius converses with the Lady Philosophy who appears to him in his prison. In the first book he defends his innocence, while she reminds him of the sufferings of Socrates and encourages him to Socratic detachment from the world. The second book develops the Stoic theme, that matters within the province of fortune are insignificant by comparison with values within one's self. Boethius has received many good things from fortune, and he must accept the evil also which she sends. The message that happiness is not to be found in wealth, power, or fame is then reinforced with material from Plato and Aristotle: true happiness is to be found only in God. Indeed, to become happy is to acquire divinity: every happy man is God, though there is only one God by nature. The fourth book tackles the problem of evil, in the form of the question 'Why do the wicked prosper?'; arguments familiar from Plato are presented to show that their prosperity is only apparent.

Throughout the first four books Lady Philosophy has had much to say about Lady Luck. But the fifth book, which is philosophically far the most interesting, addresses the question: in a world governed by divine providence, can there be any such thing as luck or chance? Boethius is able to distinguish between random chance and human choice, but he accepts that free human choice, even if not random, is difficult to reconcile with the existence of a God who foresees everything that is to happen. 'If God foresees all and cannot in any way be mistaken, then that must necessarily happen which in his providence he foresees will be.'

Boethius' problem is not the same as Augustine's: he is talking not about predestination (God's *willing* humans to act virtuously and be saved) but simply about foreknowledge (God's *knowing* what humans will do or not do). It seems that if we say that humans are free to act in any way other than that in which God sees they will act, then they have the power to put God in the wrong. For 'if human deeds can be turned aside into a different way from that foreseen, then there will no longer be firm foreknowledge of the future, but rather uncertain opinion'. Boethius accepts that a genuinely free action cannot be certainly foreseen, even by God; and he takes refuge in the notion of divine timelessness, saying that God's seeing is not really a *fore*seeing.

> The same future event, when it is related to divine knowledge, is necessary, but when it is considered in its own nature it seems to be quite free and independent. . . . God beholds as present those future events which happen because of free will.

There are two kinds of necessity, Boethius explains. There is plain or straightforward necessity, illustrated by the proposition:

> Necessarily, all men are mortal.

and there is conditional necessity, illustrated by the proposition:

> Necessarily, if you know that I am walking, I am walking.

The future events which God sees as present are not straightforwardly necessary, but only conditionally necessary.

Problems remain with Boethius' treatment of the dilemma he posed with unparalleled clarity. Surely, matters really are as God sees them; so if God sees tomorrow's sea battle as present, then it really is present already. However,

Boethius' theory was to remain the classic solution of the problem for centuries to come.

Boethius has been called 'Last of the Romans, first of the scholastics'. Certainly, in his work he links classical philosophy with the technical philosophy of the medieval schools, more even than Augustine does. But he was not the last Christian philosopher of antiquity: that distinction belongs to a scholar of the Eastern Empire, John the Grammarian, or John **Philoponus**.

Philoponus flourished in the reign of Justinian, who became Emperor in the East in 527, three years after the execution of Boethius. Justinian was the Emperor who closed the schools of Athens and who is famous for having presided over the codification of Roman Law. His generals also conquered, for a while, substantial portions of the former Western Empire. Philoponus, as a Christian based in Alexandria, was unperturbed by the closure of the pagan schools in Athens, and could look with satisfaction on the downfall of their foremost scholar, the Aristotelian commentator Simplicius. For it was as a radical critic of Aristotle that Philoponus made his name, and Simplicius was his most distinguished contemporary adversary.

First, Philoponus attacked Aristotle's doctrine that the world had always existed. Some pagan philosophers were willing to accept that God was the creator of the world, in the sense that the world's existence had, from all eternity, been causally dependent on God. Others were prepared to accept that the world had had a beginning, in the sense that the orderly cosmos we know had, at a particular time, been brought out of chaos. But all the pagan philosophers of the time accepted the eternity of matter, and this, Christians believed, was incompatible with the Genesis account of the creation of heaven and earth out of nothing. More to the point, Philoponus insisted in his book *On the Eternity of the World*, it was inconsistent with Aristotle's own view that nothing could traverse through more than a finite number of temporal periods. For if the world had no beginning then it must have endured through an infinite number of years, and worse still, through 365 times an infinite number of days.

Secondly, Philoponus attacked Aristotle's dynamics. Aristotle's theory of natural and violent motion encountered a difficulty in explaining the movement of projectiles. If I throw a stone, what makes it move upward and onward when it leaves my hand? Its natural motion is downwards, and my hand is no longer in contact with it to impart its violent motion upwards. Aristotle's answer had been that the stone was pushed on, at any given point, by the air immediately behind it. The lameness of this account was exposed by Philoponus, who proposed instead that the thrower impressed upon the projectile an internal force, or impetus.

The notion of natural motion in Aristotle is tied to the notion of natural place, the natural motion of an element being motion towards its natural place. Philoponus thought that the concept of natural place was appropriate only if we thought of the universe as a whole as something similar to an animal with a head and limbs and other bodily parts. This, in turn, was conceivable only if we regarded the universe as having been designed by a Creator.

In his work *The Manufacture of the Universe* Philoponus applied his impetus theory widely throughout the cosmos. The heavenly bodies, for instance, rotate in their orbits not because they have souls, but because God gave them the appropriate impetus when he created them. The theory of impetus did away with the mixture of physics and psychology in Aristotle's astronomy. It made possible a unified theory of dynamics which was a great improvement on Aristotle's, and it was not surpassed until the introduction of the theory of inertia in the age of Galileo and Newton.

Philoponus rejected Aristotle's thesis that the heavenly bodies were made out of a non-terrestrial element, the imperishable quintessence. This rejection was necessary if the impetus theory was to be extended to the heavens as well as to the earth. But it was also congenial to Christian piety to demolish the notion that the world of the sun and moon and stars was something supernatural, standing in a relation to God different from that of the earth on which his human creatures lived.

Philoponus was indeed a theologian as well as a philosopher, and wrote, in later life, a number of treatises on Christian doctrine. Unfortunately, his treatment of the Trinity laid him open to charges of tritheism (the belief that there are three Gods) and his treatment of the Incarnation explicitly defended the monophysite heresy (the denial that Christ had two natures). When summoned to Constantinople by Justinian to defend his views on the Incarnation, Philoponus failed to appear; and when after his death his teaching on the Trinity was examined by the ecclesiastical authorities it was condemned as heretical. Consequently, his influence on Christian thinking was minimal. But his influence was felt outside the bounds of the old Roman Empire; and it was there, in the centuries between Justinian and William the Conqueror, that the most significant philosophers are to be found.

VII

EARLY MEDIEVAL PHILOSOPHY

JOHN THE SCOT

For two centuries after the death of Philoponus there is nothing for the historian of philosophy to record. During that period, however, two events altered beyond recognition the world which had fostered classical and patristic philosophy. The first was the spread of Islam; the second was the emergence of the Holy Roman Empire.

Within ten years of the death of the Prophet Muhammad in 633 the religion of Islam had spread by conquest from its native Arabia throughout the neighbouring Persian Empire and the Roman provinces of Syria, Palestine, and Egypt. In 698 the Muslims captured Carthage, and ten years later they were masters of all North Africa. In 711 they crossed the Straits of Gibraltar, easily defeated the Gothic Christians, and flooded through Spain. By 717 their empire stretched from the Atlantic to the Great Wall of China. Their advance into Northern Europe was halted only in 732, when they were defeated at Poitiers by the Frankish leader Charles Martel.

Charles Martel's grandson, Charlemagne, who became king of the Franks in 768, drove the Muslims back to the Pyrenees, but he did no more than nibble at their Spanish dominions. His military and political ambitions for France were more concerned with its Eastern frontier. He conquered Lombardy, Bavaria, and Saxony and had his son proclaimed king of Italy. After rescuing Pope Leo III from a revolution in Rome, he had himself crowned Roman Emperor in St Peter's on Christmas Day 800. When Charlemagne died in 814 almost all the Christian inhabitants of continental Western Europe were united under his rule. Formidable as a general, and ruthless when provoked, he had a high ideal of his vocation as ruler of Christendom, and one of his favourite books was *The City of God*. He was anxious to revive the study of letters, and brought scholars from all over Europe to join the learned Alcuin of York in a school, based at Aachen, whose members, though mainly concerned with other disciplines, sometimes displayed an amateur interest in philosophy.

It was at the court of Charles's grandson, Charles the Bald, that we find the most significant Western philosopher of the ninth century, John the Scot. John was born not in Charles's dominions, but in Ireland, and for the avoidance of doubt he added to his name 'Scottus' the surname 'Eriugena', which means Son of Erin. He first engaged in philosophy in 852 when invited by the Archbishop of Rheims to write a treatise to prove heretical the ideas of a learned and pessimistic monk, Gottschalk. Gottschalk's alleged offence was to have maintained that there was a double divine predestination, one of the saints to heaven, and one of the damned to hell; a doctrine which he claimed, reasonably enough, to have found implicit in Augustine. Archbishop Hincmar, like the monks of Augustine's time, thought this a doctrine inimical to good discipline; hence his invitation to Eriugena.

Eriugena's refutation (*On Predestination*) was, from Hincmar's point of view, a remedy worse than the disease. In the first place, his arguments against Gottschalk were silly: there could not be a double predestination, because God was simple and undivided, and there was no such thing as *pre*destination because God was eternal. Secondly, he tried to draw the sting out of the destiny of the damned by maintaining that there was no physical hell; the wicked want to flee from God to Unbeing, and God punishes them only by preventing their annihilation. The fire of judgement spoken of in the Gospels is common to both good and bad; the difference between them is that the blessed turn into ether and the damned into air. Gottschalk and Eriugena both found themselves condemned by Church Councils, one at Quiersy in 853, the other at Valence in 855.

Despite this, Charles the Bald commissioned Eriugena to translate into Latin the works of Dionysius the Areopagite. These were four treatises, Neo-Platonic in content and probably written in the sixth century, which were wrongly believed to be the work of an Athenian convert of the Apostle Paul. Eriugena, whose knowledge of Greek indicates the high level of Irish culture in the ninth century, went to work with a will, and produced a commentary as well as translation.

These tasks whetted his appetite to produce his own system, which he did in the five books of his *Periphyseon*, or *On Nature*. Nature is divided into four: nature creating and uncreated; nature created and creating; nature created and uncreating; and nature uncreated and uncreating. The first, obviously enough, is God. The second, nature created and creating, is the world of intellect, the home of the Platonic Ideas, which are created in God the Son. This second nature creates the third, nature created and uncreating; that is the everyday world of the things we can see and feel in space and time, such as animals, plants, and rocks. The fourth, nature uncreated and uncreating, is once again the uncreated God, conceived now not as the creator but as the ultimate end to which all things return.

Eriugena's language about God is highly agnostic. God cannot be described in human language; he does not fit into any of Aristotle's ten categories. God therefore is beyond all being, and so it is more correct to say that He does not exist than that He exists. Eriugena tries to save himself from sheer atheism by saying that what God is doing is something better than existing. What the Bible says of God, he says, is not to be taken literally; but in every verse there are innumerable meanings, like the colours in a peacock's tail.

It is not easy to see where human beings fit into Eriugena's fourfold scheme. They seem to straddle uneasily between the second and the third. Our animal bodies seem clearly to belong with the third; but they are created by our souls, which have more affinity with the objects in the second. And at one point Eriugena seems to suggest that the entire human being has its home in the second: 'Man is a certain intellectual notion, eternally made in the divine mind'. He must be thinking of the Idea of Man; systematically, in Platonic style, he insists that species are more real than their members, universals more real than individuals. When the world ends, place and time will disappear, and all creatures will find salvation in the nature that is uncreated and uncreating.

Despite the influence of Greek sources, Eriugena's ideas are often original and imaginative; but his teaching is obviously difficult to reconcile with Christian orthodoxy, and it is unsurprising that *On Nature* was repeatedly condemned. Three and a half centuries after its publication a Pope ordered, ineffectively, that all copies of it should be burnt.

ALKINDI AND AVICENNA

Paradoxically, the Christian Eriugena was a much less important precursor of Western medieval philosophy than a series of Muslim thinkers in the countries that are now Iraq and Iran. Besides being significant philosophers in their own right, these Muslims provided the route through which much Greek learning was made available to the Latin West.

In the fourth century a group of Syrian Christians had made a serious study of Greek philosophy and medicine. Towards the end of the fifth century the Emperor Zeno closed their school as heretical and they moved to Persia. After the Islamic conquest of Persia and Syria, they were taken under the patronage of the enlightened Caliphs of Baghdad in the era of the *Arabian Nights*. Between 750 and 900 these Syrians translated Aristotle into Arabic, and made available to the Muslim world the scientific and medical works of Euclid, Archimedes, Hippocrates, and Galen. At the same time, mathematical and astronomical works were imported from India and 'Arabic' numerals were adopted.

Arabic thinkers were quick to exploit the patrimony of Greek learning. **Alkindi**, a contemporary of Eriugena's, wrote a commentary on Aristotle's *De Anima*. He offered a remarkable interpretation of the baffling passage in which Aristotle speaks of the two minds, a mind to make things and a mind to become things. The making mind, he said, was a single super-human intelligence; this operated upon individual passive intelligences (the minds 'to become') in order to produce human thought. Alfarabi, who died in Baghdad in 950, followed this interpretation; as a member of the sect of Sufis he gave it a mystical flavour.

The most significant Muslim philosopher of the time was Ibn Sina or **Avicenna** (980–1037). Born near Bokhara, he was a precocious student who mastered logic, mathematics, physics, medicine and metaphysics in his teens, and published an encyclopedia of these disciplines when he was twenty. His medical skill was unrivalled and much in demand: he spent the latter part of his life as court physician to the ruler of Isfahan. He wrote a few works in Persian and many in Arabic; over one hundred have survived, in the original or in Latin translations. His *Canon of Medicine*, which adds his own observations to a careful assembly of Greek and Arabic clinical material, was used by practitioners in Europe until the seventeenth century. It was through Avicenna that they learnt the theory of the four humours, or bodily fluids (blood, phlegm, choler, and black bile) which were supposed to determine people's health and character, making them sanguine, phlegmatic, choleric, or melancholic as the case might be.

Avicenna's metaphysical system was based on Aristotle's, but he modified it in ways which were highly significant for later Aristotelianism. He took over the doctrine of matter and form and elaborated it in his own manner: any bodily entity consisted of matter under a substantial form, which made it a body (a 'form of corporeality'). All bodily creatures belonged to particular species, but any such creature, e.g. a dog, had not just one but many substantial forms, such as animality, which made it an animal, and caninity, which made it a dog.

Since souls, for an Aristotelian, are forms, a human being, on this theory, has three souls: a vegetative soul (responsible for nutrition, growth, and reproduction), an animal soul (responsible for movement and perception), and a rational soul (responsible for intellectual thought). None of the souls exist prior to the body, but while the two inferior souls are mortal, the superior one is immortal and survives death in a condition either of bliss or of frustration, in accordance with the life it has led. Following Alfarabi's interpretation of Aristotle, he distinguished between two intellectual faculties: the receptive human intellect which absorbs information received through the senses, and a single superhuman active intellect which communicates to humans the ability to grasp universal concepts and principles.

The active intellect plays a central role in Avicenna's system: it not only illuminates the human soul, but is the cause of its existence. The matter and the varied forms of the world are emanations of the active intellect, which is itself the last member of a series of intellectual emanations of the unchanging and eternal First Cause, namely God.

In describing the unique nature of God, Avicenna introduces a celebrated distinction, that between essence and existence. This arises out of his account of universal terms such as 'horse'. In the material world, there are only individual horses; the term 'horse', however, can be applied to many different individuals. Different from both of these is the essence *horseness*, which in itself is neither one nor many, and is neutral between the existence and non-existence of any actual horses.

Whatever kind of creature we take, we will find nothing in its essence which will account for the existence of things of that kind. Not even the fullest investigation into *what kind* of thing something is will show *that* it exists. If we find, then, things of a certain kind existing, we must look for an external cause which added existence to essence. There may be a series of such causes, but it cannot go on for ever. The series must come to an end with an entity whose essence *does* account for its existence, something whose existence is derived from nothing outside itself, but is entailed by its essence. Such a being is called by Avicenna a necessary existent: and of course only God fills the bill. It is God who gives existence to the essences of all other beings. Since God's existence depends upon nothing but his essence, his existence is eternal; and since God is eternal, Avicenna concluded, so is the world which emanates from him.

Avicenna was a sincere Muslim, and he was careful to reconcile his philosophical scheme with the teaching and commands of the Prophet, which he regarded as a unique enlightenment from the Active Intellect. Just as Greek philosophy operated within the context of the Homeric poems, and the stage is set for Jewish and Christian philosophy by the Old and New Testaments, so Muslim philosophy takes as its backdrop the Koran. But Avicenna's interpretations of the sacred book were taken by conservatives to be unorthodox, and his influence was to be greater among Christians than among Muslims.

THE FEUDAL SYSTEM

At the time of Avicenna's death great changes were taking place in Christendom. Charlemagne's unification of Europe did not last long, and few of his successors as Holy Roman Emperors were able to exercise effective rule outside the bounds of Germany. They occupied, however, the highest point of an elaborate pyramidal social and political structure, the feudal system. Throughout Europe, smaller or larger manors were ruled by local lords with their own courts and soldiers, who pledged their allegiance to greater lords, promising, in return for their protection, military and financial support. These greater lords in turn were the subordinates, or vassals, of kings. While the feudal system, for much of the time, preserved the peace in a fragmented Europe, warfare often broke out over contested issues of vassalage. When the Norman William the Conqueror invaded England in 1066, he justified his conquest on the grounds that the last Saxon king, Harold, had sworn allegiance to him and broken his oath by assuming the crown of England.

While local land ownership and the personal engagement of vassal to overlord were the foundations of secular society, the organization of the Church was becoming more centralized. True, the abbeys in which monks lived in community were great landowners, and abbots and bishops were powerful feudal lords; but as the eleventh century progressed, they were brought to an ever greater degree under the control of the Holy See in Rome. A line of unedifying and ineffective Popes in the tenth and early eleventh century gave way to a series of reformers, who sought to eradicate the ignorance, intemperance and corruption of many of the clergy, and to end clerical concubinage by enforcing a rule of celibacy. Chief among the reformers was Pope Gregory VII, whose high view of the Papal calling brought him into conflict with the equally energetic German Emperor, Henry IV.

According to almost all medieval thinkers, Church and State were each, independently, of divine origin, and neither institution derived its authority from the other. Despite the great variety of institutions at lower levels – feudal lordships and monarchies in the State, bishoprics, abbeys, and religious orders in the Church – each institution acknowledged a universal head: the Holy Roman Emperor and the Pope. The purposes of the two institutions were distinct: the State was to provide for the security and well-being of citizens in this world, the Church to minister to the spiritual needs of believers on their journey towards heaven. The jurisdictions, therefore, were in principle complementary rather than competing. But there were many areas where in fact they overlapped and could conflict.

The quarrel between Gregory and Henry concerned the nomination and confirmation of bishops. This was obviously the concern of the Church, since a bishopric was a spiritual office; but bishops were often also substantial landowners with a feudal following, and lay rulers often took a keen interest in their appointment. Disregarding a Papal prohibition, the Emperor Henry IV personally appointed bishops in Germany; Pope Gregory, who claimed the power to depose all princes, excommunicated him, that is to say, banned him from participation in the activities of the Church. This had the effect of absolving the Emperor's vassals from their allegiance, and to restore it, he had to abase himself before the Pope in the snow at Canossa.

SAINT ANSELM

In England too, under William the Conqueror's successors relations between Church and State were often strained; and the quarrels between Pope and King played an important part in the life of the most important philosopher of the eleventh century, St Anselm of Canterbury. Anselm, who was born just before Avicenna's death, resembled him as a philosopher in several ways, but began from a very different starting point. An Italian by birth, he studied the works of Augustine at the Norman abbey of Bec, under Lanfranc, who later became William the Conqueror's Archbishop of Canterbury. As a monk, prior, and finally Abbot of Bec, Anselm wrote a series of brief philosophical and meditative works. In *On the Grammarian* he reflected on the interface between grammar and logic, and the relationships between signifiers and signified; he explored, for instance, the contrast between a noun and an adjective, and the contrast between a substance and a quality, and wrote on the relationship between the two contrasts. In his soliloquy *Monologion* he offered a number of arguments for the existence of God, including one which goes as follows. Everything which exists exists through something or other. But not everything can exist through something else; therefore there must be something which exists through itself. This argument would have interested Avicenna, but Anselm did not find it wholly satisfactory, and in a meditation addressed to God entitled *Proslogion* he offered a different argument, which was the one that made him famous in the history of philosophy.

Anselm addresses God thus:

> We believe that thou art a being than which nothing greater can be conceived. Or is there no such nature, since the fool hath said in his heart, there is no God? (Psalm 14: 1) But at any rate, this very fool, when he hears of this being of which I speak – a being than which nothing greater can be conceived – understands what he hears, and what he understands is in his understanding; although he does not understand it to exist. For, it is one thing for an object to be in the understanding, and another to understand that the object exists. . . . Even the fool is convinced that something exists in the understanding, at least, than which nothing greater can be conceived. For, when he hears of this, he understands it. And whatever is understood, exists in the understanding. And assuredly that, than which nothing greater can be conceived, cannot exist in the understanding alone. For, suppose it exists in the understanding alone: then it can be conceived to exist in reality; which is greater.
>
> Therefore, if that, than which nothing greater can be conceived, exists in the understanding alone, the very being than which nothing greater can be conceived is one than which a greater can be conceived. But obviously this is impossible. Hence there is no doubt that there exists a being than which nothing greater can be conceived, and it exists both in the understanding and in reality.

Whereas Avicenna was the first to say that God's *essence* entailed his existence, Anselm claims that the very *concept* of God shows that he exists. If we know what we mean when we talk about God, then we automatically know there is a God; if you deny his existence you do not know what you are talking about.

Is Anselm's argument valid? The answer has been debated from his day to ours. A neighbouring monk, Gaunilo, said that one could prove by the same route that the most fabulously beautiful island must exist, otherwise one would be able to imagine one more fabulously beautiful. Anselm replied that the cases were different, because even the most beautiful imaginable island could be conceived not to exist, since we can imagine it going out of existence, whereas God cannot in that way be conceived not to exist.

It is important to note that Anselm is not saying that God is the greatest conceivable thing. Indeed, he expressly says that God is *not* conceivable; he is greater than anything that can be conceived. On the face of it, there is nothing self-contradictory in saying that that than which no greater can be conceived is itself too great for conception. I can say that my copy of the *Proslogion* is something than which nothing larger will fit into my pocket. That is true, but it does not mean that my copy of the *Proslogion* will itself fit into my pocket; in fact it is far too big to do so.

The real difficulty for Anselm is in explaining how something which cannot be conceived can be in the understanding at all. To be sure, we understand each of the words in the phrase 'that than which no greater can be conceived'. But is this enough to ensure that we grasp what the whole phrase means? If so, then it seems that we can indeed conceive God, even though of course we have no exhaustive understanding of him. If not, then we have no guarantee that that than which no greater can be conceived exists even in the intellect, or that 'that than which no greater can be conceived' expresses an intelligible thought. Philosophers in the twentieth century have discussed the expression 'The least natural number not nameable in fewer than twenty-two syllables'. This sounds a readily intelligible designation of a number – until the paradox dawns on us that the expression itself names the number in twenty-one syllables. However, even philosophers who have agreed with each other that Anselm's proof is invalid have rarely agreed what is wrong with it, and whenever it appears finally refuted, someone revives it in a new guise.

Equally original and influential was Anselm's attempt, in his book *Cur Deus Homo*, to give a reasoned justification for the Christian doctrine of the incarnation. The title of the book means 'Why did God become man?' Anselm's answer turns on the principle that justice demands that where there is an offence, there must be satisfaction. Satisfaction must be made by an offender, and it must be a recompense which is equal and opposite to the offence. The magnitude of an offence is judged by the importance of the person offended; the magnitude of satisfaction is judged by the importance of the person making the recompense. So Adam's sin was an infinite offence, since it was an offence against God; but any satisfaction that mere human beings can make is only finite, since it is made by finite creatures. It is impossible, therefore, for the human race, unaided, to make up for Adam's sin. Satisfaction can only be adequate if it is made by one who is human (and therefore an heir of Adam) and one who is divine (and can therefore make infinite recompense). Hence, the incarnation of God is necessary if original sin is to be wiped out and the human race is to be redeemed.

Anselm's theory influenced theologians until long after the Reformation; but his notion of satisfaction was also incorporated into some philosophical theories of the justification of punishment.

By the time he wrote *Cur Deus Homo* Anselm had succeeded Lanfranc as Archbishop of Canterbury. His last years were much occupied with the quarrels over jurisdiction between king William II and Pope Urban II, which in some ways recapitulated that between Gregory VII and Henry IV a few years before. Anselm died in Canterbury in 1109 and is buried in the Cathedral there.

ABELARD AND HÉLOÏSE

Peter Abelard was just thirty years old when Anselm died. Born into a knightly family in Brittany in 1079, he was educated at Tours and went to Paris in about 1100 to join the school attached to the Cathedral of Notre Dame, run by William of Champeaux. Falling out with his teacher, he went to Melun to found a school of his own, and later set up a rival school in Paris on Mont Ste Geneviève. From 1113 he was William's successor at Notre Dame. While teaching there he took lodgings with Fulbert, a canon of the Cathedral, and became tutor to his niece Héloïse. He became her lover probably in 1116, and when she became pregnant married her secretly. Héloïse had been reluctant to marry, and shortly after the wedding retired to live in a convent. Fulbert, outraged by Abelard's treatment of his niece, sent two henchmen to his room at night to castrate him. Abelard became a monk in the abbey of St Denis, near Paris, while Héloïse took the veil as a nun at Argenteuil. Our knowledge of Abelard's life up to this point depends heavily upon a long autobiographical letter which he wrote to Héloïse some years later, *History of my Calamities*. It is the most lively exercise in autobiography since Augustine's *Confessions*.

From St Denis, Abelard continued to teach (partly in order to support Héloïse). He began to write theology, but his first work, the *Theology of the Highest Good*, was condemned by a synod at Soissons in 1121 as unsound about the Trinity. After a brief imprisonment Abelard was sent back to St Denis, but made himself unpopular there and had to leave Paris. From 1125 to 1132 he was abbot of St Gildas, a corrupt and boisterous abbey in a remote part of Brittany. He was miserable there, and his attempts at reform were met with threats of murder. Héloïse meanwhile had become prioress of Argenteuil, but she and her nuns were made homeless in 1129. Abelard was able to found and support a new convent for them, the Paraclete, in Champagne. By 1136 he was back in Paris, lecturing once more on Mont Ste Geneviève. His teaching attracted the critical attention of St Bernard, Abbot of Clairvaux and second founder of the Cistercian order, the preacher of the Second Crusade. St Bernard denounced Abelard's teaching to the Pope, and had him condemned at a Council at Sens in 1140. Abelard appealed unsuccessfully to Rome against the condemnation, but was ordered to give up teaching and retire to the Abbey of Cluny. There, two years later, he ended his days peacefully; his edifying death was described by the Abbot, Peter the Venerable, in a letter to Héloïse.

Abelard is unusual in the history of philosophy as being also one the world's most famous lovers, even if he was tragically forced into the celibacy which is more typical of great philosophers, whether medieval or modern. It is as a lover, an ill-fated Lancelot or Romeo, rather than a philosopher, that he has been celebrated in literary classics. In Pope's *Epistle of Héloïse to Abelard*, Héloïse, from her chill cloister, reminds Abelard of the dreadful day on which he lay before her, a naked lover bound and bleeding; she pleads with him not to forsake their love.

> Come! with thy looks, thy words, relieve my woe;
> Those still at least are left thee to bestow.
> Still on that breast enamour'd let me lie,
> Still drink delicious poison from thy eye
> Pant on thy lip, and to thy heart be prest;
> Give all thou canst – and let me dream the rest.
> Ah no! instruct me other joys to prize
> With other beauties charm my partial eyes,
> Full in my view set all the bright abode
> And make my soul quit Abelard for God.

ABELARD'S LOGIC

Abelard's importance as a philosopher is due above all to his contribution to logic and the philosophy of language. Logic, when he began his teaching career, was studied in the West mainly from Aristotle's *Categories* and *On Interpretation*, plus Porphyry's introduction and some works of Cicero and Boethius. Aristotle's major logical works were not known, nor were his physical and metaphysical treatises. Abelard's logical researches, therefore, were less well informed than those, say, of Avicenna; but he was gifted with remarkable insight and originality. He wrote three separate treatises of Logic over the period from 1118 to 1140.

A major interest of twelfth-century logicians was the problem of universals: the status of a word like 'man' in sentences such as 'Socrates is a man', and 'Adam is a man'. Abelard was a combative writer, and describes his own position on the issue as having evolved out of dissatisfaction with the answer given by successive teachers to the question: what is it that, according to these sentences, Adam and Socrates have in common? Roscelin, his first teacher, said that all they had in common was the *noun* – the mere sound of the breath in 'man'. He was, as later philosophers would say, a nominalist, *nomen* being the Latin word for 'noun'. William of Champeaux, Abelard's second teacher, said that there was a very important *thing* which they had in common, namely the human species. He was, in the later terminology, a *realist*, the Latin word for 'thing' being *res*.

Abelard rejected the accounts of both his teachers, and offered a middle way between them. On the one hand, it was absurd to say that Adam and Socrates had only the noun in common; the noun applied to each of them in virtue of their objective likeness to each other. On the other hand, a resemblance is not a substantial thing like a horse or a cabbage; only individual things exist, and it would be ridiculous to maintain that the entire human species was present in each individual. We must reject both nominalism and realism.

> When we maintain that the likeness between things is not a thing, we must avoid it seeming as if we were treating them as having nothing in common; since what in fact we say is that the one and the other resemble each other in their being human, that is, in that they are both human beings. We mean nothing more than that they are human beings and do not differ at all in this regard.

Their being human, which is not a thing, is the common cause of the application of the noun to the individuals.

The dichotomy posed by nominalists and realists is, Abelard showed, an inadequate one. Besides words and things, we have to take into account our own understanding, our concepts: it is these which enable us to talk about things, and turn vocal sounds into meaningful words. There is no universal *man* distinct from the universal noun 'man'; but the sound 'man' is turned into a universal noun by our understanding. In the same way, Abelard suggests, a lump of stone is turned into a statue by a sculptor; so we can say, if we like, that universals are created by the mind just as we say that a statue is created by its sculptor.

It is our concepts which give words meaning – but meaning itself is not, for Abelard, a simple notion. He makes a distinction between what a word signifies and what it stands for. Consider the word 'boy'. Wherever this occurs in a sentence, it signifies the same ('young human male'). In 'a boy is running across the grass', where it occurs in the subject, it also stands for a boy; whereas in 'this old man was a boy', where it occurs in the predicate, it does not stand for anything. Roughly speaking, 'boy' stands for something in a given context only if, in that context, it makes sense to ask 'which boy?'

Abelard's treatment of predicates shows many original logical insights. Aristotle, and many philosophers after him, worried about the meaning of 'is' in 'Socrates is wise' or 'Socrates is white'. Abelard thinks this is unnecessary: we should regard 'to be wise' or 'to be white' as a single verbal unit, with the verb 'to be' simply as part of the predicate. What of 'is' when it is equivalent to 'exists'? Abelard says that in the sentence 'A father exists' we should not take 'A father' as standing for anything; rather, the sentence is equivalent to 'Something is a father'. This proposal of Abelard's contained great possibilities for the development of logic, but they were not properly followed up in the Middle Ages, and the device had to await the nineteenth century to be reinvented.

ABELARD'S ETHICS

Abelard was an innovator in ethics no less than in logic. He was the first medieval writer to give a treatise the title *Ethics*, and unlike his medieval successors he did not have Aristotle's *Ethics* to take as a starting point. But here his innovations were less happy. Abelard objected to the common teaching that killing people or committing adultery was wrong. What is wrong, he said, is not the action, but the state of mind in which it is done. It is incorrect, however, to say that what matters is a persons's will, if by 'will' we mean a desire for something for its own sake. There can be sin without will (as when a fugitive kills in self-defence) and there can be bad will without sin (such as lustful desires one cannot help). True, all sins are voluntary in the sense that they are not unavoidable, and that they are the result of some desire or other (e.g. the fugitive's wish to escape). But what really matters, Abelard says, is the sinner's intention or consent, by which he means primarily the sinner's knowledge of what he is doing. He argues that since one can perform a prohibited act innocently – e.g. marry one's sister unaware that she is one's sister – the evil must be not in the act but in the consent. 'It is not what is done, but with what mind it is done, that God weighs; the desert and praise of the agent rests not in his action but in his intention.'

Thus, Abelard says, a bad intention may ruin a good act. Two men may hang a criminal, one out of zeal for justice, the other out of inveterate hatred; the act is just, but one does well, the other ill. A good intention may justify a prohibited action. Those who were cured by Jesus did well to disobey his order to keep the cure secret, for their motive in publicizing it was a good one. God himself, when he ordered Abraham to kill Isaac, performed a wrong act with a right intention.

A good intention not carried out may be as praiseworthy as a good action: if, for instance, you resolve to build an almshouse, but are robbed of your money. Similarly, bad intentions are as blameworthy as bad actions. Why then punish actions rather than intentions? Human punishment, Abelard replies, may be justified where there is no guilt; a woman who has overlain her infant unawares is punished to make others more careful. The reason we punish actions rather than intentions is that human frailty regards a more manifest evil as being a greater evil. But God will not judge thus.

Abelard's teaching did not exactly amount to 'It doesn't matter what you do as long as you're sincere', but it did come very close to allowing that the end could justify the means. But what most shocked his contemporaries was his claim that those who, in good faith, persecuted Christians – indeed those who killed Christ himself, not knowing what they did – were free from sin. This thesis was made the subject of one of the condemnations of Sens.

Abelard experimented in theology no less recklessly than in ethics. One example must suffice: his novel treatment of God's almighty power. He raised the questions whether God can make more things, or better things, than the things he has made, and whether he can refrain from acting as he does. Whichever way we answer, he said, we find ourselves in difficulty.

On the one hand, if God can make more and better things than those he has made, is it not mean of him not to do so? After all, it costs him no effort!

Whatever he does or leaves undone is right and just; hence it would be unjust for him to have acted otherwise than he has done. So he can only act as he has in fact acted.

On the other hand, if we take any sinner on his way to damnation, it is clear that he could be better than he is; for if not, he is not to be blamed for his sins. But he would be better than he is only if God were to make him better; so there are at least some things which God can make better than he has.

Abelard opts for the first horn of the dilemma. Suppose it is now not raining. Since this has come about by the will of the wise God, it must now not be a suitable time for rain. So if we say God could now make it rain, we are attributing to him the power to do something foolish. Whatever God wants to do he can; but if he doesn't want to do something, then he can't.

Critics objected that this thesis was an insult to God's power: even we poor creatures can act otherwise than we do. Abelard replied that the power to act otherwise is not something to be proud of, but a mark of infirmity, like the ability to walk, eat, and sin. We would all be better off if we could only do what we ought to do.

What of the argument that the sinner will be saved only if God saves him, therefore if the sinner can be saved God can save him? Abelard rejects the logical principle which underlies the argument, namely, that if p entails q, then possibly p entails possibly q. He gives a counterexample. If a sound is heard, then somebody hears it; but a sound can be audible without anyone being able to hear it. (Maybe there is no one within earshot.)

Abelard's discussion of omnipotence is a splendid piece of dialectic; but it cannot be said to amount to a credible account of the concept, and it certainly did not convince his contemporaries, notably St Bernard. One of the propositions condemned at the Council of Sens was this: God can act and refrain from acting only in the manner and at the time that he actually does act and refrain from acting, and in no other way.

AVERROES

Abelard was far the most brilliant Christian thinker of the twelfth century. The other significant philosophers of the age were the Arab Averroes and the Jew Maimonides. Both of them were natives of Cordoba in Muslim Spain, then the foremost centre of artistic and literary culture in the whole of Europe.

Averroes' real name was Ibn Rushd. He was born in 1126, the son and grandson of lawyers and judges. Little certain is known about his education, but he acquired a knowledge of medicine which he incorporated into a textbook called *Kulliyat*. He travelled to Marrakesh, where he secured the patronage of the sultan. The sighting there of a star not visible in Spain convinced him of the truth of Aristotle's claim that the world was round. He acquired a great enthusiasm for all of Aristotle's philosophy, and the caliph encouraged him to begin work on a series of commentaries on the philosopher's treatises.

In 1169 Averroes was appointed a judge in Seville; later he returned to Cordoba and was promoted to chief judge. However, he retained his links with Marrakesh, and went back there to die in 1198, having fallen under suspicion of heresy.

Earlier in his life, Averroes had had to defend his philosophical activities against a more conservative Muslim thinker, Al-Ghazali, who had written an attack on rationalism in religion, entitled *The Incoherence of the Philosophers*. Averroes responded with *The Incoherence of the Incoherence*, asserting the right of human reason to investigate theological matters.

Averroes' importance on the history of philosophy derives from his commentaries on Aristotle. These came in three sizes: short, intermediate, and long. For some of Aristotle's works all three commentaries are extant, for some two, and for some only one; some survive in the original Arabic, some in translations into Hebrew and Latin. Averroes also commented on Plato's *Republic*, but his enormous admiration for Aristotle ('his mind is the supreme expression of the human mind') did not extend in the same degree to Plato. Indeed, he saw it as one of his tasks as a commentator to free Aristotle from Neo-Platonic overlay, even though in fact he preserved more Platonic elements than he realized.

Averroes was not an original thinker like Avicenna, but his encyclopaedic work was to prove the vehicle through which the interpretation of Aristotle was mediated to the Latin Middle Ages. His desire to free Aristotle from later accretions made him depart from Avicenna in a number of ways. Thus, he abandoned the series of emanations which in Avicenna led from the first cause to the active intellect, and he denied that the active intellect produced the natural forms of the visible world. But in one respect he moved further away than Avicenna from the most plausible interpretation of Aristotle. After some hesitation, he reached the conclusion that neither the active intellect nor the passive intellect is a faculty of individual human beings; the passive intellect, no less than the active, is a single, eternal, incorporeal substance. This substance intervenes, in a mysterious way, in the mental life of human individuals. It is only because of the role played in our thinking by the individual corporeal imagination that you and I can claim any thoughts as our own.

Because the truly intellectual element in thought is non-personal, there is no personal immortality for the individual human being. After death, souls merge with each other. Averroes argues for this in a manner which resembles the Third Man argument in Plato's *Parmenides*.

Zaid and Amr are numerically different but identical in form. If, for example, the soul of Zaid were numerically different from the soul of Amr in the way Zaid is numerically different from Amr, the soul of Zaid and the soul of Amr would be numerically two, but one in their form, and the soul would possess another soul. The necessary conclusion is therefore that the soul of Zaid and the soul of Amr are identical in their form. An identical form inheres in a numerical, i.e. a divisible multiplicity, only through the multiplicity of matter. If then the soul does not die when the body dies, or if it possesses an immortal element, it must, when it has left the body, form a numerical unity.

At death the soul passes into the universal intelligence like a drop into the sea.

Averroes was, at least in intention, an orthodox Muslim. In his treatise *On the Harmony between Religion and Philosophy* he spoke of several levels of access to the truth. All classes of men need, and can assimilate, the teaching of the Prophet. The simple believer accepts the literal word of Scripture as expounded by his teachers. The educated person can appreciate probable, 'dialectical' arguments in support of revelation. Finally, that rare being, the genuine philosopher, needs, and can find, compelling proofs of the truth. This doctrine was crudely misunderstood by Averroes' intellectual posterity as a doctrine of double truth: the doctrine that something can be true in philosophy which is not true in religion, and vice versa.

Averroes made little mark on his fellow Muslims, among whom his type of philosophy rapidly fell into disfavour. But after his writings had been translated into Latin, his influence was very great: he set the agenda for the major thinkers of the thirteenth century, including Thomas Aquinas. Dante gave him an honoured place in his Inferno as the author of the great commentary; and Aristotelian scholars, for centuries, referred to him simply as *the* Commentator.

MAIMONIDES

Rabbi Moses ben Maimon, better known to later writers by the name of Maimonides, was nine years younger than Averroes. He left his birthplace, Cordoba, when thirteen. Muslim Spain, which had provided a tolerant environment for Jews hitherto, was overrun by the fanatical Almohads, and Maimonides' family migrated to Fez and later to Palestine. For the last forty years of his life he lived in Egypt, and he died in Cairo in 1204.

Maimonides wrote copiously, in both Hebrew and Arabic, on rabbinic law and on medicine, but as a philosopher he is known for his book *The Guide for the Perplexed*, which was designed to reconcile the apparent contradictions between philosophy and religion which troubled believers. Much of the Bible, he thought, would be harmful if interpreted in a literal sense, and philosophy is necessary to determine its true meaning. We cannot say anything positive about God, since he has nothing in common with creatures like us. He is a simple unity, and does not have distinct attributes such as justice and wisdom. When we attach predicates to the divine name, as when we say 'God is wise', what we are really doing is saying what God is *not*; we mean that God is not foolish. (Foolishness, unlike divine wisdom, is something of which we have ample experience.)

> The meaning of 'knowledge' the meaning of 'purpose' and the meaning of 'providence', when ascribed to us, are different from the meanings of these terms when ascribed to Him. When the two providences or knowledges or purposes are taken to have one and the same meaning, difficulties and doubts arise. When, on the other hand, it is known that everything that is ascribed to us is different from everything that is ascribed to Him, truth becomes manifest. The differences between the things ascribed to Him and those ascribed to us are expressly stated in the text *Your ways are not my ways.* (Isaiah 55: 8)

This 'negative theology' was to have great influence on Christian as well as Jewish philosophers.

The only positive knowledge of God which is possible for human beings – even for so favoured a man as Moses – is knowledge of the workings of the natural world which is governed by him. We are not to think, however, that God's governance is concerned with every individual event in the world; his providence concerns human beings individually, but concerns other creatures only in general.

> Divine providence watches only over the individuals belonging to the human species, and in this species alone all the circumstances of the individuals and the good and evil that befall them are consequent upon their deserts. But regarding all the other animals and, all the more, the plants and other things, my opinion is that of Aristotle. For I do not at all believe that this particular leaf has fallen because of a providence watching over it . . . nor that the spittle spat by Zayd has moved till it came down in one particular place upon a gnat and killed it by a divine decree. . . . All this is in my opinion due to pure chance, just as Aristotle holds.

Maimonides' account of the structure and operation of the natural world was indeed taken largely from Aristotle, 'the summit of human intelligence'. But as a believer in the Jewish doctrine that the world was created within time to fulfil a divine purpose, he rejected the Aristotelian conception of an eternal universe with fixed and necessary species. It is disgraceful to think, he says, that God could not lengthen the wing of a fly.

The aim of life, for Maimonides, is to know, love, and imitate God. Both the prophet and the philosopher can come to the knowledge of whatever can be known about God, but the prophet can do so more swiftly and surely. Knowledge is to lead to love, and love finds expression in the passionless imitation of divine action which we find in the accounts of the prophets and lawgivers in the Bible. Those who are not gifted with prophetic or philosophical knowledge have to be kept under control by beliefs which are not strictly true, such as that God is prompt to answer prayer and is angry at sinners' wrongdoing.

Like Abelard among the Christians and Averroes among the Muslims, Maimonides was accused by his co-religionists of impiety and blasphemy. Such was the common fate of philosophical speculation by religious thinkers in the twelfth century. Christendom in the thirteenth century will offer something new: a series of philosophers of the first rank who were also venerated as saints in their own religious community.

VIII

PHILOSOPHY IN THE THIRTEENTH CENTURY

An Age of Innovation

The thirteenth century was the apogee of the Christian Middle Ages. The great projects of Christendom in the twelfth century had been military ventures: the Crusades. The century had begun with the bloody recovery of Jerusalem from the Saracens in the First Crusade. It had ended with the preaching of the Fourth Crusade, whose only achievement was the sack of the Greek Christian capital of Constantinople. In between, neither the fiery preaching of St Bernard to the Second Crusaders, nor the military prowess of Richard the Lion Heart in the Third Crusade, had been able to prevent the Christian Kingdom of Jerusalem from returning and remaining under Muslim rule. Taken all in all, the Crusades had been an expense of spirit in a waste of shame. Expeditions projected with devout intent were disfigured by avarice, treachery, cruelty and massacre, until they became paradigms of unjust warfare.

The thirteenth century was more auspicious than the twelfth. Crusades continued, but avoided the excesses that had disfigured the First and Fourth. The Emperor Frederick II secured a treaty in 1229 which briefly returned Jerusalem to Christian rule; his expedition achieved more with less outlay than any other, even though it is not numbered in the traditional list of crusades. The Fifth crusade, which took up much of the life of the saintly King Louis of France, was considerably less brutal than its predecessors; but it was no more successful, and he died in 1270 without reaching the holy city, with the words 'Jerusalem, Jerusalem' on his lips.

Early in the century the imperious reforming Pope Innocent III convened the first great Church Council in the West – the Lateran Council attended by twelve hundred prelates. This entrenched reforms in clerical discipline and established the rule that Christians should make a yearly confession to a priest and take part in the Eucharist at Eastertime. The pattern was now established in Catholic Christendom of the seven sacraments, or official ceremonies, which marked the main events, and catered for the spiritual needs, in the lives of the faithful from

---

131

womb to tomb: baptism in infancy, confirmation in childhood, matrimony and holy orders to inaugurate a secular or clerical vocation, penance and eucharist to cleanse and feed the soul, the last anointing to comfort the sick and the dying. The provision of the sacraments was the major function of the institutional Church, and the sacraments were held to be essential if the believer was to achieve the holiness of life, or at least the holiness at the hour of death, which was needed to gain eternal life in heaven and avoid eternal punishment in hell.

It was in the thirteenth century that architects, in churches and cathedrals across the continent, showed what could be achieved with the pointed arch, the feature which sets Gothic apart from classical architecture. While sturdy Latin prose continued to be written, and Latin poetry of the quality of the *Dies Irae*, in Italy a vernacular literature grew up, which culminated in Dante's *Divine Comedy*, set in the final year of the century. As the century drew to its close, Dante's friend Giotto began to paint in a novel way, linking the Byzantine icons of the past with the Italian Renaissance of the future. Within a comparatively peaceful Christendom, individual nations began to take shape, and to establish their national institutions. In England, the year 1215 saw the signing of Magna Carta, and in 1258 Simon de Montfort convened the first English Parliament.

The great universities of Northern Europe established themselves in the thirteenth century. The University of Paris received its charter in 1215: in the previous century Abelard, at the height of his academic career, had been no more than a schoolmaster. One year earlier a Papal Legate had confirmed the status of the infant University of Oxford. The Universities of Salerno and Bologna, specializing in medicine and law respectively, were older than either Paris or Oxford, but during the high Middle Ages they did not achieve a similar dominant position.

Universities are a medieval invention, if by 'university' we mean a corporation of people engaged professionally, full-time, in the teaching and expansion of a corpus of knowledge, handing it on to their pupils, with an agreed syllabus, agreed methods of teaching, and agreed professional standards. A typical university consisted of four faculties: the universal undergraduate faculty of Arts, and the three higher faculties of theology, law, and medicine, each linked to a profession. Someone who was licensed to teach in one university could teach in any university and, in an age when all academics used the common language of Latin, there was considerable migration of graduates. The teaching programme was built around set texts. In Arts, as we shall see, it was the works of Aristotle, in Latin versions, which provided the canon. In medical faculties the texts varied; in faculties of law, Justinian's codification of Roman Law provided the core of the syllabus. In theology the text on which lectures were based, in addition to the Bible, was a work known as the *Sentences* – a compilation, by the twelfth-century Bishop of Paris Peter Lombard, of authoritative texts drawn from the Old and New Testaments, Church Councils, and Church Fathers, grouped topic by topic, for and against particular theological theses.

A student in a medieval university learnt both by listening to lectures from his seniors, and, as he progressed, by giving lectures to his juniors. But a particularly prized method of instruction was the academic disputation. A teacher would put up some of his pupils – a senior student, plus one or more juniors – to dispute an issue. The senior pupil would have the duty to defend some particular thesis – for instance, that the world was not created in time; or, for that matter, that the world *was* created in time. This thesis would be attacked, and the opposite thesis would be presented, by other pupils. In arguing the matter out with each other the students had to observe strict formal rules of logic. After each side had presented its case, the instructor then settled the dispute, trying to bring out what was true in what had been said by the one, and what was sound in the criticisms made by the others.

Universities, like Parliaments, are legacies of the Middle Ages from which we continue to benefit. Equally important in the short run, for the intellectual as well as the devotional life of the age, was the foundation of the religious orders of begging ('mendicant') friars, the Franciscans and the Dominicans.

St Francis of Assisi secured Papal approval in 1210 for the rule he had laid down for his small community of wandering preachers. Of all medieval saints, he has enjoyed the greatest popularity within and without his Church: ascetic but joyful, poet of nature, inventor of the Christmas crib, preacher to the birds, bearer in his person of the wounds of the Saviour on the cross. He even visited the Sultan to try to convert him to Christianity by methods closer to the Gospel than the behaviour of the Crusaders.

St Dominic, on the other hand, has never attracted much affection outside his own order. He devoted much of his life to the fight against heresy, in particular the Albigensian heresy then thriving in Provence, a resurgent Manicheism. To this end he founded convents of nuns to pray and communities of poor friars to preach; but senior Church authorities preferred bloodier methods and Albigensianism was made the target of a new type of Crusade. In the last years of his life Dominic travelled throughout Europe setting up convents for men and women, and his Order was approved by the Pope in 1216. Like the Franciscans ('Friars Minor') the Dominicans ('Friars Preachers') were to live on alms, but from the outset their ethos was less romantic and more scholarly. It was the eventual involvement of the Dominicans with the Inquisition which, more than anything else, associated St Dominic in the popular imagination with gloom and terror.

After the death of St Francis, the Franciscans rapidly became just as successful academically as the Dominicans. By 1219 both Orders were established in the University of Paris, and from that time until the Reformation, with few exceptions, the most distinguished philosophers and theologians came from one or other mendicant order. In the thirteenth century, two thinkers stand out above all others: St Bonaventure the Franciscan, and St Thomas Aquinas the Dominican. The two were exact contemporaries: born within a few years of each other in the twenties of the century, they took their degree together on the same day in Paris, and were both to die in the same year, 1274. Significant differences separate them, however, both in philosophy and in theology, and in respect of the relationship between the two.

SAINT BONAVENTURE

Bonaventure was the son of an Italian physician, and was said to have been healed of a childish illness by St Francis. He become a friar in 1243, and studied under Alexander of Hales, the first head of the Franciscan school in Paris and the author of a vast theological anthology which served as a textbook for the order. Having received his licence to teach in 1248, Bonaventure wrote a great Commentary on the Sentences, and became head of the Paris Franciscans in 1253. He held the post for only four years, and was then elected Minister General of the Franciscans. The Order was in some disarray, with different factions, after St Francis' death in 1226, claiming to be the sole authentic perpetuators of his spirit. Bonaventure, a capable administrator as well as a model ascetic, reunited and reorganized the Order; he wrote the official life of St Francis, and attempted to have all others destroyed. He was made a Cardinal in 1273, and a year later he died at the Council of Lyons, which briefly reunited the separated Greek and Latin churches. His administrative duties allowed him little time for study during his later years, but he retained his interest in philosophy. His best known work is a short mystical treatise entitled *The Journey of the Mind to God*.

Bonaventure writes in the tradition of Augustine, and is explicitly a Platonist, welcoming many Neo-Platonic elements deriving from Hellenistic and Arabic sources, which he knew from Hales' anthology. Plato's Ideas exist only in the divine mind, as 'eternal reasons'; but they are the primary objects of human knowledge. Only in another life, when the blessed see God face to face, can the human mind be directly acquainted with these Ideas; but in the present life we acquire knowledge of necessary and eternal truths through their reflected light. Thus our minds are illuminated by the unseen God, just as our eyes see everything by the light of the sun, even though they cannot look on the sun itself.

According to Bonaventure we do acquire information through our senses, but this by itself is inadequate to generate the clarity and certainty necessary for real knowledge. Only our inborn knowledge of God and his eternal reasons enables us to achieve the unchanging truth. Bonaventure accepts the distinction between the active and the receptive intellect, but unlike the Arabic philosophers he thinks they are both faculties of the individual soul. Together these faculties are sufficient to enable the human mind to think intellectual thoughts – to understand the sentences of our language. But only by divine illumination can we determine whether these thoughts are true or not, whether they correspond to anything outside our minds.

Light, both literal and metaphorical, plays an important part in Bonaventure's metaphysics. 'Let there be light' was God's first command in Genesis; this means that light was the first form given to prime matter, and light is the basic substantial form of all bodies, corresponding to what others had called the form of corporeality. Bodily creatures contain many other forms in addition: humans, for instance, in addition to the basic form of light, and the supreme form which is their rational soul, have one form which makes them living creatures, and another form which makes them animals. Matter, on the other hand, from the outset, was not a mere empty receptacle of form; it contained genetic tendencies (*rationes seminales*) which contained in germ the history of its future changes. Everything other than God is composed of matter and form; even angelic spirits who lack bodies, we are told, contain 'spiritual matter' – a notion which might appear to the uninstructed to be self-contradictory.

Bonaventure, though willing to make use of concepts drawn from Aristotle, was highly suspicious of the Aristotelianism just becoming fashionable in university faculties of Arts. In the latter half of the twelfth century many hitherto unknown texts of Aristotle had been translated into Latin; early in the thirteenth century these new versions flooded into the libraries of Western Europe. Aristotle's *Analytics* and *Topics* were available by 1159, a 'New Logic' to add to the *Categories* and *De Interpretatione* which had formed part of the traditional corpus deriving from Boethius. James of Venice, who translated part of the new logic, also put into Latin the *Physics*, the *De Anima* and part of the *Metaphysics*. Translations were made not only from Greek: Gerard of Cremona travelled to Spain to translate Arabic versions of Aristotle's scientific works. In the 1220s Michael Scot translated into Latin not only the rest of the *Metaphysics* but also substantial portions of Averroes' commentaries on several texts. Aristotle's *Nicomachean Ethics* was translated in several spurts; the first complete version was made in mid-thirteenth century by Robert Grosseteste, first Chancellor of Oxford University and himself no mean philosopher. Last and most important of the translators was William of Moerbeke, who between 1260 and 1280 retranslated or revised almost all the known works, and completed the corpus with some which had so far not been available in Latin.

The University of Paris did not at first welcome this wealth of new material, which was to transform Latin philosophy. In 1210 an edict forbade any lectures on Aristotle's natural philosophy, and ordered his texts to be burnt. The condemnation was reinforced by Papal bulls, but seems to have rapidly become a dead letter. By 1255 the university had been thoroughly converted; not only Aristotle's physics, but his metaphysics and his ethics, and indeed all his known works, were made compulsory parts of the syllabus in Arts.

THIRTEENTH-CENTURY LOGIC

One of the first disciplines to flourish in the new environment was formal logic, where the recovery of Aristotle's entire corpus prompted new developments, to be observed in two thirteenth-century Paris textbooks, one by the Englishman William of Sherwood, the other by Peter of Spain.

These books presented the rules of Aristotle's syllogistic, and provided doggerel verses to make them memorable and easy to operate. The best known such verse begins with the following line:

Barbara celarent darii ferio baralipton.

Each word represents a particular type of valid syllogism, with the vowels indicating the nature of the three propositions which make it up. The letter 'a', for instance, stands for a universal affirmative proposition, and 'e' a universal negative proposition. A syllogism in Barbara, therefore, contains three universal propositions (e.g. 'All puppies are dogs; all dogs are animals; so all puppies are animals'). A syllogism in Celarent, by contrast, has as premises one universal negative and one universal affirmative, with a universal negative conclusion (e.g. 'No dogs are birds; all puppies are dogs; so no puppies are birds'). The consonants in the words also have a function, indicating how syllogisms are to be classified and how they can be transformed into equivalent syllogisms of different classes. Verses of this kind were mocked in the Renaissance as, literally, barbaric; but they served a useful, if modest, purpose as mnemonics.

More important for the development of logic was the medieval logicians' treatment of terms, the elements which go to make up propositions. First, they divided terms into categorematic terms (the words which give a sentence its content, such as 'dog', 'puppy', 'animal', and 'bird' in the examples above), and syncategorematic terms, function words like 'and', 'or', 'not', 'if', 'all', 'every', 'some', 'only', and 'except' which exhibit the structure of sentences and the form of arguments. It is the syncategorematic terms which are the special subject matter of logic.

Medieval logicians, while not as such interested in the meaning of particular categorematic terms, had much to say about the different ways in which such terms could have meaning. They studied, as we might say in a modern terminology, the semantic properties of words, classifying the different ways in which they might be used. One of the properties most thoroughly investigated was one they called 'supposition'. Roughly speaking, the supposition of a term is what it stands for; but this is not at all a simple matter.

First, we must distinguish between material and formal supposition. This distinction is made in modern languages by the use of quotation marks: if we wish to mention a word, rather than use it in the normal way, we put it in inverted commas. Consider the word 'water'. 'Water' contains two syllables, and 'water' is a noun. In such a sentence, the medievals would say that the word has material supposition. We are talking primarily about the physical symbol, rather than what it means or stands for. When we use the word 'water' in the normal way to talk about water, then we are using it with formal supposition. (The sound of the word is its matter, its meaning is its form.)

However, formal supposition comes in several kinds. The medievals made a distinction between simple supposition and personal supposition. This distinction corresponds, in English sentences but not in Latin, to the presence or absence of an indefinite article before a noun. Thus, in 'man is mortal' there is no article and the word has simple supposition; but in 'a man is knocking at the door' the word has personal supposition. Further technical terms were introduced to mark the differences between 'pepper is hot' and 'pepper is sold in Rome' (every bit of pepper is hot, but not every bit is sold in Rome) and between 'man is an animal' and 'an animal has broken into the garden' (in the second case, but not the first, it makes sense to ask 'which animal?').

The medieval classifications of the properties of terms drew attention to grammatical differences of genuine logical importance which are still relevant to the serious study of semantics. Their terminology may seem cumbrous to us who do not have medieval Latin as our native tongue; but it is partly due to the reflections of medieval logicians that in the modern languages we learned as children we have been able to master other, more streamlined, ways of marking these distinctions.

Another way in which medieval logicians improved upon Aristotle was in the development of modal logic, the logic of arguments which turn on the meanings of 'necessary' and 'possible'. In this area they were building on the work of Boethius, and like Boethius, as we shall see, medieval philosophers made use of the lessons of modal logic in attempting to dissolve thorny issues of divine omniscience and human action, and of freedom and determinism.

AQUINAS' LIFE AND WORKS

Among the professors at Paris University in the thirteenth century was the philosopher who more than any other brought Christian philosophy to terms with Aristotle: **St Thomas Aquinas**.

Thomas was born about 1225 at Roccasecca near Aquino in Italy. He was schooled by the Benedictine monks of Monte Cassino and studied liberal arts at the University of Naples. Against the bitter opposition of his family he joined the Dominicans in 1244 and studied philosophy and theology at Paris and at Cologne. He studied under an older Dominican, Albert the Great, a man of enormous and indiscriminating erudition, then newly started on a gigantic project of commenting on Aristotle's works, some of them more than once.

Aquinas was a devoted pupil of Albert, who quickly recognized his genius. From 1254 to 1259 he lectured at Paris, becoming a full professor ('regent master') in 1256. During the decade 1259–69 Aquinas was in Italy, occupying various posts in his order and in the service of the Popes at Orvieto, Rome, and Viterbo. From 1269 to 1272 he taught for a second period in the University of Paris during a period of lively theological and philosophical controversy. His teaching career was brought to an end by ill health in 1273, after a year at the University of Naples where he had begun his career as an undergraduate. He died at Fossanova on 7 March 1274 while journeying to Lyons to take part in the Council which was to unite the Greek and Latin churches.

Aquinas' works, though all written within twenty years, are enormously voluminous. Because his works were among the first to be put into machine-readable form, we are in a position to say that he produced 8,686,577 words. Best known are his two massive syntheses of philosophy and theology, the *Summa contra Gentiles* (against the Errors of the Infidels) some 325,000 words long, and the *Summa Theologiae* which, in a million and a half words, expounds his mature thought at even greater length. These encyclopaedic works, though theological in intent, and largely in subject matter, contain much material that is philosophical in method and content. The earliest of Aquinas' theological syntheses, his commentary on the *Sentences* of Peter Lombard, then a century old, is the least philosophically rewarding to read. Most explicitly philosophical is the series of commentaries on Aristotle and a number of pamphlets written during his Paris sojourns for didactic or polemical purposes (such as the *De Ente et Essentia*, a juvenile work on being and essence, the *De Unitate Intellectus* attacking the Averroist view that the whole of mankind has only a single intellect, and the *De Aeternitate Mundi* arguing that philosophy cannot prove that the cosmos had a beginning in time). Among the most lively of Aquinas' remains are the *Quaestiones Disputatae*, records of live academic debates on a variety of theological and philosophical topics. Matter of philosophical interest can be found even in Aquinas' commentaries on the Bible, such as his exposition of the Book of Job.

Aquinas wrote a dense, lucid and passionless Latin which, though condemned as barbaric by Renaissance taste, can serve as a model of philosophical discourse. The structure of the individual sections ('articles') of the *Summa Theologiae* is derived from the method of academic disputation. Whenever Aquinas is going to present a particular thesis, he begins by presenting the strongest reasons he can think of against its truth; these will sometimes be authoritative texts, more often arguments depending on an analysis of the concepts employed in the proposition which is up for question. Secondly, there follows the *sed contra*, a reason in favour of the view which he thinks correct; this is often no more than some familiar tag or preacher's text. Then the real reasons for Aquinas' position are stated, in the central body of the article. Finally, the article concludes with responses to the objections initially stated. This structure is not easy to follow at first, but anyone familiar with it quickly comes to see that it provides a marvellous intellectual discipline.

Aquinas' first service to philosophy was to make the works of Aristotle known and acceptable to his Christian colleagues, against the lifelong opposition of conservative theologians such as Bonaventure who were suspicious of a pagan philosopher filtered through Muslim commentaries. Aquinas' commentaries on the translations of his friend William of Moerbeke made students in Western universities familiar with Aristotle's own ideas, and in his theological writings he showed to what a considerable extent it was possible to combine Aristotelian positions in philosophy with Christian doctrines in theology. Though his principal philosophical themes and techniques are Aristotelian, Aquinas was no more a mere echo of Aristotle than Aristotle was of Plato. In addition to working out the relationship between Aristotelianism and Christianity Aquinas develops and modifies Aristotle's ideas within the area of philosophy itself.

Naturally Aquinas' philosophy of physics has been antiquated by the progress of natural science, and his treatment of logic has been rendered archaic by the development of mathematical logic in the nineteenth and twentieth centuries. But his contributions to metaphysics, philosophy of religion, philosophical psychology and moral philosophy entitle him to an enduring place in the first rank of philosophers.

Bertrand Russell wrote: 'There is little of the true philosophic spirit in Aquinas. He does not, like the Platonic Socrates, set out to follow wherever the argument may lead. Before he begins to philosophize, he already knows the truth; it is declared in the Catholic faith. . . . The finding of arguments for a conclusion given in advance is not philosophy, but special pleading.' It has often been remarked that this last remark comes oddly from a philosopher who (as we shall see) in his book *Principia Mathematica* takes hundreds of pages to prove that one and one make two. In fact, many of the conclusions Aquinas reached were novel in his time, and several of them seemed highly suspicious to conservatives. Moreover, he is very discriminating in his evaluation of the arguments of others, and never endorsed an argument simply because it supports a position he accepts himself. Thus, he offered a refutation of Anselm's argument for the existence of God, and he dismissed the arguments of those who thought they could show by pure reason that the world had a beginning in time.

Aquinas' Natural Theology

Aquinas' most famous contribution to the philosophy of religion is the Five Ways or proofs of the existence of God to which he refers early in his *Summa Theologiae*. Motion in the world, Aquinas argues, is only explicable if there is a first unmoved mover; the series of efficient causes in the world must lead to an uncaused cause;

contingent and corruptible beings must depend on an independent and incorruptible necessary being; the varying degrees of reality and goodnesss in the world must be approximations to a subsistent maximum of reality and goodness; the regular teleology of non-conscious agents in the universe entails the existence of an intelligent universal Orderer. Several of the Five Ways seem to depend on antiquated physics, and none of them has yet been restated in a manner clear of fallacy. Recently, philosophical interest has turned to the long and complicated argument for God's existence presented in the *Summa contra Gentiles*; it will be interesting to see whether it can be restated in a way which will carry conviction to the unbeliever.

The most valuable part of Aquinas' philosophy of religion is his examination of the traditional attributes of God, such as eternity, omnipotence, omniscience, benevolence. He takes great trouble with the exposition and resolution of many of the philosophical problems which they raise. In the wider area of philosophy of religion Aquinas' most infuential contribution was his account of the relationship between faith and reason, and his defence of the independence of philosophy from theology. According to Aquinas faith is a conviction as unshakeable as knowledge, but unlike knowledge it is not based on rational vision; it depends instead on the acceptance of something that presents itself as a revelation from God. The conclusions of faith cannot contradict those of philosophy, but they are neither derived from philosophical reasoning nor are they the necessary basis of philosophical argument. Faith is, however, a reasonable and virtuous state of mind because reason can show the propriety of accepting divine revelation even when it cannot demonstrate the truth of what is revealed.

It is essentially to Aquinas that we owe the distinction, familiar to philosophers in modern times, between natural and revealed theology. Suppose a philosopher offers an argument for a theological conclusion. We can ask whether any of the premises of the argument are claimed to record specific divine revelations or not. Are any premises of the argument put forward because they occur in a sacred scripture, or are alleged to have been revealed in a private vision? Or, on the contrary, are all the premises put forward as facts of observation or straightforward truths of reason? If the former, we are dealing with revealed theology; if the latter, with natural theology. Natural theology is a part of philosophy while revealed theology is not, even though theologians may use philosophical skills in seeking to deepen their understanding of sacred texts.

Aquinas believes that there are some theological truths which can be reached by the unaided use of reason: for instance, the existence of God. Others can be grasped either by reason or by faith; for instance, divine providence and goodness. Others can be known only by revelation, such as the Trinity of persons in God and the Incarnation of God in Christ. Among those which can be known only by revelation, Aquinas believed, was the truth that the created world had a beginning. His philosophical treatment of this issue had a sophistication unmatched before or since: by patient examination he refuted not only Aristotelian arguments for the eternity of the world, but also arguments put forward by Muslims and Christians to show that the world was created in time. Neither proposition, he maintained, could be proved by reason, and philosophy must be agnostic on the issue; we should believe that creation took place in time simply because the book of Genesis told us so.

MATTER, FORM, SUBSTANCE, AND ACCIDENT

In metaphysics Aquinas was a faithful follower of Aristotle – though not a slavish one, as the example of the eternal universe illustrates. He accepted the analysis of material bodies in terms of matter and form, and the thesis that change is to be explained as the reception of different successive forms in the same matter. He also accepted the Aristotelian doctrine that matter is the principle of individuation: if two pebbles on the beach resemble each other in every possible way, they will not differ at all in form, but they will be two pebbles and not one pebble because they are two different chunks of matter.

These Aristotelian theses gave rise to problems in connection with the angels of which the Bible speaks and which Christian tradition had come to regard as non-corporeal. Aquinas regarded as implausible Bonaventure's suggestion that angels too contained matter, but matter that was spiritual. Instead, he regarded angels as being pure immaterial forms. But if matter is the principle of individuation, how can there be more than one immaterial angel? Aquinas' answer was that each angel was a form of a different kind, a species all to himself. So Michael and Gabriel would differ from each other not as Peter differs from Paul, but as a sheep differs from a cow.

Matter and *form* are the concepts used by Aristotelians to analyse substantial change, the type of change when one kind of thing turns into another. To analyse the less drastic change when one and the same thing gains or loses a transient property (e.g. grows taller or becomes sunburnt), the concepts used were *substance* and *accident*. One of the most extraordinary, but also influential, uses to which Thomas put Aristotle's concepts was in his explanation of the nature of the Christian eucharist, the sacrament which perpetuated the supper in which Jesus took bread and said 'this is my body', and spoke of wine as being his blood. Aquinas maintained that when Jesus' words were repeated by the priest, the substance of bread and wine turned into the substance of Christ's body and blood. This change was called 'transubstantiation'.

Transubstantiation is a *unique* conversion, Aquinas says, a turning of one thing into another which has no parallel. In all other cases, where A turns into B there is some stuff which is first A-ish and then B-ish; in Aristotelian terms, the same matter is first informed with A-ishness, and then with B-ishness. But in the eucharistic conversion there is no parcel of stuff which is first bread and then Christ's body; not only does one form give way to another, but one bit of matter gives way to another. In an ordinary change, where the form of A-ishness gives way to the form of B-ishness, we have a trans*form*ation. In the eucharist we have not just one form giving way to another, but one substance giving way to another: not just transformation but trans*substant*iation.

We may wonder whether anything is now left here of the notion of *turning into*, and indeed why the notion is introduced at all into the discussion of the eucharist. There is no mention in scriptural references of anything turning into anything else; why is there in Aquinas?

The notion is introduced as the only possible explanation of the presence of Christ's body under the appearances of bread and wine. After the consecration it is true to say that Christ is in such-and-such a place; on the altar, say, in the church of Bolsena. Now there are only three ways, Aquinas says, in which something can begin to exist in a place in which it did not exist before. Either it moves to that place from another place, or it is created in that place, or something which is already in that place turns, or is turned, into it. But Christ's body does not move into the place where the eucharistic appearances are, nor is it created, since it already exists. Therefore something – to wit, the bread and wine – is turned into it.

What remain, visible and tangible on the altar, are, Aquinas says, the accidents of bread and wine – shape, colour and so on; they remain, according to Aquinas, without a substance to inhere in. Aquinas did not believe that the accidents after consecration inhered in the substance of Christ's body. If this were so then, for example, the size and shape which the bread once had would become the size and shape of Christ's body, which would mean that he was round and two inches in diameter, and so on.

St Thomas attached great importance to the doctrine of transubstantiation, and he expressed his devotion to the eucharist not only in theological prose but also in the devotional hymns which he wrote for the new feast of Corpus Christi. A verse of one of them has been thus translated by Gerard Manley Hopkins.

> Seeing, touching, tasting are in thee deceived;
> How says trusty hearing? that shall be believed:
> What God's Son has told me, take for truth I do;
> Truth himself speaks truly, or there's nothing true.

Hopkins' verse is more mannered than Aquinas', but it represents accurately the sense of the original. The verse is surprising, because Aquinas' official view is that in the eucharist there is no deception of the senses: they register accurately the presence of the accidents, and it is not their job, but the intellect's, to make judgements about substance. In this extraordinary case, the intellect may be misled into judging the presence of bread: but not if it listens to the word of God.

Is the concept of accidents inherent in no substance a coherent one? On the one hand, the idea of the Cheshire cat's grin without the cat seems the very quintessence of absurdity. On the other hand, to take an example of Aquinas' own, a smell of wine can hang around after the wine has all been drunk. And perhaps the colour of the sky is an example of an accident without a substance: the blueness of the sky is not the blueness of anything real.

However, the principle that the accidents inhere in no substance leaves one problem which may be thought fatal to Aquinas' account. Among the accidental categories of Aristotle is the category of place; 'is on the altar', for instance, is an accidental predicate. But if the accidents which once belonged to the bread do not inhere after consecration in the substance of Christ, then it appears that it by no means follows from the presence of the host upon the altar that Christ is present on the altar. Thus the doctrine of transubstantiation appears in the end to fail to secure that for which alone it was originally introduced, namely the real presence of Christ's body under the sacramental appearances.

AQUINAS ON ESSENCE AND EXISTENCE

Difficulties with the notion of transubstantiation do not, of course, call in question the general concepts of substance and accident outside this particular, and perhaps perverse, theological application of them. But the Aristotelian analysis of change raises other problems which Aquinas considers. If accidental change is to be understood as one and the same substance taking on various accidents, and substantial change is to be understood as one and the same matter taking on various substantial forms, should we understand the origin of the material world itself as being a case of one and the same essence passing from non-existence to existence? This was not, of course, a question which arose for Aristotle, who did not believe in creation out of nothing; but some later Aristotelians had posed the question and answered it in the affirmative. Aquinas firmly rejects the idea: creation is totally different from change, and is not to be understood in terms of existence being fastened on to an essence.

None the less, Aquinas accepted the terminology of essence and existence and makes frequent use of it in his metaphysics. In all creatures, he taught, essence and existence were distinct; in God, however, they were identical: God's essence was his existence. This is often held to be a sublime metaphysical insight. In fact, it appears to rest on a confusion.

We should make a distinction between generic and individual essences. If we understand 'essence' in the generic sense (as being the reality which corresponds to a predicate such as '. . . is God', '. . . is human', '. . . is a Labrador'), then it is true that there is, in all creatures, a real distinction between essence and existence. That is to say, whether or not there are any instances of a particular kind of thing is quite another matter from what are the constituent characteristics of a thing of that kind – for instance, whether there are or are not unicorns is a different kind of question from the question whether unicorns are mammals. But if we take 'essence' in this sense, then the doctrine that essence and existence are identical in God is a piece of nonsense: it amounts to saying that the question 'what kind of thing is God?' is to be answered by saying 'There is a God'.

On the other hand, if we understand 'essence' in the individual sense in which we can speak of the individualized humanity possessed by Socrates and by Socrates alone, then the doctrine of the real distinction in creatures becomes obscure and groundless. As Aquinas often insists, for a human being to exist is for it to go on being a human being; Peter's existing is the very same thing as Peter's continuing to possess his essence; if he ceases to exist he ceases to be a human being and his individualized essence passes out of the nature of things.

AQUINAS' PHILOSOPHY OF MIND

In treating of the human mind Aquinas had an exacting task: he wanted to show that it was possible to accept Aristotle's psychology without following Averroes in denying the immortality of the individual human soul. Like Bonaventure, Aquinas refused to accept the Arab philosophers' theory that human beings shared a common universal intellect. The intellect which sets human beings apart from other animals can be thought of, without too much distortion of Aquinas' thought, as the capacity for thinking those thoughts that only a language-user can think. This power was, for Aquinas, a faculty of the individual human soul. Following Aristotelian tradition, he distinguished between an active intellect and a receptive intellect; both of these, he insisted, were powers which each one of us possesses. The active intellect is the capacity to form universal ideas and to attain necessary truth. The receptive intellect is the storehouse of ideas and knowledge once acquired.

According to Aquinas, the intellect acquires its concepts by reflection upon sensory experience; we have no innate ideas, nor, for everyday knowledge, do we receive any special divine illumination. Experience is necessary for human acquisition of concepts, but it is not sufficient; that is why we have a special concept-forming capacity, the active intellect. We need it, Aquinas thought, because the material objects of the world we live in are not, in themselves, fit objects for intellectual understanding. A Platonic Idea, universal, intangible, unchanging, unique, might be a suitable object for the intellect; but in our world there are no such things as Platonic Ideas, and if there are any in the mind of God that is no business of ours in our present lives. So, Aquinas concludes, we need a special power in order to create what he calls 'actually thinkable objects' by abstracting ideas from our experience of the world. This power is the active intellect.

Aquinas explains what he means by making a comparison between sight and thought. Colours are perceptible by the sense of sight: but in the dark, colours are only potentially, not actually, perceptible. The sense of vision is only actuated – a person only sees the colours – when light is present to render them actually perceptible. Similarly, Aquinas says, the things in the physical world are, in themselves, only potentially thinkable or intelligible. An animal with the same senses as ours perceives and deals with the same material objects as we do; but he cannot have intellectual thoughts about them – he cannot, for instance, have a scientific understanding of their nature – for lack of the light cast by the active intellect. We, because we can abstract ideas from the material conditions of the natural world, are able not just to perceive, but to think about, and understand, the world.

It is by means of its ideas that the mind understands the world; but this does not mean that ideas are replicas or pictures of external things from which the mind reads off their nature. However, because ideas are universal and external things are particular, it does mean that, for Aquinas, there is no purely intellectual knowledge of individuals as such. This follows from two Aristotelian theses which Aquinas accepted: that to understand something is to grasp its form without its matter; and that matter is the principle of individuation.

If Plato was wrong, as Aquinas thought he was, then there is not, outside the mind, any such thing as human nature in itself: there is only the human nature of individual human beings such as Tom, Dick, and Harry. But because the humanity of individuals is form embedded in matter, it is not something which can, as such, be the object of pure intellectual thought. To grasp the humanity of Tom, the humanity of Dick, and the humanity of Harry we need to call in aid the senses and the imagination. The humanity of an individual, in Aquinas' terminology, is 'thinkable' (because it is a form), but not 'actually thinkable' (because existing in matter). That is to say, it is, because it is a form, a fit object of the understanding; but it needs to undergo a metamorphosis if it is to be actually held in the mind. It is the active intellect which, on the basis of our experience of individual humans, creates the intellectual object, humanity as such. And humanity as such has no existence outside the mind.

Theorists of the human mind are sometimes grouped into empiricists, rationalists, and idealists. Very crudely, empiricists believe that all knowledge of the world comes from experience; rationalists believe that important knowledge about the world is inborn; idealists believe that the human mind's knowledge extends only to its own ideas. Aquinas' position differs from each of these, but shares with each some common ground. Like the empiricists, Aquinas denies that there is innate knowledge; mind without experience is a *tabula rasa*, an empty page. But he agrees with the rationalists against the empiricists that mere experience, of the kind that humans and animals share, is impotent to write anything on the empty page. Like the idealists, Aquinas believes that the immediate object of purely intellectual thought is something which is its own creation, namely, a universal concept; but, unlike many idealists, Aquinas believes that a human being, by means of these universal concepts and with the aid of the senses and the imagination, can achieve genuine knowledge of the extra-mental world.

AQUINAS' MORAL PHILOSOPHY

Aquinas' ethical system is most copiously set out in the Second Part of his *Summa Theologiae*. This, which is nearly 900,000 words long, is subdivided into a first part (the *Prima Secundae*) which contains the General Part of ethics, and the second part (the *Secunda Secundae*) which contains detailed teaching on individual moral topics. The work, in both structure and content, is modelled on Aristotle's *Nicomachean Ethics*, on which at the same time Aquinas wrote a line-by-line commentary.

Much in Aristotle was very congenial. Like Aristotle Aquinas identifies the ultimate goal of human life with happiness, and like him he thinks that happiness cannot be equated with pleasure, riches, honour, or any bodily good, but must consist in activity in accordance with virtue, especially intellectual virtue. The intellectual activity which satisfies the Aristotelian requirements for happiness is to be found perfectly only in contemplation of the essence of God; happiness in the ordinary conditions of the present life must remain imperfect. True happiness, then, even on Aristotle's terms, is to be found only in the souls of the blessed in Heaven. The Saints will in due course receive a bonus of happiness, undreamt of by Aristotle, in the resurrection of their bodies in glory. Aquinas expounds and improves upon Aristotle's account of virtue, action, and emotion before going on to relate these teachings to the specifically theological topics of divine law and divine grace.

Aquinas' lengthy discussion of human action marks a great advance on Aristotle or any previous Christian thinker. Aristotle, in his *Ethics*, introduced the concept of voluntariness: something was voluntary if it was originated by an agent free from compulsion or error. In his moral system an important role was also played by the concept of *prohairesis* or purposive choice: this was the choice of an action as part of an overall plan of life. Aristotle's concept of the voluntary was too clumsily defined, and his concept of *prohairesis* too narrowly defined, to demarcate the everyday moral choices which make up our life. (The fact that there is no English word corresponding to '*prohairesis*' is itself a mark of the awkwardness of the concept; most of Aristotle's moral terminology has been incorporated into all European languages.) While retaining Aristotle's concepts, Aquinas introduced a new one of *intention*, which filled the gap left between the two of them, and greatly facilitated moral thinking.

In Aquinas' system there are three types of action. There are those things which we do for their own sake, wanted as ends in themselves: the pursuit of philosophy, for instance. There are those things which we do because they are means to ends which we want for themselves: taking medicine for the sake of our health is Aquinas' example. It is in these actions that we exhibit intention: we intend to achieve the end by the means. Finally, there are the (perhaps unwanted) consequences and side-effects which our intentional actions bring about. These are not intentional, but merely voluntary. Voluntariness, then, is the broadest category; whatever is intentional is voluntary, but not vice versa. Intention itself, while covering a narrower area than voluntariness, is a broader concept than Aristotle's *prohairesis*.

Aquinas expounds the relation between intention and morality in the following manner. Human acts may be divided into kinds, some of which are good (e.g. using one's own property), some bad (e.g. stealing), and some indifferent (e.g. walking in the country). Every individual concrete action, however, will be performed in particular circumstances with a particular purpose. For an action to be good, the kind it belongs to must not be bad, the circumstances must be appropriate, and the intention must be virtuous. If any of these elements is missing, the act is evil. Consequently, a bad intention can spoil a good act (almsgiving out of vainglory) but a good intention cannot redeem a bad act (stealing to give to the poor).

Aquinas considers the problem of erroneous conscience, the case where someone has a false belief about the goodness or badness of a particular action. To do what one thinks wrong, he says, is always wrong; it is always a bad thing for a man's will to disaccord with his reason, even if his reason is in error. Accordingly, an erroneous conscience always binds us. However, it does not always excuse us. If the error is due to negligence, then the agent is not excused. Adultery is not excused by thinking it lawful, for such error is culpable ignorance of the law of God. But a man who, without negligence, believes another man's wife to be his own does not sin by having sex with her.

Aquinas agrees with Abelard that the goodness of a good action derives from the good will with which it is performed; but he says that will can only be good if it is willing an action of a kind reason can approve. Moreover, he insists that good will cannot be fully genuine unless it is put into action when opportunity arises. A failure to act must be an involuntary failure if it is to be irrelevant to morality. Thus Aquinas avoids the paradoxical conclusions which brought Abelard's theory of intention into disrepute.

The morality of an act, Aquinas says, may be affected by its consequences. He makes a distinction between the harm which is foreseen and intended, and that which is foreseen and not intended. As an example of the former he cites the harm resulting from the actions of a murderer or thief; to illustrate the latter he says, 'A man, crossing a field the more easily to fornicate, may damage what is sown in the field; knowingly, but without a mind to do any damage'. In these cases we have bad consequences of bad acts, and in each case the sin is aggravated. But what about the responsibility of an agent for the bad consequences of good acts? Aquinas addresses this issue when dealing with the lawfulness of killing in self defence. Augustine had taught that this was forbidden for a Christian; but authoritative legal texts said it was lawful to repel force with force. Aquinas says: an act may have two effects, one intended, and the other beside the intention; thus, the act of a man defending himself may have two effects, one the preservation of his own life, the other the death of the attacker. Provided no more violence is used than necessary, such an act is permissible; however, it is never lawful to intend to kill another, unless one is acting on public authority, like a soldier or policeman.

From remarks such as this Aquinas' followers developed the famous doctrine of double effect. If an act, not evil in istelf, has both good and bad effects, then it may be permissible if (1) the evil effect is not intended, and (2) the good effect is not produced by means of the bad, and (3) on balance, the good done outweighs the harm. There are many everyday applications of the principle of double effect: e.g. there is nothing wrong with appointing the best person to a job, though you know that by doing so you will give pain to the other candidates. The principle is fundamental to serious ethical thinking; but for reasons to be discussed later, it fell into disrepute among moralists in the early modern period.

In the *Secunda Secundae* Aquinas analyses each individual virtue in turn, and the vices and sins which conflict with it. Here, too, he is following Aristotle; but there are important additions and modifications. Christian tradition had added the three 'theological' virtues of faith, hope, and charity to the classical Greek list of wisdom, temperance, courage, and justice. Aquinas accordingly treats of the virtue of faith and the sins of unbelief, heresy, and apostasy; of the virtue of hope and the sins of despair and presumption; and of the virtue of charity and the sins of hatred, envy, discord and sedition.

Aquinas' list of moral virtues does not altogether tally with Aristotle's, though he works hard to Christianize some of the more pagan characters who appear in the *Nicomachean Ethics*. For Christians, for instance, one of the most important virtues is humility. Aristotle's good man, on the other hand, is far from humble: he is great-souled, that is to say he is a highly superior being who is very well aware of his own superiority to others. In his treatment of humility, Aquinas comments on the text of St Paul, 'let each esteem others better than themselves'. How can this be possible, and if possible, how can it be a virtue? Aquinas sensibly says that it cannot be a virtue to believe oneself the worst of sinners: if we all did that, then all but one of us would be believing a falsehood, and it cannot be the part of virtue to promote false belief. He glosses the text thus: what is good in each of us comes from God; all we can really call our own is our sinfulness. But humility does not require, he says, that someone should regard less the gifts of God in himself than the gifts of God in others.

Aquinas defines humility as the virtue which restrains the appetite from pursuing great things beyond right reason. It is the virtue which is the moderation of ambition – not its contradiction, but its moderation. It is based on, though it is not identical with, a just appreciation of one's own defects. Finally, by a remarkable piece of intellectual legerdemain, Aquinas makes it not only compatible with, but a counterpart of, the great-souled man's alleged virtue of magnanimity. Humility, he says, ensures that one's ambitions are based on a just assessment of one's defects, magnanimity that they are based on a just assessment of one's gifts.

Aquinas is anxious to reconcile the virtue-based ethic of Aristotle with the role of divine law in the Christian moral system. In Aristotle it is reason which sets the goal of action and sets the standard by which actions are to be judged; according to the Bible, the standard is set by the law. But there is no conflict, because law is a product of reason. Human legislators, the community or its delegates, use their reason to devise laws for the general good of individual states. But the world as a whole is ruled by the reason of God. The eternal plan of providential government, which exists in God as ruler of the universe, is a law in the true sense. It is a natural law, inborn in all rational creatures in the form of a natural tendency to pursue the behaviour and goals appropriate to them. The natural law is simply the sharing, by rational creatures, in the eternal law of God. It obliges us to love God and our neighbour, to accept the true faith, and to offer worship.

Many times Aquinas returns to the passage in the final book of the *Nicomachean Ethics* which values the contemplative life above the active life. He treats it in several different ways, one of the most interesting of which is his application of Aristotle's teaching to the topic of the vocations of various religious orders. All religious orders, he says, are instituted for the sake of charity: but charity includes both love of God and love of neighbour. The contemplative orders seek to spend time on God alone; the active orders seek to serve the needs of their fellows. Now which are to be preferred, contemplative or active orders? Aquinas draws a distinction between two kinds of active life. There is one kind of active life which consists entirely in external actions, such as the giving of alms, or the succour of wayfarers; but there is another kind of active life which consists in teaching and preaching. In these activities the religious person is drawing on the fruits of previous contemplation, passing on to others the truths thus grasped. While the purely contemplative life is to be preferred to the purely active life, the best life of all for the religious is the life which includes teaching and preaching. 'Just as it is better to light up others than to shine alone, it is better to share the fruits of one's contemplation with others than to contemplate in solitude.' St Thomas does not specify what religious order he has in mind; but his phrase *contemplata aliis tradere* served as a motto for the Dominican Order.

Neither in his lifetime nor for long after his death was Aquinas regarded as a uniquely authoritative Catholic thinker. Three years after his death a number of propositions resembling positions he had held were condemned by ecclesiastical authorities in Paris and Oxford, and it was half a century before he was generally regarded as theologically sound. Even after his canonization in 1323 he did not enjoy, even within his own Order, the special prestige assigned to him by Catholics in recent times. In the nineteenth century Pope Leo XIII, in an encyclical letter, gave him official status as the foremost theologian of the Church, and in the twentieth century Pope Pius X gave a similar accolade to his philosophy. This ecclesiastical endorsement harmed rather than helped Aquinas' reputation outside the Catholic Church, but at the present time his extraordinary gifts are gradually being rediscovered by secular philosophers.

IX
OXFORD PHILOSOPHERS

THE FOURTEENTH-CENTURY UNIVERSITY

Among those who were critical of Aquinas after his death were a number of Franciscans associated with Oxford. During the thirteenth century, the University of Paris had undoubtedly dominated the learned world. By the end of the century, Paris and Oxford were almost like two campuses of a single university, with many masters passing between the two institutions. But by 1320 Oxford had established itself as a firmly independent centre, and indeed had taken over from Paris the hegemony of European scholasticism. Paris continued to produce distinguished scholars: Jean Buridan, for instance, Rector of the University in 1340, who reintroduced Philoponus' theory of impetus, and Nicole Oresme, Master of the College of Navarre in 1356, who translated much of Aristotle into French and who explored, without endorsing, the hypothesis that the earth rotated daily on its axis. But the fourteenth-century thinkers who made most mark on the history of philosophy were all Oxford associates.

There were two striking, and at first sight contradictory, features of the fourteenth-century university as typified in Oxford. These were the extreme length of the curriculum, and the remarkable youthfulness of the institution. The curriculum in Arts lasted eight or nine years, with a BA in the fifth year, and an MA after the seventh. Equipped with an MA or its equivalent a typical theology student then spent four years attending lectures on the Bible and the *Sentences*; three years later he himself began to lecture, first on the *Sentences* (as a bachelor), then on the Bible (as a 'formed bachelor'). Eleven years or so after starting his theological studies he became a regent master in theology, and continued for at least another two years lecturing on the Bible and supervising students before his course was complete. A university course of studies could last from one's fourteenth to one's thirty-sixth year.

Such a long period of training might be expected to produce a gerontocracy; yet hardly anyone in the university of the period was over forty. This was because there was not the sharp division familiar in modern universities between students and faculty. Lecturing and supervision were carried out by students themselves at specified periods of their studies. Someone like Aquinas who continued teaching and writing nearly to his death at the age of fifty would have been most unusual in fourteenth-century Oxford.

Relationships between the faculties of Arts and of theology were not always easy, and in the last years of the thirteenth century Oxford, like Paris, had been affected by a backlash of Augustinian theologians against Aristotelian philosophers. In the words of Etienne Gilson, 'After a short honeymoon, theology and philosophy thought they had discovered that their marriage had been a mistake.' The theologians' principal targets were scholars who interpreted Aristotle in the style of Averroes; but they attacked also some of the philosophical teachings of Aquinas, despite the hostility he had himself shown to Averroes' teachings.

In 1277 the congregation of Oxford University formally condemned thirty theses in grammar, logic, and natural philosophy. Several of the theses which were condemned were corollaries of Aquinas' teaching that in each human being there was only a single form, namely, the intellectual soul. Congregation condemned, for instance, the view that when the intellectual soul entered the embryo, the sensitive and vegetative souls ceased to exist. The issue was of concern to theologians, not just philosophers, because Aquinas' view was taken to imply that the body of Jesus in the tomb, between his death and resurrection, had nothing in common, save bare matter, with his living body. Victory in a long-running controversy was now given to those who, like St Bonaventure, believed in a plurality of forms in an individual human being. Supporters of St Thomas tried to appeal to Rome, but came to grief.

The Oxford congregation which condemned the thesis of the single form was presided over by an Archbishop of Canterbury, Robert Kilwardby, who was, like St Thomas, a Dominican. When, shortly afterwards, Kilwardby was summoned to Rome as a Cardinal, he was succeeded as Archbishop by an Oxford Franciscan, John Peckham. Peckham persecuted with even greater vigour those who supported Aquinas on this issue. For some time to come Oxford was dominated by Franciscan thinkers who, though very well acquainted with Aristotle, in this and other matters rejected Aquinas' distinctive version of Aristotelianism.

Duns Scotus

The most distinguished of these was John **Duns Scotus**. He was born about 1266 perhaps at Duns, near Berwick-on-Tweed. He studied at Oxford between 1288 and 1301, and was ordained priest in 1291. Merton College used to claim him as a fellow, but the claim is now generally regarded as baseless. While at Oxford he lectured on the *Sentences*, and he gave similar courses in Paris in 1302–3, and possibly also at Cambridge a year later. In the last year of his short life he lectured in Cologne, where he died in 1308. His lecture courses survived in an incomplete and chaotic state, in the form both of his own corrected autographs and of the notes of his pupils. A definitive edition of his works still awaits completion. His language is crabbed, technical, and unaccommodating; but through its thickets it has always been possible to discern an intellect of unusual sophistication. Scotus well deserved his sobriquet 'The subtle doctor'.

On almost every major point of contention Scotus took the opposite side to Aquinas. In his own mind, if not in the light of history, equal importance attached to his disagreements with another of his seniors, Henry of Ghent, an independent Parisian master of the 1280s who occupied a middle position between the Augustinians and the extreme Aristotelians. Scotus was always anxious to situate his own positions in relation to Henry's stance, and it was through Henry's eyes that he saw many of his predecessors.

Aristotle had defined metaphysics as the science which studies Being qua being. Scotus makes great use of this definition, broadening its scope immeasurably by including within Being the infinite Christian God. According to Scotus for something to *be* is for it to have some predicate, positive or negative, true of it. Anything, whether substance or accident, belonging to any of Aristotle's categories has being, and is part of Being. But Being is much greater than this, for whatever falls under Aristotle's categories is finite, and Being contains the infinite. If we wish to carve up Being into its constituent parts, the very first division we must make is between the finite and the infinite.

Aquinas too had talked of Being, but he understood it in a different way. Each kind of thing had its own kind of being: for a living thing, for instance, to be was the same as to be alive; and so among living things there were as many different types of being as there were different types of life. This did not imply that the verb 'to be' had a different meaning when it was applied to different kinds of thing. When we say that robins are birds and herrings are fish, we are not making a pun with the word 'are'. The verb 'to be', in Aquinas' terms, was neither equivocal, like a pun, nor univocal, like a straightforward predicate such as 'yellow'; it was *analogous*. In this it resembled a word like 'good'. We can speak of good strawberries and good knives without punning on 'good', even though the qualities that make a strawberry good are quite different from those that make a knife good. Similarly we can speak, without equivocation, of the being of many different kinds of thing, even though what their being consists of differs from case to case.

Scotus disagreed with Aquinas here. For him 'being' was not analogous, but univocal: it had exactly the same meaning no matter what it was applied to. It meant the same whether it was applied to God or to a flea. It was, in fact, a disjunctive predicate. If you listed all possible predicates from A to Z, then the verb 'to be' was equivalent to 'to be A or B or C . . . or Z'. The meaning of 'to be', therefore, depended on the content of all the predicates; it did not in any way depend on the subject of the sentence in which it occurred. A predicate must be univocal, Scotus argued, if one is to be able to apply to it the principle of non-contradiction, and make use of it in deductive arguments.

Being, for Scotus, includes the Infinite. How does he know? How can he establish that, among the things that there are, is an infinite God? He offers a number of proofs, which at first sight resemble those of Aquinas. One proof, for instance, makes use of the concept of causality to prove the existence of a First Cause. Suppose that we have something capable of being brought into existence. What could bring it into existence? It must be something, because nothing cannot cause anything. It must be something other than itself, for nothing can cause itself. Let us call that something else A. Is A itself caused? If not, it is a First Cause. If it is, let its cause be B. We can repeat the same argument with B. Then either we go on for ever, which is impossible, or we reach an absolute First Cause.

It might be thought that Scotus could say, at this point, 'and that is what all men call God'. But no: unlike Aquinas, who took as his starting point the actual existence of causal sequences in the world, Scotus began simply with the possibility of causation. So the argument up to this point has proved only the possibility of a first cause: we still need to prove that it actually exists. Scotus in fact goes one better and proves that it *must* exist. The proof is quite short. A first cause, by definition, cannot be brought into existence by anything else; so either it just exists or it does not. If it does not exist, why not? There is nothing that could cause its non-existence, if that existence is possible at all. But we have shown that it is possible; therefore it must exist. Moreover, it must be infinite; because there cannot be anything that could limit its power. If there were any incoherence in the notion of infinite being, Scotus says, it would long ago have been detected – the ear quickly detects a discord, the intellect even more easily detects incompatibilities.

Scotus prefers his kind of proof to Aquinas' Five Ways because it begins not with contingent facts of nature, but with purely abstract possibilities. If you start from mere physics, he believed, you will never get beyond the finite cosmos; and in any case you may have got your physics wrong (as Aquinas, as it happens, had).

The infinite God, reflecting on his own essence, sees it as capable of being reproduced or imitated in various possible partial ways: it is this which, before all creation, produces the essences of things. These essences, as Scotus conceives them, are in themselves neither single nor multiple, neither universal nor particular. They resemble – and not by accident – Avicenna's *horseness*, which was not identical either with any of the many individual horses, nor with the universal concept of horse in the mind. By a sovereign and unaccountable act of will, God decrees that some of these essences should be instantiated; and thus the world is created.

Creatures in the world, for Scotus as for other scholastics, are differentiated from each other by the different forms they possess. Socrates possesses the form of humanity; a different form is possessed by Brownie the donkey (a favourite example of Franciscan philosophers). But at this point Scotus introduces a new kind of form, or quasi-form. According to Aquinas, two humans, Peter and Paul, were distinct from each other not on account of their form, but on account of their matter. Scotus rejected this, and postulated a distinct formal element for each individual: his *haecceitas* or *thisness*. Peter had a different *haecceitas* from Paul, and so, presumably, did Brownie from Eeyore.

In an individual such as Socrates we have, then, according to Scotus, both a common human nature and an individuating principle. The human nature is a real thing which is common to both Socrates and Plato; if it were not real, Socrates would not be any more like Plato than he is like a line scratched on a blackboard. Equally, the individuating principle must be a real thing, otherwise Socrates and Plato would be identical. The nature and the individuating principle must be united to each other, and neither can exist in reality apart from the other: we cannot encounter in the world a human nature that is not anyone's nature, nor can we meet an individual that is not an individual of some kind or other. Yet we cannot identify the nature with the *haecceitas*: if the nature of donkey were identical with Brownie's *thisness*, then every donkey would be Brownie.

Is the nature really distinct from the *haecceitas* or not? We seem to have reached an impasse: there are strong arguments on both sides. To solve the problem, Scotus made use of a new concept, which rapidly became famous: the objective formal distinction (*distinctio formalis a parte rei*). The nature and the haecceity are not really distinct, in the way in which Socrates and Plato are distinct, or in the way in which my two hands are distinct. Nor are they merely distinct in thought, as Socrates and the teacher of Plato are. Prior to any thought about them, they are, he says, formally distinct: they are two distinct formalities in one and the same thing. It is not clear to me, as it was not to many of Scotus' successors, how the introduction of this terminology clarifies the problem it was meant to solve. Scotus applied it not only in this context but also widely elsewhere, for instance to the relationship between the different attributes of the one God, and to the relationship between the vegetative, sensitive, and rational souls in humans.

The introduction of the notion of haecceity affects Scotus' conception of the human intellect. Aquinas had denied the possibility of purely intellectual knowledge of individuals, because the intellect could not grasp matter as such, and matter was the principle of individuation. But the *haecceitas* though not a form, is quite distinct from matter, and is sufficiently like a form to be present in the intellect. According to Scotus, because each thing has within it an intelligible principle, the human intellect can grasp the individual in its singularity.

Scotus extended the scope of the intellect also in a different direction. Aquinas maintained that in the present life the intellect was most at home in acquiring, by abstraction from experience, knowledge of the nature of material things. Scotus said that to define the proper object of the intellect in this way was like defining the object of sight as what could be seen by candlelight. The saints in heaven enjoyed the intellectual vision of God; if we were to take the future life as well as the present into account we must say that the proper object of the intellect was as wide as Being itself. Scotus did not deny that in fact all our knowledge arises from experience, but he thought that the dependence of the intellect on the senses in the present life was perhaps a punishment for sin.

Scotus makes a distinction between intuitive and abstractive knowledge. Abstractive knowledge is knowledge of the essence of an object, considered in abstraction from the question whether the object exists or not. Intuitive knowledge is knowledge of an object as existent: it comes in two kinds, perfect intuition when an object is present, and imperfect intuition which is memory of a past or anticipation of a future object.

On the relationship between the intellect and the will, Scotus once more departs from the position of St Thomas in several ways. Historians of philosophy call him a 'voluntarist', a partisan of the will against the intellect. What does this mean precisely? Scotus asks whether anything other than the will effectively causes the act of willing in the will. He replies, nothing other than the will is the total cause of its volition. Aquinas had maintained that the freedom of the will derived from an indeterminacy in practical reasoning. The reason could decide that more than one alternative was an equally good means to a good end, thus leaving the will free to choose. Scotus maintained that any such contingency must come from an undetermined cause which can only be the will itself. But in making the will the cause of its own freedom, Scotus' theory runs the danger of leading to an infinite regress of free choices, where the freedom of a choice depends on a previous free choice whose freedom depends on a previous one, and so on for ever.

This was not a danger of which Scotus was unaware, and in the course of his discussion of God's foreknowledge of free actions he introduced a new kind of potentiality, uniquely characteristic of human free choice, which holds out the possibility of avoiding the regress.

When we have a case of free action, Scotus says, this freedom is accompanied by an obvious power to do opposite things. True, the will can have no power to will X and not-will X at the same time – that would be nonsense – but there is in the will a power to will after not willing, or to a succession of opposite acts. That is to say that while A is willing X at time t, A can not-will X at time $t + 1$. This, he says, is an obvious power to do a different kind of act at a later time.

But, Scotus says, there is another non-obvious power, which is without any temporal succession. He illustrates this kind of power by imagining a case in which a created will existed only for a single instant. In that instant it could only have a single volition, but even that volition would not be necessary, but be free. The lack of succession involved in this kind of freedom is most obvious in the case of the imagined momentary will, but it is in fact there all the time. That is to say, that while A is willing X at t, not only does A have the power to not-will X at $t + 1$, but A also has the power to not-will X at t, at that very moment. This is an explicit innovation, the postulation of a non-manifest, we might even say occult, power.

Scotus carefully distinguishes this power from logical possibility; it is something which accompanies logical possibility but is not identical with it. It is not simply the fact that there would be no contradiction in A's not willing X at this very moment, it is something over and above – a real active power – and it is the heart of human freedom.

The sentence 'This will, which is willing X, can not-will X' can be taken in two ways. Taken one way ('in a composite sense') it means that 'This will, which is willing X, is not-willing X' is possibly true; and that is false. Taken another way ('in a divided sense'), as meaning that this will which is now willing X at t has the power of not-willing X at $t + 1$, it is obviously true.

But what of 'This will, which is willing X at t, can not-will X at t'? Here too, in accordance with Scotus' innovation, we can distinguish between the composite sense and the divided sense. It is not the case that it is possible that this will is simultaneously willing X at t and not-willing X at t. But it is true that it is possible that not-willing X at time t might inhere in this will which is actually willing X at time t.

Scotus at this point makes a distinction between instants of time and instants of nature: there can be more than one instant of nature at the same instant of time. We here encounter, for the first time in philosophy, what later logicians were to call 'possible worlds'. At the same instant of time, on this account, there may be several simultaneous possibilities. These synchronic possibilities need not be compatible with each other, as in the case in point: they are possible in different possible worlds, not in the same possible world.

For better or worse, the notion of possible worlds was to have a distinguished future in the history of philosophy. Scotus' account of the origin of the world, described earlier, makes God's creation a matter of choosing to actualize one among an infinite number of possible universes. Later philosophers were to separate the notion of possible worlds from the notion of creation, and to take the word 'world' in a more abstract way, so that any totality of compossible situations constitutes a possible world. This abstract notion was then used as a means of explaining every kind of power and possibility. Credit for the introduction of the notion is usually given to Leibniz, but it belongs instead to Scotus. It has proved the longest-lived of the subtleties which gave him his nickname.

Despite his uncommon ingenuity as a philosopher, Scotus in his writings systematically restricts the scope of philosophy. Aquinas had made a distinction between truths about God graspable only by faith, such as the Trinity, and other truths knowable by reason; and he had included in the latter class knowledge of all the principal attributes of God, such as omnipotence, immensity, omnipresence, and so on. Scotus, on the contrary, thought reason impotent to prove that

God was omnipotent or just or merciful. A Christian knows, he argued, that omnipotence includes the power to beget a Son; but this is not something which pure reason can prove that God possesses. In a similar way many topics which, for Aquinas, fell within the province of philosophy are by Scotus kicked upstairs for treatment by the theologian.

In theology itself, Scotus was best known for his sponsorship of belief in the immaculate conception. This doctrine is not, as is often thought, the belief that Mary conceived Jesus as a virgin; it is the belief that Mary, when herself conceived, was free from the inherited taint of original sin. (The many people nowadays who disbelieve in original sin automatically believe in the immaculate conception of Mary.) The doctrine is important in the history of philosophy because it relates to a long-standing philosophical dispute. Aquinas had denied that Mary was conceived immaculate because, following Aristotle, he did not believe that a newly conceived foetus had an intellectual soul during its first few weeks of existence. Scotus believed that the soul entered the body at the moment of conception, and the eventual acceptance by the Church of the doctrine of the immaculate conception was a victory for his thesis. This philosophical disagreement is obviously relevant to the attitude taken by Catholics in the present day on the issue of abortion.

Gerard Manley Hopkins, the most famous Scotist of modern times, singled out for special praise his championing of the immaculate conception. Ranking Scotus among the greatest of all philosophers, he describes him as:

> Of realty the rarest-veined unraveller; a not
> Rivalled insight, be rival Italy or Greece;
> Who fired France for Mary without spot.

OCKHAM'S LOGIC OF LANGUAGE

Scotus' tendency to restrict the field of operation of philosophy is carried further by his successor, William **Ockham**. William, like Scotus a Franciscan friar, came from the village of Ockham in Surrey; he was born about 1285 and studied at Oxford shortly after Scotus had left it. He lectured on the *Sentences* from 1317 to 1319, but never took his MA, having fallen foul of the Chancellor of the University, John Lutterell. He went to London where, in the 1320s, he wrote up his Oxford lectures, and composed a systematic treatise on logic as well as commentaries on Aristotle and Porphyry. In 1324 he was summoned to Avignon to answer charges of heresy brought by Lutterell, and soon afterwards gave up his interest in theoretical philosophy.

Many of Ockham's positions in logic and metaphysics were taken up either in development of, or in opposition to, Duns Scotus. Though his thought is less sophisticated than that of Scotus, his language is mercifully much clearer. Like Scotus, Ockham regards 'being' as a univocal term, applicable to God in the same sense as to creatures. He allows into his system, however, a much less extensive variety of created beings, reducing the ten Aristotelian categories to two, namely substances and qualities. Like Scotus, Ockham accepts a distinction between abstractive and intuitive knowledge; it is only by intuitive knowledge that we can know whether a contingent fact obtains or not. Ockham goes beyond Scotus, however, in allowing that God, by his almighty power, can make us have intuitive knowledge of an object that does not exist. Whatever God can do through secondary causes, he argues, God can do directly; so if God can make me know that a wall is white by causing the white wall to meet my eye, he can make me have the same belief without there being any white wall there at all. This thesis obviously opens a road to scepticism, quickly traversed by some of Ockham's followers.

Ockham's most significant disagreement with Scotus concerned the nature of universals. He rejected outright the idea that there was a common nature existing in the many individuals we call by a common name. No universal exists outside the mind; everything in the world is singular. Ockham offered many arguments against common natures, of which one of the most vivid is the following:

> It follows from that opinion that part of Christ's essence would be wretched and damned; because that same common nature really existing in Christ really exists in Judas and is damned.

Universals are not things but signs, single signs representing many things. There are natural signs and conventional signs: natural signs are the thoughts in our minds, and conventional signs are the words which we coin to express these thoughts.

Ockham's view of universals is often called nominalism; but in his system it is not only names, but concepts, which are universal. However, the title has a certain aptness, since Ockham thought of the concepts in our minds as forming a language system, a language common to all humans and prior to all the different spoken languages. In that sense it is true to say that for Ockham, only names are universal; but we have to count among names not only the names in natural languages, but the unspoken names of our mental language – a language which, as Ockham describes it, turns out to have quite a strong structural similarity to medieval Latin.

At different times in his career Ockham gives different accounts of the relationship between the names of the mental language and the things in the world. According to his earlier theory, the mind fashioned mental images or representations, which resembled real things. These 'fictions', as he called them, served as elements in mental propositions, in which they took the place of the things they resembled. Fictions could be universal in the sense of having an equal likeness to many different things. Later, Ockham ceased to believe in these fictions; names in the mental language were simply acts of thinking, items in an individual person's psychological history. These mental names occur in mental sentences (presumably as successive stages of the thinking of the sentence); a thought, or sentence, is a true thought or sentence if the successive names which occur in it are names of the same thing. Thus the thought that Socrates is a philosopher is a true thought because Socrates can be called both 'Socrates' and 'philosopher'. It is not easy to see, on this account, quite how to explain the truth conditions of a sentence such as 'Socrates is not a dog'; but Ockham, to his credit, goes to some trouble to deal with the difficult cases.

Ockham is best known for something which he never said, namely 'Entities are not to be multiplied beyond necessity'. This principle, commonly called 'Ockham's Razor', is not found in his works, though he did say similar things such as 'it is futile to do with more what can be done with fewer' or 'plurality should not be assumed without necessity'. In fact, the sentiment long antedated Ockham; but it does sum up his reductionist attitude to the technical philosophical developments of his predecessors. Sometimes this attitude enabled him to cut away fictional entities; as often as not, it led him to overlook distinctions that were philosophically significant.

OCKHAM'S POLITICAL THEORY

Ockham's summons to Avignon did not lead to a condemnation for heresy, even though a commission spent several years examining his Commentary on the *Sentences*. However, his time there did give a wholly new turn to his career. The Pope of the time, John XXII, was in conflict with the Franciscan Order on two issues concerning poverty: the historical question whether Christ and the Apostles had lived in absolute poverty, and the practical question of the ownership of property by contemporary Franciscans. Ockham became involved in this controversy, and made himself so unpopular with the Pope that, along with the head of his Order, Michael of Cesena, he had to flee from Avignon to Munich. There they were taken under the protection of the Holy Roman Emperor, Ludwig of Bavaria. According to legend Ockham said, 'Emperor, defend me with your sword and I will defend you with my pen'. Whether or not this is true, Ockham was henceforth involved in the broader issues of the relationship between Pope and Emperor, between Church and State.

In order to explain the questions at issue, we have to go back in time. The conflict over the right to appoint bishops, which surfaced in the eleventh-century quarrel between Pope Gregory VII and the Emperor Henry IV, was repeated more than once in succeeding years. In England, as we saw, St Anselm when Archbishop clashed with William II over the issue, and so did his successor Thomas Becket, with Henry II – a conflict which led to his martyrdom and canonization, and to the long train of Canterbury pilgrims.

The second major issue which set Church and State at odds was the taxation of the clergy for secular purposes. At the end of the thirteenth century King Philip the Fair of France wished to levy taxes on clerical property in order to finance his wars with England. In a bull of 1296 Pope Boniface VIII sought to ban this, though he had to relent when Philip, in retaliation, forbade the export of money from France to pay Papal taxes. The controversy continued, and Duns Scotus, who was in Paris at the time, was sent into exile for supporting the Papal party. A pamphlet war followed. Giles of Rome, a follower of St Thomas, stated the extreme Papalist position that the temporal power is subject to the spiritual power even in temporal matters. John of Paris, in support of the king, argued that the Pope was not the owner, but only the custodian of ecclesiastical property, and that he was subject to the superior authority of a General Council of the Church.

The most distinguished contributor to this debate was the poet Dante, who in his *De Monarchia* restated the traditional conception of parallel authorities pursuing temporal and eternal ends, each wielding a separate sword by divine command. The practical issues were determined, however, less by philosophical argument than by main force. In 1303 Philip the Fair sent troops to kidnap Pope Boniface in Anagni, with a view to having him tried by a Council in France. Though he failed in this attempt, he succeeded, when Boniface died shortly after, in securing the election to the Papacy of a French cardinal. The new Pope, Clement V, in 1309 transferred the Papacy to Avignon, where it remained for seventy years.

It was a third great clash between Church and State which drew in Ockham. The Avignon Pope who condemned the radical Franciscan teaching on apostolic poverty, John XXII, had previously intervened in a disputed Imperial election and opposed the eventually successful candidate, Ludwig IV. In 1324 the Pope excommunicated Ludwig, who in response appealed to a General Council to condemn the Pope as a heretic because of his attitude to the Franciscans. In 1328 Ludwig entered Rome, had himself crowned Emperor, burned John in effigy, and installed an antipope. His senior adviser in Rome was **Marsilius** of Padua, author of the recent *Defender of the Peace*, one of the most significant works on political philosophy to appear in the Middle Ages.

Marsilius had written the book at Paris, where he had briefly been rector of the University; on its appearance he had had to flee, like Ockham, to the protection of Ludwig. In the book, he mounted a sustained attack on Papal and ecclesiastical interference in what he regarded as the legitimate province of autonomous and self-sufficient states. The disorder, corruption, conflict and warfare endemic in Italy, Marsilius maintains, are all the result of Papal arrogance and ambition. But he takes his stand not just on local issues, but on general principle, and trawls through the Bible and Aristotle and classical and patristic authors to prove that the state is a 'perfect' society, that is to say one which is both supreme and self-sufficient within its own sphere.

For Marsilius there are two types of government: rule by the consent of the ruler's subjects, and rule against their will; only the former is legitimate, and the latter is tyranny. The laws of the state derive their authority from the citizens, or from the better sort among them; states may delegate the actual task of legislation to bodies or institutions, which may legitimately have a different form in different states. The prince is the executive head of the State; the citizens' consent to his rule finds its best expression if he is an elected officer, but there are other legitimate ways in which consent may be manifested. An irregular or incompetent prince should be removed from office by the legislature.

Neither Christ nor the Apostles, Marsilius insists, made any claim to temporal power, and there is no Scriptural authority for Papal claims to supremacy. The Church consists of the whole community of Christian believers, and the institution which best reflects its structure is a General Council. But even a General Council may only enforce its decisions with the approval of the temporal authorities, and if heresy is to be prosecuted, it must be by the State and not by the Church.

Ockham was in sympathy with many of Marsilius' views, but he had reservations about some of them, and in any case he was a much less systematic political thinker. His political writings are polemical pamphlets rather than textbooks of political theory. Thus, the conflict with the Pope over apostolic poverty led Ockham to formulate a theory of natural rights, and to distinguish between two classes: rights which may legitimately be renounced (such as the right to private property) and those which are inalienable (such as the right to one's own life). Ockham's most important contribution to the debate on the work of Church and State is his *Dialogues*, which is again a compilation of various pamphlets. Whereas Marsilius' conception of government is clearly shaped by conditions in the Italian city-states of his time, Ockham's immediate concerns are much more directly focused on the Holy Roman Empire.

The Emperor derives his power, he insists, not from the Pope, but from the people, through the medium of the imperial electors. What goes for the Emperor goes, *mutatis mutandis*, for other temporal sovereigns. The right to choose one's rulers is one of the natural rights of human beings. Peoples if they wish can exercise these rights by setting up a hereditary monarchy; but if such a monarch abuses his power, the people are entitled to depose him.

Ockham's hostility to the Papacy is much less radical than Marsilius'. He has no doubt that *de facto* Papal supremacy has been exercised in a tyrannical way; but he is willing to allow a *de jure* supremacy, which he envisages as a constitutional monarchy. The Papal power should be controlled by General Councils, which would resemble the representative assembly of a parliamentary democracy, with members elected by local parishes and religious communities.

THE OXFORD CALCULATORS

When Ockham died of the Black Death in Munich in 1349 it was a quarter of a century since he had left Oxford. During the period, the University had become the unquestioned intellectual centre of scholastic philosophy. It would be wrong to envisage it simply as a battleground for warring schools of thought, Thomists against Scotists, nominalists against realists and so on. During this period, Aquinas was not much followed in Oxford, even by Dominicans, and Scotism was not dominant even though in the first half of the fourteenth century the leading thinkers were Franciscans. Even Ockham left behind no characteristic nominalist school in Oxford. It was in France that nominalists like John of Mirecourt and Nicholas of Autrecourt took to lengths of extreme scepticism his teaching that God's unlimited power rendered suspect human claims to any certain knowledge of absolute truth.

Between 1320 and 1340 a group of vigorous and independent thinkers in Oxford authored developments in various parts of the curriculum. Many writers published logical treatises, expanding the traditional logic into many new areas, exploring especially propositions about motion and change, expansion and contraction, measurement and time. The most important of the logical writers was Walter Burley, whose *Pure Art of Logic* marked a high point in the formalization of logic in the Middle Ages.

Formalization became important in theology too: it reached a point where theology can almost be said to have become mathematized. Problems of maxima and minima, and questions whether continua are infinitely divisible and infinitely extendible, which might be thought to be the province of the mathematical scientist rather than the theologian, are first worked out in the analysis of the growth of grace in the souls of the faithful and in measuring the capacity for infinite beatitude of the Saints in heaven.

Whether or not these inquiries assisted the progress of theology, they were to prove most valuable in the study of physics. This was already apparent in the development, especially at Merton College, of a new mathematical physics. The method of inquiry of these Oxford 'calculators' was the presentation and solution of *sophismata*, logical puzzles and paradoxes. A proposition such as 'Socrates is infinitely whiter than Plato begins to be white' was presented and analysed, and assessed for possible truth and falsity. Bizarre as this method might seem, to the modern reader, it was in the course of resolving these *sophismata* that notions of mathematical ratio and proportions were evolved. Moreover, the new notions were given diagrammatic representation by line segments, which proved useful in measuring the interaction of motion, time, and distance. In this way the foundation was laid for the revolution in physics associated with much better known names such as that of Galileo.

One of the foremost of the Merton Calculators was Thomas Bradwardine, who developed a theory of ratios which he used to present a theory of how forces, resistances, and velocities were to be correlated in motion; this quickly superseded Aristotle's laws of motion, not only in Oxford, but also in Paris, where it was adopted by Oresme. Bradwardine was also a representative of another new tendency of the Oxford of the mid-fourteenth century, a revival of Augustinianism. Augustine had, of course, always been an authority to be quoted with reverence; but now scholars began to pay more attention to the historical context of his writing, and to take most interest in his later, anti-Pelagian work. Bradwardine, in his massive *De Causa Dei*, presented an Augustinian treatment of the issues surrounding predestination and freedom. Theological interest at this period had moved away from Trinitarian and Christological issues to such topics as grace and freedom and the limits of omnipotence. If you can resist sin for a single hour, does that mean you can resist it for a lifetime? Can God command that he be hated? What if God were to reveal to someone their future damnation?

JOHN WYCLIF

In the generation after Bradwardine (who died in 1349 shortly after becoming Archbishop of Canterbury) the most significant figure in the Augustinian revival was John **Wyclif**. Between 1360, when Wyclif was Master of Balliol, and 1372, when he took his DD, he produced a substantial corpus of philosophical writing. The most important part of it was a *Summa de Ente*, which included a treatise on universals, designed to vindicate realism against the criticism of the nominalists.

Wyclif's favourite examples of universals are species (such as *dog*) and genera (such as *animal*). A realist can define genus simply as what is predicated of many things which are different in species. A nominalist has to entangle himself in a complicated circumlocution: 'A genus is a term which is predicable, or whose counterpart is predicable, of many terms which signify things which are specifically distinct.' The nominalist cannot say that it is essential to a term to be actually predicated: perhaps there is no one around to do any predicating. He cannot say that any particular term – any particular sound or image or mark on paper – has to be predicable; most signs do not last long enough for multiple predication. (Hence the talk of 'counterparts'.) Having begun his definition by trying to identify genus with a term (that is, a sound or a mark on paper), the nominalist in the end has had to abandon his pretence that species and genus are mere signs and admit that specific difference is something belonging not to the signs but to the things signified. When we talk of species and genus, Wyclif insists, we are not talking of ink blots on paper; if we were we could change a man into a donkey by altering the significance of a term. But of course we cannot alter the species and genus of things by fiat, as we can alter the meanings of words.

Wyclif's argument for his realism is essentially simple. Anyone who believes in objective truth, he maintains, is already committed to belief in real universals. Suppose you are aware that one individual A resembles another individual B. There must be some respect C in which A resembles B. But in 'seeing that A resembles B in respect C' is the same thing as 'seeing the C-ness of A and B'; and that involves conceiving C-ness, a universal common to A and B. So anyone who can make judgements of likeness automatically knows what a universal is.

Wyclif's enthusiasm for real universals takes him far beyond the narrow ground of logic and metaphysics into that of ethics and politics. All the sin that reigns in the world, he claims, is caused by intellectual and emotional error about universals. Nominalism leads to preferring the lesser good to the greater and to valuing one's individual self over the humanity of one's fellow humans. From this early metaphysical germ he was later to develop a full-fledged theory of communism.

In 1374 Wyclif was briefly enrolled in the service of the English king and invited to take part in controversy on that perennial topic, the right of secular rulers to tax the clergy. In his book *On Civil Dominion* he propounded two startling theses: a man in sin has no right to ownership of property; a man who is in a state of grace possesses all the goods of the universe.

The first thesis is proved briskly. You cannot justly possess a thing unless you can use it justly. But every one of the actions of a sinner is unjust; therefore, no sinner can use anything justly or possess it justly.

The second thesis takes rather more proving. A just man is an adoptive son of God, and so is lord of God's realm. When God gives grace, he gives himself and all that is in himself: and in him is the ideal reality of all creatures, to which their actual existence is a mere accessory. But if each Christian in grace is lord of all, it is only on condition that he shares his lordship with all others in a state of grace.

> All the goods of God should be common. This is proved thus. Every man should be in a state of grace; and if he is in a state of grace, he is lord of the world and all it contains. So every man should be lord of the universe. But this is not consistent with there being many men, unless they ought to have everything in common. Therefore all things should be in common.

Despite their radical implications, Wyclif's writings on dominion do not seem to have caused him trouble, initially, with his superiors. The secular authorities used them in support of the disendowment of the clergy, and did not take them seriously in respect of the laity. The ecclesiastical authorities were temporarily hamstrung, because from 1378 the church was in schism, with two rival Popes, one in Rome and one in Avignon, each claiming the supreme authority and each hurling anathemas at the other. Stimulated by this latest scandal, Wyclif launched a series of attacks on the Papacy which went beyond the censures of Ockham and Marsilius.

What led to Wyclif's downfall, however, was not his assault on the Papacy, but his teaching on the Eucharist. When he denounced the Popes and questioned the validity of Papal claims he could find sympathizers even among the higher clergy; when he called for the disendowment of the Church, many laymen and begging friars found his words congenial; but when he renounced the doctrine of transubstantiation, friars, noblemen and bishops all turned against him, and even his own University of Oxford expelled him. He died, at liberty but in disgrace, at Lutterworth in 1384.

The schism in the Church continued for many years: the most valiant attempts to reconcile the rival Papal lines in Rome and Avignon led only to the creation of a third dubious Papacy in Pisa. It was not until 1415 that the Council of Constance secured the election of a Pope who was recognized throughout Christendom. Simultaneously the Council turned to the long delayed business of dealing with Wyclif's heresies (which had by this time spread, with dramatic political effect, to Bohemia). His doctrines had been banned in Oxford a few years previously; now an enormous list of Wycliffite tenets was condemned by the universal Church.

Wyclif was best known in later times as the author, or at least the inspirer, of the first complete translation of the Bible into English. On the basis of this and his writings against transubstantiation and against the Papacy he was hailed as the Morning Star of the Reformation. But he was equally the Evening Star of scholasticism. For centuries his philosophical work remained unread. Protestant writers were repelled by its scholastic subtlety; Catholic writers preferred to concentrate on scholastics who made a more orthodox end. In recent years, the publication of his major treatises has made clear that this last of the Oxford scholastics was a considerable philosophical thinker, worthy to make a third to Scotus and Ockham.

X
RENAISSANCE PHILOSOPHY

THE RENAISSANCE

There is no hard and fast line dividing the Medieval Period from the Renaissance, still less a date which can be assigned when the one ended and the other began. The developments which were characteristic of the Renaissance took place at different speeds in different spheres, and at different times in different regions. The impact of these changes on philosophy was fragmented and scattered, so that its history follows no clear line. Indeed, from many a university history course, one would gain the impression that after Ockham philosophy hibernated during the fifteenth and sixteenth centuries, not to emerge until the time of Descartes when it rose again in totally altered form.

This is an exaggeration. What is true is that the great medieval universities no longer produced philosophers of the calibre of Paris in the thirteenth century and Oxford in the fourteenth. The figures of significance in the fifteenth and sixteenth centuries are scattered around Europe, members of communities of many different kinds, or solitary thinkers enjoying the patronage of a local magnate. None of them achieved, or deserved, the lasting international significance of the greatest medieval philosophers. In the seventeenth century, when philosophers of the first rank are again to be found, we find that none of them achieved their fame as university professors.

Paris and Oxford, in their great days, had both been international universities. The universal use of Latin made academic communication and exchange easy, and those teachers who belonged to the mendicant orders enjoyed access to a continental network of communities. By the end of the fourteenth century this was changing. In all the countries of Europe vernacular literature began to thrive, and though Latin remained the language of academia, it was no longer the vehicle for the most vigorous expression of thought. In England, for instance, Wyclif's colleagues began to write and preach in English, and English was the chosen medium of the best minds among his contemporaries such as Chaucer, Langland, and Gower. The hundred years' war between England and France isolated Oxford from Paris, and each university went its separate way, impoverished.

Political changes went hand in hand with linguistic ones. The central authority of the Papacy was fatally weakened by the Great Schism. The Holy Roman Emperor was effectively Emperor only of Germany and Austria. At the Council of Constance, which re-established a single Papacy, the assembled delegates set a new precedent by voting in individual national groups. By the end of the fifteenth century, after periods of internal turmoil and civil strife, powerful, independent, centralized monarchies established themselves in England, Spain, and France. Northern Italy consisted of a set of vigorous, autonomous city-states, ruled by hereditary oligarchies or plutocratic dynasties. The Popes, re-established now in Rome without competition after the Avignon exile and the long schism, were rulers of a swathe of the central part of Italy. For years to come they devoted much of their energy to the affairs of this statelet. Their authority over the universal Catholic Church did not regain its strength until after half of Europe had been lost to Protestantism at the Reformation.

It was in Italy, and especially in Florence and Rome, that the Renaissance first flowered. The aspect of it which was seen as central at the time was the revival of ancient classical learning. This was 'humanism', not in the sense of a concern with the human race, but in the sense of a devotion to 'humane letters'. This meant, in practice, a preference for pagan Latin authors over Christian Latin authors, and an ambition to read Greek authorities in the original rather than in translation. The latter ambition was fostered by two political events. The battered Greek Empire of Constantinople, under constant pressure from the Ottoman Turks, needed military aid from Western Christians, and in 1439 Pope Eugenius IV and the Byzantine Emperor and Patriarch signed an act of Union between the Eastern and Western Churches at Florence. This Union, like its predecessor of 1270, was short-lived, but the contact with Greek scholarship had lasting effects. When, in 1453, Constantinople fell to the Turks, refugee scholars brought to the West not only their own knowledge of classical Greek, but also precious manuscripts of ancient authors. The Pope of the time, Nicholas V, a bibliophile on a grand scale, left at his death some 1,200 Greek and Latin manuscripts, which made him the effective founder of the Vatican Libary.

FREE-WILL: ROME VS. LOUVAIN

One of the humanists at the court of Nicholas was Lorenzo **Valla**, the author of an influential manual of Latin elegance, which was critical of the style of the Vulgate, the standard Latin translation of the Bible. A skilled philologist, Valla proved in 1441 that the Donation of Constantine, on which for centuries the Popes had based their claims as temporal rulers, was an anachronistic forgery. Despite this, Pope Nicholas sportingly made him Papal Secretary in 1448. Valla had an interest in philosophy, but rated it less important than rhetoric. He wrote provocative works in which he satirized Aquinas and placed Epicurus above Aristotle.

His most interesting philosophical work is a little dialogue on Free-Will, in which he criticizes Boethius' *Consolation of Philosophy*. It starts from a familiar problem. 'If God foresees that Judas will be a traitor, it is impossible for him not to become a traitor, that is, it is necessary for Judas to betray, unless – which should be far from us – we assume God to lack providence.' For most of its length the dialogue follows a set of moves and counter-moves familiar from scholastic discussions; it is like reading Scotus adapted as a high-school text, with the difficult corners cut and the style blessedly simplified. But near the end, two surprising moves are made.

First, two pagan gods appear in this scholastic context. Apollo predicted to the Roman king Tarquin that he would suffer exile and death in punishment for his arrogance and crimes. In response to Tarquin's complaints, Apollo said that he wished his prophecy were happier, but he merely knew the fates, he did not decide them; recriminations, if any were in order, would be better addressed to Jupiter.

> Jupiter, as he created the wolf fierce, the hare timid, the lion brave, the ass stupid, the dog savage, the sheep mild, so he fashioned some men hard of heart, others soft, he generated one given to evil, the other to virtue, and further, he gave a capacity for reform to one and made another incorrigible. To you, indeed he assigned an evil soul with no resource for reform. And so both you, for your inborn character, will do evil, and Jupiter, on account of your actions and their evil effects, will punish sternly.

At first, the introduction of Apollo and Jupiter seems an idle humanist flourish; but the device enables Valla, without blasphemy, to separate out the two attributes of omniscient wisdom and irresistible will which in Christian theology are inseparable in the one God. If freedom is done away with, it is not by divine foreknowledge but by divine will.

Now comes the second surprise. Rather than offer a philosophical reconciliation between divine providence and human will, Valla quotes a passage from the Epistle to the Romans about the predestination of Jacob and the reprobation of Esau. He takes refuge with Paul's words, 'O the depth of the riches both of the wisdom and knowledge of God! how unsearchable are his judgments and his ways past finding out.' Such a move would be entirely expected from an Augustine or a Calvin: but it is not at all what the reader expects to hear from a humanist with a reputation as a champion of the independence and liberty of the human will. The dialogue ends with a denunciation of the philosophers and above all of Aristotle. It is no wonder that in his table talk Luther was to describe Valla as 'the best Italian that I have seen or discovered'.

Valla's dialogue dates from the 1440s. A few years later the subject about which he wrote was the topic of fierce debate in the University of Louvain, one of the new Universities springing up in Northern Europe, founded in 1425.

In 1465 a member of the Arts faculty, **Peter de Rivo**, was asked by his students to discuss the question: was it in St Peter's power not to deny Christ after Christ had said 'Thou wilt deny me thrice'? The question, he said, had to be answered in the affirmative: but it was not possible to do so if we accepted that Christ's words were true at the time he uttered them. We must instead maintain that they were neither true nor false, but had instead a third truth-value. In support of this possibility, Peter de Rivo appealed to the authority of Aristotle.

In the ninth chapter of his *De Interpretatione* Aristotle appears to argue that if every future-tensed proposition about a particular event – such as 'There will be a sea battle tomorrow' – is either true or false, then everything happens necessarily and there is no need to deliberate or to take trouble. On the most common interpretation, Aristotle's argument is meant as a *reductio ad absurdum*: if future-tensed propositions about singular events are already true, then fatalism follows: but fatalism is absurd, therefore, since many future events are not yet determined, statements about such events are not yet true or false, though they later will be so.

Peter de Rivo's introduction of a third truth-value was attacked by his theologian colleague Henry van Zomeren. Scripture, said Henry, is full of future-tensed propositions about singular events, namely prophecies. It was insufficient to say, as Peter did, that these were propositions which were hoped to come true. Unless they were already true, the prophets were liars. Peter responded that to deny the possibility of a third truth-value was to fall into the determinism which the Council of Constance had condemned as one of Wyclif's heresies. Soon the faculties of Arts and theology were at each other's throats.

In Louvain, the senior university authorities seemed to favour Peter de Rivo. Van Zomeren decided to appeal to the Holy See. He had a friend in Rome, Bessarion, one of the Greek bishops attending the Council of Florence, who had remained in Rome and been made a Cardinal. Bessarion, before agreeing to support van Zomeren, asked advice from a Franciscan friend, Francesco della Rovere, who wrote for him a scholastic assessment of the logical issues. Della Rovere concluded against the acceptance of a third truth-value, on the grounds that heretics were condemned for denying future-tensed articles of the Creed. They could only be justly condemned for asserting a falsehood; but if a future-tensed proposition was not true but neutral, then its contradictory would be not false but neutral.

It was not until the twentieth century that the notion of three-valued logic was further explored by logicians, and logical laws such as della Rovere enunciated began to be taken seriously. Two things, however, are interesting in the fifteenth-century context. The first is that it is in scholastic Louvain, not in humanist Italy, that the stress is laid on free-will rather than on divine power. The acceptance of three-valued logic is an extreme assertion of human freedom and open choice: future-statements about human actions are not only not necessarily true, they are not true at all. The second is that the case of Peter de Rivo illustrates perfectly how arbitrary, in philosophy, is the division between the Middle Ages and the Renaissance. For the Francesco della Rovere who contributed to this typically scholastic controversy is no other than the Pope Sixtus IV who, accompanied by a brace of Papal *nipoti*, looks out at us from Melozzo da Forli's fresco of the appointment of the humanist Platina as Vatican Librarian.

The election of Pope Sixtus in 1471 was indeed a disaster for Peter de Rivo. Within three years the bull *Ad Christi Vicarii* condemned five of his propositions as scandalous and wandering from the path of Catholic faith. The two final ones read thus: 'For a proposition about the future to be true, it is not enough that what it says should be the case: it must be unpreventably the case. We must say one of two things: either there is no present and actual truth in the articles of faith about the future, or what they say is something which not even divine power could prevent.' The other three condemned propositions were ones in which Peter tried to find proofs in Scripture for his three-valued system of logic.

RENAISSANCE PLATONISM

Cardinal Bessarion, who had introduced the future Pope into this quarrel, was no enemy to Aristotle: he produced a new Latin translation of the *Metaphyiscs*. But he was himself involved in a different controversy about the relationship of Aristotle to Christian teaching. Greek scholars at the Papal court were now making the works of Plato available in Latin, but some of them were doing so with a degree of reluctance. One, George of Trebizond, published a choleric tract denouncing Plato as inferior in every respect to Aristotle (whom he presented in a highly Christianized version). Bessarion wrote a reply, published in both Greek and Latin, *Against the Calumniator of Plato*, arguing that while neither Plato nor Aristotle agreed at all fully with Christian doctrine, the points of conflict between the two of them were few, and there were at least as many points of agreement between Plato and Christianity as there were between Christianity and Aristotle. His tract was the first solidly based account of Plato's philosophy to appear in the West since classical times.

It was not in Rome, however, but in Florence – where Greek had been taught since 1396 – that Platonism flourished most vigorously. By the time of the Council of Florence the banking family of the Medici had achieved pre-eminence in the city. The head of the family, Cosimo de Medici, appears, with his grandsons Lorenzo and Giuliano, alongside the Greek Emperor and Patriarch in Benozzo Gozzoli's Magi fresco in the chapel of the Medici palace, a resplendent representation of the *dramatis personae* of the Council. It was he who ordered his court philosopher, Marsilio Ficino, to translate the entire works of Plato. This task was completed by 1469, the year in which Lorenzo the Magnificent succeeded as head of the Medici clan. Ficino gathered around him a group of wealthy students of Plato, whom he called his 'Academy'; he revered Plato not only above Aristotle but also, some of his critics complained, above Moses and Christ. Certainly, he believed that a Platonic revival was required if Christianity was to be made palatable to the intelligentsia of his age. He set out his own Neo-Platonic account of the soul, and its origin and destiny, in his work *Platonic Theology* (1474).

The most interesting member of Ficino's group of Florentine Platonists was Giovanni **Pico della Mirandola**. He was learned in Greek and Hebrew, and as a young man was impressed by the magical elements to be found in the Jewish mystical cabbala and the Greek texts of Hermes Trismegistos (a corpus of ancient alchemical and astrological writings, recently translated by Ficino). He was anxious to combine Greek, Hebrew, Muslim, Oriental, and Christian thought into a single Platonic synthesis, and at the age of twenty-four he offered to go to Rome to present and defend his system, spelt out in 900 theses. However, the disputation was forbidden, and many of his theses were condemned, among them one which affirmed 'there is no branch of science which gives us more certainty of Christ's divinity than magic and cabbala'.

Pico was not an indiscriminating admirer of the pseudo-sciences of the ancients. He wrote a work in twelve books against the pretensions of the astrologers: the heavenly bodies could affect men's bodies but not their minds, and no one could know enough about the particular influence of the stars to cast a horoscope. On the other hand, he maintained that alchemy and symbolic rituals could give a legitimate magical power, to be distinguished sharply from the black magic which operated by invoking the power of demons. The consistent drive in Pico's writing was the desire to exalt the powers of human nature: astrology was to be opposed because its determinism limited human freedom, white magic was to be encouraged because it extended human powers and made man the 'prince and master' of creation.

Lorenzo the Magnificent died in 1492; his last years had been saddened by the murder of his brother Giuliano, killed by disaffected Florentines encouraged by Pope Sixtus IV and his nephews. Two years after his death the Medici were expelled and the reforming friar Savonarola made Florence briefly into a puritan republic. Pico became Savonarola's follower, and made a pious end in 1494. One of his final writings was *De Ente et Uno*, presenting a reconciliation of Platonic and Aristotelian metaphysics.

MACHIAVELLI

Savonarola fell from favour and was burnt as a heretic in 1498, but the Florentine republic survived him. One of its officers and diplomats was Niccolò **Machiavelli**, who served in its chancellery from 1498 until 1512, when the Medici returned to power in the city. In the course of his career he became a friend and admirer of Cesare Borgia, the illegitimate son of Pope Alexander VI, a Spaniard who had succeeded to the Pontificate in 1492. Cesare, with the complaisance of his pleasure-loving father, worked by bribery and assassination to appropriate most of central Italy for the Borgia family. It was only the fact, Machiavelli believed, that Cesare was himself at death's door when Alexander died which prevented him from achieving his aim.

Upon the return of the Medici, Machiavelli was suspected of participation in a conspiracy; he was tortured and placed under house arrest. During this time he wrote *The Prince*, the best-known work of Renaissance political philosophy.

This short book is very different from scholastic treatises on politics. It does not attempt to derive, from first principles, the nature of the ideal state and the qualities of a good ruler. Rather, it offers to a would-be ruler, whose ends are a matter of his own choice, recipes for success in their pursuit. Drawing on the recent history of the Italian city-states, as well as on examples from Greek and Roman history, Machiavelli describes how provinces are won and lost and how they can best be kept under control. Cesare Borgia is held up as a model of political skill. 'Reviewing thus all the actions of the Duke, I find nothing to blame: on the contrary, I feel bound, as I have done, to hold him as an example to be imitated.'

The Prince impresses by the cool cynicism of its advice to princes: some people are shocked by its immorality, others gratified by its lack of humbug. The constant theme is that a prince should strive to appear, rather than to be, virtuous. In seeking to become a prince, one must appear to be liberal; but once one is in office, liberality is to be avoided. A prince should desire to be accounted merciful rather than cruel; but in reality it is far safer to be feared than loved. However, while imposing fear on his subjects a prince should try to avoid their hatred.

> For a man may very well be feared and yet not hated, and this will be the case so long as he does not meddle with the property or with the women of his citizens and subjects. And if constrained to put any to death, he should do so only when there is manifest cause or reasonable justification. But, above all, he must abstain from the property of others. For men will sooner forget the death of their father than the loss of their patrimony.

Machiavelli puts the question whether the Prince should keep faith. He answers that he neither can nor ought to keep his word when to keep it is hurtful to him and when the causes which led him to pledge it are removed. No prince, he says, was ever at a loss for plausible reasons to cloak breach of faith. But how will people believe princes who constantly break their word? It is simply a matter of skill in deception, and Pope Alexander VI is singled out for praise in this regard. 'No man ever had a more effective manner of asseverating, or made promises with more solemn protestations, or observed them less. And yet, because he understood this side of human nature, his frauds always succeeded.'

Summing up, then, a prince should speak and bear himself so that to see and hear him, one would think him the embodiment of mercy, good faith, integrity, humanity, and religion. But in order to preserve his princedom he will frequently have to break all rules and act in opposition to good faith, charity, humanity, and religion.

The recent monarch whom Machiavelli singles out as 'the foremost King in Christendom' is Ferdinand of Aragon. This king's achievements had indeed been formidable. With his wife Isabella of Castile he had united the kingdoms of Spain, and established peace after years of civil war. He had ended the Moorish kingdom of Granada, and encouraged Columbus in his acquisition of Spanish colonies in America. He had driven out the Jews as well as the Moors from Spain. From Pope Sixtus IV he had obtained the establishment of an independent Spanish Inquisition, and from Alexander VI a bull dividing the New World between Portugal and Spain, with Spain obtaining the lion's share. The quality which Machiavelli singles out for praise is Ferdinand's 'pious cruelty'.

Machiavelli devotes one chapter of *The Prince* to Ecclesiastical Princedoms. 'These Princes alone,' he says, 'have territories which they do not defend, and subjects whom they do not govern; yet their territories are not taken from them through not being defended, nor are their subjects concerned at not being governed, or led to think of throwing off their allegiance, nor is it in their power to do so. Accordingly these Princedoms alone are secure and happy.'

This state of things, which Machiavelli attributes to 'the venerable ordinances of religion', was hardly what obtained during the pontificate of Julius II, the warlike Pope who succeeded Alexander VI and put an end to the hopes of Cesare Borgia. As Machiavelli himself described it, 'He undertook the conquest of Bologna, the overthrow of the Venetians, and the expulsion of the French from Italy; in all which enterprises he succeeded'.

Julius II, a della Rovere nephew of Sixtus IV, was much more of a prince than a pastor. But he did not entirely fulfil Machiavelli's maxim that a prince should have no care or thought but for war. He was a great patron of artists, and the rooms which Raphael decorated for him in the Vatican contain some of the most loving representations of philosophers and philosophical topics in the history of art. He employed Michelangelo to decorate the ceiling of his uncle's Sistine Chapel, and commissioned Bramante to build a new church of St Peter, taking the hammer himself to commence the destruction of the old basilica. He even summoned a General Council at the Lateran in 1512, with a view to the emendation of a Church by now universally agreed to be in great need of reform.

Shortly after the summoning of the Council, Julius died and was succeeded by the first Medici Pope, the son of Lorenzo the Magnificent, who took the name Leo X. A genial hedonist, Leo showed little enthusiasm for reform, and the principal achievement of the council was to define the immortality of the individual soul, in opposition to a group of Paduan Aristotelians who had denied the doctrine in a reaction to the revival of Platonism.

The most important of these Paduans was Pietro **Pomponazzi**, whose book *On the Immortality of the Soul* had appeared just after the beginning of the Council. The theme of this was that if one took seriously Aristotle's identification of the soul with the form of the body it was impossible to believe that it could survive death. All human knowledge arises from the senses, and all human thought demands corporeal images. Self-consciousness is not a human privilege; it is shared by brute beasts, who love themselves and their kind. Human self-consciousness, no less than animal, is dependent on the union of soul and body. The immortality of the soul cannot be proved by appealing to the necessity for another life to provide sanctions for good or bad conduct; in the present life, virtue is its own reward, and vice its own punishment, and if these intrinsic motives are not enough, they are backed up by the sanction of the criminal law.

More's Utopia

Pomponazzi's book, swiftly condemned, did not have a great influence; but in the same year there appeared a much more popular work: *Utopia*. This was written by **Thomas More**, a London barrister in his thirties who had just entered the royal service under King Henry VIII. More was a keen humanist, anxious to promote the study of Greek and Latin literature in England, and a close friend of Desiderius Erasmus, the great Dutch scholar who was just then working on a scholarly edition of the Greek New Testament. *Utopia*, written in Latin, was a lively description of a fictional commonwealth, addressed to an audience which was agog for news of overseas discoveries.

Utopia ('Nowhereland') is an island of fifty-four cities of 6,000 households apiece, each with its own agricultural hinterland, farmed by the city-dwellers who are sent by rota to spend two-year stints in the country. Within the city, the citizens swap houses by lot every tenth year; there is no private property and nothing is ever locked up. Every citizen, in addition to farming, learns a craft, and everyone must work, but the working day is only six hours. There are no drones, as in Europe, so there are many hands to make the work light, and much leisure time for cultural activity. Only very few people are exempted from manual work, either as scholars, priests, or members of the tiers of elected magistracies which rule the community.

In Utopia, unlike Plato's republic, the primary unit of society is the family household. Women, on marriage, move to their husband's house, but males normally remain in the house where they were born under the rule of the oldest parent as long as he is fit to govern it. No household may include less than ten or more than sixteen adults; any excess members are transferred to other houses which have fallen below quota. If the number of households in a city surpasses the limit, and no other city has room for more, colonies are planted in unoccupied land overseas, and if the natives there resist the settlement, the Utopians will establish it by force of arms.

Internal travel in Utopia is regulated by passport; but once authorized, travellers are welcomed in other cities just as if they were at home. But no one, wherever he may be, is to be fed without doing his daily stint of work. The Utopians make no use of money, and employ gold and silver only to make chamberpots and criminals' fetters; diamonds and pearls are given to children to keep with their rattles and dolls. The Utopians cannot understand how other nations prize courtly honours, or enjoy gaming with dice, or delight in hunting animals.

The Utopians are no ascetics, and they regard bodily mortification for its own sake as something perverse; but they honour those who live selfless lives embracing tasks which others reject as loathsome, such as road-making or sick-nursing. Some of these people practise celibacy and vegetarianism; others eat flesh and live normal family lives. The Utopians regard the former as holier, and the latter as wiser.

Men marry at twenty-two and women at eighteen; premarital sex is forbidden, but bridegroom and bride must thoroughly inspect each other naked before the wedding. The Utopians are monogamous, and in principle marriage is lifelong; however, adultery may break a marriage, and in that case the innocent, but not the adulterous, spouse is allowed to remarry. Adultery is severely punished, and repeated adultery carries the death penalty. The Utopians believe that if promiscuity were allowed, few would be willing to accept the burdens of monogamous matrimony.

The Utopians do not regard war as glorious, but they are not pacifists either. Men and women receive military training, and the nation will go to war to repel invaders or to liberate peoples oppressed by tyranny. Rather than engage in pitched battle, they prefer to win a war by having the enemy rulers assassinated; and if battles overseas cannot be avoided, they employ foreign mercenaries. In wars of defence, husbands and wives stand in the battle line or man the ramparts side by side. 'It is a great reproach and dishonesty for the husband to come home without his wife, or the wife without her husband.'

Most Utopians worship a single invisible supreme being, 'the father of all'; there are married priests of both sexes, men and women of extraordinary holiness 'and therefore very few'. Utopians do not impose their religious beliefs on others; tolerance is the rule, and any harassment in proselytizing, such as Christian hell-fire preaching, is punished with banishment. All Utopians, however, believe in immortality and a blissful afterlife; the dead, they think, revisit their friends as invisible protectors. Suicide on private initiative is not permitted, but those who are incurably and painfully sick may be counselled by the priests and magistrates to take their own lives. The manner of meeting one's death is of the highest moment; those who die reluctantly are gloomily buried, those who die cheerfully are cremated with songs of joy.

Like Plato's republic, Utopia contains attractive and repellent features, and alternates devices that seem practicable with others that seem fantastic. Like Plato before him, More uses the depiction of an imaginary society as a vehicle for theories of political philosophy and criticism of contemporary social institutions. Again like Plato, More often leaves his readers to guess how far the arrangements he describes are serious political proposals and how far they merely present a mocking mirror to the distortions of real-life societies.

THE REFORMATION

The society in which More had grown up was about to be changed dramatically, and in his opinion, greatly for the worse. In 1517 a professor of theology at Wittenberg threw down a challenge to the Pope's pretensions that was to lead half Europe to reject Papal authority. Martin **Luther**, an Augustinian monk of the monastery of Erfurt, had made a study of St Paul's Epistle to the Romans which led him to question fundamentally the ethos of Renaissance Catholicism. The occasion of his public protest was the proclamation of an indulgence in return for contributions to the building of the great new church of St Peter's in Rome. The offer of an indulgence – that is, of remission of punishment due to sin – was a normal part of Catholic practice; but this particular indulgence was promoted in such an irregular and catchpenny manner as to be a scandal even by the lax standards of the period.

Luther's attack on Catholic practices soon went much further than indulgences. By 1520 he had questioned the status of four of the Church's seven sacraments, arguing that only baptism, the eucharist, and penance had Gospel sanction. In his book *The Liberty of the Christian Man* he stated his cardinal doctrine that the one thing needful for the justification of the sinner is faith, or trust in the merits of Christ; without this faith nothing avails, with it everything is possible. Pope Leo X condemned his teaching in the bull *Exsurge Domine* in 1520. Luther, when it reached him, burnt the bull before a great crowd; he was excommunicated in 1521. King Henry VIII, with some help from More and his friends, published *An Assertion of the Seven Sacraments* in confutation of Lutheran doctrine. Pope Leo, in gratitude, gave him the title 'Defender of the Faith'.

Luther lived in Saxony, part of the Holy Roman Empire, which was now ruled by the Austrian Habsburg Emperor Charles V. Charles was king also of the Spanish dominions which he had inherited from his grandparents Ferdinand and Isabella, and so was ruler of much of Europe and parts of America. He summoned Luther to a meeting of the Imperial council at Worms. The reformer refused to recant any of his teaching, and was sentenced to banishment from the Empire. But the Duke of Saxony offered him asylum, under the guise of house arrest in the Wartburg.

During the next few years, Luther wrote furiously. He tanslated the Bible into clear and vigorous German, a model for future translators in other languages. He dashed off a contemptuous and vituperative reply to Henry VIII; More, on the king's behalf, wrote a no less scurrilous riposte. Luther's teaching that man of himself is not free to choose between good and evil had been attacked by Erasmus in a pamphlet *On Free Will*, resembling in some ways Valla's dialogue. Erasmus was a better humanist than Valla, but he was not his equal as a philosopher, and when Luther responded in *On the Bondage of the Will* it was he who had the better of the argument. Not that Luther was, or wished to be, a philosopher. He denounced Aristotle, and in particular his *Ethics*, 'the vilest enemy of grace'.

The movement which Luther had begun did not long remain under his control. Independent groups of reformers, especially in France and Switzerland, under Jean Calvin and Ulrich Zwingli, shared his opposition to the Pope but differed from him on the nature of the eucharist and the distribution of grace. The Peasants' Revolt of 1524 showed that insubordination to Church hierarchies could be followed by insurrection against State institutions. A concordat between the Protestant sects was engineered at Augsburg by Luther's eirenic lieutenant Melanchthon in 1530.

While Protestantism grew, the Catholic monarchs quarrelled, and the Popes dithered. In 1523 Leo X was succeeded, after a brief intervening pontificate, by his Medici cousin Clement VII. The Church's opposition to usury was fast becoming a dead letter when the foremost bankers of Europe could occupy the Papacy for two generations in succession. The Emperor Charles enrolled Henry VIII in a league against Francis I of France. Pope Clement could not make up his mind whether to support Charles or Francis; his tergiversation irritated Charles and in 1527 the Holy City was sacked by the Lutheran troops of the Catholic Emperor. Clement was asked by Henry VIII to annul his long-standing marriage with Queen Catherine of Aragon, Charles's aunt; his reluctance to do so led Henry to break with the Holy See in 1533.

Thomas More, unwilling to assist King Henry with his divorce, fell from royal favour, and was beheaded, a martyr for the Papal supremacy, in 1535. He spent much of the last years of his life in controversy with Lutherans, and especially with William Tyndale, who had adopted many of Luther's doctrines and, following Luther's example, had in 1526 produced a superb vernacular New Testament, a template for all future English versions.

The controversy between More and the Lutherans illustrates vividly the negative side of humanist education. The subjects of their quarrel had been matters of controversy among scholastics for centuries; the scholastic debates, if sometimes arid, had commonly been sober and courteous. In humanist education the study of formal patterns of argument had now been replaced by the systematic quest for rhetorical effect. Admiration for Cicero as a model of style meant that humanist controversialists treated their opponents like barristers hectoring a hostile witness. Thomas More, writing against Luther, is far removed from Thomas Aquinas, always anxious to put the best possible interpretation on the position of those he disagrees with. Luther shared More's disdain for recent scholasticism, and More's enthusiasm for elaborate and rhetorical abuse on the classical model. The pugnacious conventions of humanist debate were a factor which led to the hardening of positions on either side of the Reformation divide.

A Catholic counter-reformation began under the pontificate of Paul III (1534–49). Himself a survivor from the riotous days of the Borgias, he now promoted to the Cardinalate a group of austere ascetics who would transform the Papal court. In 1540 he approved the new religious order of the Jesuits, founded by the ex-soldier Ignatius Loyola on principles of unquestioning obedience and loyalty to the Papacy. In 1545 Pope Paul convened the Council of Trent, which continued, with interruptions, until 1563. The Council reformed Church discipline, and established seminaries for the training of priests. It condemned the Lutheran doctrine of justification by faith alone, and proclaimed that human free-will had not been extinguished by Adam's fall. It reaffirmed the doctrine of transubstantiation and the traditional seven sacraments, and emphasized the authority of ecclesiastical tradition alongside Scripture.

By the time the Council had finished its work, Calvin was dying and Luther was dead. So too was Charles V who, after an inconclusive war against the Protestant princes, had accepted the partition of Germany between Lutherans and Catholics at the peace of Augsburg (1555). England had lurched from schismatic Catholicism under Henry VIII, to Calvinism under his son Edward VI, to counter-reformation Catholicism under his elder daughter Mary and her husband Philip II of Spain, and finally to an Anglican compromise under his younger daughter Elizabeth I.

The work of the Counter-Reformation reached its apogee under Pope Pius V, the most devout and one of the most intransigent of sixteenth-century Popes. It was in his reign that Turkish expansion into the Mediterranean was halted at the naval battle of Lepanto. He strengthened Papal censorship and introduced an Index of books which Catholics were forbidden to read or possess. He built a grand palace for the Holy Office or Inquisition, the Church's official thought police. He excommunicated Queen Elizabeth and released her subjects from obedience to her: the one serious attempt to put this sentence into effect came to grief when Philip II's Spanish Armada was defeated and wrecked in 1588.

The sixteenth century was a barren one for philosophy. While in the Middle Ages many of the best minds had been devoted to metaphysics, the Renaissance turned men's attention to literature, and the Reformation and Counter-Reformation turned it to sectarian controversy. The division of Christendom was, from a religious point of view, an unnecessary tragedy. The theological issues which separated Luther and Calvin from their Catholic opponents had been debated many times in the Middle Ages without leading to sectarian warfare. Few twentieth-century Catholics and Protestants, if not professionally trained in theology, are aware of the real nature of the differences between the contrasting theories of the eucharist, of grace, and of predestination which in the sixteenth century led to anathemas and bloodshed. It comes as a surprise to most Catholics, for instance, to discover that they are bound to believe that no one reaches heaven who is not predestined; and few Protestants can explain the exact difference between Catholic transubstantiation and Lutheran real presence. Professional theologians in this century have shown that if the doctrinal issues had been handled in the Reformation era with the good will and the patient subtlety which characterized the best scholastics there would have been no difficulty in finding formulas of reconciliation between positions which instead hardened into intransigence.

Questions of authority, of course, are easier to understand and more difficult to arbitrate than questions of doctrine. But the unity of Christendom could have been maintained under a constitutional Papacy subject to general councils, such as Ockham had suggested, such as had been the practice in the fifteenth century, and such as even Thomas More, for the greater part of his life, believed to be the divine design for the Church.

But of course it was not theology, much less philosophy, that was the predominant force in the break-up of Europe's religious unity: rather, it was the ambition and avarice of kings and popes, and the growth of nationalist feeling resentful of international control. But the impact of Reformation and Counter-Reformation on philosophy was considerable in several ways.

The first and immediate effect was a crackdown on freedom of thought. To be sure, heresy had been persecuted in the Middle Ages, and many poor people had suffered grievously for following unorthodox preachers who were seen as a threat to established society. However, the authorities had been comparatively lenient in dealing with the hardy innovations of university teachers: Wyclif retained his Oxford post for years after propounding doctrines which in the sixteenth century would have brought him to the prisons of the Inquisition. The curriculum of medieval universities, though tied to set texts, allowed the commentator a much greater liberty of speculation than the rigid prescriptions for courses in post-Tridentine seminaries. The invention of printing permitted ideas to be disseminated much more widely than hitherto; but the Index of prohibited books set much stricter limits on which ideas could be disseminated.

The extent of thought control was particularly noticeable in Catholic countries; but it was quite perceptible in many Protestant jurisdictions, even in comparatively liberal Holland. The fact that there was no longer one single standard of orthodoxy partially compensated for the increase in local enforcement: when philosophers on the different sides of the religious divisions could read each others' works they became aware of the limits of religious consensus. But the benefits of this would only be felt in the long term.

POST-REFORMATION PHILOSOPHY

The Reformation disputes also affected the areas on which philosophers concentrated. We can illustrate this in three instances: formal logic, scepticism, and free-will.

Formal logic had progressed steadily in the Middle Ages, building on the foundations laid by Aristotle and the Stoics. This study continued in sixteenth-century universities, but humanist scholars were impatient with it, regarding its terminology as barbarous and its complexities as pettifogging. The Parisian Peter **Ramus** (1515–72), who according to legend defended for his Master's degree the thesis that everything Aristotle had taught was false, published a new model logic textbook in French which he claimed represented the natural movement of thought. Modern historians of logic can find little of value in his book, and the best of it seems to be merely a truncated Aristotle. However, Ramus, having turned Protestant in 1561, was killed in the terrible Paris massacre of heretics on St Bartholomew's day, and his status as a martyr gave his writings a prestige they could never have earned on their own merits. Their popularity impoverished the study of logic for centuries to come and it was only in the twentieth century that many of the medieval developments in logic were independently discovered by mathematical logicians.

When speculative philosophy had been brought into disrepute by the Renaissance, and dogmatic theology had been turned by the Reformation into a battlefield of contradictions, contemplative minds began to feel the attractions of scepticism. This was greatly reinforced when the works of the ancient sceptic, Sextus Empiricus, became available in mid-century. The essayist Michel de **Montaigne**, in his *Apology for Raimond Sebond*, presented in superb French prose the ancient arguments against the possibility of genuine knowledge: the deceptiveness of the senses, the difficulty of distinguishing between dreams and waking life, the delusions produced by drunkenness or disease, the variety of human judgements, the contradictions between philosophical systems.

Montaigne had a poor estimate of the humanistic and scientific achievements of his age, and questioned most of his contemporaries' most cherished beliefs. He contrasted civilized Europeans, to their disadvantage, with the simplicity and nobility of the inhabitants of the New World. He was not sceptical of Christianity: on the contrary, he maintained that of all the ancient philosophies, scepticism was the one most congenial to the Christian religion, which, as St Paul said, had been concealed from the wise and revealed to the ignorant. Grace and faith, not philosophy, showed us the only way to truth.

The foundation of the Society of Jesus gave rise to a new regiment of Catholic philosophers to fight beside the Dominicans and Franciscans in the battle against heresy. In terms of sheer intellectual power, the Jesuit Francisco **Suarez** has a strong claim to be the most formidable philosopher of the century. But in the history of philosophy he does not have a place commensurate to his gifts, because most of his work is a restatement and a refinement of medieval themes, rather than an exploration of new territory. His writings provide a reminder that in spite of all the criticism and competition, Aristotelianism continued to thrive in many quarters throughout the sixteenth century.

The most purely philosophical issue dividing the Catholic and Protestant camps was human free-will, the reality of which had been proclaimed at the Council of Trent in opposition to Luther's determinism. The matter was taken up with enthusiasm by Suarez and his Jesuit colleague Luis de Molina. They offered a formulation of free agency which was to become classic: 'That agent is called free which in the presence of all necessary conditions for action can act and refrain from action or can do one thing while being able to do its opposite.' Freedom, thus defined in terms of the ability for alternative action, became known as 'liberty of indifference'.

Molina's most original contribution to philosophy is his account of divine foreknowledge. Scotus had said that God knew what human beings would do through knowing his own divine decrees; this too was Luther's account. This theory, Molina believed, is incompatible with belief in human freedom; what really happens is something quite different. We have to go back in thought beyond God's decree to create, when the world is not yet actual and many different worlds are possible. God knows what any possible creature would freely do in any possible circumstances: by knowing this, and by knowing which creatures he intends to create and in which circumstances he intends to place them, God knows what actual creatures will in fact do.

Molina said that God had three different kinds of knowledge. There is, first, his natural knowledge, by which he knows his own nature and all the things which are possible to him either by his own action or by the action of free possible creatures. Then there is God's free knowledge: his knowledge of what will actually happen after the free divine decision has been taken to create certain free creatures and to place them in certain circumstances. Between the two there is God's 'middle knowledge': this is his knowledge of what any possible creature would do in any possible world. Middle knowledge, Molina claims, is the key to reconciling divine foreknowledge and human freedom. Because middle knowledge is based on creatures' hypothetical decisions, human autonomy is upheld; because middle knowledge is prior to God's decision to create, his omniscience about the actual world is preserved.

Molina's ingenious solution was not popular among his own co-religionists. Dominicans, no less than Lutherans and Calvinists, saw it as excessively exalting human freedom and derogating from divine power. The dispute on this issue between Jesuits and Dominicans became so fierce that in 1605 Pope Clement VIII had to issue a decree imposing silence on both sides. Ironically, a reformed divine of Leiden, Arminius, began to defend doctrines very similar to Molina's, and it fell to the Synod of Dort in 1619 to declare that they were not tenable by orthodox Calvinists.

BRUNO AND GALILEO

The great intellectual advance of the sixteenth century was not in philosophy itself, but in the separation that was achieved between the philosophy of nature and the science of physics. Both disciplines endeavour to understand the same subject matter; but scientific physics proceeds by observation and hypothesis, not by *a priori* speculation or conceptual analysis. As scientific physics progresses, philosophy in this area retains only a diminished role as the philosophy of science itself.

The contrast between physics and natural philosophy is illustrated vividly by two thinkers active at the end of the century: Giordano Bruno and Galileo Galilei. Both men were greatly influenced by the writings of Nicholas Copernicus (1473–1543) who, in a book dedicated to Pope Paul III, had proposed the hypothesis that the earth rotates round the sun and that the sun, not the earth, is the centre of the planetary system. But there were great differences between the ways in which each developed Copernicus' revolutionary conception.

Bruno (1548–1600), an Italian wandering scholar, once a Dominican, starts from a Neo-Platonist position. The phenomena we see in the world are the effects of a world-soul which animates nature and makes it into a single organism. In Bruno's thought God sometimes seems distant and unknowable; at other times God seems to be totally identified with the world of nature. In Bruno's august but not wholly intelligible expression, God is the Nature which causes Nature (*natura naturans*) which manifests itself in the Nature which is caused by Nature (*natura naturata*).

The world of nature, for Bruno, is infinite, with no edge, surface, or limit. In this boundless space there are many solar systems; our sun is just one star among others, and no one star can be called the centre of the universe, since all position is relative. Our earth enjoys no unique privilege; for all we know intelligent life is present elsewhere in the universe. Solar systems rise, glow, and perish, pulsating moments in the life of the single organism whose soul is the world-soul. The universe is built up of atoms, physical and spiritual; each human being is a conscious, immortal, atom, mirroring in itself the entire universe.

Bruno's opinions, unsurprisingly, did not find favour with the Church. He was passed from one Inquisition to another, and, having refused to recant, was burnt in Rome in 1600. His theories anticipate, in an exciting way, scientific discoveries of later ages and speculations which remain popular with scientists at the present day. But that is what they are, speculations; so far as we know he devoted no time to observation or experiment.

Matters are very different when we turn to Bruno's younger contemporary, **Galileo** Galilei (1564–1642), long-time professor at Padua University and court mathematician to the Medici Grand Duke of Tuscany. Galileo was, indeed, a distinguished philosopher of science, with a firmer grasp than anyone previously of the importance of mathematics in physics. The book of the universe, he wrote, cannot be read until we learn the letters and language in which it is written. 'It is written in the language of mathematics, and its letters are triangles, circles, and other geometrical figures, without which it is impossible to understand a single word.' But it was not his philosophy but his experimental work which set Galileo apart from and above his predecessors.

Using the newly discovered telescope, Galileo was able to observe the mountains of the moon and the spots on the sun; this showed that the heavenly bodies were made not out of Aristotle's quintessence, but of the same sort of material as our earth. His observations of the phases of Venus provided fresh evidence in favour of Copernicus' heliocentric hypothesis. By experiments on the inclined plane and with freely falling bodies, Galileo sought to establish the law of inertia and to show that falling bodies accelerate uniformly over time. In a brief period he was able to refute experimentally many of the aspects of Aristotle's physics which had been criticized, but not experimentally disproved, by philosophers since the time of John Philoponus.

Galileo's work naturally made him unpopular with academics who had a vested interest in Aristotelianism; but what got him into trouble with the Inquisition were his comments on the relationship between the heliocentric hypothesis and Biblical texts describing the sun as moving through the sky. Galileo claimed that in these passages the sacred author was simply adopting a popular manner of speaking, which must give way to scientific certainty. The Jesuit Cardinal Bellarmine retorted that heliocentrism, though supported by a handful of confirmatory observations, was only a hypothesis, not yet established with certainty. In this exchange there is an agreeable irony, with the physicist showing himself the better biblical critic, and the Cardinal showing himself the better philosopher of science. But neither party emerged with any glory; Galileo recanted his theories, and the Inquisitors sentenced him to indefinite imprisonment. Despite Pope Urban VIII's commutation of the sentence, the episode has stood ever since as a prime example of the baneful effect of the Counter-Reformation on scientific research.

FRANCIS BACON

The most distinguished philosopher of science during the Renaissance period was not himself a researcher. The essayist Francis Bacon (1561–1626) was almost the same age as Galileo; educated at Trinity College, Cambridge, and Gray's Inn, he followed a career at the Bar and in the House of Commons. In 1591 he became a client of Queen Elizabeth's favourite, the Earl of Essex; then, when Essex proved treasonable, he took a leading part in his prosecution. He was knighted by James I on his accession in 1603, and became Solicitor-General. In 1605 he wrote the first of his major philosophical writings, *The Advancement of Learning*, an elaborate classification of all possible sciences. He was soon promoted to be Attorney-General and finally in 1618 Lord Chancellor, as Lord Verulam. In 1620 his second major work, the *Novum Organum*, was published; it was intended as part of an enormous project, the *Instauratio Magna*, which was to take all knowledge for its province. In 1621, subjected to a Parliamentary inquiry, he pleaded guilty to charges of bribery, and was exiled from court and temporarily imprisoned. He died at Highgate in 1626, from a cold caught, so it was said, while stuffing a hen with snow in order to observe the effect of cold on the preservation of meat.

Bacon divided the mind into three faculties: memory, imagination, and reason. To each of these there corresponds a field of learning: history, poesy, and philosophy. History includes not only 'civil history', to which Bacon contributed a narrative of the reign of Henry VII, but also 'natural history', which falls into three parts, one treating of the normal course of nature, a second of extraordinary marvels, and a third of technology. Bacon himself contributed to natural history two compilations of research data, a History of the Winds, and a History of Life and Death. Poesy he describes, after the fashion of Aristotle's *Poetics*, as 'feigned history': it includes prose fiction as well as poetry in verse. Poesy may be narrative or dramatic or 'parabolical', this last kind being illustrated by Aesop's fables. Finally we come to philosophy, whose divisions and classifications form the main topic of *The Advancement of Learning*.

Philosophy falls into three divisions. The first is divine philosophy, which others called natural theology, which Bacon treats perfunctorily. The other two are natural philosophy, and human philosophy, which are defined at much greater length. These three are the branches of a tree of which the trunk is first philosophy, the discipline which others (but not Bacon) called metaphysics. Metaphysics, for Bacon himself, is one part of speculative natural philosophy, the part which deals with formal and final causes, while the other part, physics, deals with efficient and material causes. Besides speculative natural philosophy, there is operative natural philosophy, roughly speaking technology, which is further divided into mechanics and magic; mechanics is the application to practice of physics, magic is the application to practice of metaphysics.

Both the traditional Aristotelian terminology of the four causes and the provocative word 'magic' are misleading. Bacon's natural magic, he tells us, is to be sharply distinguished from the 'credulous and superstitious conceits' of alchemy and astrology. Moreover, though it is the practical application of metaphysics, natural magic makes no real use of final causes, and when Bacon speaks of 'forms' he tells us that he means laws: the form of heat or the form of light is the same thing as the law of heat or the law of light.

> To enquire the Form of a lion, of an oak, of gold, nay of water, of air, is a vain pursuit: but to enquire the Forms of sense, of voluntary motion, of vegetation, of colours, of gravity and levity, of density, of tenuity, of heat of cold, and all other natures and qualities, which like an alphabet are not many, and which the essences (upheld by matter) of all creatures do consist; to enquire I say the true forms of these, is that part of Metaphysics which we now define.

The forms which are the alphabet of Bacon's world are obscure characters in comparison with the mathematical shapes and symbols of Galileo's world alphabet. It is a systematic weakness of Bacon's philosophy of science that he underestimates mathematics: in his classification it appears as a mere appendix to natural philosophy.

The other great division of philosophy, human philosophy, corresponds to anatomy, psychology, and what would now be called the social sciences. Logic and ethics appear as branches of psychology, in a reckless confusion between normative disciplines and empirical sciences. Political theory is a part of civil philosophy, that branch of philosophy which is concerned with the benefits which humans derive from living in society.

In *The Advancement of Learning* Bacon observes that current logic is deficient because it lacks a theory of scientific discovery.

> Like as the West-Indies had never been discovered if the use of the mariner's needle had not been first discovered, though the one be vast regions and the other a small motion; so it cannot be found strange if sciences be no further discovered if the art itself of invention and discovery hath been passed over.

Bacon sought to remedy this lack with his *Novum Organum*, designed, as its title indicated, to supersede Aristotelian logic, and to replace it with something different and more useful.

Utility, indeed, is for Bacon the chief goal of science. The purpose of investigation is to extend the power of the human race over nature. Syllogisms will not produce new concepts or extend knowledge. What we need is *induction* – not hasty generalization from inadequate sampling of nature, but a carefully schematized procedure, mounting gradually from particular instances to axioms of gradually increasing generality.

In order to introduce discipline into the art of scientific generalization we must first make ourselves aware of the factors that can introduce bias into our observations. These are what Bacon calls 'the idols': the idols of the tribe, the idols of the den, the idols of the market-place, and the idols of the theatre. The idols of the tribe are the temptations common to all humans: the tendency to judge things by surface appearances and to acquiesce in received opinions. The idols of the den are peculiarities of particular types of character: some people, for instance, are innately too conservative, others are too attracted by novelties. The idols of the market-place are snares concealed in the language we use, which contains meaningless, ambiguous, and ill-defined words. The idols of the theatre are false systems of philosophy, whether 'sophistical' like Aristotle's, or excessively 'empirical' like that of William Gilbert (in fact a perfectly reputable scientist, discoverer of the magnetic pole), or 'superstitious' like the Neo-Platonists who do not distinguish sufficiently between theology and philosophy.

Bacon's positive proposals are more helpful, if less vivid, than his denunciations of others. Induction is the search for the hidden forms of things, and it must begin with precise and regular record of observations. If, for instance, we wish to discover the form of heat, we must make a table of cases in which heat is present (e.g. the rays of the sun, and the sparks of a flint), cases in which it is absent (e.g. the rays of the moon and the stars), and cases in which it is present in different degrees (e.g. in animals at different times and in different conditions). When we compare the tables we will discover what is always present when heat is present, what is always absent when it is absent, and what varies in proportion to its presence. This method can be generalized.

Macaulay, otherwise a great admirer of Bacon's philosophy, mocked his inductive method as being the merest common sense. He imagines a man whose stomach is out of order reasoning in the following way. 'I ate minced pies on Monday and Wednesday, and I was kept awake by indigestion all night. I did not eat any on Tuesday and Friday, and I was quite well. I ate very sparingly of them on Sunday, and was very slightly indisposed in the evening. But on Christmas-day I almost dined on them, and was so ill that I was in great danger. It cannot have been the brandy which I took with them. For I have drunk brandy daily for years without being the worse for it.' The invalid, in strict accord with Baconian principles, then concludes that mince pies do not agree with him.

What Macaulay failed to realize was that the most important step in Bacon's method is the use of his tables to exclude various candidates for being identical with the form which is sought. Negative instances are more important, in the process of establishing laws, than positive ones. Bacon, it has been said, was the first person to point out that laws of nature cannot be conclusively verified, but can be conclusively falsified.

In an age which placed excessive emphasis on the power of individual genius, Bacon was one of the first to realize that natural science could make progress only by co-operative effort on a gigantic scale. In the *New Atlantis*, which he left unfinished at his death, he pictures an island containing an institute known as Solomon's House, which turns out to be a research establishment, working on projects for – among other things – telephones, submarines, and aeroplanes. The president of the institute describes its purpose thus:

> The End of our Foundation is the knowledge of Causes, and secret motions of things, and the enlarging of the bound of Human Empire, to the effecting of all things possible.

This sums up Bacon's view of the nature and purpose of science: it was a vision which was accepted by those of his compatriots who, thirty-five years later, founded the Royal Society.

XI
THE AGE OF DESCARTES

The Wars of Religion

In the first half of the seventeenth century Europe worked out, by political and military means, the consequences of the religious reformation. It was the age of the wars of religion. In France, three decades of civil war between Catholic and Calvinist came to an end in 1598 when the Calvinist leader, Henri de Navarre, having converted to Rome and succeeded to the throne as Henri IV, established by the Edict of Nantes toleration for Calvinists within a Catholic state. In 1618 the Holy Roman Emperor Ferdinand II formed a Catholic League to fight the German Protestant princes; it defeated the Protestant elector Frederick V at the battle of the White Mountain near Prague, and reimposed Catholicism in Bohemia. But this Catholic victory was followed by a succesion of Protestant victories won by the Swedish king, Gustavus Adolphus. After his death the Thirty Years War was brought to an end in 1648 by the Peace of Westphalia, which established co-existence in the Empire between the two religions.

In Britain, after the defeat of the Spanish Armada in 1588, and the enthrone-ment in England in 1603 of King James I from Calvinist Scotland, there was little serious chance of England returning to Catholicism, despite the fantasies of the Gunpowder Plotters in 1605. But the English Civil War, which led to the execu-tion of James's son Charles I in 1649, was, in the minds of many participants, a conflict not only between King and Parliament but also between the Church of England and other Protestant sects. But after 1650 it could no longer be said that Europe was divided into two hostile military camps, one Catholic and one Prot-estant. Indeed, that had already ceased to be true when, in the later stages of the Thirty Years War, the France of Louis XIII, under Cardinal Richelieu, had taken sides with the Protestant king of Sweden against the Austrian Catholic Emperor.

During the wars of religion there appeared the first full-length philosophical treatment of the ethics of war, *On the Rights and Wrongs of War and Peace* by Hugo **Grotius**, published in 1625. Though there was no longer any international authority universally recognized throughout Europe, Grotius maintained that there was a common law among nations, valid alike in peace and war. War did not terminate, or suspend, moral relationships between the warring parties; war could be justly undertaken, but only if certain moral principles were scrupulously observed.

Though there were medieval precedents, Grotius can claim to be the principal author of the theory of the just war. According to this theory, a war may only be waged in order to right a specific wrong: that is what gives the right to go to war, the *ius ad bellum*. War should be taken up only as a last resort, when other measures of redressing the grievance or preventing aggression have failed. There must be good hope of victory, and the good to be obtained by the righting of the wrong must outweigh the harm which will be done by the choice of war as a means. Finally, one must observe certain rules in the actual conduct of the war: that is, justice in war itself, the *ius in bello*. The deliberate killing of non-combatants and the ill-treatment of prisoners of war will render unjust a war which may have initially begun with solid justification. The system elaborated by Grotius and his successors remains to this day the most satisfactory framework for the discussion of the ethics of war.

THE LIFE OF DESCARTES

Among those who fought on the Catholic side in the Thirty Years War was the most important philosopher of the seventeenth century, René **Descartes**. Descartes was born in 1596, in a village which is now called La-Haye-Descartes. He was educated by the Jesuits and remained a Catholic throughout his life; but he chose to spend most of his adult life in Protestant Holland. He was a man of the world, a gentleman of leisure living on his fortune; he never lectured in a university and commonly wrote for the general reader. His most famous work, the *Discourse on Method*, was written not in academic Latin, but in good plain French, so that it could be understood, as he put it, 'even by women'.

While serving in the Emperor's army, Descartes acquired a conviction of his mission as a philosopher. On a winter's day in 1619 he conceived the idea of undertaking, single-handed, a reform of human learning that would display all disciplines as branches of a single wonderful science. When he went to sleep, full of ardour for his project, he had three dreams that he regarded as prophetic signs of divine vocation.

In pursuit of his goal Descartes was an innovator in many disciplines. Nowadays it is his philosophical works which are most read: in his own time his reputation rested as much on his mathematical and scientific works. He was the founder of analytical geometry, and the Cartesian co-ordinates which enable arithmetical and geometrical methods to be combined derive their name from his Latin surname, Cartesius. In his thirties he wrote a significant treatise on dioptrics, the result of careful theoretical and experimental work on the nature of the eye and of light. He also composed one of the first scientific treatises on meteorology, in which he put forward a theory of the nature of rainbows.

The culmination of his early scientific work was a treatise called *The World*. In it he set out to give an exhaustive scientific account of the origin and nature of the universe, and of the working of the human body. Like Galileo he adopted the hypothesis that the earth rotated round the sun; but before the work was complete he learnt of Galileo's condemnation. He decided against publication and henceforth kept his heliocentrism private. This decision was undoubtedly motivated by caution, not conviction; but there is no need to doubt the genuineness of his fundamental religious beliefs.

In 1637 he decided to publish three shorter treatises, on dioptrics, geometry, and meteorology, which he prefaced with a brief *Discourse on Method*. The three scientific treatises are now read only by specialists in the history of science; but the preface has been translated into more than a hundred languages, and is still read with pleasure by millions. It is written in the style of an autobiography, and presents in miniature a summary of his scientific system and his philosophical method. It is an excellent illustration of Descartes' gift for presenting complicated philosophical doctrines so elegantly that they appear fully intelligible on first reading and yet still provide matter for reflection to the most advanced specialists. He prided himself that his works could be read 'just like novels'. Indeed, his main ideas can be so concisely expressed that they could be written on the back of a postcard; and yet they were so revolutionary that they changed the course of philosophy for centuries.

If you wanted to put Descartes' main ideas on the back of a postcard you would need just two sentences: man is a thinking mind; matter is extension in motion. Everything, in Descartes' system, is to be explained in terms of this dualism of mind and matter. Indeed, we owe to Descartes that we think of mind and matter as the two great, mutually exclusive and mutually exhaustive, divisions of the universe we inhabit.

For Descartes, a human being is a thinking substance. He rejected the Aristotelian doctrine that the soul was the form of the body, with the corollary that disembodied existence, if possible at all, was something incomplete. Whereas, for a medieval Aristotelian, man was a rational animal, for Descartes, man's whole essence is mind. In the *Discourse* he says 'I recognised that I was a substance whose whole essence or nature is to think, and whose being requires no place and depends on no material thing.' In our present life, he agreed, our minds are intimately united with our bodies, but it is not our bodies that make us what we really are. Moreover, in Descartes' system the mind is conceived in a new way: the essence of the human mind is not intelligence but consciousness, the awareness of one's own thoughts and their objects.

Contrasted with mind is matter. For Descartes, matter is extension in motion. By 'extension' is meant what has the geometrical properties of shape, size, divisibility and so on; these were the *only* properties which Descartes attributed, at a fundamental level, to matter. In his suppressed treatise on the World, and in the revised elements of it which he published in his lifetime, he offered to explain all of the phenomena of heat, light, colour, and sound in terms of the motion of small particles of different sizes and shapes.

Like Bacon, Descartes compared knowledge to a tree; but for him the tree's roots were metaphysics, its trunk was physics, and its fruitful branches were the moral and useful sciences. His own writings, after the *Discourse*, followed the order thus suggested. In 1641 he wrote his metaphysical *Meditations*, in 1644 his *Principles of Philosophy* (an edited version of *The World*), and in 1649 a *Treatise on the Passions* which is largely an ethical treatise. The 1640s were the final, most philosophically fruitful, decade of his life.

THE DOUBT AND THE *COGITO*

Descartes insisted that the first task in philosophy is to rid oneself of all prejudice by calling in doubt all that can be doubted. The second task of the philosopher, having raised these doubts, is to prevent them leading to scepticism. This strategy comes out clearly in Descartes' *Meditations*. As the title suggests, the work is not intended to be read as an academic treatise. It is meant to be followed in the frame of mind of a religious retreat, such as St Ignatius Loyola's *Spiritual Exercises*. It is to provide a form of thought therapy, detaching the mind from false approaches to the truth in the way that religious meditation detaches the soul from the world and the flesh.

In this intellectual discipline, the deliverances of the senses are called in question, first by considerations drawn from sense-deception, and then by an argument from dreaming.

> What I have so far accepted as true *par excellence*, I have got either from the senses or by means of the senses. Now I have sometimes caught the senses deceiving me; and a wise man never entirely trusts those who have once cheated him.
>
> But although the senses may sometimes deceive us about some minute or remote objects, yet there are many other facts as to which doubt is plainly impossible, although these are gathered from the same source; e.g. that I am here, sitting by the fire, wearing a winter cloak, holding this paper in my hands, and so on.
>
> A fine argument! As though I were not a man who habitually sleeps at night and has the same impressions (or even wilder ones) in sleep as these men do when awake! How often in the still of the night, I have the familiar conviction that I am here, wearing a cloak, sitting by the fire – when really I am undressed and lying in bed!

But even if the senses are deceptive, and waking life is as illusory as a dream, surely reason can be relied on, and the knowledge of a science such as mathematics is secure!

Whether I am awake or asleep, two and three add up to five, and a square has only four sides; and it seems impossible for such obvious truths to fall under a suspicion of being false.

But there has been implanted in my mind the old opinion that there is a God who can do everything, and who made me such as I am. How do I know he has not brought it about that, while in fact there is no earth, no sky, no extended objects, no shape, no size, no place, yet all these things should appear to exist as they do now? Moreover, I judge that other men sometimes go wrong over what they think they know perfectly well; may not God likewise make me go wrong, whenever I add two and three, or count the sides of a square, or do any simpler thing that might be imagined? But perhaps it was not God's will to deceive me so; he is after all called supremely good.

But even if God is no deceiver, how do I know that there is not some evil spirit, supremely powerful and intelligent, who does his utmost to deceive me? If I am to avoid the possibility of assenting to falsehood, I must consider that all external objects are delusive dreams, and that I have no body but only a false belief in one.

These doubts are brought to an end by Descartes' famous argument for his own existence. However much the evil genius may deceive him, it can never deceive him into thinking that he exists when he does not. 'Undoubtedly I exist if he deceives me; let him deceive me as much as he can, he will never bring it about that I am nothing while I am thinking that I am something.' 'I exist' cannot but be true when thought of; but it has to be thought of to be doubted. Once this is seen 'I exist' is indubitable, because whenever I try to doubt it I automatically see that it is true.

Descartes' argument is usually presented in the terser form he used in the *Discourse*: *Cogito, ergo sum*: 'I am thinking, therefore I exist'. From these few words Descartes not only derives a proof of his existence, but also seeks to discover his own essence, to demonstrate the existence of God, and to provide the criterion to guide the mind in its search for truth. No wonder that every word of the *cogito* has been weighed a thousand times by philosophers.

'I am thinking'. What is 'thinking' here? From what Descartes says elsewhere, it is clear that any form of inner conscious activity counts as thought; but of course the thought in question here is the self-reflexive thought that he is thinking. How important is the 'I' in 'I am thinking'? In ordinary life the word 'I' gets its meaning in connection with the body which gives it utterance; is someone who doubts whether he has a body entitled to use 'I' in a soliloquy? Some critics have thought that he should really have said only 'There is thinking going on'.

'Therefore'. This word makes the *cogito* look like an argument from a premiss to a conclusion. Elsewhere Descartes speaks as if his own existence is something he intuits immediately. Accordingly, there has been much discussion whether the *cogito* is an inference or an intuition. Probably Descartes meant it to be an inference, but an inference that was immediate, rather than one which presupposed some more general principle such as 'Whatever is thinking exists'.

'I exist'. If the premise should have been 'thinking is going on', should the conclusion be only 'existing is going on'? Critics have argued that the doubting Descartes has no right to draw the conclusion that there is an enduring, substantial self. Perhaps he should have concluded rather to a fleeting subject for a transient thought; or perhaps, even, there can be thoughts with no owners. Can Descartes assume that the 'I' revealed by the methodical doubt is the same person who, unpurified by doubt, answered to the name of 'René Descartes'? Once the link has been severed between body and mind, how can anyone be certain of the identity of the thinker of the *Meditations*?

These questions have been pressed with great force in the philosophy of the last two centuries. In Descartes' own time, it was asked how 'I am thinking, therefore I exist' differs from 'I am walking, therefore I exist'. Descartes' answer is that as an argument the one is as good as the other; but the premiss of the first is indubitable, whereas the premiss of the second is vulnerable to doubt. If I have no body, then I am not walking, even if I believe I am; but however much I doubt, then by the very fact of doubting, I am thinking. But 'I think I am walking, therefore I exist' is a perfectly valid form of the *cogito*.

THE ESSENCE OF MIND

In the rest of the *Meditations* Descartes proceeds to answer the question '*What am I, this I whom I know to exist?*' The immediate answer is that I am a thing which thinks (*res cogitans*). 'What is a thing which thinks? It is a thing which doubts, understands, conceives, affirms, denies, wills, refuses, which also imagines and feels.' 'Think' is being used in a wide sense: for Descartes, to think is not always to think *that* something or other, and thinking includes not only intellectual meditation, but also volition, emotion, pain, pleasure, mental images, and sensations. No previous author had used the word with such a wide extension. But Descartes did not believe that he was altering the sense of the word: he applied it to the new items because he believed that if they were properly understood, they could be seen to possess the feature which was the most important characteristic of the traditional items if *they* were properly understood. This feature was immediate consciousness, which for him was the defining feature of thought. 'I use this term to include everything that is within us in such a way that we are immediately conscious of it. Thus, all the operations of the will, the intellect, the imagination and the senses are thoughts.'

The thing which thinks is a thing which 'understands, conceives'. The mastery of concepts and the formulation of articulate thoughts are, for Descartes as for medieval philosophers, operations of the intellect, and thoughts or perceptions which are both clear and distinct are for him operations of the intellect *par excellence*. However, Descartes makes a much sharper distinction than his predecessors did between intellection and judgement. Descartes does not regard the mind's consciousness of its own thoughts as a case of judgement; simply to register the contents of the mind, an idea or set of ideas, is not to make a judgement.

Understanding the proposition '115 + 28 = 143' is a perception of the intellect; but making the judgement that the proposition is true, asserting that 115 plus 28 makes 143, is an act not of the intellect, according to Descartes, but of the will. The intellect provides the ideas which are the content on which the will is to judge. In many cases, the will can refrain from making a judgement about the ideas which the intellect presents; but this is not so when the intellectual perception is clear and distinct. A clear and distinct perception is one which forces the will, a perception which cannot be doubted however hard one tries. Such is the perception of one's own existence produced by the *cogito*.

In addition to understanding and perceiving, then, a thinking being affirms and denies, wills and refuses. The will says 'yes' or 'no' to propositions (about what is the case) and projects (about what to do). The human will is, in a certain sense, infinite in power. 'The will, or freedom of choice, which I experience in myself is so great that the idea of any greater faculty is beyond my grasp.' Because of this infinity it is the will which in human beings is the especial image and likeness of God.

It would be wrong, however, to think of Descartes as an indeterminist, like the Jesuit believers in liberty of indifference. The form of freedom which Descartes most valued was not liberty of indifference, but liberty of spontaneity, which is defined as the ability to do what we want, the ability to follow our desires. Clear and distinct perception, which leaves the will with no alternative but to assent, takes away liberty of indifference but not liberty of spontaneity. 'If we see very clearly that something is good for us it is very difficult – and on my view impossible, as long as one continues in the same thought – to stop the course of our desires.' The human mind is at its best, for Descartes, when assenting, spontaneously but not indifferently, to the data of clear and distinct perception.

Finally, the *res cogitans* 'imagines and feels'. Imagination and sensation are understood by Descartes sometimes broadly and sometimes narrowly. Taken in the broad interpretation, sensation and imagination are impossible without a body, because sensation involves the operation of bodily organs, and even imagination, at least as conceived by Descartes, involves the inspection of images in the brain. But taken in the narrow sense – as they are in the definition of the *res cogitans* – sensation and imagination are nothing other than modes of thought. As Descartes puts it, as he emerges from his doubt: 'I am now seeing light, hearing a noise, feeling heat. These objects are unreal, for I am asleep; but at least I seem to see, to hear, to be warmed. This cannot be unreal, and this is what is properly called my sensation.' Descartes here isolates an indubitable immediate experience, the seeming-to-see-a-light which cannot be mistaken, the item that is common to both veridical and hallucinatory experience. It is this which is, for

Descartes, 'sensation strictly so called' and which is a pure thought. It does not involve any judgement; on the contrary, it is a thought which I can have while refraining, as part of the discipline of Cartesian doubt, from making any judgements at all.

GOD, MIND, AND BODY

The upshot of the Cartesian doubt and the *cogito* is Descartes' conclusion that he is a thing that thinks, a conscious being. But is that *all* he is? Well, at this stage, this is all that he is certain of. 'There is thought: of this and this only I cannot be deprived. I am, I exist; that is certain. For how long? For as long as I am thinking; maybe if I wholly ceased to think, I should at once wholly cease to be. For the present I am admitting only what is necessarily true; I am, with this qualification, no more than a thinking thing.' Later, Descartes concludes 'my essence consists solely in the fact that I am a thinking thing'.

Now of course not being certain that I have any essence other than thought is not at all the same thing as being certain that I do not have any essence other than thought. Scholars still debate whether Descartes failed to distinguish between the two. But in his *Meditations*, for his last word on the relation between mind and body, we have to wait until he has considered the existence and nature of God.

In the *Fifth Meditation* Descartes tells us that he finds in himself the idea of God, of a supremely perfect being, and that he clearly and distinctly perceives that everlasting existence belongs to God's nature. This perception is just as clear as anything in arithmetic or geometry; and if we reflect on it, we see that God must exist.

> Existence can no more be taken away from the divine essence than the magnitude of its three angles together (that is, their being equal to two right angles) can be taken away from the essence of a triangle; or than the idea of a valley can be taken away from the idea of a hill. So it is not less absurd to think of God (that is, a supremely perfect being) lacking existence (that is, lacking a certain perfection), than to think of a hill without a valley.

One's first reaction to this argument (usually called Descartes' 'ontological argument' for the existence of God) is that it is a simple begging of the question of God's existence. But Descartes clearly thought that theorems could be proved about triangles, whether or not there was actually anything in the world that was triangular. Similarly, therefore, theorems could be stated about God in abstraction from the question whether there exists any such being. One such theorem is that God is a totally perfect being, that is, he contains all perfections. But existence itself is a perfection; hence, God, who contains all perfections, must exist.

Before Descartes published his *Meditations*, he arranged for the manuscript to be circulated to a number of savants for their comments, which were eventually printed, along with his responses, in the published version. One of the critics, the mathematician Pierre Gassendi, objected that existence could not be treated in this way.

> Neither in God nor in anything else is existence a perfection, but rather that without which there are no perfections. . . . Existence cannot be said to exist in a thing like a perfection; and if a thing lacks existence, then it is not just imperfect or lacking perfection; it is nothing at all.

Descartes had no ultimately convincing answer to this objection. The non-question-begging way of stating the theorem about triangles is to say: if anything is triangular, then it has its three angles equal to two right angles. Similarly, the non-question-begging way of stating the theorem about perfection is to say that if anything is perfect, then it exists. That may perhaps be true: but it is perfectly compatible with there being nothing that is perfect. But if nothing is perfect, then nothing is divine and there is no God, and so Descartes' proof fails.

The argument which we have just presented and criticized seeks to show the existence of God by starting simply from the content of the idea of God. Else-where, Descartes seeks to show God's existence not just from the content of the idea, but from the occurrence of an idea with that content in a finite mind like his own. Thus, in the *Third Meditation*, he argues that while most of his ideas – such as thought, substance, duration, number – may very well have originated in himself, there is one idea, that of God, which could not have himself as its author. I cannot, he argues, have drawn the attributes of infinity, independence, supreme intelligence, and supreme power from reflection on a limited, dependent, ignorant, impotent creature like myself. But the cause of an idea must be no less real than the idea itself; only God could cause the idea of God, so God must be no less real than I and my idea are. Here the weakness in the argument seems to lie in an ambiguity in the notion of 'reality' (as in 'Zeus was not real, but mythical' vs. 'Zeus was a real thug').

Descartes' proofs differ from proofs like Aquinas' Five Ways which argue to the existence of God from features of the world we live in. Both of the *Meditations* arguments are designed to be deployed while Descartes is still in doubt whether anything exists besides himself and his ideas. This is an important matter, since the existence of God is an essential step for Descartes towards establishing the existence of the external world. It is only because God is truthful that the appear-ances of bodies independent of our minds cannot be wholly deceptive. Because of God's veracity, we can be sure that whatever we clearly and distinctly perceive is true; and if we stick to clear and distinct perception, we will not be misled about the world around us.

Antoine Arnauld, one of those who were invited to submit comments on the *Meditations*, thought he detected a circle in Descartes' appeal to God as the guarantor of the truth of clear and distinct perception. 'We can be sure that God exists, only because we clearly and evidently perceive that he does; therefore, prior to being certain that God exists, we need to be certain that whatever we clearly and evidently perceive is true.'

There is not, in fact, any circularity in Descartes' argument. To see this we must make a distinction between particular clear and distinct perceptions (such as that I exist, or that two and three make five) and the general principle that what we clearly and distinctly perceive is true. Individual intuitions cannot be doubted as long as I continue clearly and distinctly to perceive them. But prior to proving God's existence it is possible for me to doubt the general proposition that whatever I clearly and distinctly perceive is true.

Again, propositions which I have intuited in the past can be doubted when I am no longer adverting to them. I can wonder now whether what I intuited five minutes ago was really true. Since simple intuitions cannot be doubted while they are before the mind, no argument is needed to establish them; indeed, for Descartes, intuition is superior to argument as a method of attaining truth. It is only in connection with the general principle, and in connection with the round-about doubt of the particular propositions, that appeal to God's truthfulness is necessary. Hence Descartes is innocent of the circularity alleged by Arnauld.

In the *Sixth Meditation* Descartes says that he knows that if he can clearly and distinctly understand one thing without another, that shows that the two things are distinct, because God at least can separate them. Since he knows that he exists, but observes nothing else as belonging to his nature other than that he is a thinking thing, he concludes that his nature or essence consists simply in being a thinking thing; he is really distinct from his body and could exist without it.

None the less, he does have a body closely attached to him; but his reason for believing this is that he now knows there is a God, and that God cannot deceive. God has given him a nature which teaches him that he has a body which is injured when he feels pain, which needs food and drink when he feels hunger or thirst. Nature teaches him also that he is not in his body like a pilot in a ship, but that he is tightly bound up in it so as to form a single unit with it. If these teachings of nature were false in spite of being clear and distinct, then God, the author of nature, would turn out to be a deceiver, which is absurd. Descartes concludes therefore that human beings are compounded of mind and body.

However, the nature of this composition, this 'intimate union' between mind and body, is one of the most puzzling features of the Cartesian system. The matter is made even more obscure when we are told that the mind is not directly affected by any part of the body other than the pineal gland in the brain. All sensations consist of motions in the body which travel through the nerves to this gland and there give a signal to the mind which calls up a certain experience.

The transactions in the gland, at the mind–body interface, are highly mysterious. Is there a causal action of matter on mind or of mind on matter? Surely not, for the only form of material causation in Descartes' system is the communication of motion; and the mind, as such, is not the kind of thing to move around in space. Or does the commerce between mind and brain resemble intercourse between one human being and another, with the mind reading off messages and symbols presented by the brain? If so, then the mind is in effect being conceived as a homunculus, a man within a man. The mind–body problem is not solved, but merely miniaturized, by the introduction of the pineal gland.

THE MATERIAL WORLD

Descartes' *Meditations* brought him fame throughout Europe. He entered into correspondence and controversy with most of the learned men of his time, especially through the intermediary of a learned Franciscan, Marin Mersenne. Some of his friends began to teach his views in universities; and in the *Principles of Philosophy* he set out his metaphysics and his physics in the form of a textbook. Other professors, seeing their Aristotelian system threatened, subjected the new doctrines to violent attack. However, Descartes did not lack powerful friends and so he was never in real danger.

One of his correspondents was Princess Elizabeth of the Palatine, the niece of King Charles I of England. She presented a number of shrewd objections to Descartes' account of the interaction of mind and body, to which he was unable to give a satisfactory answer. Out of their correspondence grew the last of his full-length works, the *Passions of the Soul*. When it was published, however, this book was dedicated not to Elizabeth but to another royal lady who had interested herself in philosophy, Queen Christina of Sweden. Against his better judgement Descartes was persuaded to accept appointment as court philosopher to Queen Christina, who sent an admiral with a battleship to fetch him from Holland. The Queen insisted on being given her philosophy lessons at 5 o'clock in the morning. Under this regime Descartes, a lifelong late riser, fell victim to the rigours of a Swedish winter and died in 1650.

Some of the most important of Descartes' doctrines were not fully spelt out in his published works, and only became clear when his voluminous correspondence was published after his death. One such is his doctrine of the creation of the eternal truths; another is the theory that animals are unconscious automata.

In 1630 Descartes wrote to Mersenne:

> The mathematical truths which you call eternal have been laid down by God and depend on Him entirely no less than the rest of his creatures. Indeed to say that these truths are independent of God is to talk of Him as if He were Jupiter or Saturn and to subject him to the Styx and the Fates. Please do not hesitate to assert

and proclaim everywhere that it is God who has laid down these laws in nature just as a king lays down laws in his kingdom. . . . It will be said that if God had established these truths He could change them as a king changes his laws. To this the answer is 'Yes he can, if His will can change'. 'But I understand them to be eternal and unchangeable' – 'I make the same judgment about God' 'But His will is free.' – 'Yes, but His power is incomprehensible.'

It was an innovation to make the truths of logic and mathematics depend on God's will. It was not that previous philosophers thought such truths were totally independent of God; according to most thinkers, they were independent of God's will, but dependent upon, indeed in some sense identified with, his essence. Descartes was the first to make the world of mathematics a separate creature, dependent, like the physical world, upon God's sovereign will.

This doctrine, Descartes said, was the necessary foundation of his physical theory. He rejected, systematically, the Aristotelian apparatus of real qualities and substantial forms, both of which he regarded as chimerical entities. The essences of things, he maintained, are not forms as conceived by Aristotle; they are simply the eternal truths, which include the law of inertia and other laws of motion as well as the truths of logic and mathematics. Now in the Aristotelian system it was the forms and essences that provided the element of stability in the flux of phenomena which made it possible for there to be universally valid scientific knowledge. Having rejected essences and forms, Descartes needed a new foundation for the certain and immutable physics that he wished to establish. If there are no substantial forms, what connects one moment of a thing's history to another? Descartes' answer is: nothing but the immutable will of God. And to reassure ourselves that the laws of nature will not at some point change, we have once again to appeal to the veracity of God, who would be a deceiver if he let our inductions go astray.

In Descartes' system we have a world of physics governed by deterministic laws of nature, and we have the mental world of the solitary consciousness. Human beings, as compounds of mind and body, straddle both worlds uncomfortably. Where do non-human animals fit in?

According to most thinkers before Descartes, animals differ from human beings by lacking rationality, but resemble them in possessing the capacity for sensation. But Descartes' account of the nature of sensation makes it difficult to attribute it to animals in the same sense as we attribute it to human beings. In a human, according to Descartes, there are two elements in sensation: on the one hand, there is a thought (e.g. a pain, or an experience as it were of seeing a light), and on the other hand, there are the mechanical motions in the body which give rise to that thought. The same mechanical motions may occur in the body of an animal as occur in the body of a human, and if we like we can, in a broad sense, call these sensations; but an animal cannot have a thought, and it is thought in which sensation, strictly so called, consists. It follows that, for Descartes, an animal cannot have a pain, though the machine of its body may cause it to react in a way which, in a human, would be the expression of a pain. As Descartes wrote to an English nobleman:

> I see no argument for animals having thoughts except the fact that since they have eyes, ears, tongues, and other sense-organs like ours, it seems likely that they have sensations like us; and since thought is included in our mode of sensation, similar thought seems to be attributable to them. This argument, which is very obvious, has taken possession of the minds of all men from their earliest age. But there are other arguments, stronger and more numerous, but not so obvious to everyone, which strongly urge the opposite.

This doctrine did not seem quite as shocking to Descartes' contemporaries as it does to most people nowadays; but they reacted with horror when some of his disciples claimed that human beings, no less than animals, were only complicated machines.

Descartes' two great principles – that man is a thinking substance, and that matter is extension in motion – are radically misconceived. In his own lifetime phenomena were discovered which were incapable of straightforward explanation in terms of matter in motion. The circulation of the blood and the action of the heart, as discovered by the English physician William Harvey, demanded the operation of forces such as elasticity for which there was no room in Descartes' system. None the less, his scientific account of the origin and nature of the world was fashionable for a century or so after his death; and for a while other, more fruitful, scientific conceptions of nature felt obliged to define their position in relation to his.

Descartes' view of the nature of mind endured much longer than his view of matter: indeed, throughout the West, it is still the most widespread view of mind among educated people who are not professional philosophers. As we shall see, it was later to be subjected to searching criticism by Kant, and was decisively refuted in the twentieth century by Wittgenstein, who showed that even when we think our most private and spiritual thoughts we are employing the medium of a language which cannot be severed from its public and bodily expression. The Cartesian dichotomy of mind and matter is, in the last analysis, untenable. But once grasped, its influence can never wholly be shaken off.

More than any other philosopher, Descartes stands out as a solitary original genius, creating from his own head a system of thought to dominate his intellectual world. It is true that there is hardly a philosophical argument in his works which does not make its appearance, somewhere or other, in the writings of earlier philosophers whom he had not read. But no one else ever displayed the ability to combine such thoughts into a single integrated system, and offer them to the general reader in texts which can be read in an afternoon, but which provide material for meditation over decades.

XII

ENGLISH PHILOSOPHY IN THE SEVENTEENTH CENTURY

THE EMPIRICISM OF THOMAS HOBBES

One of the invited commentators on Descartes' *Meditations* was Thomas **Hobbes**, the foremost English philosopher among his contemporaries. This early encounter between Anglophone and continental philosophy was not cordial. Descartes thought Hobbes' objections trivial, and Hobbes is reported to have said 'that had Des Cartes kept himself wholly to Geometry he had been the best Geometer in the world, but his head did not lie for Philosophy'.

Hobbes was eight years Descartes' senior, born just as the Armada arrived off England in 1588. After education at Oxford he was employed as a tutor by the Cavendish family, and spent much time on the continent. It was in Paris, during the English Civil War, that he wrote his most famous work on political philosophy, *Leviathan*. Three years after the execution of King Charles he returned to England to live in the household of his former pupil, now the Earl of Devonshire. He published two volumes of natural philosophy, and in old age translated into English the whole of Homer, as in youth he had translated Thucydides. He died, aged 91, in 1679.

Hobbes stands squarely and bluntly in the tradition of British empiricism which looks back to Ockham and looks forward to Hume. 'There is no conception in a man's mind which hath not at first, totally or by parts, been begotten upon the organs of Sense.' There are two kinds of knowledge, knowledge of fact, and knowledge of consequence. Knowledge of fact is given by sense or memory: it is the knowledge required of a witness. Knowledge of consequence is the knowledge of what follows from what: it is the knowledge required of a philosopher. In our minds there is a constant succession or train of thoughts, which constitutes mental discourse; in the philosopher this train is governed by the search for causes. These causes will be expressed in language by conditional laws, of the form 'If A, then B'.

It is important, Hobbes believes, for the philosopher to grasp the nature of language. The purpose of speech is to transfer the train of our thoughts into a train of words; and it has four uses.

> First, to register, what by cogitation, we find to be the cause of any thing, present or past; and what we find things present or past may produce, or effect: which in sum is acquiring of Arts. Secondly, to shew to others that knowledge which we have attained; which is, to Counsell and Teach one another. Thirdly, to make known to others our wills, and purposes, that we may have the mutuall help of one another. Fourthly, to please and delight our selves, and others, by playing with our words, for pleasure or ornament, innocently.

Hobbes is a staunch nominalist. Universal names like 'man' and 'tree' do not name any thing in the world or any idea in the mind, but name many individuals, 'there being nothing in the world Universall but Names; for the things named, are every one of them Individual and Singular'. Sentences consist of pairs of names joined together; and sentences are true when both members of the pairs are names of the same thing. One who seeks truth must therefore take great care what names he uses, and in particular must avoid the use of empty names or insignificant sounds. These, Hobbes observes, are coined in abundance by scholastic philosophers, who put names together in inconsistent pairs. He gives as an example 'incorporeall substance', which he says is as absurd as 'round quadrangle'.

The example was chosen as a provocative manifesto of materialism. All substances are necessarily bodies, and when philosophy seeks for the causes of changes in bodies the one universal cause which it discovers is motion. In saying this, Hobbes was very close to one half of Descartes' philosophy, his philosophy of matter. But in opposition to the other half of that philosophy, Hobbes denied the existence of mind in the sense in which Descartes understood it. Historians disagree whether Hobbes' materialism involved a denial of the existence of God, or simply implied that God was a body of some infinite and invisible kind. But whether or not Hobbes was an atheist, which seems unlikely, he certainly denied the existence of human Cartesian spirits.

While Descartes exaggerates the difference between humans and animals, Hobbes minimizes it, and explains human action as a particular form of animal behaviour. There are two kinds of motion in animals, he says, one called vital and one called voluntary. Vital motions include breathing, digestion, and the course of the blood. Voluntary motion is 'to go, to speak, to move any of our limbs, in such manner as is first fancied in our minds'. Sensation is caused by the direct or indirect pressure of an external object on a sense-organ 'which pressure, by the mediation of Nerves, and other strings and membranes of the body, continued inwards to the Brain, and Heart, causeth there a resistance, or counter-pressure, or endeavour of the heart, to deliver it self: which endeavour, because outward, seemeth to be some matter without'. It is this seeming which constitutes colours, sounds, tastes, odours etc.; which in the originating objects are nothing but motion.

The activities thus described correspond to those which Aristotelians attributed to the vegetative and sensitive souls. What of the rational soul, with its faculties of intellect and will, which for Aristotelians made the difference between men and animals? In Hobbes, this is replaced by the imagination, which is a faculty common to all animals, and whose operation is again given a mechanical explanation, all thoughts of any kind being small motions in the head. If a particular imagining is caused by words or other signs, it is called 'understanding', and this too is common to men and beasts, 'for a dog by custom will understand the call or the rating of his Master; and so will many other Beasts'. The kind of understanding that is peculiar to humans is 'when imagining any thing whatsoever, we seek all the possible effects, that can by it be produced; that is to say, we imagine what we can do with it, when we have it. Of which I have not at any time seen any sign, but in men only.'

This difference Hobbes attributes not to a difference in the human intellect, but in the human will, which includes a great variety of passions unshared by animals. The human will, no less than animal desire, is itself a consequence of mechanical forces. 'Beasts that have deliberation, must necessarily also have Will.' The will is, indeed, nothing but the desire which comes at the end of deliberation; and the freedom of the will is no greater in humans than in animals. 'Such a liberty as is free from necessity is not to be found in the will either of men or beasts. But if by liberty we understand the faculty or power, not of willing, but of doing what they will, then certainly that liberty is to be allowed to both, and both may equally have it.'

HOBBES' POLITICAL PHILOSOPHY

Hobbes' determinism allows him to extend the search for causal laws beyond natural philosophy (which seeks for the causes of the phenomena of natural bodies) into civil philosophy (which seeks for the causes of the phenomena of political bodies). It is this which is the subject matter of *Leviathan*, which is not only a masterpiece of political philosophy but also one of the greatest works of English prose.

The book sets out to describe the interplay of forces which cause the institution of the State or, in his term, the Commonwealth. It starts by describing what it is like for men to live outside a commonwealth, in a state of nature. Since men are roughly equal in their natural abilities, and are equally self-interested, there will be constant quarrelsome and unregulated competition for goods, power, and glory. This can be described as a natural state of war. In such conditions, Hobbes says, there will be no industry, agriculture, or commerce:

no knowledge of the face of the earth; no account of time; no arts; no letters; no society; and, which is worst of all, continual fear and danger of violent death; and the life of man, solitary, poor, nasty, brutish and short.

Whether or not there was ever, historically, such a state throughout the world, we can see instances of it, Hobbes says, in contemporary America, and we can see evidence of it in the precautions which men even in civilized countries take against their fellows.

In a state of nature there are no laws in the true sense. But there are 'laws of nature' in the form of principles of rational self-interest, recipes for maximizing the chances of survival. Such laws urge men in their natural state to seek peace, and to give up some of their unfettered liberty in return for equal concessions by others. These laws lead them to give up all their rights, except that of self-defence, to a central power which is able to enforce the laws of nature by punishment. This central power may be an individual, or an assembly; whether single or plural, it is the supreme sovereign, a single will representing the wills of every member of the community.

The sovereign is instituted by a covenant of every man with every man, each one yielding up their rights on condition that every other does likewise. 'This done, the multitude so united in one person, is called a Commonwealth. This is the generation of that great Leviathan, or rather, to speak more reverently, of that mortal god, to which we owe under the immortal God our peace and defence.'

The covenant and the sovereign come into existence simultaneously. The sovereign is himself not a party to the covenant, and therefore cannot be in breach of it. That covenants should be observed is a law of nature; but 'covenants without the sword are but breath', and it is the function of the sovereign to enforce, not only the original covenant which constitutes the State, but individual covenants which his subjects make with each other.

Commonwealths can come into existence not only by free covenant, but also by warfare. In each case it is fear which is the basis of the subjects' subjection to the sovereign, and in each case the sovereign enjoys equal and inalienable rights. Every subject is the author of every action of the sovereign 'and consequently he that complaineth of injury from his Sovereign complaineth of that of which he is the author'.

The sovereign is the source of law and property rights, and is the supreme governor of the Church. It is the sovereign, and not any presbytery or Bishop, which has the right to interpret Scripture and determine correct doctrine. The insolent interpretations of fanatical sectaries have been the cause of civil war in England; but the greatest usurpation of sovereignty in the name of religion is to be found in Rome. 'If a man will consider the originall of this great Ecclesiastical Dominion, he will easily perceive, that the Papacy is no other, than the Ghost of the deceased Roman Empire, sitting crowned upon the grave thereof.'

Under a sovereign so powerful, what liberty is left to the subject? In general, liberty is no more than the silence of the law: the subject has liberty to do whatever the sovereign has not troubled to make a law against. But no one, says Hobbes, with doubtful consistency, is obliged at the sovereign's command to kill himself, or incriminate himself, or even to go into battle. Moreover, if the sovereign fails to fulfil his principal function, that of protecting his subjects, then their obligation to him lapses. It was presumably this axiom that Hobbes had in mind when, having written *Leviathan* as a royalist exile in Paris, he made his peace with Cromwell in 1652.

Hobbes had never been a supporter of the divine right of kings, nor did he believe in a totalitarian state. The state exists for the sake of the citizens, not the other way round; and the rights of the sovereign derive not from God but from the rights of those individuals who renounce them to become his subjects. It was not during the civil war, nor during the commonwealth, but in the reign of Charles II, after the restoration of the Stuart monarchy, that the theory of divine right became an issue for philosophers. The debate started with the publication in 1680 of Sir Robert Filmer's *Patriarcha*, which claimed that the King's authority derived by patriarchal descent from the royal authority of Adam, and should thus be free of restraint by Parliament. This presented an easy target for the most influential political philosopher of the seventeenth century, John Locke.

THE POLITICAL THEORY OF JOHN LOCKE

Locke had been born in 1632. After education at Westminster School he took his MA at Christ Church, Oxford, in 1658. He qualified in medicine and became physician to Lord Shaftesbury, a member of the inner cabinet of King Charles II. Charles had returned from exile in 1660 on a wave of popular reaction against the tyranny and austerity of Cromwellian rule. As his reign progressed, however, royalty became less popular, especially as the heir to the throne, the King's brother James, was a sturdy Catholic. Shaftesbury led the Whig party, which sought to exclude James from the succession; he had to flee the country after being implicated in a plot against the royal brothers in 1683. Locke accompanied him to Holland, and spent the years of his exile composing his greatest philosophical work, the *Essay Concerning Human Understanding*, which was published in several editions in the later years of his life.

In 1688 the 'Glorious Revolution' drove out James II and replaced him with William of Orange, placing the English monarchy on a new legal basis, with a Bill of Rights and a much enhanced role for Parliament. Locke followed William to England and became the theorist of the new constitution. In 1609 he published *Two Treatises of Civil Government*, which became classics of liberal thought. He worked at the Board of Trade in the 1690s, and died in 1704.

In the first of his *Treatises* Locke makes short work of Filmer's case for the divine right of kings. Filmer's fundamental error is to deny that human beings are naturally free and equal to each other. In the second *Treatise* Locke gives his own account of the state of nature, which contrasts interestingly with that of Hobbes.

Before there are any states to make statutes, Locke maintains, men are aware of a natural law, which teaches that all men are equal and independent, and that no one ought to harm another in his life, health, liberty, or possession. These men, with no earthly superior above them, are in a state of liberty, but not a state of licence. Besides being bound by natural law, humans possess natural rights, in particular the right to life, self-defence, and freedom. They have also duties; in particular, the duty not to give away their rights.

A significant natural right is the right to property. God does not assign particular properties to particular individuals, but the existence of a system of private property is part of God's plan for the world. In the state of nature, people acquire property by 'mixing their labour' with natural goods, whether by drawing water, collecting fruit, or tilling the soil. Locke believed that there was a natural right not just to acquire, but also to inherit, private property.

Locke is obviously much less pessimistic about the state of nature than Hobbes was. His view resembles more the optimism of Pope's later *Essay on Man*.

> Nor think, in Nature's State they blindly trod;
> The state of Nature was the reign of God:
> Self-love and social at her birth began,
> Union the bond of all things, and of Man.
> Pride then was not; nor Arts, that Pride to aid;
> Man walk'd with beast, joint tenant of the shade;
> The same his table, and the same his bed;
> No murder cloath'd him, and no murder fed.
> In the same temple, the resounding wood,
> All vocal beings hym'd their equal God.

In the state of nature, however, men have only a precarious hold on any property more substantial than the shade they share with the beasts. Everyone can learn the teachings of nature, and transgressors of nature's law deserve punishment. But in the state of nature everyone has to be the judge in his own case, and there may be no one with sufficient power to punish violators. It is this which leads to the institution of the state. 'The great and chief end of men uniting into commonwealths, and putting themselves under government, is the preservation of their property; to which in the state of nature there are many things wanting.'

The state is created by a social contract, with men handing over to a government their rights to see that the natural law is put into practice. They hand over to a legislature the right to make laws for the common good, and to an executive the right to enforce these laws. (Locke is aware of good reasons for separating these two branches of government.) The decision on the particular form of legislature and executive is to be made by a majority of the citizens (or at least of the property-owners).

Locke's social contract differs from Hobbes' in several ways. Locke's governors, unlike Hobbes' sovereign, are themselves parties to the initial contract. The community entrusts to the chosen type of government the protection of its rights; and if the government breaches the trust placed in it, the people can remove or alter it. If a government acts arbitrarily, or if one branch of government usurps the role of another, then the government is dissolved, and rebellion is justified. Here Locke obviously has in mind the autocratic rule of the Stuart kings and the Glorious Revolution of 1688.

Locke believed, implausibly, that social contracts of the kind he describes were historical events. But he held that the maintenance of any government, however set up, depended on the continuing consent of the citizens in each generation. Such consent, he admits, is rarely explicit; but tacit consent is given by anyone who enjoys the benefits of society, whether by accepting an inheritance, or merely by travelling on the highway. Taxation, in particular, must rest on consent: 'The supreme power cannot take from any man any part of his property without his own consent.'

Locke's political ideas were not original, but their influence was great, and continued long after people ceased to believe in the theories of the state of nature and natural law that underpinned them. Anyone who knows the Declaration of Independence and the American Constitution will find a number of Locke's ideas, and indeed phrases, very familiar.

LOCKE ON IDEAS AND QUALITIES

Locke's influence was by no means restricted to the political sphere. His *Essay Concerning Human Understanding* is often regarded as the foundation charter of a particularly British school of philosophy. Historians of philosophy often contrast British and continental philosophy in the seventeenth and eighteenth centuries: the continentals were rationalists, trusting to the speculations of reason, and the British were empiricists, basing knowledge on the experience of the senses. Descartes and Locke are often put forward as the founding fathers of these two opposing schools. In fact, in spite of the differences between them, the two philosophers share a lot of presuppositions, as we can see if we examine the famous controversy over the possibility of innate ideas, which was supposed to be the touchstone of the conflict between rationalism and empiricism.

Locke is forever talking about 'ideas'. His 'ideas' are very similar to Descartes' 'thoughts'; and indeed Descartes himself sometimes talks of thoughts as ideas. In each case there is an appeal to immediate consciousness: ideas and thoughts are what we meet when we look within ourselves. In each case it is often difficult to tell whether by 'idea' is meant the object of thought (what is being thought about) or the activity of thinking (what thinking itself consists in or amounts to). Locke says that an idea is 'whatever it is which the mind can be employed about in thinking'. There is a damaging ambiguity in the phrase 'what the mind is employed about', which can mean either what the mind is thinking of (the object) or what the mind is engaged in (the activity).

The distinction between empiricism and rationalism is not wholly without foundation, and the answers which Locke gives to philosophical questions from time to time conflict with those given by Descartes. But though the answers differ, Locke's questions are Descartes' questions. Are animals machines? Does the soul always think? Can there be space without matter? Are there innate ideas?

This last question can have several meanings, and once we break the question down, we find that there is no great gulf fixed between the positions of Locke and Descartes.

First, the question may mean 'Do infants in the womb think thoughts?' Both Descartes and Locke believed that unborn infants had simple thoughts or ideas, such as pains, and sensations of warmth. Neither Descartes nor Locke believed that infants had complicated thoughts of a philosophical kind.

Secondly, the question may be taken to concern not the activity of thinking, but simply the capacity for thought. Is there an inborn, general, capacity for understanding which is specific to human beings? Both Descartes and Locke believe that there is.

Thirdly, the question may concern not the general faculty of understanding, but assent to certain particular propositions, e.g. 'One and two are equal to three' or 'It is impossible for the same thing to be, and not to be'. Descartes and Locke agree that our assent to such self-evident truths does not depend on experience. Locke insists, however, that a process of learning must precede the grasp of these propositions. And Descartes agrees that not all innate ideas are principles assented to as soon as understood: some of them become clear and distinct only after laborious meditation.

Fourthly, we may ask whether there are any principles, whether theoretical or practical, which command universal assent. The answer, Locke thought, was no; and even if it were yes, this would not be sufficient to prove innateness, since the explanation might be a common process of learning. But Descartes can agree that universal consent does not entail innateness, and can retort that innateness does not entail universal consent either. Some people, perhaps most people, may be prevented by prejudice from assenting to innate principles.

The arguments of Locke and Descartes in fact pass each other by. Locke insists that innate concepts without experience are insufficient to account for the phenomena of human knowledge; Descartes argues that experience without an innate element is insufficient to account for what we know. It is possible for both views to be correct.

Locke claimed that the arguments of his rationalist opponents would lead one 'to suppose all our ideas of colours, sounds, taste, figure etc. innate, than which there cannot be anything more opposite to reason and experience'. Descartes would not have regarded this conclusion as at all absurd – and that for a reason which Locke would himself wholeheartedly accept, namely that our ideas of qualities such as colours, sounds, and taste are entirely subjective.

Locke divided the qualities to be found in bodies into two categories. The first group are the *primary qualities*: these are such things as solidity, extension, figure, motion, rest, bulk, number, texture, and size; these qualities, he says, are in bodies 'whether we perceive them or no'. Qualities in the second group are called '*secondary qualities*', they are such things as colours, sounds, tastes, which, according to Locke, 'are nothing in the objects themselves, but powers to produce various sensations in us by their primary qualities'. All qualities, primary or secondary, produce ideas in our minds; the difference, according to Locke, is that the qualities in objects which produce the primary qualities are really like the ideas they produce, whereas the ideas which are produced in us by secondary qualities do not resemble in any way the qualities which produce them.

There are many precursors of Locke's distinction. The Aristotelian tradition distinguished between those qualities like shape which were perceived by more than one sense ('common sensibles') and those like taste which were perceived by only a single sense ('proper sensibles'). Locke's distinction had been more fully anticipated by Galileo and Descartes. Decartes had argued that a physiological account of perception need involve only primary qualities as explanatory factors: what goes on in our bodies when we see or hear or taste is nothing more than motions of shaped matter. Even if this had turned out to be true, it would not have entailed that secondary qualities were merely subjective and did not really belong to the objects in the world which appear to posess them. But Locke offers a more sustained argument for this conclusion than any of his predecessors had done.

Locke's first claim is that only primary qualities are inseparable from their subjects: there cannot be a body without a shape or a size, as there can be a body without a smell or a taste. For instance, if you take a grain of wheat and divide it over and over again, it may lose its secondary qualities but every part retains solidity, extension, shape, and mobility. What are we to make of this argument? It may be true that a body must have some shape or other, but any particular shape can surely be lost, as a piece of wax may cease to be cubical and become spherical. What Locke says of the secondary qualities might be said also of some of the primary qualities. Motion is a primary quality, but a body may be motionless. It is only if we think of motion and rest as a pair of possible values on a single axis of 'mobility' that we can say that here we have a quality which is inseparable from bodies. But in the same sense we can think of heat and cold as values on a single scale of temperature, and say that a body must have some temperature or other. After all, in 1665 the physicist Robert Hooke had already established a thermometer scale.

Locke says that secondary qualities are nothing but a power to produce sensations in us. Let us grant that this is true, or at least a good approximation to truth. It does not mean that secondary qualities are merely subjective, that is to say that they are not genuine properties of the objects that appear to possess them. To take a parallel case, to be poisonous is simply to have a power to produce a certain effect in an animal; but it is an objective matter, a matter of ascertainable fact, whether something is poisonous or not. We may agree with Locke that secondary qualities are defined by their relationship to human perceivers; but a property can be relational while being perfectly objective. 'Being higher than Mont Blanc' is a relational property; but it is a straightforward question of fact whether or not Kanchenjunga is higher than Mont Blanc.

Locke claims that what produces in us the ideas of secondary qualities is nothing but the primary qualities of the object which has the power. The sensation of heat, for instance, is caused by the corpuscles of some other body causing an increase or diminution of the motion of the minute parts of our bodies. But even if primary qualities alone figure in the corpuscularian explanation, why should one conclude that the sensation of heat is nothing but 'a sort and degree of motion in the minute particles of our nerves'? Locke here seems to be appealing to the archaic principle that like causes like. But what reason is there to accept this principle? Surely a substance can cause illness without itself being sick.

Locke claims that secondary qualities do not exist unperceived. But this consorts ill with his view that secondary qualities are powers. They are powers which are exercised when they cause sensations in a perceiver. But powers can exist when they are not being exercised – most of us have the ability to recite *Three Blind Mice*, but we very rarely exercise it. So there is no reason why we should not say that the secondary qualities are powers which continue to exist, but are not exercised save when the qualities are perceived. The candy is always sweet, but it only actually tastes sweet when someone is tasting it. Aristotle was clearer here than Locke: a piece of candy's tasting sweet to me is one and the same thing as my tasting the sweetness of the candy, but the sense-quality and the sense-faculty are two different powers, each of which continues to exist in the absence of the other. Locke claimed that objects had no colours in the dark; but this is a conclusion from, not an argument for, his thesis.

Locke denies that whiteness and coldness are really in objects, because he says the ideas of such secondary qualities do not resemble the qualities in the bodies themselves. This argument trades on the ambiguity, remarked above, in Locke's notion of idea. If an idea of X is a case of perceiving X, then there is no more reason to expect perceiving a colour to resemble that colour than there is to expect eating a potato to resemble a potato. But if, on the other hand, an idea of X is an image of X, then we must reply that when I see a delphinium, what I see is not an image of blueness, but blueness itself. Locke can only deny this by assuming what he is setting out to prove.

Finally, Locke argues from an analogy between feeling and sensation. If I put my hand in the fire, the fire causes both heat and pain; the pain is not in the object, why should we think that the heat is? Once again, the analogy is being drawn in the wrong way. The fire is painful as well as hot. In saying it is painful no one is claiming that it feels pain; equally, in saying it is hot, no one is claiming that it feels heat. If Locke's argument worked, it could be turned against himself. When I cut myself, I feel the slash of the knife as well as the pain: is motion then a secondary quality?

Locke is basically correct in thinking that secondary qualities are powers to produce sensations in human beings, and he has familiar arguments to show that the sensations produced by the same object will vary with circumstances (luke-warm water will appear hot to a cold hand, and cold to a hot hand; colours look very different under a microscope). But from the fact that the secondary qualities are anthropocentric and relative it does not follow that they are subjective or in any way fictional. In a striking image suggested by the Irish chemist Robert Boyle, the secondary qualities are keys which fit particular locks, the locks being the different human senses. Once we grasp this, we can accept, in spite of Locke, that grass really is green, and snow really is cold.

SUBSTANCES AND PERSONS

In the Aristotelian tradition, qualities, like other accidents, belonged to *substances*. In Descartes, too, the notion of substance is of prime importance. Locke says that the notion of substance arises from our observation that certain ideas constantly go together. No one has any clear idea of substance, but 'only a supposition of he knows not what support of such qualities, which are capable of producing simple ideas in us'.

The ideas of particular kinds of substance such as *horse* or *gold* are not simple ideas, but complex ideas. Locke calls them *sortal* ideas: collections of simple co-occurrent ideas plus this general confused idea of a something, we know not what, in addition to its observable qualities. Particular substances are concrete individuals which belong to these different sorts or species. They fall into the two general categories of material and spiritual: material substances, which are characterized by the primary qualities, and spiritual substances, which are characterized by the possession of intellect and will and the power to cause motion.

Substances such as humans and trees have essences: to be a man, or to be an oak, is to have the essence of man or the essence of oak. But there are, for Locke, two kinds of essence. There is the nominal essence, the right to bear a particular name. Nominal essences are the largely arbitrary creation of human language. But things also have real essences, the work of nature, not of man; these are commonly quite unknown to us, at least in advance of experimental inquiry.

Locke's notion of substance is impenetrably obscure. He seems to maintain that substance itself is indescribable because it is propertyless: but can one seriously argue that substance has no properties because it is what *has* the properties? On his own account of the origin of ideas, it is very difficult to account for the emergence of the confused general idea of substance. Substance seems to have been postulated because of the need of a subject for items to belong to, or for items to inhere in. But what, in Locke's system, does the inhering? Shall we say 'qualities'? But qualities, in Locke's system, are hidden behind the veil which ideas place between them and the perceiver. Shall we then say 'ideas'? But ideas already have something to inhere in, namely the mind of the perceiver. The trail is laid for Berkeley's later destructive criticism of the whole notion of material substance.

In the Aristotelian tradition there was no such thing as propertyless substance, a something which could be identified as a particular individual without reference to any sortal. Fido is an individual substance only so long as he remains a dog, only so long as the sortal 'dog' can be truly applied to him. All identity is relative identity, in the sense that we cannot sensibly ask whether A is the same individual as B without asking whether A is the same individual F as B, where 'F' holds a place for some sortal. (A may be the same book as B, but a different edition; or the same edition, but a different copy.) Locke's confused doctrine of substance led him into insoluble difficulties about identity and individuation; but it also stimulated some of his most interesting philosophical writing, in his discussion of the problem of personal identity.

Philosophical problems about identity arise in many different contexts. Some are religious contexts. Can any of us survive the death of our body? If an immortal soul outlives death, is it still a human being? Can a single soul inhabit two different bodies in succession? Can two souls or spirits inhabit the same body at the same time? Other contexts are scientific or medical. When a single human body, at different periods, exhibits different cognitive capacities and contrasting patterns of behaviour, it is natural to talk of split or dual personality. But can a single body really be two different persons at two different times? If the link is cut between the left and right hemispheres of a single brain, the capacities and behaviour of the two halves of a single body may become dissociated. Is this a case of two persons in a single body at one and the same time? Problems like this call for reflection on the concepts of body, soul, mind, person, and on the criteria for identification and re-identification which go with each concept.

It was, however, the religious problems which provided the backdrop for Locke's discussion. Christians believed that the dead would rise again on the last day:

what was the link between a body now dead and turned to clay and a future body gloriously risen? Between death and resurrection, so Catholics believed, individual disembodied souls rejoiced in heaven or suffered in hell or purgatory. Christian Aristotelians strove to reconcile this with their philosophical belief that matter is the principle of individuation. But since disembodied souls are immaterial, what makes the disembodied soul of Peter distinct from the disembodied soul of Paul?

Locke saw clearly that the problems of personal identity could only be resolved if one accepted that identity was relative: that A can be the same F as B without being the same G as B. A colt, he says, growing up to a horse, sometimes fat, sometimes lean, is all the while the same horse, though not the same mass of matter. 'In these two cases of a Mass of Matter, and a living Body, *Identity* is not applied to the same thing.'

The identity of plants and animals consists in continuous life in accordance with the characteristic metabolism of the organism. But in what, Locke asks, does the identity of the same *Man* consist? (By 'man', of course, he means 'human being' including either sex.) A similar answer must be given: a man is 'one fitly organized Body taken in any one instant, and from thence continued under one Organization of Life in several successively fleeting Particles of Matter united to it'. This is the only definition which will enable us to accept that an embryo and an aged lunatic can be the same man, without having to accept that Socrates, Pilate, and Ceasar Borgia are the same men. If we say that having the same soul is enough to make the same man, we cannot exclude the possibility of the transmigration of souls and reincarnation. We have to insist that man is an animal of a certain kind, indeed an animal of a certain shape.

But Locke makes a distinction between the concept *man* and the concept *person*. A person is a being capable of thought, reason, and self-consciousness; and the identity of a person is the identity of self-consciousness. 'As far as this consciousness can be extended backwards to any past Action or Thought, so far reached the Identity of that *Person*; it is the same *self* now it was then; and 'tis by the same *self* with this present one that now reflects on it, that that Action was done.'

Here Locke's principle is that where there is the same self-consciousness, there there is consciousness of the same self. But the passage contains a fatal ambiguity. What is it for my present consciousness to extend backwards?

If my present consciousness extends backwards for so long as this consciousness has a continuous history, the question remains to be answered: what makes *this* consciousness the individual consciousness it is? Locke has debarred himself from answering that *this* consciousness is the consciousness of *this* human being, since he has made his distinction between *man* and *person*.

If, on the other hand, my present consciousness extends backwards only as far as I remember, then my past is no longer my past if I forget it, and I can disown the actions I no longer recall. Locke sometimes seems prepared to accept this; I am not the same person, but only the same man, who did the actions I have forgotten, and I should not be punished for them, since punishment should be directed at persons, not men. However, he seems unwilling to contemplate the further consequence that if I erroneously think I remember being King Herod ordering the massacre of the innocents then I can justly be punished for their murder.

According to Locke I am at one and the same time a man, a spirit, and a person, that is to say, a human animal, an immaterial substance, and a centre of self-consciousness. These three entities are all distinguishable, and in theory may be combined in a variety of ways. We can imagine a single spirit in two different bodies (if, for instance, the soul of the wicked emperor Heliogabalus passed into one of his hogs). We can imagine a single person united to two spirits: if, for instance, the present mayor of Queensborough shared the same consciousness with Socrates. Or we can imagine a single spirit united to two persons (such was the belief of a Christian Platonist friend of Locke's who thought his soul had once been the soul of Socrates). Locke goes on to explore more complicated combinations, which we need not consider, such as one case to illustrate one person, one soul and two men, and another case to illustrate two persons, one soul, and one man.

What are we to make of Locke's trinity, of spirit, person and man? There are difficulties, by no means peculiar to Locke's system, of making sense of immaterial substance, and few of Locke's present-day admirers employ the notion. But the identification of personality with self-consciousness remains popular in some quarters. The main difficulty with it, pointed out in the eighteenth century by Bishop Joseph Butler, arises in connection with the concept of memory.

If Smith claims to remember doing something, or being somewhere, we can, from a common-sense point of view, check whether this memory is accurate by seeing whether Smith in fact did the deed, or was present on the appropriate occasion; and we do so by investigating the whereabouts and activities of Smith's body. But Locke's distinction between person and human being means that this investigation will tell us nothing about the person Smith, but only about the man Smith. Nor can Smith himself, from within, distinguish between genuine memories and present images of past events which offer themselves, delusively, as memories. The way in which Locke conceives of consciousness makes it difficult to draw the distinction between veracious and deceptive memories at all. The distinction can only be made if we are willing to join together what Locke has put asunder, and recognize that persons are human beings.

Locke was not as influential as a theoretical philosopher as he was as a political philosopher; but his influence was none the less extensive, the more so because his name was often linked with that of his compatriot and younger contemporary, Sir Isaac **Newton**. In 1687 Newton published his *Philosophiae naturalis principia mathematica*, which caused a revolution in science of much more enduring importance than the Glorious Revolution of the following year.

Among many scientific achievements, Newton's greatest was the establishment of a universal law of gravitation, showing that bodies are attracted to each other by a force in direct proportion to their masses and in inverse proportion to the distance between them. This enabled him to bring under a single law not only the motion of falling bodies on earth, but also the motion of the moon around the earth and the planets round the sun. In showing that terrestrial and celestial bodies obey the same laws, he dealt the final death blow to the Aristotelian physics. But he also refuted the mechanistic system of Descartes, because the force of gravity was something above and beyond the mere motion of extended matter. Descartes himself, indeed, had considered the notion of attraction between bodies, but had rejected it as resembling Aristotelian final causes, and involving the attribution of consciousness to inert masses.

Newton's physics, therefore, was quite different from the competing systems it replaced; and for the next two centuries physics simply *was* Newtonian physics. The separation of physics from the philosophy of nature, set in train by Galileo, was now complete. The work of Newton and his successors is the province not of the historian of philosophy, but of the historian of science.

XIII

CONTINENTAL PHILOSOPHY IN THE AGE OF LOUIS XIV

Blaise Pascal

Two years after the publication of Descartes' *Meditations*, King Louis XIV succeeded to the throne of France. For the first eighteen years of his reign he was a minor, and the government was in the hands of his mother, Anne of Austria, and her chief minister Cardinal Mazarin. At the latter's death in 1661 Louis began to rule himself, and became the most absolute of all Europe's absolute monarchs. Within France, all political life was centred within his Court. 'L'état, c'est moi' he said famously: I am the state. At Versailles he built a magnificent palace to reflect his own splendour as the Sun King. He revoked the Edict of Nantes, and persecuted the Protestants in his kingdom; at the same time he made his Catholic clergy repudiate much of the jurisdiction claimed by the Pope. During his reign French drama achieved the classic perfection of Corneille and Racine; French painting found magnificent expression in the work of Poussin and Claude.

Louis brought the French army to an unparalleled level of efficiency, and made France the most powerful single power in Europe. He adopted an aggressive policy towards his neighbours, Holland and Spain; and in the earlier part of his reign he showed skill in dividing potential enemies, enrolling Charles II of England as an ally in his Dutch Wars. Only alliances of other European powers in concert could hold his territorial ambitions in check. Even a succession of military defeats inflicted by the allies under the English Duke of Marlborough could not prevent him, at the Peace of Utrecht in 1713, establishing a branch of his own Bourbon family on the throne of Spain. But when he died in 1715 he left a nation that was almost bankrupt.

During his reign, philosophical thought was centred on the legacy of Descartes. We have seen how Descartes' philosophy of nature was destroyed by English scientists; but English philosophers continued to accept, consciously or unconsciously, his dualism of matter and mind. Across the channel, his admirers and critics focused more on the tensions within his dualism, and on the relationship, in his system, between mind, body, and God. The three most significant continental philosophers of the generation succeeding him were all, in very different ways, deeply religious men: Pascal, Spinoza, and Malebranche.

Pascal, like Descartes, was a mathematician as well as a philosopher. Indeed, it is doubtful whether he considered himself a philosopher at all. Born in the Auvergne in 1623 and active in geometry and physics until 1654, he then underwent a religious conversion, which brought him into close contact with the ascetics associated with the convent of Port-Royal. These were called 'Jansenists' because they revered the memory of Bishop Jansenius, who had written a commentary on Augustine which, in the eyes of Church authorities, sailed too close to the Calvinist wind. In accord with Jansenist devaluation of the powers of fallen human nature, Pascal was sceptical of the value of philosophy, especially in relation to knowledge of God. 'We do not think that the whole of philosophy is worth an hour's labour', he once wrote; and stitched into his coat when he died in 1662 was a paper with the words 'God of Abraham, God of Isaac, God of Jacob, not of the philosophers and scholars'.

The Jansenists, because of the poor view they took of human free-will, were constantly at war with its defenders the Jesuits. Pascal wrote a book, *The Provinical Letters*, in which he attacked Jesuit moral theology, and the laxity which, he alleged, Jesuit confessors encouraged in their worldly clients. A particular target of attack was the Jesuit practice of 'direction of intention'. The imaginary Jesuit in his book says, 'Our method of direction consists in proposing to onself, as the end of one's actions, a permitted object. As far as we can we turn men away from forbidden things, but when we cannot prevent the action at least we purify the intention.' Thus, for instance, it is allowable to kill a man in return for an insult. 'All you have to do is to turn your intention from the desire for vengeance, which is criminal, to the desire to defend one's honour, which is permitted.' Such direction of intention, obviously enough, is simply a performance in the imagination which has little to do with genuine intention, which is expressed in the means one chooses to one's ends. It was this doctrine, and Pascal's attack on it, which brought into disrepute the doctrine of double effect we saw in Aquinas, according to which there is an important moral distinction between the intended and unintended effects of one's actions. If the theory of double effect is conjoined with the Jesuitical practice of direction of intention, it simply becomes a hypocritical cloak for the justification of the means by the end.

Pascal was, like Heraclitus, a master of aphorism, and many of his sayings have become familiar quotations. 'Man is only a reed, the weakest thing in nature; but he is a thinking reed.' 'We die alone.' 'Had Cleopatra's nose been shorter, the whole face of the world would have been changed.' Unlike Heraclitus, however, Pascal left a context for his remarks; they belong to a collection of *Pensées* which was intended as a treatise of Christian apologetics, but which was left incomplete at his death. Reading his remarks in context, we can sometimes see that he did not mean them to be taken at their face value. One of the most famous of them is 'The heart has its reasons of which reason knows nothing.' If we study his use of the word 'heart' we can see that he is not here placing feeling above rationality; he is contrasting intuitive with deductive knowledge. It is the heart, he tells us, which teaches us the foundations of geometry.

He did, however, draw attention to the fact that it is possible to have reasons for believing a proposition without having evidence for its truth. He was interested in, and took part in, the contemporary development of the mathematical theory of probability; and he can claim to be one of the founders of game theory. His most famous application of the nascent discipline was to the existence of God. The believer addresses the unbeliever:

> Either God exists or not. Which side shall we take? Reason can determine nothing here. An infinite abyss separates us; and across this infinite distance a game is played, which will turn out heads or tails. What will you bet?

You have no choice whether or not to bet; that does not depend on your will, the game has already begun, and the chances, so far as reason can show, are equal on either side. Suppose that you bet that God exists. If you win, God exists and you can gain infinite happiness; if you lose, then God does not exist, and what you lose is nothing. So the bet is a good one. But how much should one bet? Suppose that you were offered three lives of happiness in return for betting your present life – assuming, as before, that the chances of winning or losing are fifty–fifty. Would it not make sense to bet your whole life on the issue? But in fact, you are offered an eternity of happy life, not just three lifetimes; so the bet is infinitely attractive. The proportion of infinite happiness, in comparison with what is on offer in the present life, is such that the bet on God's existence is a good one even if the odds against winning are enormous, as long as they are only a finite number.

Pascal's wager resembles Anselm's proof of God's existence in that most people who learn of it, whether theist or atheist, smell something wrong with it, without being able to agree exactly what. In both cases the method, if it works at all, seems to work too well, and leads us to accept the existence not only of God but of many grand purely imaginary beings. In the case of the wager, it is not at all clear what it is to bet on the existence of God. Pascal clearly meant it to be roughly equivalent to leading the life of an austere Jansenist. But if, as Pascal thought, reason alone can tell us nothing about either the existence or the nature of God, how can we be sure that that is the kind of life which He will reward with eternal happiness? Perhaps we are being invited to bet on the existence, not just of God, but of the Jansenist God. But if so, what are we to do if someone else invites us to bet on the Jesuit God, or the Lutheran God, or the Muslim God?

SPINOZA AND MALEBRANCHE

The most important of Descartes' continental successors was in fact concerned with the relationship between Cartesian philosophy and the God of the Hebrews. Baruch **Spinoza** was born into a Spanish-speaking Jewish family living in Amsterdam. He was educated as an orthodox Jew, but he early rejected a number of Jewish doctrines, and in 1656, at the age of twenty-four, he was expelled from the synagogue. He earned his living polishing lenses for spectacles and telescopes, first at Amsterdam and later at Leiden and the Hague. He never married and lived the life of a solitary thinker, refusing to accept any academic appointments, though he was offered a chair at Heidelberg and corresponded with a number of savants including Henry Oldenburg, the first Secretary of the Royal Society. He died in 1677 of phthisis, due in part to the inhalation of glass-dust, an occupational hazard for a lens-grinder.

Spinoza's first published work – the only one he published under his own name – was a rendering into geometrical form of Descartes' *Principles of Philosophy*. The features of this early work – the influence of Descartes and the concern for geometrical rigour – are to be found in his mature masterpiece, the *Ethics*, which was written in the 1660s but not published until after his death. Between these two there had appeared, anonymously, a theologico-political treatise (*Tractatus Theologico-Politicus*). This argued for a late dating, and a liberal interpretation, of the books of the Old Testament. It also presented a political theory which, starting from a Hobbes-like view of human beings in a state of nature, derived thence the necessity of democratic government, freedom of speech, and religious toleration.

Spinoza's *Ethics* is set out like Euclid's geometry. Its five parts deal with God, the mind, the emotions, and human bondage and freedom. Each of its parts begins with a set of definitions and axioms and proceeds to offer formal proofs of numbered propositions, each containing, we are to believe, nothing which does not follow from the axioms and definitions, and concluding with QED. This is the best way, Spinoza believed, for a philosopher to make plain his starting assumptions and to bring out the logical relationships between the various theses of his system. But the elucidation of logical connections is not simply to serve clarity of thought; for Spinoza, the logical connections are what holds the universe together. For him, the order and connection of ideas is the same as the order and connection of things.

The key to Spinoza's philosophy is his monism: that is to say, the idea that there is only one single substance, the infinite divine substance which is identical with Nature: *Deus sive Natura*, 'God or nature'. The identification of God and Nature can be understood in two quite different ways. If one takes 'God' in his system to be just a coded way of referring to the ordered system of the natural universe, then Spinoza will appear as a less than candid atheist. On the other hand, if one takes him to be saying that when scientists talk of 'Nature' they are really talking all the time about God, then he will appear to be, in Kierkegaard's words, a 'God-intoxicated man'.

The official starting point of Spinoza's monism is Descartes' definition of substance, as 'that which requires nothing but itself in order to exist'. This definition applies literally only to God, since everything else needs to be created by him and could be annihilated by him. But Descartes counted as substances not only God, but also created matter and finite minds. Spinoza took the definition more seriously than Descartes himself did, and drew from it the conclusion that there is only one substance, God. Mind and matter are not substances; thought and extension, their defining characteristics, are in fact attributes of God, so that God is both a thinking and an extended thing. Because God is infinite, Spinoza argues, he must have an infinite number of attributes; but thought and extension are the only two we know.

There are no substances other than God, for if there were they would present limitations on God, and God would not be, as He is, infinite. Individual minds and bodies are not substances, but just modes, or particular configurations, of the two divine attributes of thought and extension. Because of this, the idea of any individual thing involves the eternal and infinite essence of God.

In traditional theology, all finite substances were dependent on God as their creator and first cause. What Spinoza does is to represent the relationship between God and creatures not in the physical terms of cause and effect, but in the logical terms of subject and predicate. Any apparent statement about a finite substance is in reality a predication about God: the proper way of referring to creatures like us is to use not a noun but an adjective.

Since 'substance', for Spinoza, has such a profound significance, we cannot take it for granted that there is any such thing as substance at all. Nor does Spinoza himself take it for granted: the existence of substance is not one of his axioms. Substance first appears not in an axiom, but in a definition: it is 'that which is in itself and is conceived through itself'. Another one of the initial definitions offers a definition of God as an infinite substance. The first propositions of the ethics are devoted to proving that there is at most one substance. It is not until proposition XI that we are told that there is at least one substance. This one substance is infinite, and is therefore God.

Spinoza's proof of the existence of substance is a version of the ontological argument for the existence of God: it goes like this. A substance A cannot be brought into existence by some other thing B; for if it could, the notion of B would be essential to the conception of A; and therefore A would not satisfy the definition of substance given above. So any substance must be its own cause and contain its own explanation; existence must be part of its essence. Suppose now that God does not exist. In that case his essence does not involve existence, and therefore he is not a substance. But that is absurd, since God is a substance by definition. Therefore, by *reductio ad absurdum*, God exists.

The weakest point in this argument seems to be the claim that if B is the cause of A, then the concept of B must be part of the concept of A. This amounts to an unwarranted identification between causal relationships and logical relationships. It is not possible to know what lung cancer is without knowing what a lung is; but is it not possible to know what lung cancer is without knowing what the cause of lung cancer is? The identification of causality and logic is smuggled in through the original definition of substance, which lumps together being and being conceived.

While Spinoza's proof of God's existence has convinced few, many people share his vision of nature as a single whole, a unified system containing within itself the explanation of all of itself. Many too have followed Spinoza in concluding that if the universe contains its own explanation, then everything that happens is determined, and there is no possibility of any sequence of events other than the actual one. 'In nature there is nothing contingent; everything is determined by the necessity of the divine nature to exist and operate in a certain manner.'

Despite the necessity with which nature operates, Spinoza claims that God is free. This does not mean that he has any choices, but simply that he exists by the mere necessity of his own nature and is free from external determination. God and creatures are determined, but God is self-determined while creatures are determined by God. There are, however, degrees of freedom even for humans. The last two books of the *Ethics* are called 'of human bondage' and 'of human freedom'. Human bondage is slavery to our passions; human freedom is liberation by our intellect.

Human beings wrongly believe themselves to be making free, undetermined, choices; because we do not know the causes of our choices, we assume they have none. The only true liberation possible for us is to make ourselves conscious of the hidden causes. Everything, Spinoza teaches, endeavours to persist in its own being; the essence of anything is indeed its drive towards persistence. In human beings this tendency is accompanied by consciousness, and this conscious tendency is called 'desire'. Pleasure and pain are the consciousness of a transition to a higher or lower level of perfection in mind and body. The other emotions are all derived from the fundamental feelings of desire, pleasure, and pain. But we must distinguish between active and passive emotions. Passive emotions, like fear and anger, are generated by external forces; active emotions arise from the mind's understanding of the human condition. Once we have a clear and distinct idea of a passive emotion it becomes an active emotion; and the replacement of passive emotions by active ones is the path to liberation.

In particular, we must give up the passion of fear, and especially the fear of death. 'A free man thinks of nothing less than of death; and his wisdom is a meditation not of death but of life.' The key to moral progress is the appreciation of the necessity of all things. We will cease to feel hatred for others when we realize that their acts are determined by nature. Returning hatred only increases it; but reciprocating it with love vanquishes it. What we need to do is to take a God's-eye-view of the whole necessary natural scheme of things, seeing it 'in the light of eternity'. This vision is at the same time an intellectual love of God, since God and Nature are one, and the more one understands God the more one loves God.

The mind's intellectual love of God is the very same thing as God's love for men: it is, that is to say, the expression of God's self-love through the attribute of thought. But on the other hand, Spinoza warns that 'he who loves God cannot endeavour that God should love him in return'. Indeed, if you want God to love you in return for your love you want God not to be God.

Clearly, Spinoza rejected the idea of a personal God as conceived by orthodox Jews and Christians. He also regarded as an illusion the religious idea of the immortality of the soul. For Spinoza mind and body are inseparable: the human mind is in fact simply the idea of the human body. 'Our mind can only be said to endure, and its existence can be given temporal limits, only in so far as it involves the actual existence of the body.' But when the mind views things in the light of eternity, time ceases to matter; past, present, and future are all equal and time is unreal.

We think of the past as what cannot be changed, and the future as being open to alternatives. But in Spinoza's deterministic universe, the future is no less fixed than the past. The difference, therefore, between past and future should play no part in the reflections of a wise man; we should not worry about the future nor feel remorse about the past. The once-for-all existence of any given mind as part of the single, infinite, necessary universe is an eternal truth; and by looking at things in the light of the eternal truths, the mind reaches throughout the unending, necessary, eternal universe. In that sense any mind is eternal, and can be thought of as having existed before birth as well as after death. But all this is something very different from the personal survival in an afterlife to which popular piety looked forward. It enabled Spinoza to greet his own death with tranquillity, but it was no wonder that both Jews and Christians looked upon him as a heretic.

A Christian contemporary who stands in the middle between Spinoza and Descartes is Nicolas **Malebranche**. Born in Paris in 1638, he became a priest of the order of the Oratory in 1664 and wrote a series of philosophical and theological treatises, remaining productive right up to his death in 1715. In philosophy, he followed Descartes closely in detail; but like many others, from Princess Elizabeth onwards, he found it impossible to accept Descartes' teaching on the interaction between mind and body.

For Malebranche, it was obvious that a spiritual being, like the human will, was incapable of moving the smallest particle of matter. If I will to move my arm, my will does not truly cause the movement of my arm. The only true cause is God, who, upon the occasion of my willing the movement, makes my arm move. The only sense in which we humans are causes is that we provide the occasion for God to do the real causing. This is Malebranche's famous 'occasionalism'.

If there is no genuine output from mind to body, equally there is no true input from body to mind. If minds are incapable of moving bodies, bodies are equally incapable of putting ideas into minds. Our minds are passive, not active, and cannot create their own ideas. These can only have come from God. If I prick my finger with a needle, the pain does not come from the needle; it is directly caused by God. We see all things in God: God is the environment in which minds live, just as space is the environment in which bodies are located.

Malebranche was far from being the first to say that we see the eternal truths by coming in contact, in some mysterious way, with ideas in the mind of God. But it was a new move to say that our knowledge of the contingent history of material and changeable bodies comes directly from God. Descartes, of course, thought that only God's truthfulness could show that our empirical knowledge of the external world was not deceptive. But for Malebranche, there is no such thing as empirical knowledge of the external world; its existence is a revelation, contained, along with other truths necessary for salvation, in the Bible.

Like Descartes, therefore, and unlike Spinoza, Malebranche accepts the existence of finite substances, material and mental. But unlike Descartes and like Spinoza, he thinks that mind's relation to God, and matter's relation to God, are both much closer than the relation of mind and matter to each other.

LEIBNIZ

Both Malebranche and Spinoza were important influences on the thinking of Gottfried Wilhelm Leibniz. Leibniz was born in 1646, the son of a professor of philosophy at Leipzig university. He started to read metaphysics in early youth, and by the age of thirteen became familiar with the writings of the scholastics, to which he remained much more sympathetic than most of his contemporaries. He studed mathematics at Jena and law at Altdorf, where he was offered, and refused, a professorship at the age of twenty-one. He entered the service of the Archbishop of Mainz, and on a diplomatic mission to Paris met many of the leading thinkers of the day, and came under the influence of Descartes' successors. There, in 1676, he invented the infinitesimal calculus, unaware of Newton's earlier but as yet unpublished discoveries. On his way back to Germany he visited Spinoza, and studied the *Ethics* in manuscript.

From 1676 until the end of his life Leibniz was a courtier to successive electors of Hanover. He was the librarian of the court library at Wolfenbüttel, and spent many years compiling the history of the House of Brunswick. He founded learned societies and became the first president of the Prussian Academy. He was ecumenical in theology as well as in philosophy, and made several attempts to reunite the Christian churches and to set up a European federation. When in 1714 the elector George of Hanover became King George I of the United Kingdom, Leibniz was left behind. No doubt he would have been unwelcome in England because he had quarrelled with Newton over the ownership of the infinitesimal calculus. He died, embittered, in 1716.

Throughout his life Leibniz wrote highly original work on many branches of philosophy, but he published only a few comparatively short treatises. His earliest treatise was the brief *Discourse on Metaphysics* which he sent in 1686 to Antoine Arnauld, the Jansenist author of the *Port Royal Logic*. This was followed in 1695 by the *New System of Nature*. The longest work published in his lifetime was *Essays in Theodicy*, a vindication of divine justice in the face of the evils of the world, dedicated to Queen Charlotte of Prussia. Two of Leibniz's most important short treatises appeared in 1714: the *Monadology* and *The Principles of Nature and of Grace*. A substantial criticism of Locke's empiricism, *New Essays on Human Understanding*, did not appear until nearly fifty years after his death. Much of his most interesting work was not published until the nineteenth and twentieth centuries.

Since Leibniz kept many of his most powerful ideas out of his published work, the correct interpretation of his philosophy continues to be a matter of controversy. He wrote much on logic, metaphysics, ethics, and philosophical theology; his knowledge of all these subjects was encyclopaedic, and indeed he projected a comprehensive encyclopedia of human knowledge, to be produced by co-operation between learned societies and religious orders.

It remains unclear how far Leibniz's significant contributions to these different disciplines are consistent with each other, and which parts of his system are foundation and which are superstructure. But there are close links between parts of his output which seem at first sight poles apart. In his *De Arte Combinatoria* he put forward the idea of an alphabet of human thought into which all truths could be analysed, and he wanted to develop a single, universal, language which would mirror the structure of the world. His interest in this was generated partly by his desire to unite the Christian confessions, whose differences, he believed, were generated by the imperfections and ambiguities of the various natural languages of Europe. Such a language would also promote international co-operation between scientists of different nations.

Since Leibniz never published his philosophy systematically, we have to consider his opinions piecemeal. In logic he distinguishes between truths of reason and truths of fact. Truths of reason are necessary, and their opposite is impossible; truths of fact are contingent and their opposite is possible. Truths of fact, unlike truths of reason, are based not on the principle of contradiction, but on a different principle: the principle that nothing happens without a sufficient reason why it should be thus rather than otherwise. This principle of sufficient reason was an innovation of Leibniz, and as we shall see, it was to lead to some astonishing conclusions.

All necessary truths are analytic: 'when a truth is necessary, the reason for it can be found by analysis, that is, by resolving it into simpler ideas and truths until the primary ones are reached'. Contingent propositions, or truths of fact, are not in any obvious sense analytic, and men can discover them only by empirical investigation. But from God's viewpoint, they are analytic.

Consider the history of Alexander the Great, which consists in a series of truths of fact. God, seeing the individual notion of Alexander, sees contained in it all the predicates truly attributable to him: whether he conquered Darius, whether he died a natural death, and so on. In 'Alexander conquered Darius' the predicate is in a manner contained in the subject; it must make its appearance in a complete and perfect idea of Alexander. A person of whom that predicate could not be asserted would not be our Alexander, but somebody else. Hence, the proposition is in a sense analytic. But the analysis necessary to exhibit this would be an infinite one, which only God could complete. And while any possible Alexander would possess all those properties, the actual *existence* of Alexander is a contingent matter, even from God's point of view. The only necessary existence is God's own existence.

Leibniz told Arnauld that the theory that every true predicate is contained in the notion of the subject entailed that every soul was a world apart, independent of everything else except God. A 'world apart' of this kind was what Leibniz later called a 'monad', and in his *Monadology* Leibniz presented a system which resembles that of Malebranche. But he reached this position by a novel route.

Whatever is complex, Leibniz argued, is made up of what is simple, and whatever is simple is unextended, for if it were extended it could be further divided. But whatever is material is extended, hence there must be simple immaterial, soul-like entities. These are the monads. Whereas for Spinoza there is only one substance, with the attributes of both thought and extension, and whereas for Malebranche there are independent substances, some with the properties of matter, and some with the properties of mind, for Leibniz there are infinitely many substances, with the properties only of mind.

Like Malebranche's substances, Leibniz's monads cannot be causally affected by any other creatures. 'Monads have no windows, by which anything could come in or go out.' Because they have no parts, they cannot grow or decay: they can begin only by creation, and end only by annihilation. They can, however, change; indeed they change constantly; but they change from within. Since they have no physical properties to alter, their changes must be changes of mental states: the life of a monad, Leibniz says, is a series of perceptions.

But does not perception involve causation? When I see a rose, is not my vision caused by the rose? No, replies Leibniz, once again in accord with Malebranche. A monad mirrors the world, not because it is affected by the world, but because God has programmed it to change in synchrony with the world. A good clockmaker can construct two clocks which will keep such perfect time that they forever strike the hours at the same moment. In relation to all his creatures, God is such a clockmaker: at the very beginning of things he pre-established the harmony of the universe.

All monads have perception, that is to say, they have an internal state which is a representation of all the other items in the universe. This inner state will change as the environment changes, not because of the environmental change, but because of the internal drive or 'appetition' which has been programmed into them by God. Monads are incorporeal automata: when Leibniz wishes to stress this aspect of them he calls them 'entelechies'.

> There is a world of created beings – living things, animals, entelechies and souls – in the least part of matter. Each portion of matter may be conceived as a garden full of plants, and as a pond full of fish. But every branch of each plant, every member of each animal, and every drop of their liquid parts is itself likewise a similar garden or pond.

We are nowadays familiar with the idea of the human body as an assemblage of cells, each living an individual life. The monads which – in Leibniz's system – corresponded to a human body were like cells in having an individual life-history, but unlike cells in being immaterial and immortal. Each animal has an entelechy which is its soul; but the members of its body are full of other living things which have their own souls. Within the human being the dominant monad is the rational soul. This dominant monad, in comparison with other monads, has a more vivid mental life and a more imperious appetition. It has not just perception but 'apperception', that is to say consciousness or reflective knowledge of the inner state, which is perception. Its own good is the goal, or final cause, not just of its own activity but also of all the other monads which it dominates. This is all that is left, in Leibniz's system, of Descartes' notion that the soul acts upon the body.

In all this, is any room left for free-will? Human beings, like all agents, finite or infinite, need a reason for acting: that follows from Leibniz's 'principle of sufficient reason'. But in the case of free agents, he maintains, the motives which provide the sufficient reason 'incline without necessitating'. But it is hard to see how he can make room for a special kind of freedom for human beings. True, in his system no agent of any kind is acted on from outside; all are completely self-determining. But no agent, whether rational or not, can step outside the life-history laid out for it in the pre-established harmony. Hence it seems that Leibniz's 'freedom of spontaneity' – the freedom to act upon one's motives – is an illusory liberty.

Leibniz has an answer to this objection, which resembles the thesis of the Jesuit Molina about the relationship between God and the created universe. Before deciding to create the world, Leibniz maintains, God surveys the infinite number of possible creatures. Among the possible creatures there will be many possible

Julius Caesars: and among these there will be one Julius Caesar who crosses the Rubicon and one who does not. Each of these possible Caesars will act for a reason, and neither of them will be necessitated (there is no law of logic saying that the Rubicon will be crossed, or that it will not be crossed). When, therefore, God decides to give existence to the Rubicon-crossing Caesar he is making actual a freely-choosing Caesar. Hence, our actual Caesar crossed the Rubicon freely.

But what of God's own choice to give existence to the actual world we live in, in contrast to the myriad other possible worlds he might have created? Was there a reason for that choice, and was it a free choice? Leibniz's answer is that God chose freely to make the best of all possible worlds; otherwise he could have had no sufficient reason to create this world rather than another.

Not all things which are possible in advance can be made actual together: in Leibniz's terms, A and B may each be possible, but A and B may not be compossible. Any created world is therefore a system of compossibles, and the best possible world is the system which has the greatest surplus of good over evil. A world in which there is free-will which is sometimes sinfully misused is better than a world in which there is neither freedom nor sin. Hence the evil in the world provides no argument against the goodness of God. Because God is good, and necessarily good, he chooses the most perfect world. Yet he acts freely, because though he cannot create anything but the best, he need not have created at all.

It is interesting to compare Leibniz's position here with that of Descartes and Aquinas. Descartes' God was totally free: even the laws of logic were the result of his arbitrary *fiat*. Leibniz, like Aquinas before him, maintained that the eternal truths depended not on God's will but on his understanding; where logic was concerned God had no choice. Aquinas' God, though not as free as Descartes', is less constrained than Leibniz's. For, according to Aquinas, though whatever God does is good, he is never obliged to do what is best. Indeed, for Aquinas, given God's omnipotence, the notion of 'the best of all possible worlds' is every bit as nonsensical as that of 'the greatest of all possible numbers'.

Leibniz's optimistic theory was memorably mocked by Voltaire in his novel *Candide*, in which the Leibnizian Dr Pangloss responds to a series of miseries and catastrophes with the incantation 'All is for the best in the best of all possible worlds'.

The Leibnizian monadology is a baroque effloresence of Cartesian metaphysics. His work marks the high point of continental rationalism; his sucessors in Germany, especially Wolff, developed a dogmatic scholasticism which was the system in which Immanuel Kant was brought up, and which was to be the target, in his maturity, of his devastating criticism. Leibniz's claim to greatness lies not in his systematic creations, but in the conceptions and distinctions which he contributed to many different branches of philosophy, and which became standard coin among succeeding philosophers.

Several of these – the distinction between different kinds of truths, the notions of analyticity and compossibility – we have already met. We may add, finally, Leibniz's treatment of identity. From the principle of sufficient reason Leibniz concluded that there were not in nature two beings indiscernible from each other; for if there were, God would act without reason in treating one differently from the other. From this principle of the Identity of Indiscernibles, he derives a definition of the identity of terms. 'Terms are identical which can be substituted one for another wherever we please without altering the truth of any statement.' If whatever is true of A is true of B, and vice versa, then A = B. This account of identity, known as Leibniz's law, though it is less subtle than that of Locke, has been taken by most subsequent philosophers as the basis of their discussions of identity.

XIV

BRITISH PHILOSOPHY IN THE EIGHTEENTH CENTURY

BERKELEY

In 1715 King Louis XIV of France died. A year earlier Queen Anne, the last of the Stuart monarchs of England, had died, and on her death, the English crown was given to the dynasty of Hanover, in order to preserve the Protestant succession. The Hanoverian King Georges were able to maintain their throne against attempts by the son and grandson of James II (the 'Old and Young Pretenders') to restore the Stuart line. At the beginning of the eighteenth century, in the reign of Anne, the crowns of England and Scotland were united; and those of England and Ireland were united at the end of the century, in the reign of George III. Thus was formed the United Kingdom of Great Britain and Ireland. As it turned out, the ablest philosophers writing in English in the eighteenth century were Irish or Scottish, though all of them saw themselves as carrying on the tradition of the Englishman John Locke.

George **Berkeley** was born in Ireland in 1685, and after graduating from Trinity College, Dublin, he published a number of short but important philosophical works. His *New Theory of Vision* appeared in 1709, *Principles of Human Knowledge* in 1710, and *Three Dialogues* in 1713. In 1713 he came to England and became a member of the circle of Swift and Pope. He travelled in Europe and America, and at one time planned to set up a missionary college in the Bermudas. He became Bishop of Cloyne in 1734 and in 1753 died in retirement in Oxford, where he is buried in Christ Church Cathedral. A College at Yale and a university town in California are named after him.

Berkeley's starting point in philosophy is Locke's theory of language. According to Locke words have meaning by standing for ideas, and general words, such as sortal predicates, correspond to abstract general ideas. The ability to form such ideas is the most important difference between humans and dumb animals.

Berkeley extracts from Locke's *Essay* two different accounts of the meanings of general terms. One, which we may call the representational theory, is that a general idea is a particular idea which has been made general by being made to stand for all of a kind, in the way in which a geometry teacher draws a particular triangle to represent all triangles. Another, which we may call the eliminative theory, is that a general idea is a particular idea which contains only what is common to all particulars of the same kind: the abstract idea of man eliminates what is peculiar to Peter, James, and John, and retains only what is common to them all. Thus, the abstract idea of man contains colour, but no particular colour, stature, but no particular stature, and so on. There is one passage in which Locke combines features of the two theories, where he explains that it takes pains and skill to form the general idea of a triangle 'for it must be neither oblique nor rectangle, neither equilateral, equicrural nor scalenon; but all and none of these at once'.

Berkeley protests that this is absurd. 'The idea of man that I frame myself must be either of a white, or a black, or a tawny, a straight, or a crooked, a tall, or a low, or a middle-sized man. I cannot by any effort of thought conceive the abstract idea.' If by 'idea' Berkeley here means an image, his criticism seems mistaken. Mental images do not need to have all the properties of that of which they are images, any more than a portrait on canvas has to represent all the features of the sitter. A dress pattern need not specify the colour of the dress, even though any actual dress must have some particular colour. A mental image of a dress of no particular colour is no more problematic than a non-specific dress pattern. There would, indeed, be something odd about an image which had all colours and no colours at once, as Lock's triangle had all shapes and no shape at once. But it is unfair to judge Locke's account by this single rhetorical passage.

Where Locke really goes astray is in thinking that the possession of a concept (which is standardly manifested by the ability to use a word) is to be explained by the having of images. To use a figure, or an image, to represent an X, one must already have a concept of an X. Moreover, concepts cannot be acquired simply by stripping off features from images. Apart from anything else, there are some concepts to which no image corresponds: logical concepts, for instance, such as those corresponding to the words 'all' and 'not'. There are other concepts which could never be unambiguously related to images, for instance arithmetical concepts. One and the same image may represent four legs and one horse, or seven trees and one copse.

Berkeley was correct, against Locke, in thinking that one can separate the mastery of language from the possession of abstract general images; but his own alternative solution, that names 'signify indifferently a great number of particular ideas', was equally mistaken. Once concept-possession is distinguished from image-mongering, mental images become philosophically unimportant. Imaging is no more essential to thinking than illustrations are to a book. It is not our images which explain our possession of concepts, but our concepts which confer meaning on our images.

Berkeley's arguments against abstract ideas are most fully presented in his *Principles of Human Knowledge*; his other criticisms of Locke are most elegantly developed in his *Three Dialogues between Hylas and Philonous*. Berkeley's own philosophical system is encapsulated in the motto *esse est percipi*: for unthinking things, to exist is nothing other than to be perceived.

In the *Three Dialogues*, the system is developed in four stages. First, Berkeley argues that all sensible qualities are ideas. Secondly, he demolishes the notion of inert matter. Thirdly, he proves the existence of God. Fourthly, he reinterprets ordinary language to match his own metaphysics, and defends the orthodoxy of his system. Berkeley's language is economical, lucid, and stylish, and the task of distinguishing between his sound and unsound arguments is not a difficult one, so that the *Dialogues* provide an ideal text for a beginners' class in philosophy.

In the first dialogue Berkeley argues for the subjectivity of secondary qualities, using Locke as an ally; then he turns the tables against Locke by producing parallel arguments for the subjectivity of primary qualities. Starting from Locke's premiss that only ideas are immediately perceived, Berkeley reaches the conclusion that no ideas, not even those of primary qualities, are resemblances of objects.

The two characters in the dialogue are Hylas, the Lockean friend of matter, and Philonous, the Berkeleian spokesman for idealism. Hylas turns out, right from the start, to be a very faint-hearted friend of matter, because he accepts without argument the premiss that we do not perceive material things in themselves, but only their sensible qualities. 'Sensible things,' he says, 'are nothing else but so many sensible qualities.' Material things may be inferred, but they are not perceived. 'The senses perceive nothing which they do not perceive immediately; for they make no inferences.'

Hylas does, however, maintain the objectivity of sensible qualities, and in order to destroy this position Berkeley makes Philonous expound the line of argument used by Locke to show the subjectivity of heat. There are, as we have seen, a number of fallacies in the argument. It is in the mouth of Hylas that Berkeley cunningly places many of the false moves, as in the following passage:

Phil. *Heat* then is a sensible thing?

Hyl. Certainly.

Phil. Doth the reality of sensible things consist in being perceived? or is it something distinct from their being perceived, and that bears no relation to the mind?

Hyl. To exist is one thing, and to be perceived is another.

Phil. I speak with regard to sensible things only. And of these I ask, whether by their real existence you mean a substance exterior to the mind, and distinct from their being perceived?

Hyl. I mean a real absolute being, distinct from, and without any relation to, their being perceived.

A shrewder defender of the objectivity of qualities might have admitted that they may have a relation to being perceived, while still insisting that they are distinct from actual perception.

Stripped of its dialogue form, the argument goes as follows. All degrees of heat are perceived by the senses, and the greater the heat, the more sensibly it is perceived. But a great degree of heat is a great pain; material substance is incapable of feeling pain, and therefore the great heat cannot be in the material substance. All degrees of heat are equally real, and so if a great heat is not something in an external object, neither is any heat.

Hylas is always answering 'yes' or 'no' to Philonous' leading questions, when he should be making distinctions. When Philonous asks 'Is not the most vehement and intense degree of heat a very great pain?' Hylas should have replied: the *sensation* of heat is a pain, maybe; the heat itself is a pain, no. It is true that unperceiving things are not capable of feeling pain; that does not mean they are incapable of being painful. Again, when Philonous asks 'Is your material substance a senseless being, or a being endowed with sense and perception?' Hylas should reply: some material substances (e.g. rocks) are senseless; others (e.g. cats) have senses. It would be tedious to follow, line by line, the sleight of hand by which Hylas is tricked into denying the objectivity of the sensation of heat. Parallel fallacies are committed in the arguments about tastes, odours, sounds, and colours.

At the conclusion of the first dialogue, Philonous asks whether it is at all possible for ideas to be like things. How can a visible colour be like a real thing which is in itself invisible? Can anything be like a sensation or idea, but another sensation or idea? Hylas concurs that nothing but an idea can be like an idea, and no idea can exist without the mind; hence he is quite unable to defend the reality of material substances.

In the second dialogue, however, Hylas tries to fight back, and presents many defences of the existence of matter; each of them is swiftly despatched. Matter is not perceived, because it has been agreed that only ideas are perceived. Matter, Philonous persuades Hylas to agree, is an extended, solid, moveable, unthinking, inactive substance. Such a thing cannot be the cause of our ideas; for what is unthinking cannot be the cause of thought. Should we say that Matter is an instrument of the one divine cause? Surely God, who can act merely by willing, has no need of lifeless tools! Or should we say that Matter provides the occasion for God to act? But surely the all-wise one has no need of prompting!

'Do you not at length perceive', taunts Philonous, 'that in all these different acceptations of Matter, you have been only supposing you know not what, for no manner of reason, and to no kind of use?' Matter cannot be defended whether it is conceived as object, *substratum*, cause, instrument, or occasion. It cannot even be brought under the most abstract possible notion of *entity*; for it does not exist in place, it has no manner of existence. Since it corresponds to no notion in the mind, it might just as well be nothing.

Matter was fantasized in order to be the basis for our ideas. But that role, in Berkeley's system, belongs not to matter, but to God; and the existence of the sensible world provides a proof of the existence of God. The world consists only of ideas, and no idea can exist otherwise than in a mind. But sensible things have an existence exterior to my mind, since they are quite independent of it. They must therefore exist in some other mind, while I am not perceiving them. 'And as the same is true with regard to all other finite created spirits, it necessarily follows that there is an omnipresent eternal Mind, which knows and comprehends all things.'

Even if we grant that the sensible world consists only of ideas, there seems to be a flaw in this proof of God's existence. One cannot, without fallacy, pass from the premiss 'There is no finite mind in which everything exists' to the conclusion 'therefore there is an infinite mind in which everything exists'. (Compare 'There is no nation-state of which everyone is a citizen; therefore there is an international state of which everyone is a citizen.')

The final task which Berkeley entrusts to Philonous is to reinterpret ordinary language so that our everyday beliefs about the world turn out to be true after all. Statements about material substances have to be translated into statements about collections of ideas. 'The real things are those very things I see and feel, and perceive by my senses. . . . A piece of sensible bread, for instance, would stay my stomach better than ten thousand times as much of that insensible, unintelligible, real bread you speak of.'

A material substance is a collection of sensible impressions or ideas perceived by various senses, treated as a unit by the mind because of their constant conjunction with each other. This thesis, which is called 'phenomenalism', is, according to Berkeley, perfectly reconcilable with the use of instruments in scientific explanation and with the framing of natural laws: they state relationships not between things but between phenomena, that is to say, ideas. What we normally consider to be the difference between appearance and reality is to be explained simply in terms of the greater or lesser vividness of ideas, and the varying degrees of voluntary control which accompany them.

Berkeley concludes his exposition with a series of reassurances to orthodox readers. The thesis that the world consists of ideas in the mind of God does not lead to the conclusion that God suffers pain, or that he is the author of sin, or that he is an inadequate creator who cannot produce anything real outside himself.

Berkeley's system is more counterintuitive than Locke's in that it denies the reality of matter and all extra-mental existence, and that it makes no room for any causation other than the voluntary agency of finite or infinite spirits. On the other hand, unlike Locke, Berkeley will allow that qualities genuinely belong to objects, and that sense objects can be genuinely known to exist. If neither system is in the end remotely credible, that is because of the root error common to both, namely the thesis that ideas, and ideas only, are perceived. But the philosopher in whose work we can see most fully the consequences of the empiricist assumptions is David Hume.

HUME'S PHILOSOPHY OF MIND

Hume was born in Edinburgh in 1711. He was a precocious philosopher, and his major work, *A Treatise of Human Nature*, was written in his twenties. In his own words it 'fell dead-born from the press'; unsurprisingly, perhaps, in view of its mannered, meandering, and repetitious style. He rewrote much of its content in two more popular volumes: *An Enquiry concerning Human Understanding* (1748) and *An Enquiry concerning the Principles of Morals* (1751). He tried, and failed, to obtain a professorship in Edinburgh, and in his lifetime he was better known as a historian than as a philosopher, for between 1754 and 1761 he wrote a six-volume history of England with a strong Tory bias. In the 1760s he was secretary to the British Embassy in Paris. He was a genial man, who did his best to befriend the difficult philosopher Rousseau, and was described by the economist Adam Smith as having come as near to perfection as any human being possibly could. In his last years he wrote a philosophical attack on natural theology, *Dialogues concerning Natural Religion*, which was published, three years after his death, in 1776. To the disappointment of James Boswell (who recorded his final illness in detail) he died serenely, having rejected the consolations of religion.

The *Treatise of Human Nature* begins by dividing the contents ('perceptions') of the mind into two classes, impressions and ideas, instead of following Locke in calling them all 'ideas'. Impressions are more forceful, more vivid, than ideas. Impressions include sensations and emotions, ideas are what are involved in thinking and reasoning. It is never quite clear, in Hume, what is meant by vividness: it seems to be a matter sometimes of how much detail a perception contains, sometimes of how much emotional colouring it has, sometimes of how great an effect it has on action. The notion is too vague to make a sharp distinction, and the use of it to differentiate thought and feeling makes each appear too like the other.

Ideas, Hume says, are copies of impressions. This looks at first like a definition, but Hume appeals to experience in support of it. From time to time he invites the reader to look within himself to verify the principle, and we are told that it is supported by the fact that a man born blind has no idea of colours. Whether it is a definition or hypothesis, the thesis is intended to apply only to simple ideas.

I can construct a complex idea of the New Jerusalem, without ever having seen any such city. But in the case of simple ideas, Hume says, the rule holds almost without exception that there is a one-to-one correspondence between ideas and impressions. The meaning of 'simple' turns out to be as slippery as that of 'vivid'. But whenever he wishes to attack metaphysics, Hume puts the principle 'no idea without antecedent impression' to vigorous use.

Hume tells us that there are two ways in which impressions reappear as ideas: there are ideas of memory and ideas of imagination. Ideas of memory differ from ideas of imagination in two respects: they are more vivid, and they preserve the order in time and space of the original impressions. Once again, it is not clear exactly what distinction is here being made. Are these differences supposed to distinguish genuine from delusory memory? The second criterion would suffice to make the distinction, but of course no one could ever apply it in his own case to tell whether any particular memory was genuine. Or are the criteria meant to distinguish would-be memory, whether accurate or mistaken, from the free play of the imagination? Here the first criterion might be tried, but it would be unreliable, since fantasies can be more obsessive than memories.

When Hume talks of memory, he always seems to have in mind the reliving in imagination of past events; but of course that is only one, and not the most important, exercise of our knowledge of the past. If 'memory' is a word that catches many different things, 'imagination' covers an even wider variety of different events, capacities, and mistakes. Imagination may be, *inter alia*, misperception ('is that a knock at the door, or am I only imagining it?'), misremembering ('did I post the letter, or am I only imagining I did?'), unsupported belief ('I imagine it won't be long before he's sorry he married her'), the entertainment of hypotheses ('imagine the consequences of a nuclear war between India and Pakistan'), and creative originality ('Blake's imagination was unsurpassed'). Not all these kinds of imagination necessarily involve the kind of mental imagery which Hume takes as the paradigm.

When imagery *is* involved, its role is quite different from that assigned to it by Hume. He believed that the meaning of the words of our language consisted in their relation to impressions and ideas. According to him, it is the flow of impressions and ideas in our minds which ensures that our utterances are not empty sounds, but the expression of thought; and if a word cannot be shown to refer to an impression or to an idea it must be discarded as meaningless.

In fact, the relation between language and images is the other way round. When we think in images it is the thought that confers meaning on the images, and not vice versa. When we talk silently to ourselves, the words we utter in imagination would not have the meaning they do were it not for our intellectual mastery of the language to which they belong. And when we think in visual images as well as in unuttered words, the images merely provide the illustration to a text whose meaning is given by the words which express the thoughts. We grasp the meaning of words not by solitary introspection, but by sharing with others in the communal enterprise of language.

The difference between remembering and imagining might be thought to be best made out in terms of *belief*. If I take myself to be remembering that *p*, then I believe that *p*; but I can imagine *p*'s being the case without any such belief. As Hume says, we conceive many things which we do not believe. But he finds it difficult, in fact, to fit belief into his plan of the furniture of the mind.

What, in Hume's system, is the difference between merely having the thought that *p*, and actually believing that *p*? It is not a difference of content; if it were, it would involve adding to the thought a new idea – perhaps the idea of existence. But, Hume says, there is no such idea. When, after conceiving something, we conceive it as existent, we add nothing to our first idea.

> Thus when we affirm, that God is existent, we simply form the idea of such a being, as he is represented to us; nor is the existence, which we attribute to him, conceiv'd by a particular idea, which we join to the idea of his other qualities, and can again separate and distinguish from them.

The difference between conception and belief, then, must lie not in the idea involved, but in the manner in which we grasp it. Belief consists in the vividness of the idea, and in its association with some current impression – the impression, whichever it is, which is the ground of our belief. 'Belief is a lively idea produc'd by a relation to a present impression.'

Hume is right that believing and conceiving need not differ in content. As he says, if A believes that *p* and B does not believe that *p*, they are disagreeing about the same idea. But having a thought about God and believing that God exists are two quite different things; and Hume is wrong to say that there is no concept of existence. How, if his account were right, could we judge that something does *not* exist? We may agree that the concept of existence is a totally different kind of concept from the concept of God or the concept of a unicorn. But Hume's difficulty in admitting that there can be a concept of existence arises from the empiricist prejudice that a concept must be a mental image.

There are several difficulties in Hume's account of vivacity as a mark of belief. Some of them are internal to his system. We may wonder, for instance, why this feeling attaching to an idea is not an impression, and how we are to distinguish belief from memory since vivacity is the criterion of each. Other difficulties are not merely internal. The crucial one is that belief need not involve imagery at all (when I sit down, I believe the chair will support me: but no thought about the matter enters my mind). And when imagery is involved in belief, an obsessive imagination (of a spouse's infidelity, for instance) may be livelier than genuine belief.

Hume's account of psychological concepts is flawed because he relies on an appeal to first-person introspection to establish the meaning of psychological terms, rather than exploring how human beings apply psychological verbs to each other in the public world. The consequences of the reliance on introspection are most vividly brought out when Hume considers his own existence.

> When I enter most intimately into what I call *myself* I always stumble on some particular perception or other, of heat or cold, light or shade, love or hatred, pain or pleasure. I never catch *myself* at any time without a perception and never can observe anything but the perception.

Berkeley had maintained that ideas inhered in nothing outside the mind; Hume now insists that there is nothing inside for them to inhere in either. There is no impression of the self, and therefore no idea of the self; there are simply bundles of impressions.

This conclusion is the end of the road which begins with the assumption, common to all the empiricists, that thoughts are images and the relation between a thinker and his thoughts is that of an inner eye to an inner picture gallery. Just as one cannot see one's own eye, one cannot perceive one's own self. But it is a mistake to regard imagination as an inner sense. The entertaining of mental images is not a peculiar kind of sensation; it is ordinary sensation phantasized. The notion of an inner sense leads to the idea of a self that is the subject of inner sensation. The self, in the tradition of Locke and Berkeley, is the eye of inner vision, the ear of inner hearing; or rather, it is the possessor of both inner eye and inner ear. Hume showed that this inner subject was illusory; but he did not expose the underlying error which led the empiricists to espouse the myth of the inner self. The real way out of the impasse is to reject the identification of thought and image, and to accept that a thinker is not a solitary inner perceiver, but an embodied human being living in a public world.

Hume prided himself on doing for psychology what Newton had done for physics. He offered a (vacuous) theory of the association of ideas as the counterpart to the theory of gravitation. But it would be unfair to blame Hume because his philosophical psychology is so jejune; he inherited an impoverished philosophy of mind from his seventeenth-century forebears, and one of his merits is that he draws out, with considerable candour, the stultifying conclusions which are implicit in the empiricist assumptions. But what gives him his substantial place in the history of philosophy is his account of causation.

HUME ON CAUSATION

If we look for the origin of the idea of causation, Hume says, we find that it cannot be any particular inherent quality of objects; for objects of the most different kinds can be causes and effects. We must look instead for relationships between objects. We find, indeed, that causes and effects must be contiguous to each other, and that causes must be prior to their effects. But this is not enough: we feel that there must be a necessary connection between cause and effect, though the nature of this connection is difficult to establish.

Hume denies that whatever begins to exist must have a cause of existence.

> As all distinct ideas are separable from each other, and as the ideas of cause and effect are evidently distinct, 'twill be easy for us to conceive any object to be non-existent this moment, and existent the next, without conjoining to it the distinct idea of a cause or productive principle.

Of course, 'cause' and 'effect' are correlative terms, like 'husband' and 'wife', and every effect must have a cause, just as every husband must have a wife. But this does not prove that every event must have a cause, any more than it follows, because every husband must have a wife, that therefore every man must be married. For all we know, there may be events which lack causes, just as there are men who lack wives.

If there is no absurdity in conceiving something coming into existence, or undergoing a change, without any cause at all, there is *a fortiori* no absurdity in conceiving of an event occurring without a cause of some particular kind. Because many different effects are logically conceivable as arising from a particular cause, only experience leads us to expect the actual one. But on what basis?

What happens, says Hume, is that we observe individuals of one species to have been constantly attended by individuals of another. 'Contiguity and succession are not sufficient to make us pronounce any two objects to be cause and effect, unless we percieve that these two relations are preserved in several instances.' But how does this take us any further? If the causal relationship was not to be detected in a single instance, how can it be detected in repeated instances, since the resembling instances are all independent of each other and do not influence each other?

Hume's answer is that the observation of the resemblance produces a new impression *in the mind*. Once we have observed a sufficient number of instances of B following A, we feel a determination of the mind to pass from A to B. It is here that we find the origin of the idea of necessary connection. Necessity is 'nothing but an internal impression of the mind, or a determination to carry our thoughts from one object to another'. The felt expectation of the effect when the cause presents itself, an impression produced by customary conjunction, is the impression from which the idea of necessary connection is derived.

Paradoxical as it may seem, it is not our inference that depends on the necessary connection between cause and effect, but the necessary connection that depends on the inference we draw from the one to the other. Hume offers not one, but two, definitions of causation. The first is this: a cause is 'an object precedent and contiguous to another and where all the objects resembling the former are placed in a like relation of priority and contiguity to those objects that resemble the latter'. In this definition, nothing is said about necessary connection, and no reference is made to the activity of the mind. Accordingly, we are offered a second, more philosophical definition. A cause is 'an object precedent and contiguous to another, and so united with it in the imagination that the idea of the one determines the mind to form the idea of the other, and the impression of the one to form a more lively idea of the other'.

It is noticeable that in this second definition of 'cause' the mind is said to be 'determined' to form one idea by the presence of another idea. This appears to import a circularity in the definition: for is not 'determination' synonymous with, or closely connected with, 'causation'? The circularity cannot be avoided by saying that the determination here spoken of is in the mind, not in the world. For the theory of causation is intended to apply to moral necessity as well as to natural necessity, to social as well as natural sciences.

The originality and power of Hume's analysis of causation is concealed by the language in which it is embedded, and which suffers from all the obscurity of the machinery of impressions and ideas. But we can separate out from the psychological apparatus three novel principles of great importance.

(a) Cause and effect must be distinct existences, each conceivable without the other.
(b) The causal relation is to be analysed in terms of contiguity, precedence, and constant conjunction.
(c) It is not a necessary truth that every beginning of existence has a cause.

Each of these principles deserves, and has received, intense philosophical scrutiny. Some of them were, as we shall see, subjected to searching criticism by Kant, and others have been modified or rejected by more recent philosophers. But to this day the agenda for the discussion of the causal relationship is the one set by Hume.

Hume defines the human will as 'the internal impression we feel and are conscious of when we knowingly give rise to any new motion of our body, or new perception of our mind'. Given Hume's theory of causation, we may wonder what right 'give rise to' has to appear in this definition. Yet if we replace 'we knowingly give rise to any new motion' with 'any new motion is observed to arise', the definition no longer looks at all plausible.

Hume regarded human actions as being no more and no less necessary than the operations of any other natural agents. Whatever we do is necessitated by causal links between motive and behaviour. The examples which he gives to prove constant conjunction in such cases are snobbish, provincial, and unconvincing. ('The skin, pores, muscles, and nerves of a day-labourer are different from those of a man of quality: So are his sentiments, actions and manners.') None the less, his arguments against free-will were to be deployed many times by other philosophers after his death.

Can experience prove free-will? Hume accepts the traditional distinction between liberty of spontaneity and liberty of indifference. Experience does exhibit our liberty of spontaneity – we often do what we want to do – but it cannot provide genuine evidence for liberty of indifference, that is to say, the ability to do otherwise than we in fact do. We may imagine we feel a liberty within ourselves, 'but a spectator can commonly infer our actions from our motives and character; and even where he cannot, he concludes in general, that he might, were he perfectly acquainted with every circumstance of our situation and temper, and the most secret springs of our complexion and disposition'.

Given Hume's official philosophy of mind and his official account of causation, there seems to be no room for talking of 'secret springs' of action. In fact, his thesis that the will is causally necessitated is difficult to make consistent either with his own definition of the will or with his own theory of causation.

Hume has been much studied and imitated in the twentieth century. His hostility to religion and metaphysics, in particular, has made him many admirers. But his importance in the history of philosophy depends on his analysis of causation, and on the intrepidity with which he followed the presuppositions of empiricism wheresoever they led.

REID AND COMMON SENSE

The definitive demolition of empiricism was to be the work of a Prussian philosopher at the end of the eighteenth century and an Austrian philosopher in the middle of the twentieth. But to the credit of British philosophy, many of the later criticisms of Wittgenstein and Kant were anticipated by a contemporary of Hume's, Thomas **Reid**. Reid was professor of moral philosophy at Glasgow, in succession to the economist Adam Smith, and he was the founder of the Scottish school of common-sense philosophy. In 1764 Reid published *An Inquiry into the Human Mind on the Principles of Common Sense* in response to Hume's *Treatise* and *Essays*, and he followed this up in the 1780s with two essays on the intellectual and active powers of man.

Initially, Reid, like many of his contemporaries, had accepted the theory of ideas; but he was brought up short by reading the *Treatise of Human Nature*. 'Your system,' he wrote to Hume, 'appears to me not only coherent in all its parts, but likewise justly deduced from principles which I never thought of calling in question, until the conclusions you draw from them made me suspect them.' Reflection on Hume made Reid see that there was something radically wrong not only with the empiricism of Locke and Berkeley, but also with the use made of ideas in the system of Descartes.

When we find the gravest philosophers, from Des Cartes down to Bishop Berkeley, mustering up arguments to prove the existence of a material world, and unable to find any that will bear examination; when we find Bishop Berkeley and Mr. Hume, the acutest metaphysicians of the age, maintaining that there is no such thing as matter in the universe – that sun, moon, and stars, the earth which we inhabit, our own bodies, and those of our friends, are only ideas in our minds, and have no existence but in thought; when we find the last maintaining that there is neither body nor mind – nothing in nature but ideas and impressions – that there is no certainty, nor indeed probability, even in mathematical axioms: I say, when we consider such extravagancies of many of the most acute writers on this subject, we may be apt to think the whole to be only a dream of fanciful men, who have entangled themselves in cobwebs spun out of their own brain.

In fact, the recent history of philosophy shows how even the most intelligent people can go wrong if they start from false first principles.

The initial problem with the theory of ideas is the ambiguity of the word 'idea'. In ordinary language, Reid maintains, it means an act of mind: to have an idea of anything is to conceive it. But philosophers have given it a different meaning, whereby it does not signify the act of conceiving, but some object of thought. These ideas are first introduced into philosophy 'in the humble character of images or representatives of things' but by degrees they have 'supplanted their constituents and undermined everything but themselves'.

In fact, Reid maintains, ideas in the philosophical sense are mere fictions. We do indeed have conceptions of many things; but a conception is not an image, and the postulation of ideas which are images is neither necessary nor sufficient to explain how we acquire and use these concepts. Not only do philosophers like Locke confuse concepts with images, but they start from the wrong end when they consider concepts themselves. They talk as if knowledge begins with bare conception, separate from belief, and that belief arises from the comparison of simple ideas. The truth is the reverse: we begin with natural and original judgements, and we later analyse them into individual concepts. Seeing a tree, for instance, does not give us a mere idea of a tree, but involves the judgement that it exists with a certain shape, size, and position.

The initial furniture of the mind is not a set of disconnected ideas, but a system of original and natural judgements. 'They are a part of our constitution, and all the discoveries of our reason are grounded upon them. They make up what is called the *common sense of mankind*; and what is manifestly contrary to any of those first principles is what we call *absurd*.' The common principles which are the foundation of reasoning include some which have been called in question by Hume: first, that sensible qualities must have a subject which we call body, and conscious thoughts must have a subject which we call mind; secondly, that whatever begins to exist must have a cause which produced it. Reid's blunt affirmation of these principles in the face of Hume's detailed criticism has a certain air of dogmatism; but he would respond that principles so fundamental neither require nor admit of proof.

Reid is willing to go along with Locke in distinguishing between primary and secondary qualities. But unlike Locke, he thinks that a secondary quality such as colour is a real quality of bodies: it is not identical with the sensation of colour which we have, but it is its cause. No one, he says, thinks that the colour of a red body has changed because we look at it through green glass. It is no objection to the objectivity of a quality that we can only detect it by its effects: the same is true of gravity and magnetism. 'Red' means what the common man means by it, and its meaning cannot be arbitrarily changed by philosophers. 'The vulgar have undoubted right to give names to things which they are daily conversant about; and philosophers seem justly chargeable with an abuse of language, when they change the meaning of a common word, without giving warning.'

But while Reid is firm that ordinary language sets the standard for the meaning of words, he by no means implies that the beliefs of the vulgar are to be preferred to the results of scientific investigation. On the contrary, Reid regarded himself as an experimental scientist, and kept himself fully up to date with recent work about the nature of vision. Indeed, in studying the geometry of visible objects, he showed great scientific ingenuity, and anticipated the development of non-Euclidean geometries. What Reid wanted to show was that the realism of the common man was fully compatible with the pursuit of science, and with the experimental study of the mind itself.

Reid was one of the ornaments of the eighteenth-century Scottish Enlightenment; he long continued to be influential in his own country, and his importance has been rediscovered in our own time. But in the mainstream of European thought his work was overshadowed by the more popular figures of the European Enlightenment, and his brusque rebuttal of empiricism was superseded by the more sophisticated critique of Kant.

XV

THE ENLIGHTENMENT

THE *PHILOSOPHES*

In the eighteenth century, social and political philosophy in France, as in Britain, was influenced by Locke. But whereas in England, under a constitutional monarchy, government was parliamentary if not democratic, and there was religious toleration for all except Catholics, in France the monarchy was absolute, and once Louis XIV revoked the Edict of Nantes in 1685 only Catholicism was officially tolerated. However, in the reign of his grandson, Louis XV, a degree of freedom of thought was permitted, through indolence rather than policy, and a group of thinkers, the *philosophes* of the French Enlightenment, created a climate of thought hostile to the *status quo* in Church and State. Their manifesto was the *Encyclopédie* edited in the 1750s by Denis Diderot and Jean d'Alembert.

Like Hume, the philosophers of the Enlightenment aimed to establish a science of human affairs which would match the science which Newton had established for the physical universe. They saw the power of the Church as an obstacle to the development of such a science, and they saw it as their mission to replace superstition with reason. Already at the end of the seventeenth century Pierre Bayle had argued in his *Dictionnaire historique et critique* that in view of the unending conflicts within both natural and revealed theology, moral teaching should be made totally independent of religion. A belief in immortality was not necessary for morality, and there was no reason why there could not be a virtuous community of atheists.

Voltaire, the best known of the *philosophes*, agreed with Bayle on the first point, but not with the second. He thought that the existence of a spiritual, separable, soul was unprovable and probably false; but he thought that the world as explained by Newton manifested the existence of God just as much as a watch shows the existence of a watchmaker. If God did not exist, he said, it would be necessary to invent him in order to back up the moral law. But Voltaire did not believe that God had created the world by choice. If he had done so, we would have to blame Him for such evils as the catastrophic earthquake which struck

Lisbon in 1755. The world was not a free creation, but a necessary and eternal consequence of God's existence. Voltaire, to use the technical term, was not an atheist but a deist.

In human affairs, too, Voltaire regarded freedom as an illusion, fostered by historians' habits of dwelling on the actions of great kings and generals. Voltaire himself wrote voluminous works of history, emphasizing the importance of the domestic, artistic, and industrial aspects of past ages. In politics, however, he was neither a populist nor a democrat; his ideal was the rule of an enlightened despot, such as his one-time patron, Frederick the Great of Prussia. The liberty he cared most about was freedom of speech, even though it is not certain that he ever said 'I disapprove of what you say, but I will defend to the death your right to say it.'

More significant as a political philosopher was the Baron de **Montesquieu**, author of the *Persian Letters*, a risqué satire on French political and ecclesiastical life, and *The Spirit of the Laws*, a vast treatise which seeks to base a theory of the nature of the state on a mountain of sociological evidence. There are three main kinds of government: republican, monarchical, and despotic. One cannot single out one kind of government as everywhere preferable: the government should be fitted to the climate, the wealth, and the national character of a country. Thus, republics suit cold climates, and despotism hot climates; freedom is easier to maintain on islands and in mountains than on level continents; a constitution suitable for Sicilians would not suit Englishmen, and so on.

Montesquieu, who lived in England for a year, was a great admirer of the British constitution, in particular because of its separation of powers, which he saw as a necessary condition of liberty. The legislative, executive, and judicial branches of government should not be combined in a single person or institution. If they are separated from each other, they act as checks and balances on each other, and provide a bulwark against tyranny. Whether or not Montesquieu's understanding of the British parliamentary monarchy was accurate, his theory has had a lasting influence, particularly through its embodiment in the American constitution.

Rousseau

Of all French philosophers of the eighteenth century the most influential was Jean Jacques Rousseau, though his influence was greater outside philosophical circles than among professional philosophers. Like St Augustine, he wrote a book of autobiographical *Confessions*; his confessions are more vivid and more detailed than the Saint's, and contain more sins, less philosophy, and no prayers. He was born in Geneva, he tells us, and brought up as a Calvinist; at sixteen, a runaway apprentice, he became a Catholic in Turin. In 1731 he was befriended by the Baronne de Warens, with whom he lived for nine years. His first job was as secretary to the French ambassador in Venice in 1743; having quarrelled with him he went to Paris and met Voltaire and Diderot. In 1745 he began a lifelong relationship with a servant girl, and had by her five children whom he dumped, one after the other, in a foundling hospital. He achieved fame in 1750 by publishing a prize-winning essay in which he argued, to the horror of the Encyclopaedists, that the arts and sciences had a baneful effect on mankind. This was followed up, four years later, by a 'Discourse on Inequality', which argued that man was naturally good, and corrupted by institutions. The two works held up the ideal of the 'noble savage' whose simple goodness put civilized man to shame.

In 1754 Rousseau returned to Geneva and became Protestant once more. After a bitter quarrel with Voltaire, he returned to France and wrote a novel, *La Nouvelle Héloïse*, a treatise on education, *Emile*, and a major work of political philosophy, *The Social Contract*. As a result of the inflammatory doctrines of these works, he had to flee to Switzerland in 1762 but he was driven out of Geneva also. In 1776 he was given sanctuary in England by David Hume, who secured him a pension from King George III. But soon his paranoid ingratitude became too much even for Hume's patience, and he returned to France in spite of the risk of arrest. In his last years he was poor and vilified, and when he died in 1778 some thought that he had killed himself.

The Social Contract is very readable, as befits a work by a philosopher who was also a best-selling novelist. Its first words are memorable, though misleading. 'Man is born free, and everywhere he is in chains. Many a man believes himself to be the master of others who is, no less than they, a slave.' Readers of Rousseau's previous works assume that the chains are those of social institutions. Shall we reject the social order then? No, we are told, it is a sacred right which is the basis of all other rights. Social institutions, Rousseau now thinks, liberate rather than enslave.

Like Hobbes, Rousseau believes that society originates when life in the original state of nature becomes intolerable. A social contract is drawn up to ensure that the whole strength of the community is enlisted for the protection of each member's person and property. Every member has to alienate all his rights to the community and give up any claim against it. But how can this be done in such a way that each man, united to his fellows, remains as free as he was before?

The solution is to be found in the theory of the general will. The social contract creates a moral and collective body, the State or Sovereign People. Every individual as a citizen shares in the sovereign's authority, as a subject owes obedience to the state's laws. The sovereign people, having no existence outside that of the individuals who compose it, can have no interest at variance with theirs: hence it expresses the general will, and it cannot go wrong in its pursuit of the public good. An individual's will may go contrary to the general will, but he can be constrained by the whole body of his fellow citizens to conform to it – 'which is no more than to say that it may be necessary to compel a man to be free'. Under Rousseau's social contract, men lose their natural liberty to lay hands on whatever tempts them, but they gain civil liberty, which permits the stable ownership of property. So men are, genuinely, more free than they were. But the freedom which Rousseau attributes to the imprisoned malefactor is the rather rarefied freedom to participate in the expression of the general will.

The sovereign people is an abstract entity: it is not to be identified with any particular government, of whatever form. Hence, the theory of the general will is not the doctrine that whatever the government does is right. How, then, is the general will to be ascertained? By holding a referendum? No: for Rousseau 'the general will' is not the same as 'the will of all'. 'There is often considerable difference between the will of all and the general will. The latter is concerned only with the common interest, the former with interests that are partial, being itself but the sum of particular wills.' The deliberations of a popular assembly, even when it is unanimous, are by no means infallible. This is because each voter may suffer from ignorance or be swayed by individual self-interest.

The general will, according to Rousseau, could be ascertained by plebiscite on two conditions: first, that every voter was fully informed; second, that no two voters held any communication with each other. The second condition is there to prevent the formation of groups or parties less than the whole community. For it is only within the context of the entire state that the differences between the self-interest of individuals will cancel out and yield the self-interest of sovereign people. 'It is therefore essential, if the general will is to be able to express itself, that there should be no partial society within the State, and that each citizen should think only his own thoughts.'

The sovereignty of the people is indivisible: if you separate the powers of the legislative and executive branches you make the sovereign a fantastic creature of shreds and patches. But sovereignty is also limited: it must be concerned only with matters of extreme generality. 'Just as the will of the individual cannot represent the general will, so, too, the general will changes its nature when called upon to pronounce upon a particular object.' Because of this the people, while the supreme legislative power, has to exert its executive power, which is concerned with particular acts, through an agent, namely the government.

A government is 'an intermediate body set up to serve as a means of communication between subjects and sovereign, charged with the execution of the laws and the maintenance of liberty'. Rulers are employees of the people: the government receives from the sovereign the orders which it passes on to the people. Like Montesquieu, Rousseau refuses to specify a single form of government as being appropriate to all circumstances. But ideally, the form of government, as well as the individual rulers, should be endorsed by periodic assemblies of the people. At this point Rousseau's affection for the procedures of a Swiss canton seem to have overcome his principle that the sovereign should concern itself only with general issues.

In spite of his concern with the general will of the people, Rousseau was not a wholehearted supporter of democracy in practice. 'Were there such a thing as a nation of Gods, it would be a democracy. So perfect a form of government is not suited to men.' He was thinking, of course, of direct democracy, government by popular assembly, and his worry was that in such a state the rulers would be unprofessional and quarrelsome. His favoured form of government is an elective aristocracy. 'It is the best and most natural arrangement that can be made that the wise should govern the masses.' The great merit of this system is that it demands fewer virtues than popular government; it does not call for a strict insistence on equality, all it requires is a spirit of moderation in the rich and of contentment in the poor. Naturally, the rich will do most of the governing; they have more time to spare. But from time to time, a poor man should be elected to office, to cheer up the populace.

After the rousing rhetoric of 'Man is born free and is everywhere in chains' this seems rather a tame and bourgeois conclusion. None the less, *The Social Contract* was seen as a threat by those in power at the time, and was venerated as a Bible by the revolutionaries who were shortly to take their place. It was not the social contract of the book's title which enraged or excited people: as we have seen, such contract theories were by now two-a-penny. What inflamed readers was the new notion of the general will.

Looked at soberly, the notion is theoretically incoherent and practically vacuous. It is not true, as a matter of logic, that if A wills A's good and B wills B's good then A and B jointly wish the good of A and B: to see this we need only consider the case where A sees as his good the annihilation of B, and B sees as his good the annihilation of A. What makes Rousseau's notion useless in practice is the difficulty of ascertaining what the general will prescribes. As we have seen, he laid down as conditions for its expression that every citizen should be fully informed and that no two citizens should be allowed to combine with each other. The fulfilment of the second condition would demand a total tyranny of the state; the first condition could never be fulfilled in a community of real human beings.

Revolution and Romanticism

It was, of course, the vacuousness of the notion of the general will which made it so valuable for political purposes. Eleven years after Rousseau's death the French Revolution swept away the regime which had banned *The Social Contract*. After a series of moderate and overdue reforms had been secured from King Louis XVI, the Revolution gathered momentum, abolished the monarchy itself, and executed the King. The Jacobin party came to power, under Robespierre, and in a reign of terror guillotined not only the surviving aristocrats of the *ancien régime* but many democrats of different colours. Robespierre could proclaim that the will of the

Jacobins was the general will, and that his despotic government was forcing citizens to be free.

The Revolution could claim to be the offspring not only of Rousseau but also of the enlightenment *philosophes* whom he opposed. The revolutionaries did their best to destroy the Catholic Church not only because of the political and economic power it had enjoyed in the *ancien régime* but also because of their belief that it was an obstacle to scientific progress. In the Cathedral of Notre Dame an actress was enthroned as a goddess of Reason. Ex-priests, retrained as deists, were sent round to country parishes as 'Apostles of Reason'.

The Revolution that had taken from Rousseau its slogans of liberty and equality ended by handing over the expression of the general will to Napoleon Bonaparte, who for a decade enjoyed more power in Europe than any single man since Charlemagne. But long after the Revolution had blown itself out, Rousseau's influence was still to be felt throughout the continent in quite a different way, through the romantic movement.

It was not the Rousseau of *The Social Contract*, but the Rousseau of the *Confessions* and of the *Discourses* who shaped the romantic outlook. Rousseau's writings sought to revive, in eighteenth-century France, the contempt for the artificial life of city and court and the cult of rustic crudity which had characterised the Cynics of ancient Greece. 'Sensibility' was already much in vogue in France, and the ladies of the court played at being shepherdesses in manicured gardens at Versailles. But the romantic movement was to turn what had been a pastime for pampered idlers into the inspiration of a whole way of life.

Romantics did not necessarily take any real interest in the welfare of the rural workers. They did, however, hold up the real or imagined virtues of peasants as a mirror to society; and they sought out the forested or mountainous regions in which the poorest of them lived. On the other hand, romantics scorned the amenities which can be provided only in urban communities, such as libraries, universities, and stock-exchanges. In a combination which was comprehensible, if not inevitable, the preference for the country over the town was at the same time an assertion of passion against intellect, and a craving for excitement rather than security.

Romanticism in Britain received its most eloquent expression in the writings of Wordsworth and Coleridge. In *Frost at Midnight*, Coleridge tells his baby son:

> I was rear'd
> In the great city, pent mid cloisters dim,
> And saw nought lovely but the sky and stars.
> But *thou*, my babe! shalt wander, like a breeze,
> By lakes and sandy shores, beneath the crags
> Of ancient mountain, and beneath the clouds,
> Which image in their bulk both lakes and shores

And mountain crags: so shalt thou see and hear
The lovely shapes and sounds intelligible
Of that eternal language, which thy God
Utters, who from eternity doth teach
Himself in all, and all things in himself.

The philosophy of the English romantics often, as in that passage, resembles the pantheism of Spinoza, whom they admired. But Wordsworth explored also Platonic themes: as in the *Immortality Ode*, which revives the doctrines of recollection and pre-existence.

Our birth is but a sleep and a forgetting;
The Soul that rises with us, our life's Star,
Hath had elsewhere its setting
And cometh from afar:
Not in entire forgetfulness,
And not in utter nakedness,
But trailing clouds of glory do we come
From God, who is our home.

Elsewhere Wordsworth expresses his worship of Nature in ways which invoke Neo-Platonic ideas.

I have felt
A presence that disturbs me with the joy
Of elevated thoughts; a sense sublime
Of something far more deeply interfused.
Whose dwelling is the light of setting suns,
And the round ocean, and the living air,
And the blue sky, and in the mind of man,
A motion and a spirit, that impels
All thinking things, all objects of all thought,
And rolls through all things.

This takes us back to the World Soul of Plotinus and of Avicenna.

In the next generation of English poets, John Keats, addressing his Grecian urn, voiced a sentiment that is sometimes taken as the quintessential credo of romanticism

When old age shall this generation waste
Thou shalt remain, in midst of other woe
Than ours, a friend to man, to whom thou say'st
'Beauty is truth, truth beauty' – that is all
Ye know on earth, and all ye need to know.

But it would be unfair to characterize romanticism in general as the substitution of beauty for truth as the supreme value. The romantics had a concern for truth in their own fashion, insisting that it was more important for emotions to be genuine than to be *comme il faut*. And pre-romantics too had placed a high value on beauty; what the romantics did was to change men's perceptions of what was beautiful. In a reaction against the age of reason, order and enlightenment, romantics felt the attraction of the Middle Ages – not of its philosophy, but of its irregular architecture and its gloomy ruins. The Gothic revival, which was to flower in the nineteenth century, began in England in the same decade as Rousseau's first *Discourse*. The last decades of the eighteenth century were the heyday of the Gothic novel, full of mystery, ghosts, and wonders. Jane Austen's novels, and her mockery of the romantics, can be seen as a last reaffirmation of the clear vision and tranquil values of the age of reason.

In his old age, Coleridge became a prolific philosopher in his own right. He attacked the utilitarianism by that time flourishing in Britain, and he introduced to English readers the philosophy which he had learned from the philosophers of Germany. For the definitive evaluation of eighteenth-century empiricism and rationalism was given not by its romantic critics, but by the author of *The Critique of Pure Reason*, Immanuel Kant.

XVI

THE CRITICAL
PHILOSOPHY OF KANT

KANT'S COPERNICAN REVOLUTION

One of the most significant events in the eighteenth century was the rise of the Kingdom of Prussia. Once a backward province of eastern Germany, Prussia became a kingdom in 1701 and under Leibniz's patron Frederick I, and his son Frederick the Great, who ruled from 1740 to 1786, it came to have great weight in the balance of power between the European monarchies. Frederick the Great built up and commanded a superb army, and after three wars he had added to his kingdom substantial portions of neighbouring Austria and Poland. By the time of his death, Prussia could challenge Austria as the leading power in Germany.

Though military efficiency was the overarching aim of his government, Frederick was a cultivated man, a gifted musician, and a fluent writer in French. He corresponded with Voltaire and brought him for a period to Berlin. During his reign were laid the first foundations not only of the nineteenth-century German Empire, but also of the nineteenth-century domination of philosophy by German thinkers.

The first and greatest of these, Immanuel **Kant** (1724–1804), lived all his life in the town of his birth, Königsberg, in what was then the eastern part of Prussia. He was brought up as a devout Lutheran; he later became liberal in his theological views but was always a man of strict life and regular habit, notorious for exact punctuality in every action. At university he was instructed in the Leibnizian metaphysics, as codified into a system by Wolff; he became disenchanted with it after reading Hume and Rousseau. After holding some temporary teaching posts and declining a chair of poetry, he became professor of logic and metaphysics in his home university in 1770. He never married or held public office, and the history of his life is the history of his ideas.

As a young man he was more interested in science than philosophy, and when he first began writing philosophy it was of a cautious and conventional kind. It was not until the age of fifty-seven that he produced the work which made him immortal, *The Critique of Pure Reason*. This appeared in 1781, at the beginning of one of the most spectacular decades in the history of human culture, in which *The Marriage of Figaro* and *Don Giovanni* were composed, in which Gibbon was publishing his *Decline and Fall*, and in which Boswell was writing his *Life of Johnson*, and the youthful Turner first exhibited in the Royal Academy. Early in the decade the constitution of the United States was drafted, and by its end the French Revolution had taken place.

The *Critique of Pure Reason* reappeared in a revised edition in 1787. It was followed by two other significant works, *The Critique of Practical Reason* (1788) and *The Critique of Judgment* in 1790. Kant's writing is not easy to read, and not all the difficulty is due to the profundity of the subject or the originality of the thought. He was overfond of inventing technical terms, and forcing ideas into rigid schematisms. But the reader who perseveres through his difficult texts will find the investment philosophically well rewarded.

Kant's aim in his first *Critique* was to make philosophy, for the first time, truly scientific. Mathematics had been scientific for many centuries, and physics had become scientific when, in the age of Bacon and Descartes, it was first realized that theory had to be confirmed by experiment and experiment had to be guided by theory. But metaphysics, the oldest discipline, and the one which 'would survive even if all the rest were swallowed up in the abyss of an all-destroying barabarism', was still immature.

To become scientific, Kant believed, philosophy needed a revolution similar to that by which Copernicus placed the sun, rather than the earth, at the centre of the system of the heavens. Copernicus showed that when we think we are observing the motion of the sun round the earth, what we see is in fact the consequence of the rotation of our own earth. Kant's Copernican revolution will do for the mind what Copernicus did for the sense of vision. Instead of asking how our knowledge can conform to its objects, we must start from the supposition that objects must conform to our knowledge. Only thus can we justify the claim of metaphysics to *a priori* knowledge, which unlike *a posteriori* knowledge comes before experience. All our knowledge begins with experience, but Kant insists that it does not follow that all of it arises from experience.

The marks of *a priori* knowledge are necessity and universality. Unlike Hume, Kant maintains that the proposition 'every change has a cause' expresses a judgement which is strictly necessary and strictly universal. 'All bodies are heavy', on the other hand, is simply a generalization to which no exceptions have been observed; it is an *a posteriori* judgement.

In addition to the distinction between *a priori* and *a posteriori* judgement, Kant employs a distinction between analytic and synthetic judgements. In any judgement of the form 'A is B', he says, either the predicate B is contained in the concept A, or it lies outside it. If the former, then the judgement is analytic; if the latter, then it is synthetic. Kant's examples are 'all bodies are extended' and 'all bodies are heavy'.

What Kant means here is not altogether clear. The distinction is clearly intended to be universally applicable to propositions, yet not all propositions are structured in the simple subject–predicate form he uses in his definition. The notion of 'containing' is metaphorical; and Kant's discussion of the distinction does not make it unambiguous whether he saw it as a logical or a psychological one.

One thing, however, is quite clear: for Kant a judgement cannot be both analytic and *a posteriori*. But the possibility is left open that a proposition may be both synthetic and *a priori*. In Kant's system, indeed, the realm of the synthetic *a priori* is extensive and important. It includes the whole of mathematics: arithmetic and geometry are synthetic, since they go far beyond pure logic, and yet they are *a priori*, because they are known in advance of experience.

How such synthetic *a priori* judgements are possible is the principal problem for philosophy, and only if it can be solved is a science of metaphysics possible. If it cannot, then metaphysics is nothing more than a natural disposition to ask certain types of questions, questions for instance about the universe as a whole. Nothing guarantees that these questions are not completely idle.

Reason's first task is to understand the nature and limits of its own power. Reason must be used critically, not dogmatically, and scientific metaphysics must begin with a 'Critique of Pure Reason'. The critique of pure reason, that is, of reason divorced from experience, prepares us for the general study of *a priori* knowledge, which Kant calls 'transcendental metaphysics'. 'Transcendental' is one of Kant's favourite words: he used it with several meanings, but common to all of them is the notion of something which goes beyond and behind the deliverances of actual experience.

Human knowledge arises from the combined operation of the senses and the understanding. Through the senses, objects are given to us; through understanding, they are made thinkable. The structure of our senses determines the content of our experience; the constitution of our understanding determines its structure. The philosopher has to study both sense and understanding: Kant calls the former study 'the transcendental aesthetic' and the latter 'the transcendental logic'.

THE TRANSCENDENTAL AESTHETIC

Like his seventeenth- and eighteenth-century predecessors, Kant thinks of a sense-faculty as being in itself a passive power of receiving representations. However, he makes a distinction between the matter and the form of our experience: the matter is what derives directly from sensation, the form given by our understanding is what permits the chaos of appearance to take on order. The matter of sensations would include what makes the difference between a glimpse of blue and a glimpse of green, or the smell of a rose and the smell of a cheese. But what Kant is interested in is only the form.

In human experience any object of sense is also an object of thought: whatever is experienced is classified and codified, that is to say, it is brought by the understanding under one or more concepts. Kant wants to isolate sense-experience by taking away from it everything which really belongs to the understanding, so that nothing may be left save immediate empirical experience and its *a priori* form. 'In the course of this investigation,' Kant says, 'it will be found that there are two pure forms of sensory awareness, serving as principles of *a priori* knowledge, namely, space and time.'

Like his predecessors Kant accepts a distinction between inner and outer senses. Space is the form of outer sense, by which we 'represent to ourselves objects as outside us, and all without exception in space'. Time is the form of inner sense by means of which the mind experiences its own inner states, all ordered in time.

'What, then, are space and time? Are they real existences? Are they only determinations or relations of things, yet such as would belong to things even if they were not intuited? Or are space and time such that they belong only to the form of awareness, and therefore to the subjective constitution of our mind, apart from which they could not be ascribed to anything whatsoever?'

A dogmatic, uncritical, metaphysician will tell us that space and time are presupposed by, not derived from, experience; that we can imagine space and time without objects, but not objects without space and time; and that there is only a single space and a single time, infinite in each case. But a critical philosopher will ask how it is that we can know truths about space and time which are based on awareness (because they are not analytic), and yet are *a priori* (because they are prior to any experience). Kant's answer it that the knowledge of synthetic *a priori* truths about space and time is only explicable if they are *a priori* forms of sense-experience, rather than properties of things in themselves.

Does this mean that space and time are unreal? Kant's answer is that empirically they are real, but transcendentally they are ideal. 'If we take away the subject, space and time disappear: these as phenomena cannot exist in themselves but only in us.' What things are in themselves, beyond the phenomena, is something which is unknown to us.

Does this then mean that everything is mere appearance? Not in the ordinary sense. We commonly distinguish in experience between that which holds for all human beings and that which is incidental to a single standpoint. The rainbow in a sunny shower may be called a mere appearance, while the rain is regarded as a thing in itself. In this sense, we may grant that not everything is mere appearance. But this distinction between appearance and reality, Kant says, is something merely empirical. When we look deeper, we realize that 'not only are the drops of rain mere appearances, but that even their round shape, nay even the space in which they fall, are nothing in themselves, but merely modifications or fundamental forms of our sensible awareness, and that the transcendental object remains unknown to us'.

This conclusion may seem unpalatable, but it is forced on us, Kant believes, if we consider the nature of geometry. Geometry is a splendid achievement of the human intellect: but on what does it rest? It cannot rest on experience, because it is universal and necessary. It cannot rest on mere concepts because concepts alone will not tell you there can be no such thing as a two-sided figure. Therefore it must be a synthetic discipline resting on *a priori* awareness.

Kant's transcendental aesthetic is one of the least successful parts of his enterprise. At the time he wrote, Euclidean geometry was regarded as the only possible theory of space; shortly afterwards it was shown that there were other consistent non-Euclidean geometries. Moreover, the question whether the fundamental structure of the world we live in is Euclidean or non-Euclidean was a matter for scientific investigation to settle. But this would be impossible if spatiality was something constructed by the mind in a single, inescapably Euclidean, form.

THE TRANSCENDENTAL ANALYTIC:
THE DEDUCTION OF THE CATEGORIES

The transcendental aesthetic is followed in Kant's system by the transcendental logic, which is the study of the understanding, the creative part of the mind. It is the understanding that makes the objects of sensible awareness into objects of thought. Understanding and sense are equal and interdependent. 'Without the senses no object would be given to us, without understanding no object would be thought. Thoughts without content are empty, awareness without concepts is blind. . . . The understanding is aware of nothing, the senses can think nothing. Only through their union can knowledge arise.'

By 'logic' Kant means the rules by which the understanding operates. He is interested not in the methodology of particular sciences, but in the 'absolutely necessary rules of thought without which there can be no employment whatsoever of the understanding'. The pure logic which is his concern treats only of the form and not of the content of thought. It is distinct from, and independent of, psychology; it has no interest in the origin or history of our thoughts.

Kant was not himself concerned to expound or develop formal logic itself; in fact he accepted uncritically the logic of his day. His transcendental logic is meant to be something different: it is an inquiry into what can be known *a priori* about the applicability of logic. The task of transcendental logic is comprised in two major enterprises: the *analytic* and the *dialectic*. The transcendental analytic sets out the criteria for the valid empirical employment of the understanding; the transcendental dialectic offers a critique of the illusory dogmatic employment of the reason.

Kant distinguishes between two powers of the mind: the understanding and the judgement. The understanding is the power to form concepts, the judgement is the power to apply them. The operations of the understanding find expression in individual words, the operations of the judging faculty find expression in whole sentences. Concepts which are *a priori* are categories; judgements which are *a priori* are called principles. Kant's transcendental analytic consists of two corresponding parts: the analytic of concepts and the analytic of principles. Kant devotes much the larger part of his transcendental analytic to the analytic of concepts, which is also called the deduction of the categories.

What is meant by all this terminology? We may start from the notion of 'category', which Kant took over from Aristotle, while rejecting Aristotle's list as hopelessly unsystematic. In its place he offers a list based on the relationship between concepts and judgement. A concept is in fact nothing other than a power to make judgements of certain kinds. (To possess the concept *metal*, for instance, is to have the power to make judgements expressible by sentences containing the word 'metal' or its equivalent.) The different possible types of concept are therefore to be determined by setting out the different possible types of judgement.

Kant took over from contemporary logicians distinctions between different kinds of judgement. He classes judgements as universal ('Every man is mortal'), particular ('Some men are mortal'), or singular ('Socrates is mortal'). Again, he classifies them as affirmative ('The soul is mortal'), negative ('The soul is not mortal'), and infinite ('The soul is non-mortal'). Finally, he divides judgements into the three classes of categorical ('There is a perfect justice'), or hypothetical ('If there is a perfect justice, the obstinately wicked are punished'), or disjunctive ('The world exists either through blind chance, or through inner necessity, or through an external cause').

Kant claims to derive from these familiar classifications of judgements a new and fundamental classification of concepts. For instance, he relates categorical judgements to the category of substance, hypothetical judgements to the category of cause, and disjunctive judgements to the category of interaction. It would be difficult, and unrewarding, to try to follow the detailed steps of this derivation; it is more important to interpret the thesis that a concept is essentially a power of judgement.

Commentators have suggested various analogies for the role which Kant attributed to the categories. Some have suggested that if we compare language to a board game in which pieces are moved, then the categories are a listing of the ultimate possible moves available (forward, backward, sideways, diagonally, etc.). Alternatively, if we think of language as a tool for coping with the world, we might think of the list of categories as similar to the specification of an all-purpose tool (it must be able to cut, drill, polish and so on).

Leaving metaphor aside, we may ask whether Kant is right that there are some concepts which are indispensable if anything is to count as the operation of understanding. We might put the question in a linguistic form: are there any concepts indispensable for a fully-fledged language? The answer seems to be that any language-users – however alien to us – need to have a concept of negation, and the ability to use quantifiers such as 'all' and 'some'. If they are to be rational language-users they will also need the ability to draw conclusions from premises, which is expressed in the mastery of words like 'if', 'then', and 'therefore'. Kant was correct to link concepts with judgements, and to see that certain concepts must be fundamental to all understanding, whether or not he was well inspired when he drew up his own particular list.

If we accept that there must be a nucleus of indispensable categories, there remains the crucial question where this comes from, and how we acquire our grasp of it. Kant calls his answer to this question 'The transcendental deduction of the categories'.

'Deduction' in Kant's terminology is a quasi-legal term, a metaphor from genealogy and inheritance. A deduction of a concept is a proof that we have a title to use it, that in using it we are acting within our epistemological rights. A deduction of the categories is a proof that we have the right to apply these *a priori* concepts to objects. A deduction of an *a priori* concept cannot be a mere empirical explanation of how we come by it: it must be a proof which is, in Kant's term 'transcendental', that is to say, one which shows that the concept is necessary if there is to be any such thing as experience at all.

Consider, for instance, the concept of 'cause', which appears in Kant's list of categories. If it is *a priori* then experience cannot be cited as its origin; indeed, experience – as Hume had shown – could never establish the necessity and universality of the link binding cause and effect together. No doubt our experience does suggest to us various generalizations. But might there not be a world of experience in which such great chaos reigned that nothing could be identified as cause and effect? The thrust of the transcendental deduction is that if we did not have the concepts of the categories, including those of substance and cause, we could not understand – could not conceptualize – even the most fragmentary and disordered experience. Unless we can conceptualize objects whose existence is more than mere appearance, we cannot conceptualize sensory awareness at all.

Three elements are involved in the conceptualization of experience. First, there is the ordering of intuitions in time; secondly, there is the union of intuitions in a single consciousness; and finally, the conscious subject brings the intuitions under concepts. All this, Kant argues, involves the permanent possibility of self-consciousness.

It is not possible for me to *discover* that something is an item of *my* consciousness. I cannot be, as it were, faced with an item of consciousness, go on to wonder to whom it belongs, and conclude, upon inquiry, that it belongs to none other than myself. I can, through reflection, become aware of various features of my conscious experience; but I cannot become aware that it is *mine*. The self-conscious discoveries which one can make about one's experience are called by Kant 'apperceptions'. Kant puts the point that one does not rely on experience to recognize one's consciousness as one's own by saying that one's ownership of one's own consciousness is not an empirical apperception, but a 'transcendental apperception'.

Awareness of experiences as mine is at the same time awareness of experiences as belonging to a single consciousness. But what unites these experiences is not experience itself; in themselves my experiences are, as Kant says, 'many coloured and diverse'. Once again it is the *a priori* activity of the understanding which is at work, making what Kant calls a 'synthesis' of intuitions, combining them into the unity of a single consciousness. This Kant calls 'the transcendental unity of apperception'.

The possibility of self-consciousness, in turn, presupposes the possibility of the consciousness of extra-mental objects. This is because self-ascription of experience is only possible because of the unity and connectedness of a temporal sequence of awareness, and this same unity and connectedness is what makes it possible for a succession of experiences to constitute a single objective world.

Kant goes all the way to meet the empiricist, and then shows him on his own ground that empiricism is not enough. He agrees that for any knowledge of objects – even of oneself as an object – experience is necessary. The original unity of apperception gives me only the concept of myself; for any *knowledge* of myself, empirical awareness is necessary. But empirical knowledge, whether of myself or of anything else, involves judgement; and there cannot be judgement without concepts. Among concepts, there cannot be ones which are derived from experience without ones which are presupposed by experience; and therefore knowledge even of appearances, knowledge even of myself, must be subject to the categories.

The source of the objective order of nature is the transcendental self: the self which is shown, but not yet known, in the transcendental unity of apperception. It is thus from the transcendental unity of apperception that Kant seeks to derive the objective nature of the world, and seeks to show that there is a difference between reality and appearance. For the transcendental unity of apperception is possible only if our experience is experience of a world which is describable by the categories. That is, in essence, the transcendental deduction of the categories.

The details of the argument remain obscure. Kant states and restates it, in many different forms; in each statement there always seems to be one or other link missing in the chain of reasoning. The reader is able to glimpse isolated flashes of amazing insight without being given an overview of a compelling argument. Kant's transcendental deduction makes a damaging attack on empiricism, but it does not succeed in dealing the death blow. That had to wait for the twentieth century.

THE TRANSCENDENTAL ANALYTIC:
THE SYSTEM OF PRINCIPLES

None the less, Kant's exploration of the principles underlying our judgements is of the highest interest. *A priori* judgements, we recall, may be analytic or synthetic. The highest principle of analytic judgements is the principle of non-contradiction: a self-contradictory judgement is void, and the mark of an analytic judgement is that the contradiction of it is self-contradictory. But the principle of non-contradiction will not take us beyond the field of analytic propositions: it is a necessary, but not a sufficient condition for the truth of synthetic propositions.

In a synthetic judgement two non-identical concepts are put together. Kant lists four groups of principles which underpin synthetic judgements: he gives them technical terms, but we need not concern ourselves with these since they are more confusing than helpful.

The first of these principles is that all experiences are extensive magnitudes. Whatever we experience is extended – that is, has parts distinct from other parts – either in space or in time. 'All appearances,' Kant says, 'are experienced as aggregates, as complexes of previously given parts.' It is this, according to Kant, which underpins geometrical axioms, such as the axiom that between two points only one straight line is possible.

The second principle is that in all appearances the object of sensation has intensive magnitude. For instance, if you feel a certain degree of heat, you are aware that you could be feeling something hotter or less hot: what you are feeling is a point on a scale which extends in both directions. Similarly, to see a colour is to see something which is located on a spectrum. Kant calls this an 'anticipation of perception', but the term is an unfortunate one: it is as if he is saying that whenever you have a feeling, you can know *a priori* what feeling is going to come next. But of course only experience could show that; as Kant says, 'sensation is just that element which cannot be anticipated'. When I have a sensation what is known *a priori* is simply the logical possibility of similar sensations at other points upon a common scale. To catch Kant's sense a better word than 'anticipation' might be 'projection'.

The third principle is this: experience is only possible if necessary connections are to be found among our perceptions. There are two main stages on the way to establishing this. (a) If I am to have experience at all I must have experience of an objective realm: and this must contain enduring substances. (b) If I am to have experience of an objective realm I must have experience of causally ordered interacting substances. Each of these stages takes off from reflection on our awareness of time: time considered first as duration, and then as succession.

First, Kant points out that time itself cannot be perceived. In the experience of a moment, considered simply as an inner event, there is nothing to show when the experience occurs, or whether it occurs before or after any other given momentary experience. Our awareness of time, then, must be a relating of phenomena to some permanent, substantial, substratum.

If there is to be such a thing as change (as opposed to mere disconnected sequence) then there must be something which is first one thing and then another. But this permanent element cannot be supplied by our experience, which itself is in constant flux; it must therefore be supplied by something objective, which we may call 'substance'. 'All existence and all change in time have thus to be viewed as simply a mode of the existence of that which remains and persists.'

There are a number of ambiguities in this argument and its conclusion. It is not always clear what type of change is being talked about: does the argument concern the coming to be and passing away of substances, or is it about alteration in the properties of an enduring substance? Consequently, there is doubt as to how much is proved by the argument: is the conclusion that there must be some permanent things, or is it that there must be a single permanent thing? Kant sometimes speaks as if substance must be something everlasting; but in order to refute empiricist atomism it is sufficient to show that there must be at least some objective entities with non-momentary duration.

The second stage of the argument is based on a simple, but profound, observation. If I look at a house, there will be a certain succession in my experiences: first, perhaps, I look at the roof, then at the upper floors, then at the ground floor, then at the basement. Equally, if I stand still and watch a ship moving down a river I have a succession of different views: first of the ship upstream, then of it downstream, and so on. What distinguishes between a merely subjective succession of phenomena (the various glimpses of a house) and an objective succession (the motion of the ship downstream)? In the one case, but not the other, it would be possible for me to reverse the order of perceptions: and there is no basis for making the distinction except some necessary causal regularity. 'We never in experience attribute to an object the notion of succession . . . and distinguish it from the subjective succession of apprehension, unless when a rule lies at the foundation.'

This shows that there is something fundamentally wrong with Hume's idea that we first perceive temporal succession between events, and then go on to regard one as cause and the other as effect. Matters are the other way round: without relationships between cause and effect we cannot establish objective order in time. Moreover, Kant says, even if temporal sequence could be established independently of the cause–effect relation, bare temporal succession would be insufficient to account for causality, because cause and effect may be simultaneous. A ball, laid on a stuffed cushion, makes a hollow in the cushion as soon as it is laid on it, yet the ball is the cause, the hollow the effect. We know this because every such ball makes a dent, but not every such hollow contains a ball. The relation between time and causation is more complicated than Hume imagined.

Having refuted empiricist atomism and countered Humean scepticism about causal connections, Kant goes on to present his refutation of idealism. He has in view a twofold target: the problematic idealism of Descartes ('I exist' is the only indubitable empirical assertion), and the dogmatic idealism of Berkeley (an external world is illusory). Common to both of these is the thesis that the inner is better known than the outer, and that outer substances are inferred from inner experiences.

Kant's argument against these assumptions goes as follows. I am aware of changing mental states, and thus I am conscious of my existence in time: i.e. as having experiences first at one time and then at another. But, as has just been argued, the perception of change involves the perception of something permanent. But this something permanent is not myself: the unifying subject of my experience is not itself an object of experience. Hence, only if I have outer experience is it possible for me to make judgements about the past.

Kant's analytic closes with an insistence on the limits of the competence of the understanding. The categories cannot determine their own applicability, the principles cannot establish their own truth. Understanding alone cannot establish that there is any such thing as a substance, or that every change has a cause. All that is established *a priori*, whether by the transcendental deduction of the categories, or by the exposition of the system of the principles, is that *if experience is to be possible* certain conditions must hold. But whether experience is possible cannot be established in advance: the possibility of experience is shown only by the actual occurrence of experience itself. Concepts must be applied only to objects of possible experience; they may not be applied to things in general and in themselves. Unless we are presented in intuition with an object falling under a concept, the concept is empty and pointless.

Kant observes that philosophers make a distinction between phenomena (appearances) and noumena (objects of thought), and divide the world into a world of the senses and a world of the understanding. His own analytic has shown that there cannot be a world of mere appearances, mere objects of sense which do not fall under any categories or instantiate any rules. But we cannot conclude from this that there is a non-sensible world which is discovered by the understanding alone. Kant accepts that there are noumena in a negative sense: things which are not objects of sensible awareness. But he denies that there are noumena in a positive sense: things which are objects of a non-sensible awareness. The concept of noumenon, rightly understood, is simply a limiting concept, whose function is to set the limits of sensibility. To accept the existence of noumena as extra-sensible objects which can be studied by the use of intellect alone is to enter a realm of illusion. In his 'transcendental dialectic' Kant takes us on an exploratory tour of this world of enchantment.

THE TRANSCENDENTAL DIALECTIC:
PARALOGISMS OF PURE REASON

The analytic has set out the territory of pure understanding. That is an island of truth. But it is 'surrounded by a wide and stormy ocean, the native home of illusion, where many a fog bank and many a swiftly melting iceberg give the deceptive appearance of farther shores, deluding the adventurous seafarer ever anew with empty hopes, and engaging him in enterprises which he can never abandon and yet is unable to carry to completion'.

So, with this rare piece of romantic rhetoric, Kant begins his task of setting out the logic of illusion in the transcendental dialectic. He is not interested in contingent and accidental errors, like optical illusions or logical fallacies: his targets are much grander, namely *a priori* psychology, cosmology, and theology. All of these attempt to employ the mind in exploring a world beyond the bounds of experience, an enterprise of which illusion is the natural and inevitable result.

All our knowledge, Kant says, starts with the senses, proceeds from the senses to the understanding, and ends with reason. Reason, like understanding, operates through concepts; but while the pure concepts of understanding were categories, the concepts of pure reason are Ideas. The allusion to Plato is deliberate: Ideas, for Kant, are necessary concepts of reason to which no object corresponds in sense-experience.

The Ideas of pure reason are arrived at by taking a form of inference, and seeking to absolutize it. In ordinary life we infer conclusions from premises; the conclusions are true if the premises are true. But this seems to be only a conditional truth, since the truth of the premises themselves may be called in question. Reason looks for something unconditioned, a basis which is absolute, that is to say, derived from nothing other than itself. What is absolutely valid is valid unconditionally, in all respects, without restriction.

Kant says that there are three Ideas of pure reason; each of them is arrived at by taking a pattern of inference and striving to reach an absolute. One line of argument starts from subjective experience and concludes with the soul as permanent substantial subject. Another line of argument starts from the causal relationships between empirical objects and reaches the idea of the cosmos as a totality of causes and effects, unconditioned because it contains all conditions. A third line of argument starts from the contingency of the objects of experience and leads to the unconditioned necessity of a being of all beings, namely God. 'Pure reason thus furnishes the idea for a transcendental doctrine of the soul, for a transcendental science of the world, and finally for a transcendental knowledge of God.'

Let us consider first the illusions of *a priori* or rational psychology. Whereas empirical psychology deals with the soul as the object of inner sense, rational psychology treats of the soul as the subject of judgement. Rational psychology, Kant says, 'professes to be a science built upon the single proposition "I think"'.

It studies the transcendental subject of thinking, 'The I or he or it (the thing) which thinks' is an unknown X, the transcendental subject of the thoughts.

The 'I think' which is the text of rational psychology is the expression of the self-consciousness inseparable from thought. But how do we know that everything which thinks is self-conscious? Answer: self-consciousness is necessary to think of thinking, and in advance of experience we attribute to things those properties which are conditions of our thinking of them.

Kant lists four fallacies – he calls them 'paralogisms' or bogus syllogisms – into which we are led by our drive to transcend the limits of merely empirical psychology. In the first paralogism we proceed from the premiss 'Necessarily, the subject of thought is a subject' to the conclusion 'The subject of thought is necessarily a subject'. In the second, we pass from 'The ego cannot be divided into parts' to 'The ego is a simple substance'. In the third we move from 'Whenever I am conscious, it is the same I who am conscious' to 'Whenever I am conscious, I am conscious of the same I'. Finally, in the fourth, we argue from the truth of 'I can think of myself apart from every other thing, including my body' to the conclusion 'Apart from every other thing including my body, I can think of myself'.

In each paralogism a harmless analytical proposition is converted into a contentious synthetic *a priori* proposition. Taken together, the paralogisms add up to the claim that the self is an immaterial, incorruptible, personal, immortal entity. This is the delusion of *a priori* psychology.

THE TRANSCENDENTAL DIALECTIC:
THE ANTINOMIES OF PURE REASON

We turn next to *a priori* cosmology. Here Kant presents us with a set of antinomies. An antinomy is a pair of contrasting arguments which lead to contradictory conclusions (a thesis and an antithesis). Kant constructed a set of these to show that any attempt by reason to form 'cosmical concepts', that is to say, notions of the world as a whole, was bound to lead to irresoluble contradiction.

The first antinomy has as thesis 'The world has a beginning in time, and is also limited as regards space' and as antithesis 'The world has no beginning, and no limits in space; it is infinite as regards both time and space'.

The two propositions 'the world has a beginning in time' and 'the world has no beginning' have had, as we have seen, a long history in the works of philosophers. Aristotle thought the second could be proved. Augustine thought the first could be proved. Aquinas thought neither proposition could be proved. Kant now suggests that both propositions could be proved. That does not mean, of course, that two contradictories are both true; it is intended to show that reason has no right to talk at all about 'the world' as a whole.

The argument for the thesis starts from the definition of an infinite series as one that can never be completed, and concludes that it cannot be the case that an infinite world-series has passed away. But the argument is inconclusive. It is true that any infinite discrete series must be open at one end: no such series can be 'completed' in the sense of having two termini. But why may it not have an end in one direction, while going on for ever in the other? Elapsed time would then be 'completed' by having a terminus at the present, while reaching forever backward.

The argument from the antithesis goes thus. If the world had a beginning, then there was a time when the world did not exist. Any moment of this 'void time' is exactly like any other. Hence there can be no answer to the question 'why did the world begin when it did?' The believer in a temporally finite world can agree that it is not possible to locate the beginning of the world from outside (at such and such a point in 'void time'), while maintaining that one can locate it from within (so many time-units prior to now).

Neither of Kant's arguments is watertight, nor the parallel arguments which he offers for and against the finiteness of the world in space. Altogether, the first antinomy seems ineffective in establishing the impotence of reason.

Kant presents four antinomies in all. The second concerns simplicity and complexity; the third concerns freedom and causality; the fourth concerns necessity and contingency. In each of the antinomies, the antithesis affirms that a certain series continues for ever, the thesis that the same series comes to a full stop. Thus:

First: the series of items *next to* each other in space and in time comes to an end (thesis) / goes on for ever (antithesis)

Second: the series of items which are *parts of* others comes to an end (thesis) / goes on for ever (antithesis)

Third: the series of items *caused by* another ends in a free, naturally uncaused, event (thesis) / goes on for ever (antithesis)

Fourth: the series of items *contingent upon* another goes on for ever (antithesis) / ends with an absolutely necessary being (thesis)

Each of the italicized relationships is regarded by Kant as a form of *being conditioned* by something else: so that each of these series is a series of conditions, and each argument concludes to an unconditioned absolute.

Kant thinks that both sides to each antinomy are in error: the thesis is the error of dogmatism, the antithesis the error of empiricism. What the antinomy brings out, he maintains, is the mismatch between the scope of empirical inquiry and the pretensions of the rational ideal. The thesis always represents the world as smaller than thought: we can think beyond it. The antithesis always represents the world as larger than thought: we cannot think to the end of it. 'In all cases the cosmical idea is either too large or too small for the empirical regress.' We must match thought and the world by trimming our cosmic idea to fit the empirical inquiry.

The root error common to both the dogmatic thesis and the empiricist antithesis is the idea of the cosmic whole. In each case a task set (e.g. to trace the causal antecedents of an event) is confused with a task completed (e.g. a survey of the totality of causes). The world as a whole could never be given in experience and so 'the world as a whole' is a pseudo-concept. Hence it is not the case that the world is finite and not the case that the world is infinite.

The third antinomy differs from the previous two. In the first two antinomies both the thesis and the antithesis were rejected as false. But when Kant comes to the third antinomy he seeks to show that, properly interpreted, both thesis and antithesis are true. The thesis argues that natural causality is not sufficient to explain the phenomena of the world; in addition to determining causes we must take acount of freedom and spontaneity. The antithesis argues that to postulate transcendental freedom is to resign oneself to blind lawlessness, since the intrusion of an undetermined cause would disrupt the whole explanatory system of nature.

Kant's treatment of the third antinomy takes its place among the many attempts which have been made by philosophers to reconcile freedom and determinism. Determinists believe that every event has a cause, in the sense of a sufficient antecedent condition. There are two kinds of determinists: hard determinists, who believe that freedom is incompatible with determinism, and is therefore an illusion; and soft determinists, who believe that freedom and determinism are compatible, and can therefore accept that human freedom is genuine. Kant is a soft determinist: he seeks to show that freedom properly understood is compatible with determinism properly understood. An event may be both determined by nature and grounded in freedom.

The human will, Kant says, is sensuous but free: that is to say, it is affected by passion but it is not necessitated by passion. 'There is in man a power of self-determination, independently of any coercion through sensuous impulses.' But the exercise of this power of self-determination has two aspects, sensible (perceptible in experience) and intelligible (graspable only by the intellect). Our free agency is the intelligible cause of sensible effects; and these sensible phenomena are also part of an unbroken series in accordance with unchangeable laws. To reconcile human freedom with deterministic nature, Kant claims that nature operates in time, whereas the human will, as noumenon rather than phenomenon, is outside time.

Many soft determinists have argued that freedom and determinism are compatible because our actions, while determined, are determined by mental events in our own minds; and an action is free, it is claimed, if it is determined by inner rather than outer causes. Kant does seem to have believed in this kind of psychological determinism, but his reconciliation between freedom and nature does not depend on defining free action as action that is psychologically determined. He believed, surely correctly, that causal explanation ('I knocked him over because I was pushed') and explanation by reasons ('I knocked him over to teach him a lesson') are radically different types of explanation, and that the one is irreducible to the other. But since the reconciliation he offers takes place not at the level of experience but at the level of the noumenon, the thing in itself, his reconciling project is fatally infected with the obscurity which attends those concepts.

THE TRANSCENDENTAL DIALECTIC: CRITIQUE OF NATURAL THEOLOGY

In the fourth antinomy Kant considers arguments for and against the existence of a necessary being. He there leaves open the question whether a necessary being is to be found in the world itself, or outside the world as its cause. It is in the chapter on the Ideal of Pure Reason that he turns to consider the concept of God, the object of transcendental theology.

According to Kant all arguments to establish the existence of God must fall into one of three classes. There are ontological arguments, which take their start from the *a priori* concept of a supreme being; there are cosmological arguments, which derive from the nature of the empirical world in general; and there are physico-theological proofs, which start from particular natural phenomena.

In Kant's rational theology a very special role is assigned to the ontological argument. He claims that the cosmological argument is only the ontological argument in disguise, and he argues that the physico-theological argument by itself will lead us only to a designer, not to a genuine creator of the universe. Hence the importance of his influential critique of the ontological argument.

What is meant by calling God an absolutely necessary being? Some philosophers have defined a necessary being as one which exists in all possible worlds. If we define God in this way, then surely he exists. Our world is one possible world, otherwise it would not be actual; so if God exists in every possible world, he must exist in ours.

But is it legitimate to build existence – even possible existence – into the definition of something in this way? Kant thinks not. 'There is already a contradiction in introducing the concept of existence – no matter under what title it may be disguised – into the concept of a thing.' The ontological argument seeks to make the statement of God's existence an analytic proposition. If a proposition is analytic, then the predicate is part of the subject and cannot be denied of it. Taking the example of 'A triangle has three angles', Kant remarks:

To posit a triangle and yet to reject its three angles is self-contradictory; but there is no contradiction in rejecting the triangle together with its three angles. The same holds true of the concept of an absolutely necessary being. If its existence is rejected, we reject the thing itself with all its predicate; and no question of contradiction can then arise.

But why is Kant so sure that all existential propositions are synthetic? We can argue from concepts to non-existence: it is because we grasp the concepts 'square' and 'circle' that we know there are no square circles. Why cannot we argue similarly from concepts to existence? If 'There are no unmarried bachelors' is analytic, why not 'There is a necessary being'?

Kant's principal argument is that *being* is not a predicate, but a copula, a simple link between predicate and subject. If we say 'God is' or 'There is a God', Kant says, 'we attach no new predicate to the concept of God, but only posit the subject in itself with all its predicates'. In fact, existential propositions do not always 'posit', as Kant implies, because they may occur as sub-clauses in a larger sentence. Someone who says 'If there is a God, sinners will be punished' does not posit God's existence. None the less we may agree with Kant that 'exist' cannot be treated as a straightfoward first-order predicate.

Modern logicians, like Abelard in the twelfth century, rephrase statements of existence so that 'is' does not even look like a predicate. 'God exists' is formulated as 'Something is God'. This clarifies, but does not settle, the issues surrounding the ontological argument. For the problems about arguing from possibility to actuality return as questions about what counts as 'something': are we including in our consideration possible as well as actual objects?

Kant's principal point remains, and it is similar to a point we have seen made by Hume. 'By however many predicates we may think a thing – even if we completely determine it – we do not make the least addition to the thing when we further declare that this thing *is*. Otherwise, it would not be exactly the same thing that exists, but something more than we had thought in the concept; and we could not, therefore, say that the exact object of my concept exists.' In other words, whether there is something in reality corresponding to my concept cannot itself be part of my concept. A concept has to be determined prior to being compared to reality, otherwise we would not know *which* concept was being compared and found to correspond, or not correspond, to reality. *That* there is a God cannot be part of what we mean by 'God'; hence 'There is a God' cannot be an analyic proposition, and the ontological argument must fail.

Kant was wrong to think that the failure of the ontological argument implied that all arguments for the existence of God collapsed. What his criticism does show is that there is an incoherence in the notion of a being whose essence implies its existence. But a cosmological argument need not purport to show the existence of such a being, but only of one which is uncaused, unchanging, and everlasting, in contrast to the caused, variable, and contingent items in the world of experience.

Kant in fact has a criticism of the cosmological argument which is independent of his rebuttal of the ontological argument. All forms of the cosmological argument seek to show that a series of contingent causes, however long, can be completed only by a necessary cause. But we are faced with a dilemma if we ask whether the necessary cause is, or is not, part of the chain of causes.

If it is part of the chain, then we can raise in its case, as in the case of the other members of the chain, the question why it exists. But we cannot imagine a supreme being saying to itself 'I am from eternity to eternity, and outside me there is nothing save what is through my will, *but whence then am I?* On the other hand, if the necessary being is not part of the chain of causation, how can it be its first member and account for all the other links which end with the existence of myself?

The argument for God's existence which is most gently treated by Kant is the physico-theological proof; it must always, he said, be mentioned with respect. His aim is not to diminish its authority, but to limit the scope of its conclusion. The proof argues that everywhere in the world we find signs of order, in accordance with a determinate purpose, carried out with great wisdom. This order is alien to the individual things in the world which contribute to make it up; it must therefore have been imposed by one or more sublime wise causes, operating not blindly as nature does, but freely as humans do. Kant raises various difficulties about the analogies which this argument draws between the operation of nature and the artifice of human skill. But even if we waive these, the most the argument can prove is the existence of 'an *architect* of the world who is always very much hampered by the adaptability of the material in which he works, not a *creator* of the world to whose idea everything is subject'.

Kant called the system of the *Critique of Pure Reason*, with its constructive analytic part and its destructive dialectic part, 'transcendental idealism'. This was meant to bring out both the negative and positive aspects of the system. At the empirical level, Kant was a realist, not an idealist, like Berkeley: he did not believe that nothing existed save ideas in the mind. On the other hand, at the ultimate or transcendental level, he was an idealist, because he denied that things in themselves were knowable. Thus, he called himself a transcendental idealist.

KANT'S MORAL PHILOSOPHY

Just as the first *Critique* set out critically the synthetic *a priori* principles of theoretical reason, the *Groundwork of the Metaphysic of Morals* (1785) set out critically the synthetic *a priori* principles of practical reason. This is a brief and eloquent presentation of Kant's moral system.

In morals, Kant's starting point is that the only thing which is good without qualification is a good will. Talents, character, self-control, and fortune can be used to bad ends; even happiness can be corrupting. It is not what it achieves that constitutes the goodness of a good will; good will is good in itself alone.

> Even if, by some special disfavour of destiny, or by the niggardly endowment of stepmotherly nature, this will is entirely lacking in power to carry out its intentions; if by its utmost effort it still accomplishes nothing, and only good will is left . . . ; even then it would still shine like a jewel for its own sake as something which has its full value in itself.

It is not in order to pursue happiness that human beings have been endowed with a will; instinct would have been far more effective for this purpose. Reason was given to us in order to produce a will which was good not as a means to some further end, but good in itself. Good will is the highest good and the condition of all other goods, including happiness.

What, then, makes a will good in itself? To answer this question we must investigate the concept of *duty*. To act from duty is to exhibit good will in the face of difficulty. But we must distinguish between acting in accordance with duty, and acting from the motive of duty. A grocer who is honest from self-interest, or a philanthropist who delights in the contentment of others, may do actions which are in accord with duty. But actions of this kind, however right and amiable, have, according to Kant, no moral worth. Worth of character is shown only when someone does good not from inclination, but from duty: when, for instance, a man who has lost all taste for life and longs for death still does his best to preserve his own life in accordance with the moral law.

Kant's teaching here is directly opposed to that of Aristotle. Aristotle taught that people were not really virtuous as long as their exercise of virtue went against the grain; the really virtuous person thoroughly enjoyed performing acts of virtue. For Kant, on the other hand, it is the painfulness of well-doing that is the real mark of virtue. He realizes that he has set daunting standards for moral conduct: he is quite prepared to contemplate the possibility that there has never been, in fact, an action performed solely on moral grounds and out of a sense of duty.

What is it, then, to act from duty? To act from duty is to act out of reverence for the moral law; and the way to test whether one is so acting is to seek the maxim, or principle, on which one acts, that is to say, the imperative to which one's act conforms. There are two sorts of imperative, hypothetical and categorical. The hypothetical imperative says: If you wish to achieve a certain end, act in such-and-such a way. The categorical imperative says: No matter what end you wish to achieve, act in such-and-such a way. There are many hypothetical imperatives, because there are many different ends which humans may set themselves. There is only one categorical imperative, which is this 'Act only according to a maxim by which you can at the same time will that it shall become a universal law.'

Kant illustrates this with several examples, of which we may mention two. The first is this. Having run out of funds, I may be tempted to borrow money, though I know that I will be unable to repay it. I am acting on the maxim 'Whenever I believe myself short of money, I will borrow money and promise to pay it back, though I know that this will never be done'. I cannot will that everyone should act on this maxim, because if everyone did so the whole institution of promising would collapse. Hence, borrowing money in these circumstances would violate the categorical imperative.

A second example is this. A person who is well provided for, and is asked for help by others suffering hardship, may be tempted to respond 'What does this matter to me? Let every one be as happy as Heaven wills or as he can make himself; I won't harm him, but I won't help him either.' He cannot will this maxim to be universalized, because a situation might arise in which he himself needed love and sympathy from others.

These cases illustrate two different ways in which the categorical imperative applies. In the first case, the maxim cannot be universalized because its universalization involves contradiction (if no one keeps promises, there is no such thing as promising). In the second case, the maxim can be universalized without contradiction, but no one could rationally *will* the situation which would result from its universalization. Kant says the two different cases correspond to two different kinds of duty: strict duties, and meritorious duties.

Not all Kant's examples are convincing. He argues, for instance, that the categorical imperative excludes suicide. But however wrong suicide may be, there is nothing self-contradictory in the prospect of universal suicide; and someone sufficiently despairing might regard it as a consummation devoutly to be wished.

Kant offers a further formulation of the categorical imperative. 'Act in such a way that you always treat humanity, whether in your own person or in the person of any other, never simply as a means, but always at the same time as an end.' He claims, though he has not convinced many of his readers, that this is equivalent to the earlier imperative, and enables the same practical conclusions to be drawn. It is, in fact, more effective than the earlier formulation in ruling out suicide. To take one's own life, Kant urges, is to use one's own person as a means of bringing to an end one's discomfort and distress.

As a human being, Kant says, I am not only an end in myself, I am a member of a kingdom of ends, a union of rational beings under common laws. My will, as has been said, is rational in so far as its maxims can be made universal laws. The converse of this is that universal law is law which is made by rational wills like mine. A rational being 'is subject only to laws which are made by himself and yet are universal'. In the kingdom of ends, we are all both legislators and subjects. The reader is reminded of Rousseau's general will.

Kant concludes the exposition of his moral system with a panegyric to the dignity of virtue. In the kingdom of ends, everything has a price or a worth. If something has a price, it can be exchanged for something else. What has worth is unique and unexchangeable; it is beyond price. There are, Kant says, two kinds of price: market price, which is related to the satisfaction of need; and fancy price, which is related to the satisfaction of taste. Morality is above and beyond either kind of price.

'Morality, and humanity so far as it is capable of morality, is the only thing which has worth. Skill and diligence in work have a market price; wit, lively imagination and humour have a fancy price; but fidelity to promises and kindness based on principle (not on instinct) have an intrinsic worth.' Kant's words echoed throughout the nineteenth century, and still strike a chord with many people today.

XVII
GERMAN IDEALISM AND MATERIALISM

FICHTE

Napoleon's conquest of most of Europe can be compared with Alexander's conquests of much of Asia and parts of Africa. The spectacular military achievements were short-lived, but their cultural consequences were felt long after. After Napoleon's final defeat at Waterloo, tired monarchies were restored throughout the continent; but their tenure was precarious, and many disappeared within the next half century. French armies had carried with them the slogans of the French Revolution; and even though, in Napoleon's Empire, liberty had given way to military despotism, equality had been overlain with a new aristocracy, and fraternity had never got beyond the Cain and Abel stage, the ideal of free democracy lived on as an aspiration throughout Europe. Moreover, sentiments of nationalism had been kindled in countries which had been attacked or oppressed by Napoleon's troops. In Italy and Germany, especially, men craved to replace a patchwork of superannuated local regimes with a single, strong, national power.

One of the founders of German nationalism was the philosopher Johann Gottlieb Fichte. He was a professor at Jena and in the new University of Berlin, whose active life spanned the period between the execution of Louis XVI and the banishment of Napoleon to Elba. His Addresses to the German Nation in 1808 rebuked the Germans for the disunity which led to their defeat by Napoleon at the battle of Jena, and he served as a volunteer in the army of resistance in 1812. But his reputation as a philosopher rests on his book of 1804, *Wissenschaftslehre*.

Fichte was an admirer of Kant: his first book had been a *Critique of All Revelation*, written in the style of Kant, so successfully that it passed for the Master's work. He thought, however, that Kant's philosophy contained a radical inconsistency. Kant never gave up the notion that our experience was ultimately caused by 'things in themselves' even though we could know nothing about such things. But on his own account, the concept of cause was something which could only be applied within the sphere of phenomena. How then could there be an unknown, mind-independent cause outside this sphere?

Accordingly, in his *Wissenschaftslehre* Fichte tried to redesign Kant's system to remove the inconsistency. Two ways were possible. One way would be to allow the notion of cause to extend beyond the realm of phenomena, and allow experience to be caused by things in themselves. That is the path of dogmatism. The other would be to abandon the thing-in-itself, and to say that experience is created by the thinking subject. That is the path of idealism. That path Fichte followed, and made himself the father of German Idealism.

Fichte, starting with the Ego or pure self, set himself the task of showing how the whole of consciousness could be derived from it. His various explanations of this derivation failed to make clear, either to his admirers or to his critics, that he was not claiming that the individual self could create the whole material world. But he insisted that he was talking not of an individual self, but of a single, absolute ego, which created all phenomena and all individual selves.

This sounds rather like God, and indeed in his later, popular works, Fichte was prepared to talk in this way. 'It is not the finite self that exists, it is the divine Idea that is the foundation of all philosophy; everything that man does of himself is null and void. All existence is living and active in itself, and there is no other life than Being, and no other Being than God.' But elsewhere he said that it was superstitious to believe in a divine being which was anything more than a moral order. Fichte's populist pantheism seems to have been only a shell for a less pictorial philosophy which few could understand, and which those who claimed to understand found wanting.

HEGEL

One of those most indebted to, but also most critical of, Fichte was G. W. F. **Hegel**, by far the most influential of the German Idealists. Born in 1770, Hegel studied theology at the University of Tübingen, and taught at Jena until the University was closed down by the French invasion. In 1807 he published *The Phenomenology of Spirit*. It was not until 1816 that he became a Professor, at the University of Heidelberg; by that time he had published his major work, *The Science of Logic*. After publishing an encyclopedia of the philosophical sciences (logic, philosophy of nature, and philosophy of spirit), he was called in 1818 to a Chair in Berlin, which he held until his death from cholera in 1831.

Hegel's writings are extremely difficult to read. They also make a great immediate impression of profundity. On closer attention, some readers find that impression is enhanced, others find that it evaporates. The least difficult, and perhaps the most influential, part of Hegel's writing is his philosophy of history, so let us start with that.

Hegel believed that the philosopher had a special insight into history which ordinary historians lacked. The philosopher knows that reason is the sovereign of the world, and that the history of the world presents us with a rational process. This knowledge can be reached either by the study of a metaphysical system, or by inference from the study of history itself. It corresponds to the religious belief in providence; but it goes beyond it, because the general notion of providence is inadequate to explain history.

> To explain history is to depict the passions of mankind, the genius, the active powers, that play their part on the great stage; and the providentially determined process which these exhibit, constitutes what is generally called the 'plan' of providence. Yet it is this very plan which is supposed to be concealed from our view; which it is deemed presumption even to wish to recognize.

Only the philosopher knows the ultimate destiny of the world, and how it is to be realized. Universal history, Hegel says, consists in the development of Spirit (*Geist*) and its manifestation in concrete reality. What, then, is Spirit? It is the opposite of matter; and while the essence of matter is gravity, the essence of spirit is freedom. While matter is thus defined by the attraction its parts exercise on each other, Spirit is existence which is self-contained, independent, and self-conscious. As conscious of itself, Spirit is conscious of its own potentialities, and it possesses a drive to actualize these potentialities. Universal history, Hegel says, is 'the exhibition of Spirit in the process of working out the knowledge of that which it is potentially'.

The notion of Spirit thus introduced is likely to be found baffling on first acquaintance. Is it God? Or is 'Spirit' a misleadingly grand way of talking about individual human minds, in the way in which medical textbooks speak of 'the liver' when they are generalizing about individual people's livers? Neither of these guesses is quite right. To get a feel for what Hegel means it is better to reflect on the way in which we all talk about the human race. Without any particular metaphysical commitment, we are happy to say such things as that the human race has progressed, or is in decline, or has learnt many things in the age of science of which it was ignorant in the age of barbarism. When Hegel uses the word 'Spirit' he means much more than we do when we talk of the human race; but he is using the same kind of language.

Thus, when he says that in history Spirit progresses in consciousness of freedom, Hegel traces the growth of awareness of freedom among human beings. Those who lived under oriental despots did not know that they were free beings. The Greeks and Romans knew that they themselves were free, but their keeping of slaves showed that they did not know that man as such was free. 'The German nations, under the influence of Christianity, were the first to attain the consciousness that man, as man, is free: that it is the freedom of Spirit which constitutes its essence.'

The destiny of the world is Spirit's expansion of its freedom and its consciousness of its freedom. But this, though all-important, is an abstract statement: what are the means in the concrete by which Spirit realizes its freedom? Nothing seems to happen in the world except as the result of the self-interested actions of individuals, and history presents a dismal spectacle: it is, as Hegel puts it, the slaughterhouse in which the happiness of peoples, the wisdom of states, and the virtues of individuals are sacrificed. But gloom is not justified: for the self-interested actions of individuals are the only means by which the ideal destiny of the world can be realized. 'Nothing great in the world has been accomplished without *passion*.' The Ideal provides the warp, and human passions the woof, of the web of history. The union of the two is 'Liberty, under the conditions of morality, in a State'.

The self-interested activities of individuals are the instruments by which the World-Spirit (*Weltgeist*) achieves its object; but they are unconscious that they are doing so. They do so to greatest effect when a State is so organized that the private interests of the citizens coincide with the common interest of the State. In respect of world history, states and peoples themselves count as individuals; but there are also some unique figures who have a special role in Spirit's expression of itself: world-historical individuals such as Julius Caesar or Napoleon, whose own particular aims express the will of the World-Spirit, and who see the aspects of history which are ripe for development in their time.

These great men, however, are the exception, and the normal development of the World-Spirit is through the spirit of particular peoples or nations, the *Volksgeist*. This spirit manifests itself in a people's social and political institutions, culture, religion, and philosophy. Nations are not necessarily identical with States – indeed, it was the great task of nineteenth-century German nationalism to turn the German Nation into a German Reich – but only in a State does a nation become self-conscious of itself as a nation.

The creation of the State is indeed the high object for which the World-Spirit has been using individuals and peoples as its instruments. The State 'is the realization of Freedom, i.e. of the absolute final aim, and it exists for its own sake'. All the worth, all the spiritual reality which the individual human being possesses, he possesses only through the state. For only in participating in social and political life is he fully conscious of his own rationality, and of himself as a manifestation, through the Folk-Spirit, of the World-Spirit. The State, Hegel says, is the Divine Idea as it exists on earth.

It is the interplay between Folk-Spirits which constitutes the history of the World-Spirit and enables it to realize its destiny. In different epochs, different Folk-Spirits are the primary manifestation of the progress of the World-Spirit. The people to which it belongs will be, for one epoch, the dominant people in the world history. For each nation, the hour strikes once and only once. In Hegel's time the hour had struck for the German nation. Whereas the English can say 'we are the men who navigate the ocean, and have the commerce of the world', the German can say 'The German spirit is the spirit of the new world. Its aim is the realization of absolute Truth as the unlimited self-determination of freedom'.

German history is divided into three periods: the period up to Charlemagne, which Hegel calls the Kingdom of the Father; the period from Charlemagne to the Reformation, the Kingdom of the Son; and finally the Kingdom of the Holy Ghost, from the Reformation up to and including the Prussian monarchy. Though Prussia is almost the realization of the ideal, it is not to be the last word of the World-Spirit. One might expect, given the preference which Hegel commonly shows for wholes over their parts, that nation-states would eventually give way to a world state. But Hegel disliked the idea of a world state, because it would take away the opportunity for war, which he thought had a positive value of its own as a reminder of the transitory nature of finite existence. Instead, the future of the world lies in America 'where, in the ages that lie before us, the burden of the world's history shall reveal itself' – perhaps in a great continental struggle between North and South.

Hegel's philosophy of history, he claimed, could be deduced from his meta-physics. Only there can we see the full meaning of his invocation of World-Spirit, for the references to it are not meant to be mere metaphors for the operation of impersonal historical forces. Spirit, in Hegel's metaphysical system, resembles Kant's transcendental unity of apperception in being the subject of all experience, which cannot itself be an object of experience. Kant seems content to assume that there will be a separate such focus in the life of each individual mind. But what ground is there for this assumption? Behind Kant's transcendental self stands the Cartesian ego; and one of the first critics of Descartes' *cogito* put the question to him: how do you know that it is you who thinks, and not the world-soul that thinks in you? Hegel's spirit, then, is meant to be a centre of consciousness which is prior to any individual consciousness. One Spirit thinks severally in the thoughts of Descartes and in the thoughts of Kant, perhaps rather as I, as a single person, can feel simultaneously toothache and gout in different parts of myself.

The existence of Spirit is said, by Hegel, to be a matter of logic. Just as he sees history as a manifestation of logic, so he tends to see logic in historical, indeed military, terms. If two propositions are contradictories, Hegel will describe this as a conflict between them: one proposition will go out to do battle against another, and achieve defeat or victory against it. This is called 'dialectic', the process by which one proposition (the thesis) fights with another (the antithesis) and both are finally conquered by a third (the synthesis). Let us illustrate how Hegel uses this dialectical method in practice.

The subject matter of logic is the Absolute, the totality of reality, familiar to us from earlier philosophers as Being. We start from the thesis that the Absolute is pure Being. But pure Being without any qualities is nothing; so we are led to the antithesis 'The Absolute is nothing'. This thesis and antithesis are over-come by synthesis: the union of Being and Unbeing is becoming, and so we say 'The Absolute is Becoming'. The Absolute has a life of its own, which passes through three stages, Concept, Nature, and Spirit. These three stages are studied by three different branches of philosophy, logic, philosophy of nature, and philosophy of spirit.

Hegel often refers to the Absolute by the word 'God', and a modern Christian might think to identify the three stages in the life of the Absolute with (i) the existence of God alone before the world began, (ii) the existence of the natural creation before the evolution of man, and (iii) the history of the human race. But this would be far too simple. Hegel does make use of Aristotle's definition of God when he describes the Absolute as being the Thought which thinks itself. But it turns out that the self-awareness of the Absolute comes at the end, not at the beginning, of this life-cycle, and it is brought into existence by the philosophical reflection of human beings. It is the history of philosophy which brings the Absolute face to face with itself. Reader, I hope you realize what is happening as you are reading!

If we take Hegel seriously, however, we should stop the book at this point. For Hegel thought that with his own system, the history of philosophy comes to an end. In his *Lectures on the History of Philosophy* he displays earlier philosophies as succumbing, one by one, to a dialectical advance marching steadily in the direction of German Idealism. A new epoch has now arisen, he tells us, in which finite self-consciousness has ceased to be finite, and absolute self-consciousness has achieved reality. The sole task of the history of philosophy is to narrate the strife between finite and infinite self-consciousness; now that the battle is over, it has reached its goal.

Marx and the Young Hegelians

Hegel's importance in the history of philosophy derives not so much from the content of this writing as from the enormous influence he exercised on thinkers who followed him. Of all those whom he influenced, the one who in his turn was most influential was Karl **Marx**, who described his own philosophical vocation as 'turning Hegel upside-down'.

Marx was born in Trier, in 1818, to a liberal Protestant family of Jewish descent. He attended university first at Bonn and then at Berlin, where he studied the philosophy of Hegel under Bruno Bauer, the leader of a left-wing group known as the Young Hegelians. From Hegel and Bauer Marx learned to view history as a dialectical process. That is to say, history came in a succession of stages which followed one another, like the steps in a geometrical proof, in an order determined by fundamental logical or metaphysical principles. This was a vision which he retained throughout his life.

The Young Hegelians attached great importance to Hegel's concept of alienation, that is to say, treating as alien something with which by rights one should identify. Alienation is the state in which people view as exterior to themselves something which is truly an intrinsic element of their own being. What Hegel himself had in mind was that individuals, all of whom were manifestations of a single Spirit, saw each other as hostile rivals rather than as elements of a single unity. The Young Hegelians rejected the idea of the universal spirit, but retained the notion of alienation, locating it elsewhere in the system.

Hegel had seen his philosophy as a sophisticated and self-conscious presentation of truths which had been given uncritical and mythical expression in religious doctrines. For the Young Hegelians, religion was not to be translated, but eliminated. For Bauer, and still more for Ludwig Feuerbach, religion was the supreme form of alienation. Humans, who were the highest form of beings, projected their own life and consciousness into an unreal heaven. The essence of man is the unity of reason, will, and love; unwilling to accept limits to these perfections, we form the idea of a God of infinite knowledge, infinite will, and infinite love, and man venerates Him as an independent Being distinct from man himself. 'Religion is the separation of man from himself: he sets God over against himself as an opposed being.'

Marx was in sympathy with the Young Hegelian critique of religion, which he was later to describe as 'the opium of the people', but from an early stage he placed the focus of alienation elsewhere. He wrote:

> Money is the universal, self-constituted value of all things. Hence it has robbed the whole world, the human world as well as nature, of its proper value. Money is the alienated essence of man's labour and life, and this alien essence dominates him as he worships it.

In 1841 he wrote a critique of Hegel's philosophy of the State, in which he attacked the theory that private property was the basis of civil society. In so far as a State is based on private property it is itself an alienation of man's true nature.

In 1842 Marx became the editor of a liberal journal, the *Rheinische Zeitung*. The Prussian government regarded it as subversive, and closed it down. Marx, out of a job, and newly married, migrated to Paris with his wife, Jenny. There he found further work as a journalist, and made a number of radical friends including the revolutionary socialist Friedrich Engels who became his right-hand-man. He also made a study of the writings of British economists such as Adam Smith, and began work on his own economic theory. His basic insight was that since money is a form of alienation, all purely economic relationships – such as that between worker and employer – are alienated forms of social intercourse, and indeed a form of slavery which debases both slave and master. Only the abolition of wage slavery and the replacement of private property by communism can put an end to human alienation.

Soon he was forced to migrate again, this time to Brussels. There, with Engels, Marx wrote *The German Ideology*, a work of philosophical criticism which was not published until long after his death. In it he enunciates the principle that 'life determines consciousness, not consciousness life'. History is determined, not by the mental history of a Hegelian Spirit, nor by the thoughts and theories of human individuals, but by the processes of production of the necessities of life.

Marx had earlier reached the conclusion that human alienation would not be ended by philosophical criticism alone. It was not simply that, as he famously put it, 'The philosophers have only interpreted the world; the point is to change it'. The change that was necessary would have to be a violent one, and that called for an alliance between the philosophers and the workers. 'As philosophy finds its material weapons in the proletariat, the proletariat finds its intellectual weapons in philosophy.' In 1847 a newly-formed Communist League met in London, and Marx and Engels were commissioned to write its manifesto, which was published early in 1848, just before a series of revolutions rocked the major kingdoms of the European continent.

'The history of all hitherto existing society,' states the Manifesto, 'is the history of class struggles.' This is a consequence of the materialist theory of history. Superficially, history may appear to be a record of conflicts between different nations and different religions; but the underlying realities throughout the ages are the forces of material production and the classes which are created by the relationships between those involved in that production. The legal, political, and religious institutions which loom so large in historical narrative are only a super-structure concealing the fundamental levels of history: the forces and powers of production, and the economic relations among the producers. The philosophy, or 'ideology', which is used to justify the legal and political institutions of each epoch are merely a smokescreen concealing the vested interests of the ruling classes of the time.

CAPITALISM AND ITS DISCONTENTS

Marx developed these ideas in many later writings, culminating in his great *Capital*, written in London in the final period of his life, when he had been forced to leave France in the aftermath of the revolution of 1848. In that work he explained in detail how the course of history was dictated by the forces and relations of production.

Productive forces, in Marx's terms, include the raw materials, machinery, and labour, which go to make a finished product: as wheat, a mill, and a mill-worker are all needed to produce flour. The relations of production are economic relations which involve these forces, such as the ownership of the mill and the hiring of the worker. Developments in technology lead to different relations of produc-tion: in the age of the hand-mill, the worker is the serf of the feudal lord; in the age of the steam-mill he is the employee of the capitalist. Changes in technology can render existing relations of production obsolete: a steam-mill demands mobile workers, not serfs tied to the land. When the relations of production no longer match the productive forces, Marx believed, these relations 'turn into fetters' and a social revolution takes place.

Marx divided the past, present, and future history of the relations of production into six phases: primitive communism, slavery, feudalism, capitalism, socialism, and ultimate communism. He believed that the capitalist society in which he lived was in a state of crisis, and would shortly pass through a revolutionary change which would usher in the final stages first of socialism and then of communism. The crisis which capitalism had reached, he believed, was not a contingent historical fact; it was something inherent in the nature of capitalism itself. He based this conclusion on two economic theories: the labour theory of value, and the theory of surplus value.

Following a suggestion which goes back ultimately to Aristotle, Marx believed that the true value of any product was in proportion to the amount of labour put into it. That thesis enables us to decide what a product is worth only if we have a way of measuring the value of labour. The way to do that is to work out the cost of keeping the labourer alive and well for the time it takes to do the job. Hence, if it takes a labourer a day to produce a quantity of flour, that flour is worth the cost of one day's subsistence.

Under capitalism, however, prices in the market are determined not by true value, but by supply and demand. The capitalist, who owns the raw material and the means of production, having paid the worker a wage equal to his day's subsistence, say £1, can often sell the product for many times that sum, say £10. The difference between the subsistence wage and the market price is the surplus value, in this case £9. Under capitalism, no part of this surplus value is returned to the worker, it is all pocketed by the employer. The effect is that only one-tenth of the labourer's work is for his own benefit; nine-tenths of it is just to produce profit for the capitalist.

As technology develops, and the labourer's productivity increases accordingly, surplus value increases and the proportion of his work which is returned to him becomes smaller and smaller. Finally this exploitation is bound to reach a point at which the proletariat finds it intolerable, and rises in revolt. The capitalist system will be replaced by the dictatorship of the proletariat, which will abolish private property and introduce a socialist state in which the means of production are totally under central government control. But the socialist state will itself be only temporary, and it will wither away to be replaced by a communist society in which the interests of the individual and the community will be identical.

The theory of surplus value suffers from a fatal weakness. Marx offers no convincing reason why the capitalist, no matter how great his profits, should pay no more than a subsistence wage. But this thesis is an essential element in his prediction that capitalism would inevitably lead to revolution, and do so soonest in those states where technology, and therefore exploitation, was progressing fastest. In fact, employers soon began, and have since continued, to pay wages well above subsistence level in advanced industrialized countries. It was not in them but in backward Russia that the first proletarian revolution occurred.

If we treat Marxism as a scientific hypothesis, to be judged by the success of its predictions, it must be said that it has been totally discredited by the course of history since Marx's death. But whatever Marx himself may have thought, his theories are essentially philosophical rather than scientific; and judged from that standpoint, they can claim both successes and failures. On the one hand, though few historians nowadays accept that events are determined totally by economic factors, no historian, not even a historian of philosophy, would dare to deny the influence of those factors on politics and culture. On the other hand, even in countries which underwent socialist revolutions of a Marxist type the power wielded by individuals, such as Lenin, Stalin and Mao, has given the lie to the theory that only impersonal forces determine the course of history. Finally, the thesis that ideology is merely the smokescreen of the *status quo* is refuted by the enormous influence which has been exerted, for good or ill, by Marx's own system of ideas, considered not as a scientific theory but as an inspiration to political activism. If life determines consciousness, consciousness also determines life.

XVIII
THE UTILITARIANS

JEREMY BENTHAM

Britain survived the Napoleonic era without invasion and without revolution. Government remained in the hands of a privileged group, and in times of national crisis under Prime Ministers such as the younger Pitt and Lord Liverpool, who were highly autocratic; there was a long way yet to go before the country became a modern democracy. Reform was achieved, but in slow and constitutional stages, rather than by violent upheaval or dramatic coup d'état.

One of those who did most to make British public opinion aware of the need for reform was Jeremy Bentham, an Oxford-educated lawyer who in the year of the French Revolution, at the age of forty-one, published an *Introduction to the Principles of Morals and Legislation*. He had already, in 1776, published an anonymous attack on the English legal system as recently presented in Sir William Blackstone's commentaries. He was much interested in penal reform, and on a visit to Russia he had conceived the idea of a model prison, the Panopticon. William Pitt's government passed an Act of Parliament authorizing the scheme, but it was defeated by ducal landowners who did not want a prison near their London estates. In 1808 he became friends with James Mill and shared in the education of his young son John Stuart. He wrote many papers on legal and constitutional matters, most of which remained unpublished in his lifetime, and spent years on the preparation of a constitutional code, which was unfinished when he died. In 1817 he published a plan for parliamentary reform, followed by a draft *Radical Reform Bill*. He died in 1832 a few weeks after the Great Reform Bill had been passed, widely extending the parliamentary franchise. His body is preserved in the library of University College, London, which he helped to found.

Bentham's *Principles* is the founding document of the school of moral and political thought known as Utilitarianism, developed after him by John Stuart Mill, and continuing to flourish up to the present day. The guiding idea of the system is what Bentham calls 'the principle of utility', or 'the greatest happiness principle'. The principle of utility evaluates every action according to the tendency which it appears to have to augment or diminish happiness. The promotion of the greatest happiness of the greatest number is the only right and proper end of human action, and laws and legal systems are to be tested by their conformity, or lack of conformity, with this aim. The principle of utility enables us to distinguish good laws from bad, and it is the only source of political obligation. Belief in natural law, or natural rights, or social contracts, Bentham maintained, is nothing more than superstition.

'The greatest happiness of the greatest number' is one of those philosophical slogans, like 'the best of all possible worlds' or 'that than which nothing greater can be conceived', which are impressive on first hearing, but which when probed turn out to to have no clear meaning. It is not at all clear how we can measure happiness and compare the quantity of happiness in different people, even if we understand happiness in Bentham's rather crude way as being pleasant sensation. Again Bentham provides no consistent answer to the question 'Greatest number of *what*?' Should we add 'voters' or 'citizens' or 'human beings' or 'sentient beings'? Again, should moralists and politicians attempt to control the number of candidates for happiness, by taking steps to increase or diminish the population? If so, in which direction? Most difficult of all, how do we balance the quantity of happiness with the quantity of people? Suppose we have devised a scale from 0 to 100, on which 100 represents supreme happiness, and 0 represents supreme misery. Should we prefer a state in which 51 per cent of the people score 51, and 49 per cent score 49, to a state in which 80 per cent of the people score 100 and 20 per cent score 0? If we try, in a simple way, to operate what Bentham calls 'the felicific calculus', state A seems to score only 5002 points, and state B to score 8000 points. But anyone with a care for equality, or distributive justice, might hesitate before casting a vote for state B.

Bentham was well aware of the difficulties in putting his slogan into practice, and offers, for instance, recipes for the measurement of pleasures: they are to be valued in accordance with their intensity, duration, certainty, propinquity, fecundity, purity, and extension. He even offers a mnemonic rhyme to aid in operating the calculus:

> Intense, long, certain, speedy, fruitful, pure –
> Such marks in pleasures and in pains endure.
> Such pleasures seek if private be thy end;
> If it be public, wide let them extend.
> Such pains avoid, whichever be thy view
> If pains must come, let them extend to few.

Later Utilitarians have devoted great ingenuity to dealing with the kinds of problem outlined in the previous paragraph. But it remains true to this day that the greatest happiness principle remains the title of a research programme rather than an actual recipe for moral or political action.

Bentham's influence on moral philosophy has been enormous. We may divide moral philosophers into absolutists and consequentialists. Absolutists believe that there are some kinds of actions which are intrinsically wrong and should never be done no matter what the consequences are of refraining from doing them. Consequentialists believe that the morality of actions should be judged by their consequences, and that there is no category of act which may not, in special circumstances, be justified by its consequences. Prior to Bentham most philosophers were absolutists, because they believed in a natural law or in natural rights. If there are natural rights and a natural law, then some kinds of action, actions which violate those rights or conflict with that law, are wrong, no matter what their consequences. Bentham's attack on the notions of natural law and natural rights has been more influential than his advocacy of the principle of utility: it has had the effect of making consequentialism respectable in moral philosophy.

Consequentialists, like Bentham, judge actions by their consequences, and there is no class of actions which is ruled out in advance. A believer in natural law, told that some Herod or Nero has killed five thousand citizens guilty of no crime, can say straightway 'that was a wicked act'. The consequentialist, before making such a judgement, must say 'tell me more'. What were the consequences of the massacre? What would have happened if the ruler had allowed the five thousand to live?

The consequentialism which can trace its origin to Bentham is nowadays widespread among professional philosophers. Thoroughgoing consequentialism is probably more popular in theory than in practice: outside philosophy seminars most people probably believe that some actions are so outrageous that they should morally be ruled out in advance, and reject the idea that one should literally stop at nothing in the pursuit of desirable consequences. But in present-day discussions of, for instance, topics in medical ethics, it is consequentialists who have the greater say in the formation of policy, at least in English-speaking countries. This is because they talk in the cost–benefit terms which technologists and policy-makers instinctively understand. And among the general non-professional public, many people share Bentham's suspicion of the idea that some classes of action are absolutely prohibited.

Where, people ask, do these absolute prohibitions come from? No doubt religious believers see them as coming from God; but how can they convince unbelievers of this? Can there be a prohibition without a prohibiter? Do not those who subscribe to absolute prohibitions merely express the prejudices of their upbringing?

The answer is to be found in the nature of morality itself. There are three elements which are essential to morality: a moral community, a set of moral values, and a moral code. All three are necessary. First, it is as impossible to have a purely private morality as it is to have a purely private language, and for very similar reasons. Secondly, the moral life of the community consists in the shared pursuit of non-material values such as fairness, truth, comradeship, freedom: it is this which distinguishes between morality and economics. Thirdly, this pursuit is carried out within a framework which excludes certain prohibited types of behaviour: it is this which marks the distinction between morality and aesthetics. The answer to the question 'Who does the prohibiting?' is that it is the members of the moral community: membership of a common moral society involves subscription to a common code. In attacking the notion that some things are absolutely wrong, Bentham was attacking not just one form of morality, but something constitutive of morality as such.

Despite the baneful ethical system he originated, Bentham's detailed discussions of particular issues are often excellent. He writes briskly, and economically, making acute and relevant distinctions, and packing a great weight of argument into lucid and business-like paragraphs. Consider, as an instance, this discussion of the purpose of the penal system:

> The immediate principal end of punishment is to control action. This action is either that of the offender, or of others: that of the offender it controls by its influence, either on his will, in which case it is said to operate in the way of *reformation*; or on his physical power, in which case it is said to operate by *disablement*; that of others it can influence no otherwise than by its influence over their wills; in which case it is said to operate in the way of *example*.

Bentham rejected the retributive theory of punishment, according to which justice demands that he who has done harm shall suffer harm, whether or not his suffering has any deterrent or remedial effect on himself or others. Such retribution, plain rendering of evil for evil, would simply increase the amount of evil in the world rather than restoring any balance of justice. Since punishment involves the infliction of pain, it can only be justified if it promises to exclude some greater evil. The principal purpose of punishment, he believed, was deterrence; and punishment should not be inflicted in cases where it would have no deterrent effect, either on the offender or on others, nor should it be inflicted to any greater extent than is necessary to deter. Bentham drew up a set of rules setting out the proportion between punishments and offences, based not on the retributive principle of 'an eye for an eye, a tooth for a tooth' but on the effect which the prospect of punishment will have on the calculation by a potential offender of the profit and loss likely to follow on the offence. Any remedial effect of punishment, Bentham believed, was always bound to be subsidiary to the deterrent effect, and in practice, in the conditions of most actual prisons, was unlikely to be achieved.

Bentham also made valuable contributions in more general areas of moral philosophy. For instance, he expounded the concept of intention more lucidly than any previous writer. An act, he said, might be intentional without its consequences being so: 'thus, you may intend to touch a man without intending to hurt him: and yet, as the consequences turn out, you may chance to hurt him'. A consequence might be either directly intentional ('when the prospect of producing it constituted one of the links in the chain of causes by which the person was determined to act') or obliquely intentional (when the consequence was foreseen as likely, but the prospect of producing it formed no link in the determining chain). Among directly intentional consequences he distinguishes between those which are ultimately or immediately intentional; this corresponds to the traditional distinction between ends and means.

Bentham distinguishes between intention and motive: a man's intentions may be good and his motives bad. A, for instance, may prosecute B, out of malice, for a crime which B has not committed; A's motive is bad, but his intention may be good if he genuinely believes B to be guilty. In itself, Bentham says, no motive is either good or bad; words such as 'lust', 'avarice', and 'cruelty' denote bad motives only in the sense that they are never properly applied except where the motives they signify happen to be bad. 'Lust', for instance, is the name given to sexual desire when the effects of it are regarded as bad. For Bentham motive does not supply a separate ground for the moral qualification of an act: the only mental state primarily relevant to the morality of a voluntary act is the agent's belief about its consequences. There is something of an irony in the fact that Bentham should write so instructively about intention and motive when, in his own utilitarian system, these have less moral importance than in any other system.

John Stuart **Mill**, in his book *Utilitarianism*, summed up the issue as follows. 'He who saves a fellow-creature from drowning does what is morally right, whether his motive be duty, or the hope of being paid for his trouble; he who betrays the friend that trusts him is guilty of a crime, even if his object be to serve another friend to whom he is under greater obligation.' One motive may be preferable to another on non-moral grounds; or because it may proceed from a quality of character more likely to produce virtuous acts in the long term. But in general 'the motive has nothing to do with the morality of the action, though much with the worth of the agent'.

THE UTILITARIANISM OF J. S. MILL

Mill softened down Bentham's utilitarianism in several ways. Critics had objected that to suppose that life has no higher end than pleasure was a doctrine worthy only of swine. Mill responded by making a distinction between the quality of pleasures. 'Of two pleasures, if there be one to which all or almost all who have experience of both give a decided preference, irrespective of any feeling of moral obligation to prefer it, that is the more desirable pleasure.' Armed with this distinction, he is able to conclude that 'It is better to be a human being dissatisfied than a pig satisfied; better to be Socrates dissatisfied than a fool satisfied'. In applying the greatest happiness principle we must take account of this: the end for which all other things are desirable is an existence exempt as far as possible from pain, and as rich as possible in enjoyments in point of both quantity and quality.

Bentham's utilitarianism, with its denial of natural rights, would in principle justify, in certain circumstances, highly autocratic government and great intrusions upon individual liberty. Mill, in his writings, always strove to temper utilitarianism with liberalism, and his brief *On Liberty* is an eloquent classic of liberal individualism.

The pamphlet seeks to set out the limits to the legitimate interference of collective opinion with individual independence. He states his guiding principle in the following terms.

> The sole end for which mankind are warranted, individually or collectively, in interfering with the liberty of action of any of their number, is self-protection. The only purpose for which power can be rightfully exercised over any member of a civilised community, against his will, is to prevent harm to others. His own good, either physical or moral, is not a sufficient warrant.

The only part of anyone's conduct for which he is amenable to society is that which concerns others. Over himself, over his own body and mind, the individual is sovereign.

Mill applies his principle in particular in support of freedom of expression. If an opinion is silenced, it may, for all we know, be true; if it is not true, it may contain a portion of truth; and even if it is wholly false, it is important that the contrary opinion should be contested, otherwise it will be held either as a mere prejudice, or as a formal profession devoid of conviction. On these grounds, Mill affirms that freedom of opinion, and freedom of the expression of opinion, is a 'necessity to the mental well-being of mankind, on which all their other well-being depends'.

MILL'S LOGIC

Apart from *On Liberty* Mill's best known work is his essay on *The Subjection of Women*, written in collaboration with his wife Harriet Taylor. But Mill's reputation as a philosopher does not depend on his moral and political writings alone. He was highly learned and very industrious; he began learning Greek at the age of three, and published voluminous philosophical works while holding, for thirty-five years, a full-time job with the East India Company. In theoretical philosophy his most important work was *A System of Logic*, which he published in 1843 and which went through eight editions in his lifetime.

Mill continued in the nineteenth century the traditions of the eighteenth-century British Empiricists. He admired Berkeley, and tried to detach his theory of matter from its theological context: our belief that physical objects persist in existence when they are not perceived, he said, amounts to no more than our continuing expectation of further perceptions of the objects. Matter is defined by Mill as 'a permanent possibility of sensation'; the external world is 'the world of possible sensations succeeding one another according to laws'.

In philosophy of mind, Mill agreed with Hume that 'We have no conception of Mind itself, as distinguished from its conscious manifestations', but he was reluctant to accept that his own mind was simply a series of feelings. He had an extra difficulty about the existence of other minds. I can know the existence of minds other than my own, he had to explain, by supposing that the behaviour of others stands in a relation to sensations which is analogous to the relation in which my behaviour stands to my own sensations. This claim is not easy to reconcile with his general phenomenalist position, according to which other substances, including other people, are merely permanent possibilities of my sensation.

Unlike previous empiricists, Mill had a serious interest in formal logic and in the methodology of the sciences. His *System of Logic* (1843) begins with an analysis of language, and in particular with a theory of naming.

Mill uses the word 'name' very broadly. Not only proper names like 'Socrates' but pronouns like 'this', definite descriptions like 'the king who succeeded William the Conqueror', general terms like 'man' and 'wise', and abstract expressions like 'old age' are all counted as names in his system. Indeed, only words like 'of' and 'or' and 'if' seem *not* to be names, in his system. According to Mill, all names denote things: proper names denote the things they are names of, and general terms denote the things they are true of. Thus not only 'Socrates', but also 'man' and 'wise' denote Socrates.

For Mill, every proposition is a conjunction of names. This does not commit him to the extreme nominalist view that every sentence is to be interpreted on the model of one joining two proper names, as in 'Tully is Cicero'. A sentence joining two connotative names, like 'all men are mortal', tells us that certain attributes (those, say, of rationality and animality) are always accompanied by the attribute of mortality.

More important than what he has to say about names and propositions is Mill's theory of inference.

Inferences can be divided into real and verbal. The inference from 'no great general is a rash man' to 'no rash man is a great general' is a verbal, not a real inference; premise and conclusion say the same thing. There is real inference only when we infer to a truth, in the conclusion, which is not contained in the premises. There is, for instance, a real inference when we infer from particular cases to a general conclusion, as in 'Peter is mortal, James is mortal, John is mortal, therefore all men are mortal'. But such inference is not deductive, but inductive.

Is all deductive reasoning, then, merely verbal? Up to the time of Mill, the syllogism was the paradigm of deductive reasoning. Is syllogistic reasoning real or verbal inference? Suppose we argue from the premises 'All men are mortal, and Socrates is a man' to the conclusion 'Socrates is mortal'. It seems that if the syllogism is deductively valid, then the conclusion must somehow have already been counted in to the first premise: the mortality of Socrates must have been part of the evidence which justifies us in asserting that all men are mortal. If, on the other hand, the conclusion gives new information – if, for instance, we substitute for 'Socrates' the name of someone not yet dead (Mill used the example 'The Duke of Wellington') – then we find that it is not really being derived from the first premise. The major premise, Mill says, is merely a formula for drawing inferences, and all real inference is from particulars to particulars.

Inference beginning from particular cases had been named by logicians 'induction'. In some cases, induction appears to provide a general conclusion: from 'Peter is a Jew, James is a Jew, John is a Jew . . .', I can, having enumerated all the Apostles, conclude 'All the Apostles are Jews'. But this procedure, which is sometimes called 'perfect induction', does not, according to Mill, really take us from particular to general: the conclusion is merely an abridged notation for the particular facts enunciated in the premises. Some logicians had maintained that there was another sort of induction, imperfect induction (Mill calls it 'induction by simple enumeration'), which led from particular cases to general laws. But the purported general laws are merely formulae for making inferences. Genuine inductive inference takes us from known particulars to unknown particulars.

If induction cannot be brought within the framework of the syllogism, this does not mean that it operates without any rules of its own. Mill sets out five rules, or canons, of experimental inquiry to guide the inductive discovery of causes and effects. We may consider, as illustrations, the first two, which Mill calls respectively the method of agreement and disagreement.

The first states that if a phenomenon F appears in the conjunction of the circumstances A, B, and C, and also in the conjunction of the circumstances C, D, and E, then we are to conclude that C, the only common feature, is causally related to F. The second states that if F occurs in the presence of A, B, and C, but not in the presence of A, B, and D, then we are to conclude that C, the only feature differentiating the two cases, is causally related to F. Mill gives as an illustration of this second canon: 'When a man is shot through the heart, it is by this method we know that it was the gunshot which killed him: for he was in the fulness of life immediately before, all circumstances being the same, except the wound.'

Like all inductive procedures, Mill's methods seem to assume the constancy of general laws. As Mill explicitly says, 'The proposition that the course of Nature is uniform, is the fundamental principle, or general axiom, of Induction.' But what is the status of this principle? Mill sometimes seems to treat it as if it was an empirical generalization. He says, for instance, that it would be rash to assume that the law of causation applies on distant stars. But if this very general principle is the basis of induction, surely it cannot itself be established by induction.

It is not only the law of causation which presents difficulties for Mill's system. So too do the truths of mathematics. Mill did not think – as some other empiricists have done – that mathematical propositions were merely verbal propositions which spelt out the consequences of definitions. The fundamental axioms of arithmetic, and Euclid's axioms of geometry, he maintains, state matters of fact. Accordingly, he had in consistency to conclude that arithmetic and geometry, no less than physics, consist of empirical hypotheses. The hypotheses of mathematics are of very great generality, and have been most handsomely confirmed in our experience; none the less, they remain hypotheses, corrigible in the light of later experience.

Mill's assertion that mathematical truths were empirical generalizations was inspired by his overriding aim in *The System of Logic*, which was to refute the notion which he regarded as 'the great intellectual support of false doctrines and bad institutions', namely, the thesis that truths external to the mind may be known by intuition independent of experience. His view of mathematics was very soon to be shown as untenable by the German philosopher Gottlob Frege, and after Frege's work even those who had great sympathy with Mill's empiricism – including his godson Bertrand Russell – abandoned his philosophy of arithmetic.

After Mill's death at Avignon in 1873 an engaging *Autobiography* was published posthumously, and some essays on religious topics. In his essay *Theism*, having reflected on the problem set by the presence of evil and good in the world, Mill came to the conclusion that it could only be solved by acknowledging the existence of God while denying divine omnipotence. He concluded thus:

These, then, are the net results of natural theology on the question of the divine attributes. A being of great but limited power, how or by what limited we cannot even conjecture; of great and perhaps unlimited intelligence, but perhaps also more narrowly limited power than this, who desires and pays some regard to the happiness of his creatures, but who seems to have other motives of action which he cares more for, and who can hardly be supposed to have created the universe for that purpose alone. Such is the deity whom natural religion points to, and any idea of God more captivating than this comes only from human wishes, or from the teaching of either real or imaginary revelation.

XIX

THREE NINETEENTH-CENTURY PHILOSOPHERS

SCHOPENHAUER

The most interesting German philosopher of the nineteenth century was Arthur **Schopenhauer**, who was born in Danzig in 1788 and studied philosophy at Göttingen in 1810 after a false start as a medical student. He admired Kant but not Kant's successors. He attended the lectures of Fichte in Berlin in 1811, but was disgusted by both his obscurity and his nationalism. In the writings of Hegel and his disciples he complained of 'the narcotic effect of long-spun periods without a single idea in them'. His own style, first exhibited in his doctoral dissertation of 1813, *On the Fourfold Root of the Principle of Sufficient Reason*, was energetic and luminous, and won the praise of the great poet Goethe. In Dresden between 1814 and 1818 Schopenhauer composed his philosophical masterpiece, *The World as Will and Idea*, which he republished in an expanded form in 1844. In 1820 he went to Berlin and offered a series of lectures, but the students, injudiciously, preferred to hear Hegel who was lecturing at the same hour. The boycott of his lectures fuelled his distaste for the Hegelian system, which he regarded as mostly nonsense. In 1839 he won his first public recognition with a Norwegian prize for an *Essay on the Freedom of the Will*. Schopenhauer was a brilliant essayist, and when his essays were published in 1851 under the title *Parerga and Paralipomena* he emerged from years of obscurity and neglect to become a famous philosopher. He died in 1860.

Schopenhauer's major work, *The World as Will and Idea*, contains four books, the first and third devoted to the World as Idea, and the second and fourth to the World as Will. His philosophy of the World as Idea is closely based on Kant, but he writes so much more lucidly and wittily than Kant that the effect is rather as if a work of Henry James had been rewritten by Evelyn Waugh.

Book One begins with the statement 'The world is my idea'. By 'idea' (*Vorstellung*) Schopenhauer does not mean a concept, but a concrete, intuitive, experience. If a man is to achieve philosophical wisdom, he must accept that 'what he knows is not a sun and an earth, but only an eye that sees a sun, a hand that feels an earth'. The world exists only as idea, that is to say, exists only in relation to conscious- ness. This truth, he says, was first realized in Indian philosophy, with its doctrine of Maya or appearance, but it was rediscovered in Europe by Berkeley.

For each of us, our own body is the starting point of our perception of the world; other objects are known through their effects on each other, by means of the principle of causality, which is grasped by the understanding. Understanding is common to men and animals, because animals too perceive objects in space and time and so they too must be applying the law of causality; indeed animal sagacity sometimes surpasses human understanding. Human language-users, however, have not only understanding but reason, that is to say abstract knowledge embodied in concepts; because of this man far surpasses other animals in power and also in suffering. They live in the present alone, man lives also in the future and the past.

The three great gifts which reason gives to humans are speech, deliberation in action, and science. The importance of rational or abstract knowledge is that it can be shared and retained. For practical purposes, mere understanding may be pre- ferable: 'it is of no use to me to know in the abstract the exact angle, in degrees and minutes, at which I must apply a razor, if I do not know it intuitively, that is, if I have not got the feel of it.' But when the help of others is required, or long- term planning is necessary, abstract knowledge is essential. And conduct can only be ethical if based on principles; but principles are abstract.

All this is not very different from Kant. Schopenhauer criticizes Kant only for being half-hearted in accepting that the world is only an object in relation to a subject, and for insisting on the existence of a thing-in-itself behind the veil of appearance. It is in his presentation, in the second book, of the world as will, that Schopenhauer shows his originality.

He starts from considering the nature of sciences such as mechanics and physics. These explain the motions of bodies in terms of laws such as those of inertia and gravitation. But these laws speak of forces whose inner nature they leave completely unexplained. 'The force on account of which a stone falls to the ground or one body repels another is, in its inner nature, not less strange and mysterious than that which produces the movements and the growth of an animal.' Scientists and philosophers can never arrive at the real nature of things from without: they are like people who go around a castle looking in vain for an entrance, and con- tenting themselves with sketching its façade.

None of us would, indeed, ever be able to penetrate the meaning of the world if we were mere knowing subjects ('winged cherubs without a body'). But I am myself rooted in the world; my knowledge of it is given me through my body, which is not just one object among others, but has an active power of which I am directly conscious. It is indeed this special relationship to one body which makes me the individual I am.

> The answer to the riddle is given to the subject of knowledge, who appears as an individual, and the answer is *will*. This and this alone gives him the key to his own existence, reveals to him the significance, shows him the inner mechanism of his being, of his action, of his movements.

Acts of the will are identical with movements of the body; the will and the movement are not two different events linked by causality. The action of the body is an act of the will made perceptible, and indeed the whole body, Schopenhauer says, is nothing but objectified will, will become visible, will become idea. The body and all its parts are the visible expression of the will and its several desires: thus, 'teeth, throat and bowels are objectified hunger; the organs of generation are objectified sexual desire; the grasping hand, the hurrying feet, correspond to the more indirect desires of the will which they express'.

Each of us knows himself both as an object and as a will; and this is the key to the nature of every phenomenon in nature. The inner nature of all objects must be the same as that which in ourselves we call will. What else could it be? Besides will and idea nothing is known to us. The word 'will', Schopenhauer says, is like a magic spell which discloses to us the inmost being of everything in nature.

There are many different grades of will, and only the higher grades are accompanied by knowledge and self-determination.

> If, therefore, I say, – the force which attracts a stone to the earth is according to its nature, in itself and apart from all idea, will, I shall not be supposed to express in this opinion the insane opinion that the stone moves itself in accordance with a known motive, merely because this is the way in which will appears in man.

Will is the force which lives in the plant, the force by which crystal is formed and by which the magnet turns to the North Pole. Here at last we find what Kant looked for in vain: all ideas are phenomenal existence, the will alone is a thing in itself.

Schopenhauer's will, which is active even in inanimate objects, appears to be the same as Aristotle's natural appetite, restated in terms of Newton's laws instead of in terms of the theory of the natural place of the elements. Why does he call it 'will', then, rather than 'appetite' or simply 'force'? If we explain force in terms of will, Schopenhauer replies, we explain the less known by the better known; if, instead, we regard the will as merely a species of force, we renounce the only immediate knowledge we have of the inner nature of the world.

But there is, Schopenhauer agrees, a great difference between the higher and lower grades of will. In the higher grades individuality occupies a prominent position: each human has a strong individual personality, and so to a lesser extent do the higher species of brute animals. 'The farther down we go, the more completely is every trace of the individual character lost in the common character of the species.' In the inorganic kingdom of nature all individuality disappears.

Nature should be seen as a field of conflict between different grades of will. A magnet lifting a piece of iron is a victory of a higher form of will (electricity) over a lower (gravitation). A human being in health is a triumph of the Idea of the self-conscious organism over the physical and chemical laws which originally governed the humours of the body, and against which it is engaged in constant battle.

> Hence also in general the burden of physical life, the necessity of sleep, and, finally, of death; for at last these subdued forces of nature, assisted by circumstances, win back from the organism, wearied even by the constant victory, the matter it took from them, and attain to an unimpeded expression of their being.

The rotation of the planets round the sun, in tension between centripetal and centrifugal force, is no less an example of the universal essential conflict of the manifestation of will.

What, then, is the nature of will, which is so universally present and active? All willing, Schopenhauer says, arises from want, therefore from deficiency, and therefore from suffering. A wish may be granted; but it is succeeded by another and we have ten times more desires than we can satisfy. The fleeting gratification of a desire is 'like the alms thrown to the beggar, that keeps him alive today, that his misery may be prolonged till the morrow'. So long as our consciousness is filled by our will, we can never have happiness or peace; we can at best alternate pain with boredom.

Is there any escape from the slavery of the will? In the third book of his chief work Schopenhauer expounds a way of escape through Art. Always in animals, and for most of the time in humans, knowledge is at the service of the will, employed in securing the satisfaction of its desires. But it is possible to rise above the consideration of objects as mere instruments for the satisfaction of desire, and to adopt an attitude of pure contemplation. This attitude is most easily adopted towards beauty, whether in nature or in art. We must lose ourselves in a natural landscape or a piece of architecture; lose ourselves, literally, by forgetting our will and our individuality. We must become a simple mirror of the object of our contemplation, so that the perceiver and the perceived become one. 'In such contemplation the particular thing becomes at once the *Idea* of its species, and the perceiving individual becomes *pure subject of knowledge.*'

The Ideas which Schopenhauer is here talking of are not Lockean ideas of perception, but the Platonic Idea of the species. It is through Art, the work of genius, that we make contact with the universal which is independent of, and more real than, the individual, like the single rainbow quietly resting on the innumerable showering drops of the waterfall. Every human has the power of knowing the Ideas in things, but the genius excels ordinary mortals in possessing this knowledge more intensely and more continuously. In contemplation free from will, we lose our concern with happiness and unhappiness, and we cease to be individual. 'We are only that *one* eye of the world which looks out from all knowing creatures, but which can become perfectly free from the service of will in man alone.'

The theory of the liberating effect of aesthetic contemplation is developed in a detailed consideration of the various arts – architecture, painting, poetry, drama, and above all, music, the most powerful of the arts. Music, Schopenhauer says, is not, like the other arts, a copy of the Ideas, but is the copy of the Will itself, whose objectification the Ideas are. Schopenhauer's notion of music emptying the self was echoed by T. S. Eliot, when he wrote in *The Dry Salvages* of

> music heard so deeply
> That it is not heard at all, but you are the music
> While the music lasts.

But the person whose life was most affected by Schopenhauer's writing on music was Richard Wagner, who came to think of himself as the embodiment of Schopenhauerian genius.

The liberation offered by aesthetic contemplation, however, is only a temporary one. The only way to achieve complete freedom from the tyranny of the will is by complete renunciation. What the will wills is always life; so if we are to renounce the will we must renounce the will to live. This sounds like a recommendation of suicide; but in fact Schopenhauer regarded suicide, if sought as an escape from the miseries of the world, as a false step inspired by an over-estimate of the importance of the individual life, and motivated by a concealed will to live.

What Schopenhauer meant by renunciation is best understood by following the account he gives, in his fourth book, of different moral characters, starting with wickedness and ending with saintliness or asceticism. Moral progress consists in the gradual reduction of egoism: the tendency of the individual to make itself the centre of the world and to sacrifice everything else to its own existence and well-being.

A bad man is an egoist to the highest degree: he asserts his own will to live and denies the presence of that will in others, destroying their existence if they get in his way. A really wicked man goes beyond egoism, taking delight in the sufferings of others not just as a means to his own ends, but as an end in itself. But though the bad man regards his own person as separated by a great gulf from others, he retains a dim awareness that his own will is just the phenomenal appearance of the single will to live which is active in all. 'He dimly sees that he, the bad man, is himself this whole will; that consequently he is not only the inflicter of pain but also the endurer of it.' This is the origin of the sufferings of remorse.

Between the bad man and the good man, there is an intermediate character: the just man. Unlike the bad man, the just man does not see individuality as being an absolute wall of partition between himself and others; he is willing to recognize the will to live in others on the same level as his own, up to the point of abstaining from injury to his fellow humans. When the barrier of individuality is penetrated to a higher degree than this, then we achieve benevolence, well-doing, the love of mankind. Thus it is characteristic of the good man to make less distinction than is usually made between himself and others. 'He is just as little likely to allow others to starve, while he himself has enough and to spare, as any one would be to suffer hunger one day in order to have more the next day than he could enjoy.'

The good man loses the illusion of individuation: he recognizes himself, his will, in every being and consequently also in the sufferer. But goodness will take him a step further than benevolence.

> If he takes as much interest in the sufferings of other individuals as his own, and therefore is not only benevolent in the highest degree, but even ready to sacrifice his own individuality whenever such a sacrifice will save a number of other persons, then it clearly follows that such a man, who recognizes in all beings his own inmost and true self, must also regard the infinite suffering of all suffering beings as his own, and take on himself the pain of the whole world.

This will lead him beyond virtue to asceticism; he will have such a horror of this miserable world that it will no longer be enough to love others as himself, and to give up his own pleasures when they stand in the way of others' good. He will do all he can to disown the nature of the world as expressed in his own body, adopting chastity, poverty, abstinence, and self-chastisement, and welcoming every injury, ignominy and insult offered him by others. Thus he will break down the will, which he recognizes and abhors as the source of his own and the world's suffering existence; and when death comes he will welcome it as a deliverance. Asceticism of this kind is not a vain ideal: it can be learned through suffering, and it has been exhibited in life by many Christian, Hindu, and Buddhist saints.

Schopenhauer accepts that the life of many saints has been full of the most absurd superstition. Religious systems, he believes, are the mythical clothing of truths which are unattainable by the uneducated. But, he says, 'it is just as little needful that a saint should be a philosopher as that a philosopher should be a saint'; and this no doubt is the answer which he would give to the many people who have pointed out that his own life was very different from the ascetic ideal he painted. 'It is a strange demand upon a moralist,' he wrote, 'that he should teach no other virtue than that which he himself possesses.'

Schopenhauer's system is undeniably impressive, and each step in his argument is made persuasive by his compelling prose and enchanting metaphors. But his basic premise is untrue, and his ultimate conclusion is self-refuting. He presents no valid reason to accept the starting point that the world is my idea, and offers us no motive to adopt the ascetic programme with which he concludes. In order to distinguish the world of will from the world of the idea, and to reach a thing-in-itself distinct from mere phenomena, he has to persuade each of us that the fundamental reality is our own individuality; in order to persuade us to ascend the path through virtue to asceticism, he asks us to accept that our individuality is a mere illusion.

The complete renunciation of the will seems to be a contradiction in terms: for if the renunciation is voluntary, it is itself an act of the will; and if it is necessary then it is no real renunciation. Schopenhauer sought to avoid this contradiction by appealing, once again, to Kant's distinction between the phenomenon and the thing in itself. 'Everything is as phenomenon absolutely necessary; in itself it is will, which is perfectly free to all eternity.' But a will which is free in eternity is a will which is outside time, while the history of any saint belongs in the world of phenomena. One and the same act of self-denial cannot be both inside and outside time.

KIERKEGAARD

In the same decade as the second edition of *The World as Will and Idea* appeared, the Danish philosopher Søren **Kierkegaard** put forward a philosophy which in its practical aspect had much in common with Schopenhauer, but which rests on a totally different metaphysical foundation. Instead of being enunciated as a system in a single work, Kierkegaard's thought was presented in a variety of ways in separate essays of different styles.

Most of Kierkegaard's writings were written in his thirties, between 1843 and 1853. Brought up in a Copenhagen family of religious gloom, he revolted against theology during his time at university, and turned to philosophy. He then acquired a knowledge of, and a distaste for, Hegelianism. In 1838 he underwent a religious conversion, and gained a conviction of his philosophical vocation, which became more intense after he broke off, in 1841, his engagement to Regina Olsen. Between 1843 and 1846 he published, under different pseudonyms, a number of works, of which the most important were *Either/Or* and *Fear and Trembling*, followed by the *Concluding Unscientific Postscript* of 1846. After a mystical experience in 1848 he abandoned the use of pseudonyms and published a number of Christian discourses and *The Sickness unto Death*. Much of the latter part of his life was taken up in conflict with the established Danish Church, which he regarded as Christian only in name. He died in 1855.

Like Schopenhauer, Kierkegaard was an opponent of Hegel; but unlike Schopenhauer, he thought that Hegel's fundamental error was his undervaluation of the concrete individual. Like Schopenhauer, Kierkegaard sketches out for us a spiritual career which ends with asceticism; but each upward phase in the career, far from being a diminution or renunciation of individuality, is a stage in the affirmation of one's own unique personality.

At the lowest level, for Kierkegaard, the individual is no more than an anonymous member of a crowd; accepting unquestioningly the opinions, sentiments, and goals of the mob. The first stage towards self-realization is the entry into the aesthetic sphere. In the aesthetic stage, the individual, like Aristotle's intemperate man, has a policy of pursuing the present pleasure. He may exercise taste and discrimination: the pleasures pursued may be elegant and sophisticated. But the essential feature of the aesthetic person is that he avoids taking on any commitments, whether personal, social, or official, which would limit his field of choice and prevent him from following whatever is immediately attractive. Kierkegaard describes with great charm and insight the various forms and stages of the aesthetic life. One of its most enticing forms, obviously enough, is the gratification of sex; Kierkegaard offers, as illustrations of three different stages of erotic pursuit, three characters in Mozart's operas: Cherubino, Papageno, and finally Don Giovanni.

The aesthetic person thinks of his existence as one of freedom: but in fact it is extremely limited. A human being is like a two-storeyed house with a basement. The finest apartments, on the *piano nobile*, are intended to be inhabited by spirit; but the aesthetic person prefers to live in the cellar of sensuality. Such a person is in a state of despair, even if he does not initially realize this; but gradually he will become dissatisfied with the dissipation which is a dispersal of himself. He will then be faced with the choice of abandoning himself to despair, or of moving up to the next level by commiting himself to an ethical existence.

In the ethical stage the individual self-consciously takes his place within social institutions and accepts the obligations which flow from them. He gives up the perpetual holiday of the aesthetic life and takes a job; he forsakes the pleasures of fleeting affairs for the constancy of married life. The ethical person is quite different from the member of the crowd: he takes his place in society not unthinkingly but by an act of self-conscious choice. The ethical stage may make strict demands on the individual, and call for heroic self-sacrifice. Faced with the challenge, the individual becomes vividly conscious of human weakness; he may try to overcome it by strength of will, but find himself unable to do so. He becomes aware that his own powers are insufficient to meet the demands of the moral law. This brings him to a sense of guilt, and a consciousness of sinfulness. If he is to escape from this, he must rise from the ethical sphere to the religious sphere. For this he must make 'the leap of faith'.

The transition from the ethical to the religious sphere is most vividly portrayed in *Fear and Trembling*, which takes as its text the biblical story of God's command to Abraham to kill his son Isaac in sacrifice. Whereas an ethical hero, such as Socrates, lays down his life for the sake of a universal moral law, Abraham's heroism lay in his obedience to an individual command of God. Moreover, the command he offered to obey was a command to break a moral law: by the standards of ethics, Abraham should be convicted as a murderer. If Abraham is a hero, as the Bible portrays him, it can only be from the standpoint of faith. 'For faith is this paradox, that the particular is higher than the universal.'

Faith may demand what Kierkegaard calls 'the teleological suspension of the ethical'. Abraham's act transgressed the ethical order in view of his higher end or *telos* outside it. The demands of the unique relationship between God and an individual may override all commitments arising from general ethical laws, such as that a father should love his son more dearly than himself. But if an individual feels a call to violate an ethical law, no one can tell him whether this is a genuine command of God or a mere temptation. He cannot even know or prove it to himself: he has to make a decision in blind faith.

Partly in reaction to Hegel's rationalization of religion, Kierkegaard stresses that faith is not the outcome of any objective reasoning. In his *Concluding Unscientific Postscript* he offers a number of arguments to this effect. The form of religious faith that he has most often in mind is the Christian belief that Jesus saved the human race by his death on the Cross: a belief which involves certain historical elements. On this basis, he argues that faith cannot be rationally justified.

First of all, we can never achieve complete certainty about historical events. But a mere judgement of probability is insufficient for a religious faith which is to be the basis of eternal happiness. Secondly, historical research is never definitively concluded, so if we are to use it as the basis of our religious commitment, we must perpetually postpone that commitment. Thirdly, faith must be a passionate devotion of oneself; but objective inquiry involves an attitude of detachment. We must therefore give up the search for certainty, embrace the risk, and take the 'leap' of faith. 'Without risk there is no faith. Faith is precisely the contradiction between the infinite passion of the individual's inwardness and the objective uncertainty.'

As is obvious from all this, Kierkegaard was a deeply religious thinker; it is odd that he has had less influence within religious circles than on atheist philosophers. He saw, for instance, the progress through the aesthetic, ethical, and religious stages as a gradual appropriation of the individual's existence. To have an authentic existence one must not be a mere spectator or passenger in life, but seize control of one's own destiny. This aspect of Kierkegaard's thought was taken as a charter for 'existentialist' thinkers in the twentieth century; though some of the most influential existentialists, such as Karl Jaspers in Germany and Jean-Paul Sartre in France, severed the notion of self-appropriation from the theological conclusion which was its *raison d'être* in Kierkegaard himself.

NIETZSCHE

In the nineteenth century, all that Kierkegaard stood for was bombastically rejected by the German philosopher Friedrich **Nietzsche** (1844–1900). While for

Kierkegaard aesthetic enjoyment was the lowest form of individual existence and Christian self-denial the highest, Nietzsche regarded Christianity as the lowest debasement of the human ideal which finds its highest expression in purely aesthetic values.

After a Lutheran upbringing by his pious mother and aunts, Nietzsche felt a sense of liberation when, at the University of Leipzig in 1865, he encountered Schopenhauer's atheism. Henceforth he presented himself consistently as an opponent of the Christian ethos and the personality of Jesus. His conviction that art was the highest form of human activity found expression in his own philosophical style, which is poetic and aphoristic rather than argumentative or deductive. Appointed at the age of twenty-four to a Chair in philology at Basel, he dedicated to Richard Wagner his first book *The Birth of Tragedy from the Spirit of Music*. In it he draws a contrast between two aspects of the Greek psyche: the wild irrational passions personified in Dionysus, and the disciplined and harmonious beauty represented by Apollo. The greatness of Greek culture lay in the synthesis of the two, which was disrupted by the rationalism of Socrates; contemporary Germany could be saved from the decadence which then overtook Greece only if it looked for its salvation to Wagner.

By 1876 Nietzsche had broken with Wagner and lost his admiration for Schopenhauer. In *Human, all too Human*, he was uncharacteristically sympathetic to utilitarian morality and appeared to value science above art. But he regarded this phase of his philosophy as something to be sloughed off like the skin of a snake. After giving up his Basel Chair in 1879 he began a series of works affirming the value of Life, and denouncing, as elements hostile to life, Christian self-denial, altruistic ethics, democratic politics, and scientific positivism. The most famous of these works were *Joyful Wisdom* (1882), *Thus Spake Zarathustra* (1883–5), *Beyond Good and Evil* (1886), and *The Genealogy of Morals* (1887). By 1889 he had begun to show signs of madness, and lived in senile retirement until his death in 1900.

Nietzsche believed that history exhibits two different kinds of morality. Aristocrats, feeling themselves to belong to a higher order than their fellows, use words like 'good' to describe themselves, their ideals, and their characteristics: noble birth, riches, bravery, truthfulness, and blondeness. They despise others as plebeian, vulgar, cowardly, untruthful, and dark-coloured, and designate these characteristics as 'evil'. This is master-morality. The poor and weak, resenting the power and riches of the aristocrats, set up their own contrasting system of values, a slave-morality or herd-morality which puts a premium on character traits such as humility, sympathy, and benevolence, which benefit the underdog. The erection of this new system Nietzsche calls a 'transvaluation of values' and he attributes it to the Jews.

> It was the Jews who, in opposition to the aristocratic equation (good = aristocratic = beautiful = happy = loved by the gods), dared with a terrifying logic to suggest the

contrary equation, and indeed to maintain with the teeth of the most profound hatred (the hatred of weakness) this contrary equation, namely 'the wretched alone are the good; the poor, the weak, the lowly are alone good; the suffering, the needy, the sick, the loathsome, are the only ones who are pious, the only ones who are blessed, for them alone is salvation – but you, on the other hand, you aristocrats, you men of power, you are to all eternity the evil, the horrible, the covetous, the insatiate, the godless; eternally also shall you be the unblessed, the cursed, the damned!'

The revolt of the slaves, begun by the Jews, has now, Nietzsche said, achieved victory. Jewish hatred has triumphed under the mask of the Christian gospel of love. In Rome itself, once the paragon of aristocratic virtue, men now bow down to four Jews: Jesus, Peter, Paul, and Mary. Modern man, as a result, is a mere dwarf, who has lost the will to be truly human. Vulgarity and mediocrity become the norm: only rarely there still flashes out an embodiment of the aristocratic ideal, as in Napoleon.

The opposition between good and evil is a feature of the slave morality, now dominant. Aristocrats despised the herd as bad, but the slaves, with greater venom, condemned the aristocrats as not just bad but evil. We must fight against the domination of the slave morality: the way forward is to transcend the bounds of good and evil, and introduce a second transvaluation of values. If we can do that, then there will rise, as a synthesis to the thesis and antithesis of master and slave, the Superman.

The Superman will be the highest form of life. People are beginning to realize, Nietzsche says, that Christianity is unworthy of belief, and that God is dead. The concept of God has been the greatest obstacle to the fullness of human life: now we are free to express our will to live. But our will to live must not be, like Schopenhauer's, one which favours the weak; it must be a will to power. The will to power is the secret of all life; every living thing seeks to discharge its force, to give full scope to its ability. Knowledge is merely the instrument of power; there is no absolute truth, but only fictions which serve better or worse to fortify life. Pleasure is not the aim of action, but simply the consciousness of the exercise of power. The greatest realization of human power will be the creation of Superman.

Humanity is merely a stage on the way to Superman, who is the meaning of the earth. But Superman will not be achieved by evolution, but by an exercise of will. 'Let your will say "Superman *is to be* the meaning of the earth".' Zarathustra says:

> You could surely create the Superman! Perhaps not you yourselves, my brothers! But you could transform yourselves into forefathers and ancestors of the Superman: and let this be your finest creating!

The arrival of Superman will be the perfection of the world; but it will not be the end of history. For Nietzsche held the doctrine of eternal recurrence: history goes in cycles, and whatever has happened will happen all over again, down to the smallest detail.

It is difficult to evaluate Nietzsche coolly: the bilious unfairness of his criticism of others generates in the reader a corresponding irritable impatience with his own writing. One could say of *The Genealogy of Morals*, his last work, what he himself said of his own early work: 'It is poorly written, heavy-handed, embarrassing. The imagery is both frantic and confused. It lacks logical nicety and is so sure of its message that it dispenses with any kind of proof.'

Nietzsche quite fails to give any consistent presentation of the moral viewpoint from which he criticizes conventional morality. The nature of Superman is too sketchily described for his character to present any standard by which to make a judgement of human virtue and vice. It is difficult to find where Nietzsche himself stands on an issue such as the evaluation of cruelty. When denouncing religion and the role played by guilt in slave-morality, he describes with eloquent outrage the bitter sufferings and barbarous tortures which bigots and persecutors have inflicted. But when he describes the excesses of his aristocratic 'blonde beasts',

> who perhaps come from a ghastly bout of murder, arson, rape, and torture, with bravado and a moral equanimity, as though merely some wild student's prank had been played, perfectly convinced that the poets have now an ample theme to sing and celebrate

he seems to regard this as a peccadillo, a necessary outlet for their ebullient high spirits. It would be unphilosophical to regard Nietzsche's final insanity as a reason for discounting his philosophy; but on the other hand, it is not easy to feel much pity for one who regarded pity as the most despicable of all emotions.

XX
THREE MODERN MASTERS

CHARLES DARWIN

In his funeral oration on Karl Marx, Engels described the materialist conception of history as a scientific breakthrough comparable with Darwin's discovery of evolution by natural selection. Unlike Marx's theory, Darwin's discovery was a genuine scientific advance, and the detailed discussion of it belongs to the history of science. But it casts a backward light on several philosophical issues we have encountered earlier, and philosophical as well as scientific conclusions have been drawn from it. Hence even an outline history of philosophy would be incomplete without a brief account of the theory and its philosophical implications.

Charles Darwin was born in Shrewsbury in 1809 and attended the school there before university studies in Edinburgh and Christ's College, Cambridge. After taking his degree in 1831 he joined *HMS Beagle* on a five-year tour of the globe as resident naturalist; he published a record of his botanical and geological researches on the cruise in a series of works between 1839 and 1846. During the 1840s he began to develop the theory of natural selection which he eventually published in his great work *The Origin of Species* in 1859. This was followed by *The Descent of Man* in 1871 and a series of treatises on variations of structure and behaviour within and across species, which continued almost up to his death in 1882.

Before Darwin, biologists had worked out a classification of animals and plants into genera and species. All lions, for instance, belong to the lion species, which is a member of a genus of cats which includes also the tiger and the leopard. It is characteristic of a species that its members can breed with other members to produce offspring of the same species, and that unions between members of different species are commonly sterile.

The similarities between species which lead to their classification within a single genus may be explained in various ways. The most famous of those who drew up the classification into genus and species, the Swedish botanist Linnaeus, thought that each species had been separately created and the resemblances and difference between them reflected the design of the creator. An alternative explanation was that different species within a genus might be descended from a common ancestor. This idea long preceded Darwin: as we have seen, it was a speculation entertained by several philosophers in ancient Greece, and more recently it had been put forward by Darwin's grandfather Erasmus Darwin, and by the French naturalist Lamarck. Darwin's great innovation was to suggest the mechanism by which a new species might emerge.

Darwin observed, first, that organisms vary in the degree to which they are adapted to the environment in which they live, in particular with respect to their opportunities for obtaining food and escaping from predators. The long neck of a giraffe is an advantage in picking leaves from high trees; the long and slender legs of the wild horse help it to run fast in open plains and thus escape from its predators. Secondly, all plant and animal species are capable of breeding at a rate which would increase their populations from generation to generation. Even the elephant, the slowest breeder of all known animals, would in five hundred years produce from a single couple fifteen million offspring, if each elephant in each generation survived to breed. If an annual plant produced only two seeds a year, and their seedlings next year produced two and so on, then in twenty years there would be a million plants. The reason that species do not propagate in this way is of course that in each generation only a few specimens survive to breed. All are constantly engaged in a struggle for existence, against the climate and the elements, and against other species, striving to find food for themselves and to avoid becoming food for others.

Darwin's insight was to combine these two observations.

> Owing to this struggle for life, any variation, however slight, and from whatever cause proceeding, in its infinitely complex relations to other organic beings and to external nature, will tend to the preservation of that individual and will generally be inherited by its offspring. The offspring, also, will thus have a better chance of surviving, for, of the many individuals of any species which are periodically born, but a small number can survive.

Human husbandmen have long selected for breeding those specimens of particular kinds of plant and animal which were best adapted for their purposes, and over the years they often succeed in improving the stock, whether of potatoes or racehorses. The mechanism by which advantageous variations are preserved and extended in nature was called by Darwin 'natural selection', in parallel with the artificial selection practised by stockbreeders. Unlike his predecessor Lamarck, Darwin did not believe that the variations in adaptation were acquired by parents in their own lifetime: the variations which they passed on were ones they had themselves inherited. The origin of these variations could well be just a matter of chance.

It is easy enough to see how natural selection can operate on characteristics within a single species. Suppose that there is a population of moths, some dark and some pale, living on silver birch trees, preyed upon by hungry birds. If the trees preserve their natural colour, pale moths are better camouflaged and have a better chance of survival. If, over the course of time, the trees become blackened with soot, it will be the dark moths who have the advantage and will survive in more than average numbers. From the outside, it will appear that the species is changing its colour over time.

Darwin believed that over a very long period of time natural selection could go further, and create whole new species of plants and animals. If this were the case, that would explain the difference between the species which now exist in the world, and the quite different species from earlier ages which, in his time, were beginning to be discovered in fossil form throughout the world. In explaining even the most complex organs and instincts, he claimed, there was no need to appeal to some means superior to, though analogous with, human reason. A sufficient explanation was to be found in the accumulation of innumerable slight variations, each good for the individual possessor.

In 1871 Darwin published *The Descent of Man*, in which he explicitly extended his theory to the origin of the human species. On the basis of the similarities between humans and anthropoid apes he argued that men and apes were cousins, descended from a common ancestor.

The case for Darwin's theory was enormously strengthened in the twentieth century with the discovery of the mechanisms of heredity and the development of molecular genetics. It would not be to my purpose, and would be beyond my competence, to evaluate the scientific evidence for Darwinism. But it is necessary to spend some time on the philosophical implications of his theory, assuming that it is well established.

From Darwin's time until the present, evolutionary theory has met opposition from many Christians. At the meeting of the British Association in 1860 the evolutionist T. H. Huxley reported that the Bishop of Oxford inquired from him whether he claimed descent from an ape on his father's or his mother's side. Huxley – according to his own account – replied that he would rather have an ape for a grandfather than a man who misused his gifts to obstruct science by rhetoric.

Darwin's theory obviously clashes with a literal acceptance of the Bible account of the creation of the world in seven days. Moreover, the length of time which would be necessary for evolution to take place would be immensely longer than the six thousand years which Christian fundamentalists believed to be the age of the universe. But a non-literal interpretation of Genesis had been adopted by theologians as orthodox as St Augustine, and few Christians in the twentieth century find great difficulty in accepting that the earth may have existed for billions of years. It is more difficult to reconcile an acceptance of Darwinism with belief in original sin. If the struggle for existence had been going on for aeons before humans evolved, it is impossible to accept that it was man's first disobedience and the fruit of the forbidden tree which brought death into the world. But that is a problem for the theologian, not the philosopher, to solve.

On the other hand, it is wrong to suggest, as is often done, that Darwin disproved the existence of God. For all Darwin showed, the whole machinery of natural selection may have been part of a Creator's design for the universe. After all, belief that we humans are God's creatures has never been regarded as incompatible with our being the children of our parents; it is equally compatible with our being, on both sides, descended from the ancestors of the apes. Some theists maintain that we inherit only our bodies, and not our souls, from our parents. They can no doubt extend their thesis to Adam's inheritance from his non-human progenitor.

At most, Darwin disposed of one argument for the existence of God: namely, the argument that the adaptation of organisms to their environment shows the existence of a benevolent creator. But Darwin's theory still leaves much to be explained. The origin of individual species from earlier species may be explained by the mechanisms of evolutionary pressure and selection. But these mechanisms cannot be used to explain the origin of species as such. For one of the starting points of explanation by natural selection is the existence of true-breeding populations, namely species. Modern Darwinians, of course, do offer us explanations of the origin of speciation, and of life itself; but these explanations, whatever their merits, are not explanations by natural selection.

In the case of the human species, there is a particular difficulty in explaining by natural selection the origin of language. It is easy enough to understand how natural selection can favour a certain length of leg, because there is no difficulty in describing a single individual as long-legged, and we can see how length of legs may be advantageous to an individual. It does not seem plausible to suggest that in a parallel way the use of language might be favoured by natural selection, because it is not possible to describe an individual as a language user at a stage before there was a community of language-users. For language is a rule-governed, communal activity, totally different from the signalling systems to be found in non-humans. Because of the social and conventional nature of language there is something very odd about the idea that language may have evolved because of the advantages possessed by language-users over non-language-users. It seems almost as absurd as the suggestion that banks evolved because those born with an innate cheque-writing ability had an advantage in the struggle for life over those born without it.

The most general philosophical issue raised by Darwinism concerns the nature of causality. The fourth of Aristotle's four causes was the goal or end of a structure or activity. Explanations falling in this category were called teleological after the Greek word for end, *telos*. Teleological explanations of activity, in Aristotle, have two features. First, they explain an activity by reference not to its starting point, but to its terminus. Secondly, they do their explaining by exhibiting arrival at the terminus as being in some way good for the agent whose activity is to be explained. Thus, Aristotle will explain downward motion of heavy bodies as a movement towards their natural place, the place where it is best for them to be. Similarly, teleological explanations of structures in an organism will explain the development of the structure in the individual organism by reference to its completed state, and exhibit the benefit conferred on the organism by the structure once completed: thus, ducks grow webbed feet so that they can swim.

Descartes was contemptuous of Aristotelian teleology; he maintained that the explanation of every movement and every physical activity must be mechanistic, that is to say it must be given in terms of initial conditions described without evaluation. Descartes offered no good argument for his contention; but in the subsequent history of science, blows were dealt at each of the two elements of Aristotelian teleology, by Newton and Darwin separately. Newtonian gravity, no less than Aristotelian natural motion, provides an explanation by reference to a terminus; gravity is a centripetal force, a force 'by which bodies are drawn, or impelled, or in any way tend, towards a point as to a centre'. Where Newton's explanation differs from Aristotle's is that it involves no suggestion that it is in any way good for a body to arrive at the centre to which it tends. Darwinian explanations, like Aristotle's, demand that the terminus of the process to be explained shall be beneficial to the relevant organism; but unlike Aristotle, Darwin explains the process not by the pull of the final state but by the initial conditions in which the process began. The red teeth and red claws involved in the struggle for existence were, of course, in pursuit of a good, namely the survival of the individual organism to which they belonged; but they were not in pursuit of the good which finally emerged from the process, namely the survival of the fittest species.

Not that Darwin's discovery put an end to the search for final causes. Far from it: contemporary biologists are much keener to discern the function of structures and behaviours than their predecessors were in the period between Descartes and Darwin. What has happened is that Darwin has made teleological explanation respectable, by offering a general recipe for translating it into mechanistic explanation. His successors thus feel able to make free use of such explanations, whether or not in the particular case they have any idea how to apply the recipe.

The major philosophical question which remains is this: is teleological explanation, or mechanistic explanation, the one which operates at a fundamental level of the universe? If God created the world, then mechanistic explanation is underpinned by teleological explanation; the fundamental explanation of the existence of anything at all is the purpose of the creator. If there is no God, but the universe is due to the operation of necessary laws upon blind chance, then it is the mechanistic level of explanation which is fundamental. But even in this case there remains the question whether everything in the universe is to be explained mechanistically, or whether there are cases of teleological causation irreducible to mechanism. If determinism is true, then the answer is in the negative; mechanism rules everywhere. It is not a matter of doubt that we possess free will: but it is open for discussion whether or not free will is compatible with determinism. If the human will is free in a way that escapes determinism, then even in a universe which is mechanistic at a fundamental level, there operates a form of irreducibly teleological causality. So far as I am aware, no one, whether scientist or philosopher, has produced a definitive answer to this set of questions.

John Henry Newman

If the nineteenth century set the stage for the fiercest ever battle between science and religion, it was also spanned by the lifetime of a thinker who made a greater effort than any other to show that not just belief in God, but the acceptance of a religious creed, was a completely rational activity: John Henry Newman.

Newman was born in London in 1801, and was educated in Oxford, where he became a Fellow of Oriel in 1822, and Vicar of St Mary's in 1828. After an evangelical upbringing, he became convinced of the truth of the Catholic interpretation of Christianity, and as a founder of the Oxford movement he sought to have it accepted as authoritative within the Church of England. In 1845 he converted to the Roman Catholic Church, and worked as a priest for many years in Birmingham. He did not share the enthusiasm of Cardinal Manning, head of the Catholic Church in England, for the exaltation of Papal authority which led to the definition of Papal infallibility in 1870; but in 1879 he was made a Cardinal by Pope Leo XIII. Most of his writings are historical, theological, and devotional; but he was the author of one philosophical classic, *The Grammar of Assent*, and of all the philosophers who wrote in English his style is the most enchanting.

Newman's principal concern in philosophy is the question: how can religious belief be justified, given that the evidence for its conclusions seems so inadequate? He does not, like Kierkegaard, demand the adoption of faith in the absence of reasons, a blind leap over a precipice. He seeks to show that the commitment of faith is itself reasonable, even if no proof can be offered of the articles of faith. In the course of dealing with this question in *The Grammar of Assent*, Newman has much to say of general philosophical interest about the nature of belief, in secular as well as religious contexts.

Newman philosophized in the empiricist tradition, and disliked German metaphysics. Only the senses give us direct and immediate acquaintance with things external to us: and they take us only a little way out of ourselves. Reason is the faculty by which knowledge of things external to us, of beings, facts, and events, is attained beyond the range of sense. Unlike Kant, Newman believed that reason is unlimited in its range. 'It reaches to the ends of the universe, and to the throne of God beyond them.' Reason is the faculty of gaining knowledge upon grounds given; and its exercise lies in asserting one thing, because of some other thing.

The two great operations of the intellect, then, are inference and assent; and these two are always to be kept distinct. We often assent when we have forgotten the reasons for our assent. Arguments may be better or worse, but assent either exists or not. Some arguments may indeed force our assent, but even in the case of mathematical proof there is a difference beetween inference and assent. A mathematician would not assent to the conclusion of a complex proof he had produced himself, without going over his work and seeking the corroboration of others. Sometimes assent is given without argument, or on the basis of bad argument; and this commonly leads to error.

Is it always wrong, then, to give assent without adequate argument or evidence? Locke believed so: he gave, as a mark of the love of truth, the not entertaining any proposition with greater assurance than the proofs it is built on will warrant. 'Whatever goes beyond this measure of assent, it is plain, receives not truth in the love of it, loves not truth for truth-sake, but for some other by-end.'

If Locke were right, Newman observes, then no lover of truth could accept religious belief; and Hume and Bentham would be right to accuse believers of credulity. For, as Newman agrees, the grounds of faith are conjectural, and yet they issue in the absolute acceptance of a certain message or doctrine as divine. Faith starts from probability and ends in peremptory statements.

Newman is thinking not just of any kind of belief in the supernatural, but of faith strictly so called, contrasted on the one hand with reason and on the other hand with love. 'Faith', in the tradition in which he is writing, is used in a narrower sense than 'belief'. Aristotle believed that there was a divine prime mover unmoved; but his belief was not faith in God. On the other hand, Marlowe's Faustus, on the verge of damnation, speaks of Christ's blood streaming in the firmament; he has lost hope and charity yet retains faith. So faith contrasts both with reason and with love. Faith is belief in something as revealed by God; thus defined, it is a correlate of revelation. If we are to believe something on the word of God, it must be possible to identify something as God's word.

Faith of this kind would be condemned on Locke's criterion: for the reasons for taking any concrete event or text as a divine revelation fall short of certainty. But Newman argues that faith is not the only exercise of reason which when critically examined would be called unreasonable and yet is not so. The choice of sides in political questions, decisions for or against economic policies, tastes in literature: in all such cases if we measure people's grounds merely by the reasons they produce we have no difficulty in holding them up to ridicule, or even censure.

Many of our most solid beliefs go well beyond the flimsy evidence any of us could offer for them. We all believe that Great Britain is an island; but how many of us have circumnavigated it, or met people who have? We believe that the earth is a globe, covered with vast tracts of earth and water, whose regions see the sun by turns. I believe, with the utmost certainy, that I shall die: but what is the distinct evidence on which I believe it? On all these truths we have an immediate and unhesitating hold, nor do we think ourselves guilty of not loving truth for truth's sake because we cannot reach them through the steps of a proof.

If we refused to give assents going beyond the force of evidence, the world could not go on, and science itself could never make progress. Probability is the guide of life. If we insist upon being as sure as is conceivable, in every step of our course, we must be content to creep along the ground, and can never soar. 'If we are intended for great ends, we are called to great hazards; and whereas we are given absolute certainty in nothing, we must in all things choose between doubt and inactivity.'

Someone may object that there is a difference between religious faith and the reasonable, but insufficiently grounded, beliefs to which Newman appeals. In the ordinary cases, we are always ready to consider evidence which tells against our belief; but the religious believer adopts a certitude which refuses to entertain any doubts about the articles of faith. But Newman denies that it is wrong, even in secular matters, to hold a belief with a magisterial intolerance of contrary suggestions. If we are certain, we spontaneously reject objections as idle phantoms, however much they may be insisted on by a pertinacious opponent, or present themselves through an obsessive imagination.

> I certainly should be very intolerant of such a notion as that I shall one day be Emperor of the French; I should think it too absurd even to be ridiculous, and that I must be mad before I could entertain it. And did a man try to persuade me that treachery, cruelty, or ingratitude was as praiseworthy as honesty and temperance, and that a man who lived the life of a knave and died the death of a brute had nothing to fear from future retribution, I should think there was no call on me to listen to his arguments, except with the hope of converting him, though he called me a bigot and a coward for refusing to enter into his speculations.

To be sure, we can sometimes be certain of something and then later find out that we were wrong. This does not mean that we should give up all certainty, any more than the fact that we are sometimes told the wrong time means that we should dispense with clocks.

How does Newman apply all this to the evidences of religion? The strongest evidence for the truth of the Christian religion, he believes, is to be found in the history of Judaism and Christianity; but this evidence only carries weight to those who are already prepared to receive it. To be ready to accept it, one must already believe in the existence of God, the possibility of revelation, and the certainty of a future judgement. The persuasiveness of any proof, Newman says, depends on what the person to whom it is presented regards as antecedently probable.

311

Two objections may be made to this. The first is that antecedent probabilities may be equally available for what is true and what merely pretends to be true, for a counterfeit revelation as well as a genuine one. They supply no intelligible rule to determine what is to be believed and what not.

> If a claim of miracles is to be acknowledged because it happens to be advanced, why not for the miracles of India as well as for those of Palestine? If the abstract probability of a Revelation be the measure of genuineness in a given case, why not in the case of Mahomet as well as of the Apostles?

Newman, who is never more eloquent than when developing criticisms of his own position, nowhere succeeds in providing a satisfactory answer to this objection.

Secondly, we may ask why one should have in the first place those beliefs which Newman regards as necessary for the acceptance of the Christian revelation. What are the reasons for believing at all in God and in a future judgement? Traditional arguments offer to prove the existence of God from the nature of the physical world; but Newman himself has no great confidence in them.

> It is indeed a great question whether Atheism is not as philosophically consistent with the phenomena of the physical world, taken by themselves, as the doctrine of a creative and governing Power. But, however this be, the practical safeguard against Atheism in the case of scientific inquirers is the inward need and desire, the inward experience of that Power, existing in the mind before and independently of their examination of His material world.

The inward experience of the divine power, to which Newman here appeals, is to be found in the voice of conscience. As we conclude to the existence of an external world from the multitude of our instinctive perceptions, he says, so from the intimations of conscience, which appear as echoes of an external admonition, we form the notion of a Supreme Judge. Conscience, considered as a moral sense, involves intellectual judgement; but conscience is always emotional, therefore it involves recognition of a living object. Our affections cannot be stirred by inanimate things, they are correlative with persons.

> If, on doing wrong, we feel the same tearful, broken hearted sorrow which over-whelms us on hurting a mother; if on doing right, we enjoy the same sunny serenity of mind, the same soothing, satisfactory delight which follows on our receiving praise from a father, we certainly have within us the image of some person, to whom our love and veneration look, in whose smile we find our happiness, for whom we yearn, towards whom we direct our pleadings, in whose anger we are troubled and waste away. These feelings in us are such as require for their exciting cause an intelligent being.

It is not the mere existence of conscience which Newman regards as establishing the existence of God: intellectual judgements of right and wrong can be explained – as they are by many Christian philosophers as well as by Utilitarians – as conclusions arrived at by reason. It is the emotional colouring of conscience which Newman, implausibly, compares to our sense-experience of the external world. The feelings which he engagingly describes may indeed be appropriate only if there is a Father in heaven; but they cannot guarantee their own appropriateness. If the existence of God is intended simply as a hypothesis to explain the nature of such sentiments, then other hypotheses must also be taken into consideration. One such is that of Sigmund Freud, to whose philosophy we next turn.

SIGMUND FREUD

Freud was born into an Austrian Jewish family in 1856 and spent almost all of his life in Vienna. He trained as a doctor and went into medical practice in 1886. In 1895 he published a work on hysteria which presented a novel analysis of mental illness. Shortly afterwards he gave up normal medicine and started to practise a new form of therapy which he called psychoanalysis, consisting, as he put it himself, in nothing more than an exchange of words between patient and doctor. He continued in practice in Vienna until the 1930s, and published a series of highly readable books constantly modifying and refining his psychoanalytic theories. Fear of Nazi persecution forced him to migrate to England in 1938, and he died there at the beginning of the Second World War.

In his *Introductory Lectures on Psychoanalysis* Freud sums up psychoanalytic theory in two fundamental premises: the first is that the greater part of our mental life, whether of feeling, thought or volition, is unconscious; the second is that sexual impulses, broadly defined, are supremely important not only as potential causes of mental illness but as the motor of artistic and cultural creation. If the sexual element in the work of art and culture remains largely unconscious, this is because socialization demands the sacrifice of basic instincts, which become sublimated, that is to say, diverted from their original goals and channelled towards socially desirable activities. But sublimation is an unstable state, and untamed and unsatisfied sexual instincts may take their revenge through mental illness and disorder.

The existence of the unconscious is revealed, Freud believes, in three ways: through everyday trivial mistakes, through reports of dreams, and through the symptoms of neurosis.

What Freud called 'parapraxes', but are nowadays known as Freudian slips, are common episodes such as failure to recall names, slips of the tongue, and mislaying of objects. Freud gives many examples. A professor at Vienna, in his inaugural lecture, instead of saying, according to his script, 'I have no intention of under-rating the achievements of my illustrious predecessor' said 'I have every intention of underrating the achievements of my illustrious predecessor.' Some years after the sinking of the liner *Lusitania*, a husband, asking his estranged wife to rejoin him across the Atlantic, wrote 'Come across on the *Lusitania*', when he meant to write 'Come across on the *Mauretania*'. In each case Freud regards the slip as a better guide to the man's state of mind than the words consciously chosen.

Freud's explanations of parapraxes are most convincing where – as in the cases above – they reveal a state of mind of which the person was aware but merely did not wish to express. This reveals no very deep level of unconscious inten-tion. Matters are different when we come to the second method of tapping into the unconscious: the analysis of dream reports. 'The interpretation of dreams', Freud says, 'is the royal road to a knowledge of the unconscious activities of the mind.' Dreams, he maintained, were almost always the fulfilment, in fantasy, of a repressed wish. He admitted that comparatively few dreams are obvious repre-sentations of the satisfaction of a wish, and many dreams, such as nightmares or anxiety dreams, seem to be just the opposite. Freud dealt with this by insisting that dreams were symbolic in nature, encoded by the dreamer in order to make them appear innocuous. He distinguished between the manifest content of the dream, which is what the dreamer reports, and the latent content of the dream, which was the true meaning once the symbols had been decoded.

How is the decoding to be done? It is not difficult to give every dream a sexual significance if one takes every pointed object like an umbrella to represent a penis, and every capacious object like a handbag to represent the female genitals. But Freud did not believe that it was possible to set up a dictionary which would relate each symbol to what it symbolized. It was necessary to discover the signific-ance of a symbolic dream item for the individual dreamer, and that could only be done by exploring the associations which he attached to it in his own mind. Only when that had been done could the dream be interpreted in a way which would reveal the nature of the unconscious wish whose fulfilment the dream fantasized.

The third (though chronologically the first) method by which Freud purported to explore the unconscious was by examining the symptoms of neurotic patients. An Austrian undergraduate patient became obsessed with the (erroneous) thought that he was too fat (ich bin zu dick). He became anorexic, and wore himself out with mountain hiking. The explanation of the obsessional behaviour only became clear when the patient mentioned that at the time his fiancée's attention had been distracted from him by the company of her English cousin Dick. The unconscious purpose in slimming, Freud decided, had been to get rid of this Dick.

The unconscious motivations which surface in the psychopathology of everyday life are commonly easily recognized and acknowledged by the person in question. It is different with the significance of dreams and obsessional behaviour. This can only be detected, Freud believed, by long sessions in which the analyst invites the patient freely to associate ideas with the symbolic item or activity in question. The analyst's decoding of the symbolism is often initially rejected by the patient. For a cure to be effective, the patient has to acknowledge the desire which, according to the analyst, the decoded symbol reveals.

There is a certain circularity in Freud's procedure for discovering the unconscious. The existence of the unconscious is held to be proved by the evidence of dreams and neurotic symptoms. But dreams and neurotic symptoms do not, either on their face or as interpreted by the unaided patient, reveal the beliefs, desires, and sentiments of which the unconscious is supposed to consist. The criterion of success in decipherment is that the decoded message should accord with the analyst's notion of what the unconscious is like. But that notion was supposed to derive from, and not to precede, the exploration of dreams and symptoms.

The pattern to which the unconscious was to conform was laid out by Freud in his theory of sexual development. Infantile sexuality begins with an oral stage, in which physical pleasure is focused on the mouth. This is followed by an anal stage, between one and three, and a 'phallic' stage, in which the child focuses on its own penis or clitoris. Only at puberty does an individual's sexuality permanently focus on other persons. Freud, from an early stage in his career, regarded neurotic symptoms as the result of the repression of sexual impulses during childhood, and saw neurotic characters as fixated at an early stage of their development.

Freud attached great importance to the onset of the phallic stage. At that time, he believed, a boy was sexually attracted to his mother, and began to resent his father's possession of her. But his hostility to his father leads to fear that his father will retaliate by castrating him. So the boy abandons his sexual designs on his mother, and gradually identifies with his father. This was the Oedipus complex, a central stage in the emotional development in every boy, and also, in a modified and never fully worked out version, of every girl. The recovery of Oedipal wishes, and the history of their repression, became an important part of every analysis.

Towards the end of his life, Freud replaced the earlier dichotomy of conscious and unconscious with a threefold scheme of the mind. 'The mental apparatus,' he wrote, 'is composed of an *id* which is the repository of the instinctual impulses, of an *ego* which is the most superficial portion of the id and one which has been modified by the influence of the external world, and of a *superego* which develops out of the id, dominates the ego, and represents the inhibitions of instinct that are characteristic of man.'

Freud claimed that the modification of his earlier theory had been forced on him by the observation of his patients on the couch. Yet the mind, in this later theory, closely resembles the tripartite soul of Plato's *Republic*. The id corresponds to the appetite, the source of the desires for food and sex. Freud's id is ruled by the pleasure principle and knows no moral code; similarly, Plato tells us that if appetite is in control, pleasure and pain reign in one's soul instead of law. Both the id and the appetite contain contrary impulses perpetually at war. Some of the desires of the appetite, and all those of the id, are unconscious and surface only in dreams. Plato goes so far as to tell us that some of appetite's dreams are Oedipal: 'In phantasy it will not shrink from intercourse with a mother or anyone else, man, god, or brute, or from forbidden food or any deed of blood.'

Freud's ego has much in common with Plato's reasoning power. Reason is the part of the soul most in touch with what is real, just as the ego is devoted to the reality principle. Like reason, the ego has the task of controlling instinctual desires, providing for their harmless release. Using one of Plato's metaphors, Freud compares the ego to a rider and the id to a horse. 'The horse supplies the locomotive energy, while the rider has the privilege of deciding on the goal and guiding the powerful animal's movement.' Both Plato and Freud use hydraulic metaphors to describe the mechanism of control, seeing id and appetite as a flow of energy which can find normal discharge or be channelled into alternative outlets. But Freud departs from Plato in regarding the damming up of such energy as something which is likely to lead to disastrous results.

There remain Freud's superego and the part of the Platonic soul called 'temper'. These are alike in being non-rational, punitive forces in the service of morality, the source of shame and self-directed anger. For Freud, the superego is an agency which observes, judges, and punishes the behaviour of the ego, partly identical with the conscience, and concerned for the maintenance of ideals. It upbraids and abuses the ego, just as Plato's temper does. Superego and temper are alike the source of ambition. However, the superego's aggression is directed exclusively at the ego, whereas the temper in a Platonic soul is directed at others no less than oneself.

Both Freud and Plato regard mental health as harmony between the parts of the soul, and mental illness as unresolved conflict between them. But only Freud has a worked out theory of the relation between psychic conflict and mental disorder. The ego's whole endeavour, Freud says, is 'a reconciliation between its various dependent relationships'. In the absence of such reconciliation, particular disorders develop: the psychoses are the result of conflicts between the ego and the world, depressive neuroses are the result of conflicts between the id and the super-ego, and other neuroses are the result of conflicts between the ego and the id.

While Freud's general tripartite anatomy of the soul bears a close resemblance to Plato's, his particular treatment of the superego reminds the historian rather more of Newman's description of the conscience. Freud believed that the supergo had its origin in the injunctions and prohibitions of the child's parents, of which it was the internalized residue.

> The long period of childhood, during which the growing human being lives in dependence on his parents, leaves behind it as a precipitate the formation in his ego of a special agency in which this parental influence is prolonged. It has received the name of *superego*.

Newman's portrayal of conscience as echoing the reproaches of a mother and the approval of a father seems more like a description of the formation of the super-ego than a proof of the existence of a supernatural judge.

Freud would be indignant at figuring in a history of philosophy, since he regarded himself above all as a scientist, dedicated to discovering the rigid deter-minisms which underlay human illusions of freedom. In fact, most of his detailed theories, when they have been made precise enough to admit of experimental test-ing, have been proved to lack foundation. Among medical professionals, opinions differ whether the techniques which took their rise from his practice of psycho-analysis are, in any strict sense, effective forms of therapy. When they achieve success, it is not by uncovering unalterable deterministic mechanisms, but by expanding the freedom of choice of the individual. Despite the non-scientific nature of his work, Freud's influence on modern society has been pervasive: in relation to sexual mores, to mental illness, to art and literature, and to interpersonal relationships of many kinds.

The permissive attitude to sex of many societies in the late twentieth century is undoubtedly due not only to the increased availability of efficient contraception, but also to the ideas of Freud. He was not the first thinker to assign the sexual impulse a place of fundamental importance in the human psyche: so did all those theologians who regarded the sin of Adam, which shaped our actual human condition, as being sexual in origin, transmission, and effect. If, as some people believe, nineteenth-century prudery succeeded in concealing the importance of sex, the veil of concealment was even then easily torn away. As Schopenhauer wrote, in a passage Freud loved to quote, it is the joke of life that sex, the chief concern of man, should be pursued in secret. 'In fact', he said, 'we see it every moment seat itself, as the true hereditary lord of the world, out of the fullness of its own strength, upon the ancestral throne, and looking down from there with scornful glances, laugh at the preparations which have been made to bind it.'

Freud's emphasis on infantile sexuality was one of the elements of his teaching which contemporaries found most shocking. But the sentimental attitude to early childhood which he attacked was one of comparatively recent origin. It was not, for instance, shared by Augustine, who wrote in his *Confessions*:

> What is innocent is not the infant's mind, but the feebleness of his limbs. I have myself watched and studied a jealous baby. He could not yet speak and, pale with jealousy and bitterness, glared at his brother sharing his mother's milk. Who is unaware of this fact of experience?

What links Freud's work with modern sexual permissiveness is not medical research, but the persuasive character of his literary style. He did not assemble a statistical demonstration of a connection between sexual abstinence and mental illness; nor, in his published writings, did he recommend sexual licence. What he did do was to give widespread currency to the metaphors which he shared with Plato: the vision of sexual desire as a psychic fluid which seeks an outlet through one channel or another. Seen in the light of that metaphor, sexual abstinence appears as a dangerous damming up of forces which will eventually break through restraining barriers with devasting effect on mental health.

The very concept of mental health, in its modern form, dates from the time when Freud and his colleagues began to treat hysterical patients as genuine invalids instead of malingerers. This, it has often been said, was as much a moral decision as a medical discovery. But it was surely the right moral decision; and hysteria was close enough to the paradigm of physical illness for the concept of mental illness to have clear sense when applied to it. In ordinary illness the causes, symptoms, and remedies of disease are all physical. In mental illness, whether or not physical causes and remedies have been identified, the symptoms concern the cognitive and affective life of the patient: disorders of perception, belief, and emotion. In the diagnosis of whether perception is normal, of whether belief is rational, of whether emotion is out of proportion, there is a gentle slope which leads from clinical description to moral evaluation. This is strikingly seen in the case of homosexual attraction, which was for long regarded as a psychopathological disorder but has come to be regarded by many as a basis for the rational choice of an alternative life-style. Forms of behaviour which before Freud would have been regarded as transgressions worthy of punishment are now often judged, in the courthouse no less than in the consulting room, as symptoms of maladies fit for therapy. It is often said that Freud was not so much a medical man as a moralist; that is true, but it is truer to say that he redrew the boundaries between morals and medicine.

Perhaps Freud's greatest influence has been on art and literature. This has a certain irony, in the light of his unflattering view of artistic creation as something very similar to neurosis: a sublimation of unsatisfied libido, translating into phantasy form the unresolved conflicts of infantile sexuality. Since Freud's theories became well known, critics have delighted to interpret works of art in Oedipal terms, and historians have turned with gusto to the writing of psychobiography, analysing the actions of mature public figures on the basis of real or imagined features of their childhood. Novelists have made use of associative techniques similar to those of the analyst's couch, and painters and sculptors have taken Freudian symbols out of a dream world and given them concrete form. All of us, directly or indirectly, have imbibed so much of Freud's philosophy of mind that in discussion of our relations with our family and friends we make unselfconscious use of Freudian concepts. No other philosopher since Aristotle has made such a contribution to the everyday vocabulary of morality.

XXI

LOGIC AND THE FOUNDATIONS OF MATHEMATICS

Frege's Logic

The most important event in the history of philosophy in the nineteenth century was the invention of mathematical logic. This was not only a refoundation of the science of logic itself, but had important consequences for the philosophy of mathematics, the philosophy of language, and ultimately for philosophers' understanding of the nature of philosophy itself.

The principal founder of mathematical logic was Gottlob Frege. Born on the Baltic coast of Germany in 1848, Frege (1848–1925) took his doctorate in philosophy at Göttingen, and taught at the University of Jena from 1874 until his retirement in 1918. Apart from his intellectual activity his life was uneventful and secluded; his work was little read in his lifetime, and even after his death his influence was exercised originally through the writings of other philosophers. But gradually he came to be recognized as the greatest of all philosophers of mathematics, and as a philosopher of logic fit to be compared to Aristotle. His invention of mathematical logic was one of the major contributions to the developments in many disciplines which resulted in the invention of computers. Thus Frege affected the lives of all of us.

Frege's productive career began in 1879 with the publication of a pamphlet with the title *Begriffschrift*, or *Concept Script*. The concept script which gave the book its title was a new symbolism designed to bring out with clarity logical relationships which were concealed in ordinary language. Frege's own script, which was logically elegant but typographically cumbersome, is no longer used in symbolic logic; but the calculus which it formulated has ever since formed the basis of modern logic.

Instead of the Aristotelian syllogistic, Frege placed at the front of logic the propositional calculus first explored by the Stoics: that is to say, the branch of logic that deals with those inferences which depend on the force of negation, conjunction, disjunction etc. when applied to sentences as wholes. Its fundamental principle – which again goes back to the Stoics – is to treat the truth-value (i.e. the truth or falsehood) of sentences which contain connectives such as 'and', 'if', 'or', as being determined solely by the truth-values of the component sentences which are linked by the connectives – in the way in which the truth-value of 'John is fat and Mary is slim' depends on the truth-values of 'John is fat' and 'Mary is slim'. Composite sentences, in the logicians' technical term, are treated as *truth-functions* of the simple sentences of which they are put together. Frege's *Begriffschrift* contains the first systematic formulation of the propositional calculus; it is presented in an axiomatic manner in which all laws of logic are derived, by specified rules of inference, from a number of primitive principles.

Frege's greatest contribution to logic was his invention of quantification theory: that is to say, a method of symbolizing and rigorously displaying those inferences that depend for their validity on expressions such as 'all' or 'some', 'any' or 'every', 'no' or 'none'. This new method enabled him, among other things, to reformulate traditional syllogistic.

There is an analogy between the inference

> All men are mortal
> Socrates is a man
>
> So Socrates is mortal

and the inference

> If Socrates is a man, then Socrates is mortal
> Socrates is a man
>
> So Socrates is mortal.

The second inference is a valid inference in the propositional calculus (if p then q; but p, therefore q). But it cannot be regarded as a translation of the first, since its first premiss seems to state something about Socrates in particular, whereas if 'All men are mortal' is true, then

> if x is a man, then x is mortal

will be true no matter whose name is substituted for the variable 'x'. Indeed, it will remain true even if we substitute the name of a non-man for x, since in that case the antecedent will be false, and the whole sentence, in accordance with the truth-functional rules for 'if'-sentences, will turn out true. So we can express the traditional proposition:

> All men are mortal

in this way

> For all x, if x is a man, x is mortal.

This reformulation forms the basis of Frege's quantification theory: to see how, we have to explain how he conceived each of the items which go together to make up the complex sentence.

Frege introduced into logic the terminology of algebra. An algebraic expression such as '$x/2 + 1$' may be said to represent a *function* of x: the value of the number represented by the whole expression will depend on what we substitute for the variable 'x', or, in the technical term, what we take as the *argument* of the function. Thus 3 will be the value of the function for the argument 4, and 4 will be the value of the function for the argument 6. Frege applied the terminology of argument, function, and value to expressions of ordinary language as well as to expressions in mathematical notation. He replaced the grammatical notions of subject and predicate with the mathematical notions of argument and function, and he introduced truth-values as well as numbers as possible values for expressions. Thus 'x is a man' represents a function which for the argument Socrates takes the value *true*, and for the argument Venus takes the value *false*. The expression 'for all x', which introduces the sentence above, says, in Fregean terms, that what follows ('if x is a man, x is mortal') is a function which is true for every argument. Such an expression is called a quantifier.

Besides 'for all x', the universal quantifier, there is also the particular quantifier 'for some x' which says that what follows is true for at least one argument. Thus, 'some swans are black' can be represented in a Fregean dialect as 'For some x, x is a swan and x is black'. This sentence can be taken as equivalent to 'there are such things as black swans'; and indeed Frege made general use of the particular quantifier in order to represent existence. Thus, 'God exists' or 'there is a God' is represented in his system as 'For some x, x is God'.

Using his novel notation for quantification, Frege was able to present a calculus which formalized the theory of inference in a way more rigorous and more general than the traditional Aristotelian syllogistic which up to the time of Kant had been looked on as the be-all and end-all of logic. After Frege, for the first time, formal logic could handle arguments which involved sentences with multiple quantification, sentences which are as it were quantified at both ends, such as 'Nobody knows everybody' and 'any schoolchild can master any language'.

FREGE'S LOGICISM

In the *Begriffsschrift* and its sequels Frege was not interested in logic for its own sake. His motive in constructing the new concept script was to assist him in the philosophy of mathematics. The question which above all he wanted to answer was this: Do proofs in arithmetic rest on pure logic, being based solely upon general laws operative in every sphere of knowledge, or do they need support from empirical facts? The answer which he gave was that arithmetic itself could be shown to be a branch of logic in the sense that it could be formalized without the use of any non-logical notions or axioms. It was in the *Grundlagen der Arithmetik* (1884) that Frege first set out to establish this thesis, which is known by the name of 'logicism'.

The *Grundlagen* begins with an attack on the ideas of Frege's predecessors and contemporaries (including Kant and Mill) on the nature of numbers and of mathematical truth. Kant had maintained that the truths of mathematics were synthetic *a priori*, and that our knowledge of them depended on intuition. Mill, on the contrary, saw mathematical truths as *a posteriori*, empirical generalizations widely applicable and widely confirmed. Frege maintained that the truths of arithmetic were not synthetic at all, neither *a priori* nor *a posteriori*. Unlike geometry – which, he agreed with Kant, rested on *a priori* intuition – arithmetic was analytic, that is to say, it could be defined in purely logical terms and proved from purely logical principles.

The arithmetical notion of number in Frege's system is replaced by the logical notion of 'class': the cardinal numbers can be defined as classes of classes with the same number of members; thus the number two is the class of pairs, and the number three the class of trios. Despite appearances, this definition is not circular, because we can say what is meant by two classes having the same number of members without making use of the notion of number: thus, for instance, a waiter may know that there are as many knives as there are plates on a table without knowing how many of each there are, if he observes that there is just one knife to the right of each plate. Two classes have the same number of members if they can be mapped one-to-one on to each other; such classes are known as equivalent classes. A number, then, will be a class of equivalent classes.

Thus, we could define four as the class of all classes equivalent to the class of gospel-makers. But such a definition would be useless for purposes of reducing arithmetic to logic, since the fact that there were four gospel-makers is no part of logic. If Frege's programme is to succeed, he has to find, for each number, not only a class of the right size, but a class whose size is guaranteed by logic.

What he did was to begin with zero. Zero can be defined in purely logical terms as the class of all classes equivalent to the class of objects which are not identical with themselves. Since there are no objects which are not identical with themselves, that class has no members; and since classes which have the same members are the same classes, there is only one class which has no members, the null-class, as it is called. The fact that there is only one null-class is used in proceeding to the definition of the number one, which is defined as the class of classes equivalent to the class of null-classes. Two can then be defined as the class of classes equivalent to the class whose members are zero and one, three as the class of classes equivalent to the class whose members are zero and one and two, and so on *ad infinitum*. Thus the series of natural numbers is to be built up out of the purely logical notions of identity, class, class-membership, and class-equivalence.

In the *Grundlagen* there are two theses to which Frege attaches great importance. One is that each individual number is a self-subsistent object; the other is that the content of a statement assigning a number is an assertion about a concept. At first sight these theses may seem to conflict, but if we understand what Frege meant by 'concept' and 'object' we see that they are complementary. In saying that a number is an object, Frege is not suggesting that a number is something tangible like a tree or a table; rather, he is denying that number is a property belonging to anything, whether an individual or a collection. In saying that a number is a self-subsistent object he is denying that it is anything subjective, any mental item or any property of a mental item. Concepts are, for Frege, Platonic, mind-independent entities, and so there is no contradiction between the thesis that numbers are objective, and the thesis that number-statements are statements about concepts. Frege illustrates this latter thesis with two examples.

> If I say 'Venus has 0 moons', there simply does not exist any moon or agglomeration of moons for anything to be asserted of; but what happens is that a property is assigned to the *concept* 'moon of Venus', namely that of including nothing under it. If I say 'the king's carriage is drawn by four horses', then I assign the number four to the concept 'horse that draws the King's carriage'.

Statements of existence, Frege says, are a particular case of number statements. 'Affirmation of existence,' he says, 'is in fact nothing but denial of the number nought.' What he means is that a sentence such as 'Angels exist' is an assertion that the concept *angel* has something falling under it. And to say that a concept has something falling under it is to say that the number which belongs to that concept is something other than zero.

It is because existence is a property of concepts, Frege says, that the ontological argument for the existence of God breaks down. That-there-is-a-God cannot be a property of God; if there is in fact a God, that is a property of the concept *God*.

If number statements are statements about concepts, what kind of object is a number itself? Frege's answer is that a number is the extension of a concept. The number which belongs to the concept F, he says, is the extension of the concept 'like-numbered to the concept F'. This is equivalent to saying that it is the class of all classes which have the same number of members as the class of Fs, as was explained above. So Frege's theory that numbers are objects depends on the possibility of taking classes as objects.

FREGE'S PHILOSOPHY OF LOGIC

It will be seen that Frege's philosophy of mathematics is closely linked to his understanding of several key terms of logic and of philosophy; and indeed in the *Begriffschrift* and the *Grundlagen* Frege not only founded modern logic, but also founded the modern philosophical discipline of philosophy of logic. He did so by making a clear distinction between the philosophical treatment of logic and, on the one hand, psychology (with which it had often been confused by philosophers in the empiricist tradition) and, on the other hand, epistemology (with which it was sometimes conflated by philosophers in the Cartesian tradition). There is not, however, the same sharp distinction in his work between logic and metaphysics: indeed the two are closely related.

Corresponding to the distinction in language between functions and arguments, Frege maintained, a systematic distinction must be made between concepts and objects, which are their ontological counterparts. Objects are what proper names stand for: there are objects of many kinds, ranging from human beings to numbers. Concepts are items which have a fundamental incompleteness, corresponding to the gappiness in a function which is marked by its variable. Where other philosophers talk ambiguously of the *meaning* of an expression, Frege introduced a distinction between the *reference* of an expression (the object to which it refers, as the planet Venus is the reference of 'The Morning Star') and the *sense* of an expression. ('The Evening Star' differs in sense from 'The Morning Star' though both expressions, as astronomers discovered, refer to Venus.) Frege maintained that the reference of a sentence was its truth-value (i.e. the True, or the False), and held that in a scientifically respectable language every term must have a reference and every sentence must be either true or false. Many philosophers since have adopted his distinction between sense and reference, but most have rejected the notion that complete sentences have a reference of any kind.

The climax of Frege's career as a philosopher should have been the publication of the two volumes of *Die Grundgesetze der Arithmetik* (1893–1903), in which he set out to present in a rigorous formal manner the logicist construction of arithmetic on the basis of pure logic and set theory. This work was to execute the task which had been sketched in the earlier books on the philosophy of mathematics: it was to enunciate a set of axioms which would be recognizably truths of logic, propound a set of undoubtedly sound rules of inference, and then present, one by one, derivations by these rules from these axioms of the standard truths of arithmetic.

The magnificent project aborted before it was ever completed. The first volume was published in 1893. By the time that the second volume appeared, in 1903, it had been discovered that Frege's ingenious method of building up the series of natural numbers out of merely logical notions contains a fatal flaw. The discovery was due to the English philosopher Bertrand Russell.

RUSSELL'S PARADOX

Russell was born in 1872, the grandson of the Prime Minister Lord John Russell, and godson of John Stuart Mill. At Trinity College, Cambridge, he accepted for a while a British version of Hegelian idealism. Later, in conjunction with his friend

G. E. Moore, he abandoned idealism for an extreme realist philosophy which included a Platonist view of mathematics. It was in the course of writing a book to expound this philosophy that Russell encountered Frege's ideas, and when the book was published in 1903 as *The Principles of Mathematics* it included an account of them. Much as Russell admired Frege's writings, he detected a radical defect in his system, which he pointed out to him just as the second volume of the *Grundgesetze* was in press.

If we are to proceed from number to number in the way Frege proposes we must be able to form without restriction classes of classes, and classes of classes of classes, and so on. Classes must themselves be classifiable; they must be capable of being members of classes. Now can a class be a member of itself? Most classes are not (e.g. the class of dogs is not a dog) but some apparently are (e.g. the class of classes is surely a class). It seems therefore that classes can be divided into two kinds: there is the class of classes that are members of themselves, and the class of classes that are not members of themselves.

Consider now this second class: is it a member of itself or not? If it is a member of itself, then since it is precisely the class of classes that are *not* members of themselves, it must be not a member of itself. But, if it is not a member of itself, then it qualifies for membership of the class of classes that are not members of themselves, and therefore it is a member of itself. It seems that it must either be a member of itself or not; but whichever alternative we choose we are forced to contradict ourselves.

This discovery is called Russell's paradox; it shows that there is something vicious in the procedure of forming classes of classes *ad lib.*, and it calls into question Frege's whole logicist programme.

Russell himself was committed to logicism no less than Frege was, and he proceeded, in co-operation with A. N. Whitehead, to develop a logical system, using a notation different from Frege's, in which he set out to derive the whole of arithmetic from a purely logical basis. This work was published in the three monumental volumes of *Principia Mathematica* between 1910 and 1913.

In order to avoid the paradox which he had discovered, Russell formulated a Theory of Types. It was wrong to treat classes as randomly classifiable objects. Classes and individuals were of different logical types, and what can be true or false of one cannot be significantly asserted of the other. 'The class of dogs is a dog' should be regarded not as false but as meaningless. Similarly, what can meaningfully be said of classes cannot meaningfully be said of classes of classes, and so on through the hierarchy of logical types. If the difference of type between the different levels of the hierarchy is observed, then the paradox will not arise.

But another difficulty arises in place of the paradox. Once we prohibit the formation of classes of classes, how can we define the series of natural numbers? Russell retained the definition of zero as the class whose only member is the null-class, but he now treated the number one as the class of all classes equivalent to the class whose members are (a) the members of the null-class, plus (b) any object not a member of that class. The number two was treated in turn as the class of all classes equivalent to the class whose members are (a) the members of the class used to define one, plus (b) any object not a member of that defining class. In this way the numbers can be defined one after the other, and each number is a class of classes of individuals. But the natural-number series can be continued thus *ad infinitum* only if there is an infinite number of objects in the universe; for if there are only n individuals, then there will be no classes with $n + 1$ members, and so no cardinal number $n + 1$. Russell accepted this and therefore added to his axioms an axiom of infinity, i.e. the hypothesis that the number of objects in the universe is not finite. This hypothesis may be, as Russell thought it was, highly probable; but on the face of it it is far from being a logical truth; and the need to postulate it is therefore a sullying of the purity of the original programme of deriving arithmetic from logic alone.

When he learned of Russell's paradox, Frege was utterly downcast. He made more than one attempt to patch up his system, but these were no more successful in salvaging logicism than was Russell's theory of types. We now know that the logicist programme cannot ever be successfully carried out. The path from the axioms of logic via the axioms of arithmetic to the theorems of arithmetic is barred at two points. First, as Russell's paradox showed, the naive set theory which was part of Frege's logical basis was inconsistent in itself, and the remedies which Frege proposed for this proved ineffective. Thus, the axioms of arithmetic cannot be derived from purely logical axioms in the way Frege hoped. Secondly, the notion of 'axioms of arithmetic' was itself later called in question when the Austrian mathematician Kurt Gödel showed that it was impossible to give arithmetic a complete and consistent axiomatization in the style of *Principia Mathematica*. None the less, the concepts and insights developed by Frege and Russell in the course of expounding the logicist thesis have a permanent interest which is unimpaired by the defeat of that programme.

RUSSELL'S THEORY OF DESCRIPTIONS

In his realist period, when he wrote *The Principles of Mathematics*, Russell had believed that in order to save the objectivity of concepts and judgements it was necessary to accept the existence of Platonic ideas and of propositions which subsisted independently of their expression in sentences. Like Frege, he accepted that concepts were something independent of our thinking; but he went beyond Frege because he believed that not only relations and numbers, but also chimaeras and the Homeric gods all had being of some kind, for if not it would be impossible to make propositions about them. 'Thus being is a general attribute of everything, and to mention anything is to show that it is.'

By the time he wrote *Principia Mathematica* Russell had changed his mind. He wrote:

> Suppose we say 'the round square does not exist'. It seems plain that this is a true proposition, yet we cannot regard it as denying the existence of a certain object called 'the round square'. For if there were such an object, it would exist: we cannot first assume that there is a certain object, and then proceed to deny that there is such an object. Whenever the grammatical subject of a proposition can be supposed not to exist without rendering the proposition meaningless, it is plain that the grammatical subject is not a proper name, i.e. not a name directly representing some object. Thus in all such cases the proposition must be capable of being so analysed that what was the grammatical subject shall have disappeared. Thus, when we say 'The round square does not exist' we may, as a first attempt at such analysis, substitute 'It is false that there is an object x which is both round and square'.

So far, this account is similar to Frege's method of treating statements of existence; but Russell saw that it was necessary to give an account of the meaning of vacuous expressions such as 'the round square' and 'the present King of France' when they occurred in contexts other than statements of existence; for instance, in the sentence 'The present King of France is bald'. Russell called expressions like 'the present King of France' and 'the man who discovered oxygen' by the name 'definite descriptions'. In his article *On Denoting* of 1905 he worked out a general theory of the meaning of definite descriptions, which would take care both of the cases where there was some object answering to the description (as in 'the man who discovered oxygen') and of the cases where the description was vacuous (as in 'the present King of France').

Frege had treated definite descriptions simply as complex names, so that 'The author of Hamlet was a genius' had the same logical structure as 'Shakespeare was a genius'. This meant that he had to provide for arbitrary rules to be laid down in order to ensure that a sentence containing an empty name or vacuous definite description did not lack a truth-value. Russell thought this was unsatisfactory, and proposed to analyse sentences containing definite descriptions quite differently from those containing names. It is a mistake, he believed, to look for the meaning of definite descriptions in themselves; only the propositions in whose verbal expression they occur have a meaning.

For Russell there is a big difference between a sentence such as 'James II was deposed' (containing the name 'James II') and a sentence such as 'The brother of Charles II was deposed'. An expression such as 'The brother of Charles II' has no meaning in isolation; but the sentence 'The brother of Charles II was deposed' has a meaning none the less. It asserts three things:

(a) that some individual was brother to Charles II
(b) that only this individual was brother to Charles II
(c) that this individual was deposed.

Or, more formally:

For some *x*, (a) *x* was brother to Charles II
   and   (b) for all *y*, if *y* was brother to Charles II, $y = x$
   and   (c) *x* was deposed.

The first element of this formulation says that at least one individual was a brother of Charles II, the second that at most one individual was a brother of Charles II, so that between them they say that exactly one individual was brother to Charles II. The third element goes on to say that that unique individual was deposed. In the analysed sentence nothing appears which looks like a name of James II; instead, we have a combination of predicates and quantifiers.

What is the point of this complicated analysis? To see this we have to consider a sentence which, unlike 'The brother of Charles II was deposed', is not true. Consider the following two sentences:

(1) The sovereign of the United Kingdom is male.
(2) The sovereign of the United States is male.

Neither of these sentences is true, but the reason differs in the two cases. Everyone would agree that the first sentence is not true, but plain false, because the sovereign of the United Kingdom is female. The second fails to be true because the US has no sovereign, and on Russell's view this second sentence is not just untrue but positively false; and consequently its negation 'It is not the case that the sovereign of the US is male' is true. Sentences containing empty definite descriptions differ sharply in Russell's system from sentences containing empty names, i.e. apparent names which name no objects. For Russell a would-be sentence such as 'Slawkenburgius was a genius' is not really a sentence at all, and therefore neither true nor false, since there was never anyone of whom 'Slawkenburgius' was the proper name.

Why did Russell want to ensure that sentences containing vacuous definite descriptions should count as false? He was, like Frege, interested in constructing a precise and scientific language for purposes of logic and mathematics. Both Frege and Russell regarded it as essential that such a language should contain only expressions which had a definite sense, by which they meant that all sentences in which the expressions could occur should have a truth-value. For if we allow into our system sentences lacking a truth-value, then inference and deduction become impossible. It is easy enough to recognize that 'the round square' denotes nothing, because it is obviously self-contradictory. But prior to investigation it may not be clear whether some complicated mathematical formula contains a hidden contradiction. And if it does so, we will not be able to discover this by logical investigation unless sentences containing it are assured of a truth-value.

LOGICAL ANALYSIS

In *On Denoting* and later papers Russell constantly speaks of the activity of the philosopher as being one of analysis. By analysis he means a technique of substituting a logically clear form of words for another form of words which was in some way logically misleading. His theory of descriptions was for long a paradigm of such logical analysis. But in Russell's mind, logical analysis was far more than a device for the clarification of sentences. He came to believe that once logic had been cast into a perspicuous form it would reveal the structure of the world.

Logic contained individual variables and propositional functions: corresponding to these the world contained particulars and universals. In logic complex propositions were built up out of simple propositions as truth-functions of the simpler propositions. Similarly, in the world there were independent atomic facts corresponding to the simple propositions. Atomic facts consisted either in the possession by a particular of a characteristic, or else in a relation between two or more particulars. This theory of Russell's was called 'logical atomism'.

The theory of descriptions was the great analytic tool of logical atomism. Russell began to apply it not only to round squares and to Platonic entities, but also to many things which common sense would regard as perfectly real, such as Julius Caesar, tables, and chairs. The reason for this was that Russell came to believe that every proposition which we can understand must be composed wholly of items with which we are acquainted. 'Acquaintance' was Russell's word for immediate presentation: we were acquainted, for instance, with our own sense-data, which correspond in his system to Hume's impressions or the deliverances of Cartesian consciousness. But Russell still retained something of his earlier Platonism: he believed that we had direct acquaintance with the universals which were represented by the predicates of the reformed logical language. But the range of things which we could know by acquaintance was limited: we could not be acquainted with Queen Victoria or our own past sense-data. Those things which were not known by acquaintance were known only by description; hence the importance of the theory of descriptions.

In the sentence 'Caesar crossed the Rubicon', uttered in England now, we have a proposition in which there are apparently no individual constituents with which we are acquainted. In order to explain how we can understand the sentence Russell analyses the names 'Caesar' and 'Rubicon' as definite descriptions. The descriptions, spelt out in full, no doubt include reference to those names, but not to the objects they named. The sentence is exhibited as being about general characteristics and relations, and the names with which we become acquainted as we pronounce them.

For Russell, then, ordinary proper names were in fact disguised descriptions. A fully analysed sentence would contain only logically proper names (words referring to particulars with which we are acquainted) and universals (words referring to characters and relations). It was never altogether clear what counted as logically proper names. Sometimes Russell seemed to countenance only demonstratives such as 'this' and 'that'. An atomic proposition, therefore, would be something like '(this) red' or '(this) beside (that)'.

Logical atomism was presented in a famous series of lectures in 1918. It was far from being Russell's last word on philosophy. In the fifty-two years which remained to him Russell wrote many books and essays, some of which concern issues of logic and epistemology as well as the moral and educational topics which began to take up more and more of his attention. In his later life, and particularly after he inherited an earldom, he was known to a very wide public as a writer and campaigner on various social and political issues. But most of the work which established his reputation among professional philosophers and mathematicians was completed before 1920. Logical atomism itself, as Russell was the first to admit, was due in large part to the ideas of one of his former pupils, Ludwig Wittgenstein. It was he who was to present, in his *Tractatus Logico-Philosophicus*, the most authoritative formulation of the system. It was he too who later, having repudiated logical atomism, gradually developed the most rewarding philosophy of the twentieth century.

XXII

THE PHILOSOPHY OF WITTGENSTEIN

TRACTATUS LOGICO-PHILOSOPHICUS

Ludwig Wittgenstein was the grandson of a Jewish land-agent and the son of a steel millionaire who had nine children by a Catholic wife, and baptized all of them into the Catholic faith. Born in Vienna in 1889, he attended the *Realschule* in Linz, where he was a contemporary of Adolf Hitler. At school he lost his faith, and soon after came under the influence of Schopenhauer's idealism. After studying engineering in Berlin and Manchester he went to Cambridge, where his philosophical gifts were recognized by Russell, who devoted himself with great generosity to fostering his genius. After five terms at Cambridge he lived in isolation in Norway, and when war broke out in 1914 he enlisted as a volunteer in the Austrian artillery, and served with conspicuous courage on the Eastern and Italian fronts. During this period he wrote his masterpiece, *Tractatus Logico-Philosophicus*, which in 1918, as a prisoner of war at Monte Cassino, he sent in manuscript to Russell. The book was published in German in 1921 and shortly afterwards in German and English with an introduction by Russell.

The *Tractatus* is brief, beautiful, and very difficult. It consists of a series of numbered paragraphs, often containing no more than a single sentence. The two most famous paragraphs are the first 'The world is all that is the case' and the last 'Whereof one cannot speak, thereof one must be silent'. The book's main concern is the nature of language and its relation to the world. Its central doctrine is the picture theory of meaning. According to this theory, language consists of propositions which picture the world. Propositions are the perceptible expressions of thoughts, and thoughts are logical pictures of facts; the world is the totality of facts.

Thoughts and propositions, according to the *Tractatus*, are pictures in a literal, not just a metaphorical sense. An English sentence such as 'the rain will spread across Scotland' or 'blood is thicker than water' does not look like a picture. But that, according to Wittgenstein, is because language disguises thought beyond all recognition.

However, even in ordinary language there is a perceptibly pictorial element. Take the sentence 'Bristol is west of London'. This sentence says something quite different from another sentence made up of the same words, namely, 'London is west of Bristol'. What makes the first sentence, but not the second, mean that Bristol is west of London? It is the fact that the *word* 'Bristol' occurs to the left of the *word* 'London' in the context of the first sentence but not the second. So in that sentence, as in a map, we have a spatial relationship between words symbolizing a spatial relationship between cities. Such spatial representation of spatial relationships is pictorial in a quite straightforward way.

Few cases, however, are as simple as this. If the sentence were spoken instead of written, it would be a temporal relationship between sounds rather than a spatial relationship on the page which would represent the relationship between the cities. But this in turn is possible only because the spoken sequence and the spatial array have a certain abstract structure in common. According to the *Tractatus*, there must be something which any picture must have in common with what it depicts. This shared minimum Wittgenstein calls its logical form. Most propositions, unlike the untypical example above, do not have spatial form in common with the situation they depict; but any proposition must have logical form in common with what it depicts.

In ordinary language the logical form of thoughts is concealed. One reason for this is that many of our words, like 'Bristol' and 'London', signify complex objects. The relationship between propositions and facts will only become clear if complex objects are logically analysed into simple ones. In order to carry out this analysis, Wittgenstein made use of an extension of Russell's theory of descriptions. For instance, 'Austria-Hungary' can be regarded as a definite description of the complex object formed by the union of Austria and Hungary, and the sentence 'Austria-Hungary is fighting Russia' can be analysed, in accordance with the theory of descriptions, as follows.

$$
\begin{aligned}
\text{For some } x \text{ and some } y, \quad & x = \text{Austria} \\
\text{and} \quad & y = \text{Hungary} \\
\text{and} \quad & x \text{ is united to } y \\
\text{and} \quad & x \text{ is fighting Russia} \\
\text{and} \quad & y \text{ is fighting Russia.}
\end{aligned}
$$

In the sentence thus analysed, no mention is made of Austria-Hungary, and so we have got rid of one complex object. However, this is obviously only a first step; Austria and Hungary are each of them, in their turn, highly complex objects, consisting of many different kinds of object in spatial and other relationships.

If we proceed with the analysis of a proposition, Wittgenstein believed, we will in the end come to symbols which denote entirely non-complex objects. So a fully analysed proposition will consist of an enormously long combination of atomic propositions, each of which will contain names of simple objects, names related to each other in ways which will picture, truly or falsely, the relations between the objects they represent. Such full analysis of a proposition is no doubt humanly impossible; but the thought expressed by the proposition already has the complexity of the fully analysed proposition. The thought is related to its expression in ordinary language by extremely complicated rules which we operate unconsciously from moment to moment.

The connection between language and the world is made by the correlation between the ultimate elements of these concealed thoughts and the simple objects or atoms which constitute the substance of the world. How these correlations are made Wittgenstein does not explain; it is a deeply mysterious process which, it seems, each one of us must make for himself, creating as it were a private language.

Much of the *Tractatus* is devoted to showing how, with the aid of various logical techniques, propositions of different kinds can be analysed into combinations of atomic pictures. The truth-value of propositions of science would depend upon the truth-value of the atomic propositions from which they were built up. The propositions of logic were tautologies, that is to say, complex propositions which are true no matter what truth values their atomic propositions take; an obvious example is the proposition 'p or not p', which is true whether p is true or false. Would-be propositions which are incapable of analysis into atomic propositions reveal themselves as pseudo-propositions which yield no pictures of the world. Among these, it turns out, are the propositions of philosophy, including the propositions of the *Tractatus* itself. At the end of the book he compared it to a ladder which must be climbed and then kicked away if one is to see the world aright.

Metaphysicians attempt to describe the logical form of the world; but this is impossible. A picture must be independent of what it pictures; it must be capable of being a false picture. But since any proposition must contain the logical form of the world, it cannot picture it. What the metaphysician attempts to say cannot be said, but can only be shown. Philosophy is not a theory, but an activity: the activity of clarifying non-philosophical propositions. Once clarified, the propositions will mirror the logical form of the world, and will show what the philosopher wishes to, but cannot, say.

Neither science nor philosophy can show us the meaning of life.

> 6.52 We feel that even when all possible scientific questions have been answered, the problems of life remain completely untouched. Of course, there are then no questions left, and this itself is the answer.

Even if one could believe in immortality, it would not confer meaning on life; nothing is solved by surviving for ever. An eternal life would be as much a riddle as this one. 'God does not reveal himself *in* the world,' Wittgenstein wrote; 'it is not how things are in the world that is mystical, but *that* it exists'. Philosophy could in one sense do very little for us; but what it could do, Wittgenstein believed, had been done once for all by the *Tractatus*. The book contained all that was essential for the solutions of the problems of philosophy; and so, having written it, Wittgenstein gave up the subject.

LOGICAL POSITIVISM

The *Tractatus* quickly became famous. Oddly enough, though it was itself highly metaphysical, as well as austerely logical, its most enthusiastic admirers were the anti-metaphysical positivists of the Vienna Circle. This group, which grew up round Moritz Schlick after his appointment as Professor of the Philosophy of Science in Vienna in 1922, consisted of philosophers, mathematicians, and scientists; among its members were Friedrich Waismann, Rudolf Carnap, and Otto Neurath. In 1929, after a congress in Prague, the circle issued a manifesto, the *Wissenschaftliche Weltauffassung der Wiener Kreis*, which proclaimed the launch of a campaign against metaphysics as an outdated precursor of science. The ideas of the circle were publicized in the journal *Erkenntnis*, founded in 1930 and edited by Carnap in conjunction with Hans Reichenbach of Berlin. The circle was broken up in 1939 as a result of political pressure, after Schlick had been killed by an insane student.

What the Positivists claimed to take from the *Tractatus* was the idea that necessary truths are necessary only because they are tautologies. In the past, logical and mathematical propositions had presented serious difficulties for empiricism. Few empiricists were willing to follow Mill in denying that such propositions were necessary. It was much more attractive to accept that they were necessary but that they told us nothing about the world. Empiricists could now reaffirm their claim that knowledge about the world is acquired only by experience, and devote themselves with a clear conscience to the attack on metaphysics.

The great weapon in this attack was the Verification Principle. This, in its original form, ruled that the meaning of a proposition was the mode of its verification. Such a view of meaning enabled one to rule out of court as meaningless all statements which could neither be verified nor falsified by experience. Faced with a dispute about the nature of the Absolute, or the purpose of the Universe, or Kantian things-in-themselves, the Positivist could expose the emptiness of the quarrel by saying to the warring metaphysicians: 'What possible experience could settle the issue between you?'

Almost as soon as the Verification Principle was stated disputes broke out about its status and its formulation. The principle did not seem to be itself a tautology, a mere matter of definition. Was it, then, verifiable by experience?

If not, it seemed to stand self-condemned as meaningless. Moreover, not only metaphysical propositions, but scientific generalizations, were incapable of conclusive verification. Should we say then that the criterion of significance was not verifiability but falsifiability? Thus general propositions would be significant because they were conclusively falsifiable. But how, on this view, were assertions of existence significant? Short of an exhaustive tour of the universe, no experience could conclusively falsify them. So the principle was reformulated in a 'weak' form which laid down that a proposition was significant if there were some observations which would be *relevant* to its truth or falsity. And it was allowed that there were many significant propositions which, while 'verifiable in principle', could not be verified in practice. Even thus qualified, it was not easy to apply the Verification Principle to matters of history; and any further modifications of the principle ran the risk of making it so wide as to admit metaphysical statements.

The Positivists accepted the *Tractatus* view that the true task of philosophy was to clarify non-philosophical statements. In clarifying the language of science, the philosopher must show how all empirical statements were built up truth-functionally from elementary or 'protocol' statements, which were direct records of experience. In knowing which experiences would make one accept or reject any particular protocol one would, in virtue of the Verification Principle, understand what it meant. The words occurring in non-protocol statements derived their meaning from the possibility of the translation of such statements into protocol statements; and the words occurring in protocol statements derived their meaning from the possibility of an ostensive definition – of a gesture which would point (literally or metaphorically) to the feature of experience to which the word referred.

A difficulty here presents itself. What protocol statements record seems to be something which is private to each individual. If meaning depends on verifiability, and verification is by mental states which I alone experience, how can I ever understand anyone else's meaning? Schlick tried to answer this by making a distinction between form and content. The content of my experience – what I enjoy or live through when I look at something green – is private and incommunicable. But the form, the structural relationship, between my private experience and other people's private experience is something public and communicable. I cannot know whether, when I see a tree or a sunset, other people enjoy the same experiences as I do; for all I know, when they look at a tree they see the colour which I see when I look at a sunset. But as long as we both agree to call a tree green and a sunset red – as long, that is, as the form or structure of our experience patterns is similar – we are able to communicate with each other and construct the language of science. Few people found this answer wholly satisfactory, and the threat of solipsism was not adequately dealt with until Wittgenstein returned to philosophy.

WITTGENSTEIN'S *PHILOSOPHICAL INVESTIGATIONS*

After the war, having inherited a share of his father's fortune, Wittgenstein found himself one of the wealthiest men in Europe. Within a month of returning he gave away all his money. For some years he supported himself as a gardener or as a schoolmaster in rural schools. When his career as a schoolmaster came to an unhappy end after allegations of cruelty to his pupils, he returned to the study of philosophy and for a while he took part in the discussions of the Vienna Circle. Later, he distanced himself from the Circle and returned to Cambridge, where he submitted the *Tractatus* as a Ph.D. dissertation and was awarded a fellowship at Trinity, where, in the 1930s, he became the most influential teacher of philosophy in Britain. The philosophy which he taught in this period differed from that published in the *Tractatus*; it was not presented in print during his lifetime. During the Second World War Wittgenstein served as a medical orderly; he returned to Cambridge only briefly as Professor of Philosophy. From 1947 until his death in 1951 he lived privately, alone in Ireland, or with friends in Oxford, Cambridge, and Ithaca, New York. The book which he had long worked on was published posthumously as *Philosophical Investigations* in 1953.

After his return to philosophy in the early thirties, Wittgenstein quickly abandoned a number of the characteristic doctrines of the *Tractatus*; he ceased to believe in logical atoms, or to look for a logically articulated language cloaked in ordinary language. One of the crucial elements of logical atomism was the thesis that every atomic proposition was independent of every other one. This was clearly not true of the protocol statements which were the positivists' candidates for atomic propositions: the truth-value of 'this is a red patch' is not independent of the truth-value of 'this is a blue patch'. At one time Wittgenstein had thought that this showed that these propositions were not elementary, but needed further analysis. Now, instead, he gave up the idea that elementary propositions were independent of each other, and this led to a questioning of the distinction between elementary and non-elementary propositions. The rest of the system of logical atomism soon began to unravel. Wittgenstein gave up the idea that the ultimate elements of language were names designating simple objects, and came to believe that the words 'simple' and 'complex' have no absolute meaning, but vary in meaning according to context.

Wittgenstein retained, however, and never abandoned, the *Tractatus* view that philosophy is an activity, not a theory. Philosophy does not discover any new truths. Philosophical problems are solved not by giving new information, but by arranging what we have always known in a way which prevents us overlooking what is in itself most obvious. Philosophy allows us to have a clear view of what we are doing when we are using language non-philosophically in our ordinary life. In a striking phrase, Wittgenstein said that the function of philosophy was to untie the knots in our thinking. If this is right, the philosopher will have to make very complicated movements; but the results of philosophy will not be an elaborate structure, but something as plain as a piece of string.

Taking his cue from Freud, Wittgenstein sometimes depicts philosophy as a therapy, a therapy to cure the bruises we get by banging our understanding against the limits of language. The philosopher, like a psychoanalyst, encourages us to express doubts and puzzlement which we have been taught to repress; he cures us of the confusions we nurture in our minds by encouraging us to bring them out to the light of day, turning latent nonsense into patent nonsense.

Philosophy, Wittgenstein sometimes said, is nothing more than the dissolution of philosophical problems. But if that is what philosophy is, why do philosophy at all? If you never get as far as the problems, you will never need the solutions! Wittgenstein's answer is that while it is true that philosophy is only useful against philosophers, there is, whether we know it or not, a philosopher within each of us. In the very language we use there is a philosophy which bewitches us. This philosophy is not a set of theories or propositions: it is embodied in the misleading nature of the grammar of natural languages, which disguises the actual way in which words are used.

Philosophical misunderstanding will not harm us if we restrict ourselves to everyday tasks, using words within the contexts which are their primitive homes. But if we start upon abstract studies – of mathematics, say, or of psychology, or of theology – then our thinking will be hampered and distorted unless we can free ourselves of philosophical confusion. Intellectual inquiry will be corrupted by mythical notions of the nature of numbers or of the mind or of the soul.

Both early and late, Wittgenstein believed that the surface grammar of language concealed its true nature. But whereas in the *Tractatus* what was concealed was the complex nature of a thought buried deep in our minds, in the later philosophy what was concealed, and had to be set out in plain view, was the diversity of ways in which language functioned as a social, interpersonal, activity. Wittgenstein thought that in his earlier work he had, like other philosophers, grossly oversimplified the relation of language to the world. The connection between the two was to consist of two features only: the linking of names to objects, and the match or mismatch of propositions to facts. This, he now came to believe, was a great mistake. Words look like each other, in the same way as a clutch looks very like a foot-brake; but words differ from each other in function as much as the mechanisms which are operated by the two pedals. Wittgenstein now emphasized that language was interwoven with the world in many very different ways: and to refer to these tie-ups he coined the expression 'language-game'. 'We remain unconscious of the prodigious diversity of all the everyday language-games because the clothing of our language makes everything alike.'

Wittgenstein gives as examples of language-games obeying and giving orders, describing the appearance of objects, expressing sensations, giving measurements, constructing an object from a description, reporting an event, speculating about an event, making up stories, acting plays, guessing riddles, telling jokes, asking, cursing, greeting, and praying. He also speaks of language-games with particular words. Wittgenstein was not putting forward a general theory of language-games: the use of the expression is simply meant to stress that words cannot be understood outside the context in which they are used. We need, in giving an account of the meaning of a word, to look for the part it plays in our life. The use of 'game' is not intended to suggest that language is something trivial; the word was chosen because games exhibit the same kind of variety as linguistic activities do. Some games are competitive, others not so; some have rules, others are spontaneous; some are played with balls, others on boards; some demand skill, others do not. There is no common feature which marks all games as games: rather, different games share different features with each other as different members of the same family will resemble each other not in one single way but in a variety of ways. Similarly, there is no one feature which is essential to language; there are only family-likenesses between the countless language-games.

Philosophy does, in a sense, show us the essence of language, but not by revealing the existence of some ghostly mechanism lurking within us, but by bringing into clear view what we already confusedly know, namely, the way in which we use words. Philosophy can give us a clear view of this, and thus of the world which we grasp by means of the concepts of our language.

Like the positivists, Wittgenstein is hostile to metaphysics. But he attacks metaphysics not by the blunt instrument of some positivistic verification principle, but by the careful drawing of distinctions which enable him to disentangle the mixture of truism and nonsense in the metaphysician's concept of mind. Moreover, the kind of metaphysics which he criticizes is one of which many positivists were themselves guilty. For Wittgenstein, metaphysics consists above all of grammar masquerading as science.

Philosophers are constantly tempted to mimic the claims and methods of science. The eighteenth-century philosophers who sought to construct a Newtonian physics of the mind are conspicuous illustrations of this temptation. Wittgenstein repeatedly attacks metaphysical representations of the mind as a mysterious medium, different from a physical medium, in which special laws operate which it is the philosopher's task to discover and enuntiate. 'When philosophers use a word – "knowledge" "being" "object" "I" "proposition" "name" – and try to grasp the *essence* of the thing, one must always ask oneself: is the word ever actually used in this way in the language which is its original home? – What *we* do is to bring words back from their metaphysical to their everyday use.'

An example of Wittgenstein's criticism of the bad metaphysical conception of the mental is his attack on the notion that meaning is a mental process. Wittgenstein was no behaviourist; he did not deny that there were things which could be called 'mental processes' – a psychological process, for instance, such as the recitation of a poem in one's head. Where philosophers have gone wrong is in believing that meaning a sentence, and understanding a sentence, was a mental process under-lying the utterance, or accompanying the hearing, of the sentence. Reflection shows that this cannot be right.

If meaning was a mental process accompanying the utterance of a sentence, it should be possible for the process of meaning to take place without the sentence being uttered at all. Can one, in fact, perform the act of meaning without uttering the sentence? If you try to do so, you are likely to find yourself reciting the sentence itself under your breath. But of course it would be absurd to suggest that simultaneously with every public utterance of a sentence there is a private one too: it would surely take great skill to ensure that the two processes were exactly synchronized with each other! And how terrible if the two came slightly out of synchrony, so that the meaning of one word got mistakenly attached to the next one!

Moreover, the question whether somebody understands a sentence, and whether she really means it, can be raised about sentences uttered in the privacy of the imagination no less than about sentences uttered before a public audience. In-furiated by a curmudgeonly relation, I may mutter to myself 'I wish he would drop dead!' Luckily, I don't mean it. I hum in my mind a Russian folk-song, enchanted by the sound of the words. But I haven't the faintest idea what they mean. If understanding and meaning were processes, they would have to accom-pany private utterances as well as public utterances. So if the processes involved were some kind of inner utterance, we would be set off on an endless quest for the real understanding.

Some philosophers have thought that understanding was a mental process in rather a different sense. They have conceived the mind as a hypothetical mechan-ism postulated to explain the observable intelligent behaviour of human beings. If one conceives the mind in this way one thinks of a mental process, not as some-thing comparable to reciting the ABC in one's head, but as a process occurring in the special mental machinery. The process on this view is a mental process because it takes place in a medium which is not physical; the machinery operates according to its own mysterious laws, within a structure which is not material but spiritual; it is not accessible to empirical investigation, and could not be discovered, say, by opening up the skull of a thinker.

Such processes need not, on this view, be accessible even to the inner eye of introspection: the mental mechanism may operate too swiftly for us to be able to follow all its movements, like the pistons of a railway engine or the blades of a lawn mower. But we may feel that if only we could sharpen our faculty for introspection, or somehow get the mental machinery to run in slow motion, we might be able actually to observe the processes of meaning and understanding.

According to one version of the mental-mechanism doctrine, understanding the meaning of a word consists in calling up an appropriate image in connection with it. In general, of course, we have no such experience when we use a word and in the case of many words (such as 'the' 'if' 'impossible' 'one million') it is difficult even to suggest what would count as an appropriate image. But let us waive these points, allow that perhaps we can have images in our mind without noticing that we do, and consider only the kind of word for which this account sounds most plausible, such as colour words. We may examine the suggestion that in order to understand the order 'Bring me a red flower' one must have a red image in mind, and that it is by comparison with this image that one ascertains which flower to bring. Once we stop to think, we realize this cannot be right: otherwise how could one obey the order 'imagine a red patch?' Whatever problems there are about identifying the redness of the flower recur with identifying the redness of the patch.

It is of course true that when we talk, mental images often do pass through our minds. But it is not they which confer meanings on the words we use. It is rather the other way round: the images are like the pictures illustrating a text in the book. In general it is the text which tells us what the pictures are of, not the pictures which tell us what the words of the text mean.

In this way Wittgenstein examines, and makes us reject, various processes which might be thought of as the process of meaning. In fact, meaning and understanding are not processes at all. We are misled by grammar. Because the surface grammar of the verbs 'mean' and 'understand' resembles that of verbs like 'say' and 'breathe', we expect to find processes which correspond to them. When we cannot find an empirical process we postulate an incorporeal process.

There is another metaphysical doctrine which is closely associated with the idea that meaning is a mental process: it is the idea that naming is a mental act. This idea is the target of Wittgenstein's criticism of the notion of a private language, or more precisely, of the notion of private definition.

Wittgenstein's discussion of language-games makes clear that not all words are names; but even naming is not as simple as it appears. To name something it is not sufficient to confront it and utter a sound: the asking and giving of names is something which can be done only in the context of a language-game. This is so even in the relatively simple case of naming a material object: matters are much more complicated when we consider the names of mental events and states, such as sensations and thoughts.

Wittgenstein considers at length the way in which a word such as 'pain' functions as the name of a sensation. We are tempted to think that for each person 'pain' acquires its meaning by being correlated by him with his own private, incommunicable sensation. This temptation must be resisted: Wittgenstein showed that no word could acquire meaning in this way. One of his arguments runs as follows.

Suppose that I wish to baptize a private sensation of mine with the name 'S'. I fix my attention on the sensation in order to correlate the name with it. What does this achieve? When next I want to use the name 'S', how will I know whether I am using it rightly? Since the sensation it is to name is supposed to be a private one, no one else can check up on my use of it. But neither can I do so for myself. Before I can check up on whether the sentence 'This is S again' is true, I need to know what the sentence means. How do I know that what I now mean by 'S' was what I meant when I christened the first sensation 'S'. Can I appeal to memory? No, for to do so I must call up the right memory, the memory of S; and in order to do that I must already know what 'S' means. There is in the end no check on my use of 'S', no way of making out a difference between correct and incorrect use of it. That means that talk of 'correctness' is out of place, and shows that the private definition I have given myself is no real definition.

The conclusion of Wittgenstein's attack on private definition is that there cannot be a language whose words refer to what can only be known to the individual speaker of the language. The language-game with the English word 'pain' is not a private language, because, whatever philosophers may say, other people can very often know when a person is in pain. It is not by any solitary definition that 'pain' becomes the name of a sensation: it is rather by forming part of a communal language-game. For instance, a baby's cry is a spontaneous, pre-linguistic expression of pain; gradually the child is trained by her parents to replace this with the conventional, learned expression of pain through language. Thus pain-language is grafted on to the natural expression of pain.

What is the point of the private language argument? Who is Wittgenstein arguing against? The short answer is that he is arguing against the author of the *Tractatus*, who had given countenance to solipsism. Solipsism is the doctrine 'Only I exist'. In the *Tractatus* Wittgenstein wrote:

> what solipsism *means* is quite correct, only it cannot be *said*, but it shows itself.
> That the world is *my* world shows itself in the fact that the limits of language (*the* language which I understand) mean the limits of *my* world.

Gradually, as Wittgenstein's philosophy developed, he came to think that, even as a piece of unsayable philosophy, solipsism was a perversion of reality. The world is *my* world only if language is *my* language: a language created by my own linkage of words to the world. But language is not *my* language; it is *our* language. The private language argument shows that no purely private definitions could create a language. The home of language is not the inner world of the solipsist, but the life of the human community. Even the word 'I' only has meaning as a word in our common language.

But the scope of the private language argument extends much further than the refutation of Wittgenstein's earlier self. Descartes, in expressing his philosophical doubt, assumes that language has meaning while the existence of the body is uncertain. Hume thought it possible for thoughts and experiences to be recognized and classified while the question of the existence of the external world is held in suspense. Mill and Schopenhauer, in their different ways, thought that a man could express the contents of his mind in language while questioning the existence of other minds. All of these suppositions entail the possibility of a private language. And all of these suppositions are essential to the structure of the philosophies in question. Common to both empiricism and idealism is the doctrine that the mind has no direct knowledge of anything but its own contents. The history of both movements shows that they lead in the direction of solipsism. Wittgenstein's attack on private definition refutes solipsism by showing that the possibility of the very language in which it is expressed depends on the existence of the public and social world. The refutation of solipsism carries over into a refutation of the empiricism and idealism which inexorably involve it.

Wittgenstein did not wish to replace empiricism and idealism with a different philosophical system; his later philosophy was the very reverse of systematic. This does not mean that it lacked method, or rigour. It means rather that there was no part of philosophy which had primacy over any other part. One could start philosophizing at any point, and leave off the treatment of one problem to take up the treatment of another. Philosophy had no foundations, and did not provide foundations for other disciplines. Philosophy was not a house, nor a tree, but a web.

> The real discovery is the one that makes me capable of stopping doing philosophy when I want to. – The one that gives philosophy peace, so that it is no longer tormented by questions which bring *itself* into question. – Instead, we now demonstrate a method, by examples; and the series of examples can be broken off. Problems are solved (difficulties eliminated) not a *single* problem.

Wittgenstein believed that he had completely transformed the nature of philosophy. Certainly, his philosophy is very different from the great systems of the nineteenth century which presented philosophy as a super-science. But his thought is not as discontinuous with the great tradition of Western philosophy as he sometimes seems to have believed. Of course Wittgenstein was hostile to metaphysics, to the pretensions of rationalistic philosophy to prove the existence of God, the immortality of the soul, and to go far beyond the bounds of experience. He was hostile to that; but then so was Kant. Wittgenstein was insistent that all our intellectual inquiries depend for the possibility of their existence on all kinds of simple, natural, inexplicable, original impulses of the human mind; but so was Hume. Wittgenstein was insistent that philosophy was something which each person must do for himself, and involves the will more than the intellect; but so was Descartes. Wittgenstein was anxious that the philosopher should distinguish between parts of speech which grammarians lump together; within the broad category of verbs, for example, the philosopher has to distinguish between processes, conditions, dispositions, states, and so on. But almost word for word the distinctions which Wittgenstein makes correspond to distinctions made by Aristotle and his followers.

Though Wittgenstein, throughout his life, made a sharp distinction between philosophy and science, his philosophy has implications for other disciplines. Philosophy of mind, for instance, is important for empirical psychology. It is not that the philosopher is in possession of information which the psychologist lacks, or has explored areas of the psyche where no psychologist has ventured. What the philosopher can clarify is the psychologists' starting point, namely, the everyday concepts we use in describing the mind, and the criteria on the basis of which mental powers, states, and processes are attributed to people.

Philosophy of mind has often been a battleground between dualists and behaviourists. Dualists regard the human mind as independent of the body and separable from it; for them the connection between the two is a contingent and not a necessary one. Behaviourists regard reports of mental acts and states as disguised reports of pieces of bodily behaviour, or at best of tendencies to behave bodily in certain ways. Wittgenstein rejected both dualism and behaviourism. He agreed with dualists that particular mental events could occur without accompanying bodily behaviour; he agreed with behaviourists that the possibility of describing mental events at all depends on their having, in general, an expression in behaviour. On his view, to ascribe a mental event or state to someone is not to ascribe to her any kind of bodily behaviour; but such ascription can only sensibly be made to beings which have the capability of behaviour of the appropriate kind.

Wittgenstein was hostile not only to the behaviourist attempt to identify the mind with behaviour, but also to the materialist attempt to identify the mind with the brain. Human beings and their brains are physical objects; minds are not. This is not a metaphysical claim: to deny that a mind has a length or breadth or location is not to say that it is a spirit. Materialism is a grosser philosophical error than behaviourism because the connection between mind and behaviour is a more intimate one than that between mind and brain. The link between mind and behaviour is something prior to experience: that is to say, the concepts which we use in describing the mind and its contents have behavioural criteria for their application. But the connection between mind and brain is a contingent one, discoverable by empirical science. Aristotle's grasp of the nature of mind will stand comparison with that of many a contemporary psychologist; but he had a wildly erroneous idea of the relationship of the mind with the brain, which he believed to be an instrument to cool the blood.

Wittgenstein's philosophy of mind is closer to that of Aristotle than it is to contemporary materialist psychology. In one of his most characteristic, and most striking remarks, he goes so far as to entertain the possibility that some of our mental activities may lack any correlate in the brain.

No supposition seems to me more natural than that there is no process in the brain correlated with associating or with thinking; so that it would be impossible to read off thought-processes from brain-processes. I mean this: if I talk or write there is, I assume, a system of impulses going out from my brain and correlated with my spoken or written thoughts. But why should the *system* continue further in the direction of the centre? Why should this order not proceed, so to speak, out of chaos? It is perfectly possible that certain psychological phenomena *cannot* be identified physiologically, because physiologically nothing corresponds to them. Why should there not be a psychological regularity to which *no* physiological regularity corresponds? If this upsets our concepts of causality, then it is high time they were upset.

Here Wittgenstein makes a frontal attack on the scientism characteristic of our age: the assumption that there *must* be physical counterparts of mental phenomena. He is not defending any kind of dualism or spiritualism: what does the associating, thinking, and remembering is not a spiritual substance, but a bodily human being. But he does envisage as a possibility a pure Aristotelian soul, or entelechy, which operates with no material vehicle: a formal and final cause to which there corresponds no mechanistic efficient cause.

In his later years, in the thoughts published posthumously in *On Certainty*, Wittgenstein became interested in the propositions which make up the world-view of a society or individual. Any language-game presupposes an activity which is part of a form of life. To imagine a language, Wittgenstein says, is to imagine a form of life. To accept the rules of a language is to agree with others in a form of life. The ultimate given in philosophy is not an inner basis of private experience: it is the forms of life within which we pursue our activities and think our thoughts. Forms of life are the datum, which philosophy cannot call into question, but which any philosophical inquiry itself presupposes. What, then, is a form of life?

The paradigm of a difference between forms of life is the difference between the life of two different species of animals – animals with different 'natural histories', to use an expression beloved by Wittgenstein. Lions have a different form of life from humans; for that reason, if a lion could speak, we could not understand him.

But there can be differences between forms of life within the human species, too. Human beings share a form of life if they share a *Weltbild*, a picture of the world. A world-picture is neither true nor false. Disputes about truth are possible only within a world-picture, between disputants who share the same form of life. When one person denies what is part of the world-picture of another this may sometimes seem like lunacy, but sometimes it reflects a very deep difference of culture. If someone doubts that the world has existed before he was born we might think him mad: but in a certain culture might not a king be brought up in the belief that the world began with him?

Our world-picture includes propositions which look like scientific propositions: for instance 'water boils at 100 centigrade', 'there is a brain inside my skull'.

Others look like everyday empirical propositions: 'motor cars don't grow out of the earth' or 'the earth has existed for a long time'. But these propositions are not learnt by experience. When someone more primitive is persuaded to accept our world-picture, this is not by our giving him grounds to prove the truth of those propositions; rather, we convert him to a new way of looking at the world. The role of such propositions is quite different from those of axioms in a system: it is not as if they were learnt first and then conclusions were drawn from them. Children do not learn them: they as it were swallow them down with what they learn. When first we begin to believe anything, we believe not a single proposition, but a whole system; and the system is not a set of axioms, a point of departure, so much as the whole element in which all arguments have their life.

In discussing the propositions which make up our world-picture, Wittgenstein recognized that he was addressing the same problems as were posed by Newman in the *Grammar of Assent*: how is it possible to have unshakeable certainty which is not based on evidence. But he disapproved of the purpose for which Newman undertook his investigations, namely to prove the reasonableness of Christianity. Wittgenstein thought that Christians were obviously not reasonable; they based enormous convictions on flimsy evidence. But this did not mean that they were unreasonable; it meant that they should not treat faith as a matter of reasonability at all. In this, Wittgenstein was much closer to Kierkegaard than to Newman.

Wittgenstein was hostile to the idea that there was a branch of philosophy, natural theology, which could prove the reasonableness of belief in God. Philosophy, he thought, could not give any meaning to life; the best it could provide would be a form of wisdom. He frequently contrasts the emptiness of wisdom with the vigour of faith: faith is a passion, but wisdom is cold grey ash, covering up the glowing embers.

But though only faith, and not philosophy, can give meaning to life, that does not mean that philosophy has no rights whatever within the terrain of faith. Faith may involve talking nonsense, and philosophy may point out that it is nonsense. Wittgenstein, who once said 'Whereof one cannot speak, thereof one must be silent', later said 'Don't be afraid of talking nonsense.' But he went on to add: You must keep an eye on your nonsense.

It is philosophy that keeps an eye on the nonsense. First, it points out that the nonsense *is* nonsense: faith is no more able than philosophy, to *say* what is the meaning of life. Here Wittgenstein's old distinction between saying and showing reappears. It does not matter, he thought, if the Gospels are false. That is not a remark which could be made about something which was a *saying*, since the most important fact about sayings is that they are either true of false, and it matters greatly which. Secondly, even if religious utterances are not sayings, philosophy still has a critical role in their regard. Above all, it can distinguish faith from superstition. The attempt to make religion appear reasonable seemed to Wittgenstein to be the extreme of superstition.

AFTERWORD

Anyone looking back over the long history of philosophy is bound to wonder: does philosophy get anywhere? Have philosophers, for all their efforts over the centuries, actually learnt anything? Voltaire, talking of metaphysicians, wrote:

> They are like minuet dancers, who, being dressed to the greatest advantage, make a couple of bows, move through the room in the finest attitudes, display all their graces, are in perpetual motion without advancing a step, and finish at the identical point from which they set out.

In our own time, Wittgenstein wrote:

> You always hear people say that philosophy makes no progress and that the same philosophical problems which were already preoccupying the Greeks are still troubling us today. But people who say that do not understand the reason why it has to be so. The reason is that our language has remained the same and always introduces us to the same questions. As long as there is a verb 'be' which seems to work like 'eat' and 'drink'; as long as there are adjectives like 'identical', 'true', 'false', 'possible'; as long as people speak of the passage of time and the extent of space, and so on; as long as all this happens people will always run up against the same teasing difficulties and will stare at something which no explanation seems to remove. I read 'philosophers are no nearer to the meaning of "reality" than Plato got'. What an extraordinary thing! How remarkable that Plato could get so far! Or that we have not been able to get any further! Was it because Plato was *so* clever?

On Wittgenstein's view, it seems, there cannot be real progress in philosophy; philosophy is not like a science which progresses by adding, age by age, new layers of information upon foundations laid by previous generations. Certainly, any reader of this book will have observed how certain philosophical problems seem to remain constant, and how philosophers in later ages return again and again to themes and theories of their predecessors.

If philosophy makes no progress at all, then there seems little point in reading the history of philosophy. It is not surprising, therefore, that in his *History of*

346

Western Philosophy Bertrand Russell took up a position different from that of Voltaire and Wittgenstein. There were, he maintained, instances where philosophy had reached definitive answers to certain questions. He gave as one example the ontological argument.

> This, as we have seen, was invented by Anselm, rejected by Thomas Aquinas, accepted by Descartes, refuted by Kant, and reinstated by Hegel. I think it may be said quite decisively that as a result of analysis of the concept 'existence' modern logic has proved this argument invalid.

The ontological argument is a two-edged instance to cite. Its history does indeed show that there can be developments in philosophy: Anselm brought off the feat of inventing an argument that had not occurred to any previous philosopher. On the other hand, if the best example of philosophical progress is a case where later philosophers show up the fallacy of an earlier philosopher, it confirms the view that philosophy is only of use against philosophers. Worst of all, quite recently some contemporary philosophers, using more sophisticated forms of modern logic than were available to Russell, have claimed to reinstate the argument which he thought decisively refuted.

None the less, on this issue I believe Russell was closer to the truth than Wittgenstein. It is true that philosophy does not progress by making regular additions to a quantum of information; but philosophy offers not information, but understanding, and there are certain things which philosophers of the present day understand which even the greatest philosophers of earlier generations failed to understand. Even if we accept Wittgenstein's view that philosophy is essentially the clarification of language, there is plenty of room for progress. For instance, philosophers clarify language by distinguishing between different senses of words; and once a distinction has been made, future philosophers have to take account of it in their deliberations.

Take, as an example, the issue of free-will. Once a distinction has been made between liberty of indifference and liberty of spontaneity, the question 'do humans enjoy freedom of the will?' has to be answered in a way which takes account of the distinction. Even someone who believes that the two kinds of liberty coincide has to provide arguments to show this; he cannot simply ignore the distinction and hope to be taken seriously as a philosopher.

It often happens that after a philosophical question has been clarified by the drawing of relevant distinctions, one of the new questions which emerge from the analysis turns out not to be a philosophical question at all, but a question to be solved by some other discipline. In such a case, intellectual progress has been made, but the progress will not appear to be progress in philosophy. This process can be illustrated by reference to the question of innate ideas.

As the reader will remember, there was a keen debate in the seventeenth century about the question: which of our ideas are innate, and which are acquired?

This question involved a degree of confusion; and when clarified it broke up into two problems, one of which was psychological (what do we owe to heredity and what do we owe to environment?) and the other was epistemological (how much of our knowledge is *a priori* and how much *a posteriori*?) The question of heredity vs. environment was handed over, for better or worse, to experimental psychology, and ceased to be a philosophical question. The question how much of our knowledge is *a priori* and how much *a posteriori* was a question not about the acquisition of knowledge, but about its justification, and that, after this first split, remained within philosophy.

But that problem, too, propagated by fission into a set of questions which were philosophical and a set of questions which were not philosophical. The philosophical notions of *a priori* and *a posteriori* ramified and refined into a number of questions, one of which was Kant's question: 'Which propositions are analytic and which are synthetic?' The notion of analyticity was in the end given a precise formulation by Frege in terms of mathematical logic, and in the end the question 'Is arithmetic analytic?' was given a precise mathematical answer by Gödel's proof that arithmetic could not be completely axiomatized. But the mathematical answer to the question left behind to philosophy many remaining questions about the nature and justification of mathematical truth.

In this case, then, we began with an initial confused philosophical question – the distinction between innate and acquired ideas. This then ramified in two directions – in the direction of empirical psychology on the one hand, and in the direction of mathematical logic on the other – leaving in the middle a philosophical residue to be investigated.

Many whole disciplines which were once branches of philosophy have over the centuries become independent sciences. If we generalize from the history of philosophy, we can say that a discipline remains philosophical as long as its concepts are unclarified and its methods are controversial. Once problems can be unambiguously stated, once concepts are appropriately standardized, and once a consensus emerges for the methodology of solution, then we have an independent science rather than a branch of philosophy.

Does that mean that at some time there will be nothing left for philosophy to do? Will all problem areas be sufficiently clarified to set up as independent sciences? I believe not: the theory of meaning, epistemology, philosophy of mind, ethics, and metaphysics will always remain philosophical. Whatever new non-philosophical problems will be generated by these disciplines, to be solved by non-philosophical methods, there will always remain an irreducible core amenable only to philosophy. This is because of the self-reflexive nature of these disciplines: each of them is committed to the critical study of its own exercise.

It is for this reason that the study of the history of philosophy remains worthwhile, not just as an antiquarian enterprise, but as a method of learning the nature of philosophy itself. It is because of the irreducibly philosophical material which they contain that the ethical and metaphysical texts of Plato and Aristotle retain an interest which their writings on cosmology or zoology have lost.

The areas of philosophy which remain for ever philosophical are much more difficult to explore than those which can be, and have been, hived off into self-standing disciplines. This is because their subject matter is so all-embracing and their concepts so universally applicable. The achievement of a systematic philo-sophical overview is something so difficult that only genius can hope to achieve it. So vast is philosophy that only a wholly exceptional mind can see the con-sequences of even the simplest philosophical argument or conclusion. For all of us who are not geniuses, the best way to come to grips with philosophy is by reaching up to the minds of the great philosophers of the past.

SUGGESTIONS FOR FURTHER READING

The most impressive *History of Philosophy* by a single author is F. Copleston's nine-volume series (Burns Oates & Search Press, 1943–74). Though some readers find its style too bland, it is erudite, comprehensive and judicious. Naturally it has been superseded in detail by studies of individual philosophers, but it remains valuable to consult.

Nowadays most histories of philosophy are the work of more than one author. Such are the *Routledge History of Philosophy*, which when complete will comprise ten volumes (1993–); also *A History of Western Philosophy* published in the OPUS series by Oxford University Press (OUP) and the volumes of the *Cambridge History* published by Cambridge University Press (CUP). *Past Masters* (PM), a series of monographs on particular thinkers published by OUP, when completed and placed end to end will constitute a good introductory history of philosophy. Detailed references to individual volumes of all these works will be given below.

Other works by many hands are *The Oxford Companion to Philosophy*, ed. T. Honderich (OUP, 1995), and *The Oxford Illustrated History of Western Philosophy*, ed. A. Kenny (OUP, 1994). Useful sources for those who want to possess the works of original philosophers without great expense are the Penguin Classics (PC) and the series of World's Classics published by OUP (WC).

I am much indebted to all the authors whose works figure in this select bibliography. I have also included references to works where I have myself written at greater length on topics included in the main text.

CHAPTER ONE   *Philosophy in its Infancy*

The important texts of the philosophers discussed in this chapter are gathered in G. S. Kirk, J. Raven, and M. Schofield (eds), *The Presocratic Philosophers*, 2nd edn (CUP, 1983). A convenient collection in English is *Early Greek Philosophy* (PC, 1987), by J. Barnes, who has also published in two volumes *The Presocratic Philosophers* (Routledge, 1982). There is a brief history of the period covered in the first five chapters in T. Irwin, *Classical Thought* (OUP, 1969).

CHAPTER TWO   *The Athens of Socrates*

The complete works of Plato are translated in a single volume edited by J. M. Cooper (Hackett, 1997). The dialogues discussed in this chapter are collected in a PC, *The Last Days of Socrates*. The *Phaedo* is in WC. On Socrates, see G. Vlastos, *Socrates, Ironist and Moral Philosopher* (CUP, 1991).

CHAPTER THREE   *The Philosophy of Plato*

Most of Plato's major dialogues, including the *Republic*, have been translated in PC and WC. There is a PM by R. M. Hare (1981). See also C. Rowe, *Plato* (Harvester, 1984), and J. Annas, *An Introduction to Plato's Republic* (OUP, 1981, 1982).

CHAPTER FOUR   *The System of Aristotle*

Aristotle's complete works are translated in two volumes edited by J. Barnes (Princeton University Press, 1984). The *Nicomachean Ethics*, and the *Politics* are in PC and WC, the *De Anima* in PC, and the *Physics* in WC. There is also a collection of texts in J. Ackrill, *A New Aristotle Reader* (OUP, 1987). Barnes, *Aristotle* (PM, 1982) is one of the best in the series. See also J. L. Ackrill, *Aristotle the Philosopher* (OUP, 1981), and A. Kenny, *Aristotle's Theory of the Will* (Duckworth, 1979) and *Aristotle on the Perfect Life* (OUP, 1995).

CHAPTER FIVE   *Greek Philosophy after Aristotle*

The most important texts are collected and translated in A. A. Long and D. Sedley (eds), *The Hellenistic Philosophers* (Cambridge, 1987). See also A. A. Long, *Hellenistic Philosophy* (Duckworth, 1974) and M. Schofield, M. Burnyeat, and J. Barnes (eds), *Doubt and Dogmatism* (OUP, 1980). The thinkers discussed in this chapter and the next are covered in A. H. Armstrong (ed.), *The Cambridge History of Later Greek and Early Medieval Philosophy* (CUP, 1970). See also D. O'Meara, *Plotinus* (OUP, 1995). Plotinus' *Enneads* are available in Greek and English in the Loeb Classical Library (Heinemann, 1979).

CHAPTER SIX   *Early Christian Philosophy*

An excellent history of this period is H. Chadwick, *The Early Church* (Penguin, 1993). The relevant chapters of J. McManners (ed.), *The Oxford History of Christianity* are also useful. Augustine's *Confessions* are in WC and the *City of God* in PC. There is a PM on Augustine (1986) by H. Chadwick, who is also the author of *Boethius* (OUP, 1990). On Philoponus see R. Sorabji (ed.), *Philoponus and the Rejection of Aristotelian Science* (Duckworth, 1987).

CHAPTER SEVEN *Early Medieval Philosophy*

The topics of this and the next two chapters are covered in *The Cambridge History of Later Medieval Philosophy*, ed. N. Krezmann, A. Kenny, and J. Pinborg (CUP, 1982). A lively popular introduction to medieval philosophy is D. Knowles, *The Evolution of Medieval Thought* (Longman, 2nd edn, 1988). More up-to-date is D. Luscombe's *Medieval Thought* (OUP, 1997). For greater detail on the period covered in this chapter see *Early Medieval Philosophy*, by J. Marenbon, who is also the author of the best book on *The Philosophy of Peter Abelard* (CUP, 1997). For John the Scot, see J. J. O'Meara, *Eriugena* (OUP, 1988). The most engaging life of Anselm is R. W. Southern's *Saint Anselm* (CUP, 1990). Abelard's *Ethics* is available in translation by D. Luscombe (OUP, 1971). On the Arabic philosophers, see H. A. Davidson, *Alfarabi, Avicenna, and Averroes on Intellect* (OUP, 1992).

CHAPTER EIGHT *Philosophy in the Thirteenth Century*

The *Summa Theologiae* is available in Latin and in English in the Blackfriars edition (Eyre & Spottiswoode, from 1964). A very useful selection of Aquinas' philosophical writings, translated by Timothy McDermott, is in WC. The best biography is by J. Weisheipl, *Friar Thomas d'Aquino* (Doubleday, 1974). There is a PM (1979) by A. Kenny, also the author of *The Five Ways* (1969) and *Aquinas on Mind* (1994). See also B. Davies, *The Thought of Thomas Aquinas* (OUP, 1993), and *The Cambridge Companion to Aquinas*, ed. N. Kretzmann and Eleonore Stump. The philosophers considered in this and the succeeding chapter are dicussed in J. Marenbon, *Later Medieval Philosophy* (Routledge, 1987).

CHAPTER NINE *Oxford Philosophers*

For Oxford in the fourteenth century, see *Schools and Scholars in Fourteenth Century England* by W. J. Courtenay (Princeton University Press, 1987). There is little work of Scotus or about Scotus available in English; a collection of extracts was published by A. Wolter (Nelson, 1962). The definitive work on Ockham as a philosopher is M. Adams, *William Ockham* (Notre Dame, 1987). A selection of extracts is given in *Philosophical Writings: A Selection*, ed. by P. Boehner, and Notre Dame University Press is bringing out a multi-volume translation of his *Summa Totius Logicae*. On Ockham's politics, see A. S. McGrade, *The Political Thought of William of Ockham* (CUP, 1974). Marsilius' *Defensor Pacis* has been translated by A. Gewirth (New York, 1956). On Wyclif there is a PM (1985) by A. Kenny.

CHAPTER TEN *Renaissance Philosophy*

The best general survey is *The Cambridge History of Renaissance Philosophy*, ed. C. B. Schmitt and Q. Skinner (CUP, 1988). Briefer is B. P. Copenhaver and C. B. Schmitt,

Renaissance Philosophy (OUP, 1992). A number of texts are collected in E. Cassirer, *The Renaissance Philosophy of Man* (Chicago University Press, 1978). J. McConica's *Renaissance Thinkers* (OUP, 1993) contains four PMs – his own on Erasmus, A. Kenny's on More, P. Burke on Montaigne, and A. Quinton on Bacon. On the Reformation, see J. Bossy, *Christianity in the West, 1400–1700* (OUP, 1985) and O. Chadwick, *The Reformation* (Penguin, 1964). Giordano Bruno's main works were written while he was a double agent in the French Embassy in London, in 1583–5; there is a gripping account of his life in J. Bossy, *Giordano Bruno and the Embassy Affair* (Vintage, 1991).

CHAPTER ELEVEN *The Age of Descartes*

The best life of Descartes is S. Gaukroger, *Descartes: An Intellectual Biography* (OUP, 1994). Descartes' works are available in English in *The Philosophical Writings of Descartes* in three vols, ed. and trans. by J. Cottingham, R. Stoothoff, D. Murdoch, and A. Kenny. Short studies include A. Kenny, *Descartes* (Thoemmes, 1993) and B. Williams, *Descartes: The Project of Pure Enquiry* (Penguin, 1978).

CHAPTER TWELVE *English Philosophy in the Seventeenth Century*

Hobbes' *Leviathan* is in WC and PC. There is a PM by R. Tuck (1989), and a *Hobbes Dictionary* by R. M. Martinich (Blackwell, 1995). The complete works of John Locke are being brought out by OUP in a Clarendon edition. His *Essay concerning Human Understanding* is available in paperback (OUP, 1979). His writings on the social contract, along with those of Hume and Rousseau, are edited by E. Barker, *The Social Contract* (OUP, 1978). There is a PM by J. Dunn (1984). Other material on Locke is noted in connection with Chapter Fourteen.

CHAPTER THIRTEEN *Continental Philosophy in the Age of Louis XIV*

A general history is J. Cottingham's *The Rationalists* (OUP, 1988). Pascal's *Pensées* are in WC. Spinoza's *Ethics* and selected writings of Leibniz appeared in the Everyman Library (Dent, 1950 and 1973). There are PMs on Spinoza (by R. Scruton, 1986) and Leibniz (by G. M. Ross, 1984). See also J. Bennett, *A study of Spinoza's Ethics* (CUP, 1984) and R. M. Adams, *Leibniz: Determinist, Theist, Idealist* (OUP, 1994).

CHAPTER FOURTEEN *British Philosophy in the Eighteenth Century*

On the empiricists in general see J. Bennett, *Locke, Berkeley, Hume: Central Themes* (OUP, 1971), and R. S. Woolhouse, *The Empiricists* (OUP, 1988). Berkeley's *Principles* and *Dialogues* are in WC, as are Hume's *Dialogues concerning Natural Religion*, his *Enquiries*, his *Treatise*, and his *Selected Essays* (WC). There are PMs on Berkeley (J. O. Urmson, 1982) and Hume (A. J. Ayer, 1980). See also David Pears, *Hume's System* (OUP, 1990).

CHAPTER FIFTEEN   *The Enlightenment*

For this chapter and also Chapters Seventeen and Nineteen see R. C. Solomon, *Continental Philosophy since 1750* (OUP, 1988). Rousseau's *Discourse on Political Economy* and *Social Contract* are in WC, and his *Confessions* in PC. Several works by Voltaire are in WC and PC. There is a PM on Rousseau by R. Wokler (1995), and one on Coleridge by R. Holmes (1982).

CHAPTER SIXTEEN   *The Critical Philosophy of Kant*

The commonly used English editions of Kant's major works are *Critique of Pure Reason*, ed. N. Kemp Smith (Macmillan, 1973), *Critique of Judgment*, ed. J. Meredith (OUP, 1978) and *Groundwork of the Metaphysic of Morals*, ed. H. Paton (Hutchinson, 1955). There is a PM by R. Scruton (1982), and a *Kant Dictionary* by Howard Caygill (Blackwell, 1994). There are good studies by J. Bennett (*Kant's Analytic*, CUP, 1966, and *Kant's Dialectic*, CUP, 1974) and by P. Strawson (*The Bounds of Sense*, 1966).

CHAPTER SEVENTEEN   *German Idealism and Materialism*

There are paperback translation of parts of Hegel's work under the titles 'Hegel's Logic' and 'Hegel's Philosophy of Mind' published by OUP (1975 and 1971). OUP also issues a paperback of *The Phenomenology of Spirit* and of the introduction to his *Lectures on the History of Philosophy* (1987). There is a PM by P. Singer (1983) and a *Hegel Dictionary* by M. Inwood (Blackwell, 1993). Many of Marx's works are in PC; a Reader of his works, edited by J. Elster, has been published by CUP. There is a PM by P. Singer (1980).

CHAPTER EIGHTEEN   *The Utilitarians*

Bentham's complete works are being published in many volumes by OUP. There is a PM by John Dinwiddy (1989). His *Introduction to the Principles of Morals and Legislation* was edited by J. H. Burne and H. L. A. Hart (London, 1982). J. S. Mill's *On Liberty* and *Principles of Political Economy* are in WC.

CHAPTER NINETEEN   *Three Nineteenth-Century Philosophers*

Schopenhauer's *The World as Will and Idea* is often read in the English translation of R. B. Haldane and J. Kemp (London, 1948–50). His short essays (*Parerga and Paralipomena*, OUP, 1974) are witty and well worth reading. A recent study of his work is B. Magee, *The Philosophy of Schopenhauer* (OUP, 1987). Several of Kierkegaard's works are available in PC, and there is a PM by P. Gardiner (1988). See also A. Rudd, *Kierkegaard and the Limits of the Ethical* (OUP, 1993). Several of Nietzsche's works are in WC and PC; there is a PM by M. Tanner (1994).

CHAPTER TWENTY   *Three Modern Masters*

Darwin's *Origin of Species* is in WC and in PC. Newman's major philosophical work is *An Essay in Aid of a Grammar of Assent*, ed. I. Ker (OUP, 1985). There is a good PM by O. Chadwick (OUP, 1983). Comparatively little has been written about Newman's philosophy, but see S. A. Grave, *Conscience in Newman's Thought* (OUP, 1989). A series of inexpensive paperback English translations of the works of Freud brought out by Penguin. There is a PM on Freud by A. Storr (1989).

CHAPTER TWENTY-ONE   *Logic and the Foundations of Mathematics*

The most important philosophical texts of Frege are collected in English in *The Frege Reader*, ed. M. Beaney (Blackwell, 1997). M. Dummett's works, particularly *Frege: Philosophy of Language* (Duckworth, 2nd edn, 1981), dominate the field but are difficult for the beginner. There is no PM, but see A. Kenny, *Frege* (Penguin, 1995). Most of Russell's works are still in print; for beginners the one to read first is *Problems of Philosophy* (OUP, 1967); perhaps his best book was *Introduction to Mathematical Philosophy* (Methuen, 1919). There is a PM by A. C. Grayling (1996).

CHAPTER TWENTY-TWO   *The Philosophy of Wittgenstein*

The major texts of Wittgenstein are in English in A. Kenny, *A Wittgenstein Reader* (Blackwell, 1994). His two principal works, *Tractatus Logico-Philosophicus* and *Philosophical Investigations* are both available in English editions published by Blackwell (1961 and 1958). See A. Kenny, *Wittgenstein* (Penguin, 1973) and D. Pears, *The False Prison* (OUP, 1987–8). There is also *A Wittgenstein Dictionary* by H.-J. Glock (Blackwell, 1996).

INDEX

Blackwell Introductions to Philosophy

PHILOSOPHY THEN AND NOW: An Introductory Text with Classic Readings
Edited by N. Scott Arnold, Theodore Benditt, and George Graham
1-55786-742-9 paperback
1-55786-741-0 hardback

CONTINENTAL PHILOSOPHY: An Anthology
Edited by William McNeill and Karen S. Feldman
1-55786-561-2 paperback
1-55786-700-3 hardcover

WESTERN ETHICS:
An Anthology
Edited by Robert Arrington
0-631-19416-9 paperback
0-631-19415-0 hardcover

THE BLACKWELL COMPANION TO PHILOSOPHY
Edited by Nicholas Bunnin and Eric Tsui-James
0-631-18789-8 paperback

WESTERN PHILOSOPHY:
An Anthology
Edited by John Cottingham
0-631-18627-1 paperback

PHILOSOPHICAL WRITING: An Introduction
Second Edition
A. P. Martinich
0-631-19617-X paperback

SOCIAL ETHICS:
A Student's Guide
Jenny Teichman
0-631-19609-9 paperback

INVITATION TO PHILOSOPHY
Martin Hollis
0-631-14226-6 paperback

THE HEGEL READER
Edited by Stephen Houlgate
0-631-20347-8 paperback
0-631-20346-X hardcover

PHILOSOPHICAL INVESTIGATIONS
Ludwig Wittgenstein
Translated by G. E. M. Anscombe
0-631-20569-1 paperback

THE FREGE READER
Edited by Michael Beaney
0-631-19445-2 paperback
0-631-19444-4 hardcover

TO ORDER CALL :
1-800-216-2522 (N. America orders only) or
24-hour freephone on 0500 008205
(UK orders only)

VISIT US ON THE WEB : http://www.blackwellpublishers.co.uk